VIETNAM WAR DIARY

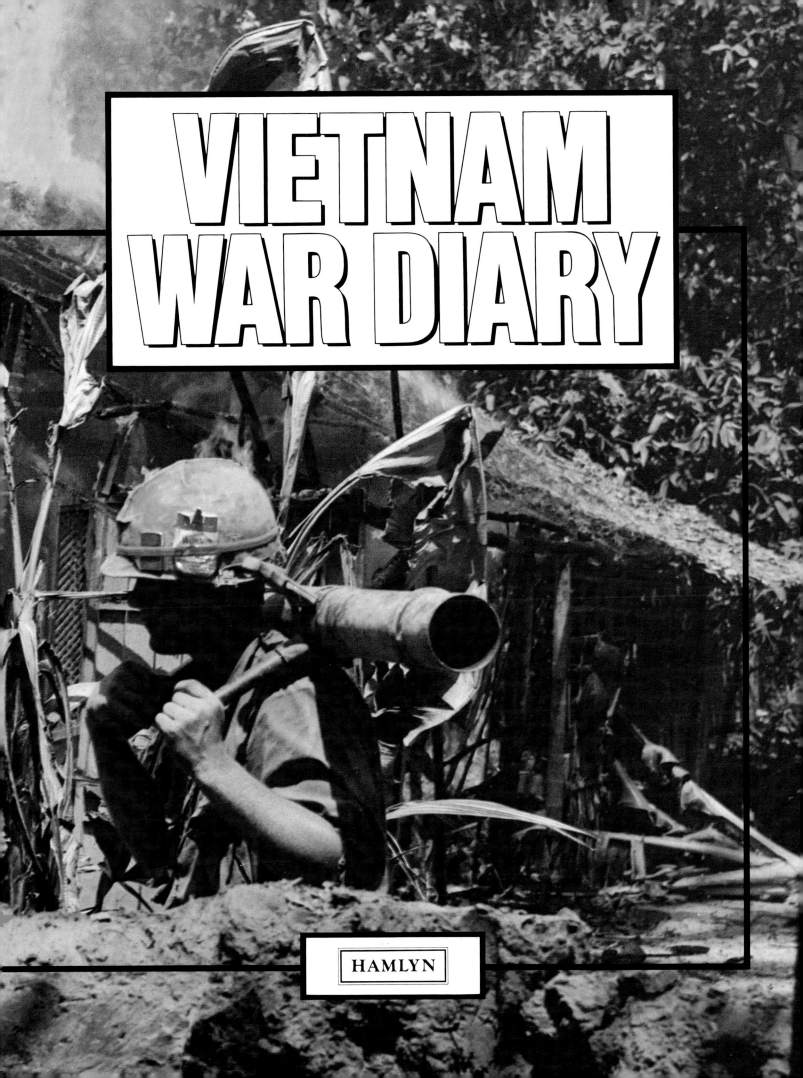

VIETNAM WAR DIARY

HAMLYN

First published in 1990 by
The Hamlyn Publishing Group,
a division of The Octopus Publishing Group
Michelin House
81 Fulham Road
London SW3 6RB

ISBN 600 55635 5

Produced by Aerospace Publishing Limited
179 Dalling Road, London W6 0ES

Produced by Mandarin Offset
Printed and bound in Hong Kong

Acknowledgments

The publishers would like to thank the following
organizations for permission to use extracts from
their publications in this book:

The New York Times
Newsweek Inc.
Time Inc.
The Washington Post

Most of the illustrations in this book were supplied by
the Department of Defense Still Media Records
Center, Washington D.C. Other organizations and
individuals who provided illustrations include:

The Associated Press
Bell Helicopters
Robert F Dorr
Grumman Aerospace Corporation

CONTENTS

INTRODUCTION

The Vietnam War has left a scar on the American soul. It was the longest conflict in American history, and it arouses more contradictory feelings than almost any other experience: feelings and emotions that are still strong today. Yet to many, it is comfortably remote, a source for Hollywood films, or for concerned television documentaries highlighting the problems of the unsettled veteran. But to many of the people of Southeast Asia, it was a long, slow end to a way of life, a tragedy that is still going on today. It was a tragedy in which all the might of American power could not defeat a poorly armed but tenacious and committed enemy. And yet, for all the shadow it casts upon the American people, the roots of the war are still misunderstood.

Southeast Asia has been a cockpit of warfare since time immemorial. For two thousand years, there has been conflict. China was usually the enemy, but wars between the Tonkinese and the Annamese, or between the Cambodians and the Thais, or any combination or permutation of combatants were common. But whatever the case, in the absence of an outside threat there has been a natural antipathy between the peoples of the north and south of what is now known as Vietnam.

In the mid-Nineteenth Century, France's colonial ambitions took the West into Indochina, and within two decades the French were in control of Vietnam, Laos and Cambodia. A century later, France's defeat by Germany and Japan's occupation of French Indochina was a signal to the native inhabitants that the Europeans were not all-powerful, and there might be a chance of throwing off the imperialist yoke. After fighting the Japanese, the nationalist Viet Minh guerrillas under Ho Chi Minh rose against post-war French rule. In 1954, the retreat from Empire and the catastrophe at Dien Bien Phu signalled the end of French occupation, their only legacy the French language, the French educational system and the Roman Catholic faith.

On July 20, 1954, an agreement was signed in Geneva which ended hostilities and paved the way for elections. Ho Chi Minh and the communists had their power base in the north, while the capitalist, Catholic politician Ngo Dinh Diem was the power in Saigon. To the age-old antipathies between north and south were added elements of Cold War hatreds. In spite of challenges to his leadership, including coup attempts, Dien consolidated his leadership with the aid of a rigged election. In the north, Ho Chi Minh made sure of his position by exterminating the last of the landowners.

In 1957, Ho unleashed 6,000 guerrillas who had remained in the south against the southern government. Known as the Viet Cong, they were assisted by the physical nature of Vietnam. A long border flanked Cambodia and Laos, ostensibly neutral nations which in fact served as communist santuaries. The mountainous north and centre of South Vietnam were sparsely populated by mountain tribes who were often at odds with Saigon, and the poor road network favoured guerrillas more than formally-constituted armed forces. Elsewhere, the ricebowl of the Mekong Delta covering most of the south of the country was another region of communist activity. In the next two or three years, infiltrations from the north grew rapidly, and it became clear that the communists were waging a co-ordinated guerrilla war against the south. And South Vietnam was being assisted by America.

This was the height of the Cold War, when the spread of world communism was perceived as the major threat to the United States. US advisers had been in Vietnam since the French departure, and plans were established to come to the aid of the South should the North mount a conventional invasion. It did not come, but it was obvious that the Army of the Republic of Vietnam was in a poor position to fight a major guerrilla war. With the assistance of US advisers, a major programme to rebuild the South Vietnamese army got under way in 1957.

The election of John F. Kennedy to the presidency in November of 1960 signalled a major change. Kennedy was a supporter of counter-insurgency concepts and a champion of the US Army's Green Berets. He was convinced that political reform and an increased US advisory/support effort could bring about peace in Vietnam. Kennedy's hopes for political reform were set back by a coup during which Diem was murdered. Twenty days later, Kennedy was himself to be killed. By the time of his assassination, there were some 16,300 US advisers and support troops (mostly helicopter transport units) in Vietnam. These were directed by the Military Assistance Command Vietnam, or MACV, which had been set up in 1962. In addition, US Air Force 'support missions' expanded into flying reconnaissance missions, air commando ground attack sorties, and defoliation from the air in an operation known as Ranch Hand.

Lyndon Johnson, thrust into the presidency by John F. Kennedy's assassination, resolved to continue his predecessor's policy in Southeast Asia. But the view from Washington was pessimistic. By the middle of 1964, the Viet Cong appeared to have the upper hand in spite of a massive US aid programme and the presence of 23,000 US advisory and support personnel. Coup followed coup in the south, and it appeared that the 'Domino' theory' theory, the fall of nation after nation to communism, would be proved in Southeast Asia. Even more assistance would be required.

Ironically, the CIA advised that the strong US presence on the island nations of the Pacific would ensure that this would not be the case. In fact, a dispassionate analysis would have shown that South Vietnam and Indochina were not and never could be vital to US interests. But nobody made that analysis. Strangely, the North Vietnamese were equally pessimistic about success with the forces available to them in south Vietnam, and so began to prepare the North Vietnamese Army (the NVA) for a more active role. So both sides were in the process of stepping up their efforts in South Vietnam.

And then, early in August 1964, a US Navy destroyer on electronic surveillance duties off the coast of North Vietnam noticed some fast-moving blips on its radar screens . . .

1964

JANUARY 1964

1st There are 16,500 US advisers in South Vietnam aiding the government in its campaign against the Viet Cong.

2nd President Johnson receives details of Oplan 34A, a proposed covert campaign against North Vietnam.

30th Major General Khanh heads a bloodless coup which topples General Minh's government in Saigon.

FEBRUARY 1964

1st Start of Oplan 34A.

16th The recent round of communist terrorist operations continues with a bomb explosion in a cinema for US personnel in Saigon.

19th A US adviser dies as two South Vietnamese Air Force aircraft are shot down by the Viet Cong.

26th Despite a five to one advantage in manpower an ARVN force fails to defeat a Viet Cong battalion near Long Dinh.

MARCH 1964

17th US announces a step-up in military and economic aid to South Vietnam.

20th Border problems come to a head as the South Vietnamese, with US military advisers, raid Chantrea in Cambodia. Prince Sihanouk of Cambodia demands reparations and a Geneva conference.

APRIL 1964

9-12th Four US advisers die in fighting in the Mekong Delta.

21st Republican Congress leaders accuse the administration of deliberately playing down the US role in Vietnam.

MAY 1964

2nd A suspected Viet Cong device sinks USNS *Card* in Saigon.

18th President Johnson requests Congress to grant a further $125 million in aid to South Vietnam.

22-31st Thailand grants base facilities for US aircraft operating against the Pathet Lao.

JUNE 1964

6-9th Two US reconnaissance aircraft are shot down over Laos by the Pathet Lao.

Tonkin Gulf
Torpedo Boat Attack

As Navy destroyers had done for years, USS *Maddox* (DD-731) steamed through whitecapped seas in the Gulf of Tonkin when out of broad daylight North Vietnamese P-4 torpedo boats cut across *Maddox*'s bow and took her under attack. It was 2 August 1964 and, as the Navy had been doing for years, *Maddox* was on a Desoto Patrol,

20th Lieutenant General William Westmoreland takes over as chief of the US MACV (Military Assistance Command Vietnam).

26th ARVN and Viet Cong forces clash at Bau Cot. 100 communists die.

JULY 1964

3-6th US personnel are killed and wounded as Viet Cong raid camps in South Vietnam.

9th China declares that it will step in if the US attacks North Vietnam.

11-12th Biggest battle of the conflict so far takes place around Chuong Thien.

gathering communications intelligence on North Vietnamese and Chinese military activities.

Exchanges of gunfire left a single bullet hole in *Maddox*'s bridge and no apparent damage to the torpedo boats. Two days later, *Maddox* was joined by USS *Turner Joy* (DD-951) and the two destroyers were on the prowl together in the Gulf of Tonkin. (Did anyone remember that Admiral Turner Joy had been a truce negotiator in the Korean War?) The ships were attacked again.

Phantom Attack

A remarkable sidelight to these two attacks – collectively to be known ever after as the Gulf of Tonkin incident – concerns Commander James Bond Stockdale, who was flying an F-8E Crusader overhead on the night of the second attack. Stockdale formed the opinion that the second attack was a "phantom", that the destroyer crews were shooting at an enemy who did not exist. He followed voice instructions from the destroyers, only to find the sea empty where the boats were supposed to be. Stockdale later became a genuine American hero, a prisoner of war, who earned the Medal of Honor for resisting his captors. He also fought valiantly, while a captive, to keep what he regarded as an important secret – that the second Gulf of Tonkin attack never took place.

To retaliate for the P-4 boat attacks, carrier-based aircraft

North Vietnamese torpedo boats leave wakes in the Gulf of Tonkin. It was boats like these which attacked the *Maddox*

from USS *Ticonderoga* (CVA-14) and USS *Constellation* (CVA-64) did exactly what the Pentagon had been thinking about for years – bombed North Vietnam. Secretary of Defense McNamara publicly named the targets while the strikes were en route. Crusaders, Skyhawks and Skyraiders dropped bombs on torpedo boat bases, petroleum facilities, and other targets. A Skyraider was shot down, its pilot killed. A Skyhawk pilot was hit, bailed out and preceded Stockdale as the first POW held "up North".

The Turning Point

It was a turning point in history. On 7 August 1964, Congress passed the Gulf of Tonkin Resolution, freezing the Commander in Chief from any legislative restraint. At the very time when Lyndon Johnson was campaigning for re-election by warning that his opponent might choose to bomb North Vietnam, Johnson was now free to do so.

Aboard *Constellation*, steaming off the North Vietnamese coast, 19-year-old seaman Jim Green followed these developments with scepticism. Shipboard duty was tough and demanding and, aboard a carrier, dangerous. Tens of thousands like Green worked fourteen-hour days, kept the aircraft flying, and had only occasional idle moments to speculate. But men like Green were not without powers of perception. "I think we're going to have to drop some more bombs on those pukes up North," Green uttered to a shipmate. "And the guy who's going to do it isn't Barry Goldwater."

US Planes K.O. 5 N. Viet Bases

U.S. Navy planes striking back at communist attackers Wednesday damaged or destroyed approximately 25 Red patrol boats at four bases in north Vietnam.

Two American planes were shot down by antiaircraft fire from ground batteries. Their pilots were presumed lost. One other plane was damaged slightly.

Besides knocking out a large portion of north Vietnam's patrol boat fleet, the U.S. planes from the carriers Ticonderoga and Constellation blew up an oil depot and other base facilities.

The low-level air attacks were carried out over a period of about five hours, from noon to 5 p.m. Vietnam time.

North Vietnam claimed to have shot down five U.S. aircraft, damaged three, and captured one American pilot during the attacks, the New China News Agency said in a broadcast monitored in Tokyo.

Stars and Stripes

The A-4 is a small, but highly effective bomber. It is heavily involved in the Navy's strikes in retaliation for communist attacks on American destroyers

96 Copters Hit Reds

Xa Ba Hao, Republic of Vietnam – One of the largest helicopter assaults of the Republic of Vietnam's war was hurled into jungles near here Wednesday where intelligence reports had indicated between 2,000 and 3,000 Viet Cong had massed for a strike.

Ninety-six helicopters, both Vietnamese and U.S. Army were thrown into attack, carrying close to 1,000 Vietnamese troops.

Stars and Stripes

27th A proposed increase in the US military presence from over 16,000 to 21,000 "advisers" is announced.

AUGUST 1964

2nd USS *Maddox* comes under attack from North Vietnamese craft in the Tonkin Gulf.

3-4th A second North Vietnamese naval assault on the *Maddox*, which is never absolutely confirmed as having taken place, leads to reprisal bombing raids on the North.

5th It is announced that the US forces in Vietnam are to be increased.

5th Lieutenant Everett Alvarez Jr becomes the first US POW of the war.

7th Public Law 88-408 – the Tonkin Gulf Resolution – is passed by the Senate. It gives the US President wide powers in Southeast Asia.

16th General Khanh becomes president of Vietnam under a new constitution which is soon withdrawn as South Vietnam erupts in anti-government violence.

29th It is disclosed that 274 US personnel have died in Vietnam since December 1961.

SEPTEMBER 1964

2-3rd General Minh reinstated as head of South Vietnamese state by Premier Khanh, though the latter is still very much in charge.

21-28th Hill tribesmen rebel against the South Vietnamese government.

26th Heavy fighting between the South Vietnamese and Viet Cong in the Mekong Delta.

30th First large-scale anti-war demonstration in US takes place at the University of California at Berkeley.

OCTOBER 1964

7th Five US personnel die when their helicopter is shot down by Viet Cong.

14th US aircraft are permitted to fly with Laotian planes on operations against communist movements on the Ho Chi Minh Trail.

NOVEMBER 1964

1st Viet Cong raid on Bien Hoa air base, 12 miles north of Saigon.

3rd Lyndon Johnson is re-elected President of the United States of America.

10th The US states that there are no plans to send combat troops to Vietnam.

18th Over 100 helicopters lift South Vietnamese troops into operations in Binh Dyong and Taynin Provinces.

28th US Ambassador to Saigon General Maxwell Taylor advocates bombing the North.

DECEMBER 1964

1-3rd A tentative agreement is reached by the President and his advisers for a proposed step-up of the bombing of the Ho Chi Minh Trail.

3rd The US announces its intention to send women military advisers to Vietnam.

5th Captain Roger Donlon becomes the first serviceman to be awarded the Congressional Medal of Honor in the Vietnam campaign.

14th Operation Barrel Roll, the escalation of bombing against targets in Laos, begins. The US public are not informed.

15th Heavy fighting in the An Loa Valley leads to the highest weekly South Vietnamese casualties so far reported.

19-20th High-ranking military officers, including General Khanh, lead another bloodless coup in Saigon.

24th Viet Cong car bomb explodes at the Brinks Hotel in Saigon, killing two Americans and wounding 65 Americans and Vietnamese. In a message to US Ambassador Taylor refusing reprisal raids against the North, President Johnson gives first hint of sending combat units to Vietnam.

28th Viet Cong take village of Bien Gia, 40 miles southeast of Saigon. It is retaken at great cost by the South Vietnamese.

Air Force Counter-Insurgency

It felt like World War II, flying with the US Air Force in Southeast Asia in the early 1960s. Men walked around barechested, carrying sub-machine guns and bandoliers of ammo slung over their shoulders. Bush hats were popular. The sound of aircraft engines on an airfield in the early morning was evocative of that early era. The wheeze of a propeller turning over, followed by a gnashing and then the cough, cough, and finally the roar of a reciprocating engine

Echoes of World War II, as a prop-driven Air Commando-piloted A-1 Skyraider dives down to lay its deadly ordnance on some Viet Cong insurgents

coming to life: It was like a time that many of the men remembered from their own experience, long before jet engines had come along.

Operating with a mix of ancient B-26 and T-28 aircraft at Bien Hoa beginning in November 1961, 200 US Air Force commandos made up the Farm Gate detachment that got everything started. At first, there was a clandestine aura to the presence of the airmen; they wore civilian clothes and kept in the background. They used a term that had become fashionable – COIN, meaning counter-insurgency.

Up through November 1964, which meant through the Diem regime and for the year that followed, it truly was a counter-insurgency air operation. Men and aircraft, working in small numbers, were effective against the Viet Cong insurgency. Throughout this period, combined VNAF

Beyond the Call

"If you lined up 100 officers and had to select the top five, he'd be one of them," a superior once said of US Army Capt. Roger Donlon, 30, of Saugerties, NY. A West Point dropout who enlisted and won a commission and the green beret of the Special Forces, Donlon was in command of a mountain outpost in Vietnam last July 6 when hordes of Viet Cong attacked by night. Shot in the stomach, he stuffed a handkerchief into the wound, cinched up his belt, and kept fighting. In fact, three more wounds didn't even slow him down. "He was a perfect target, silhouetted against the burning barracks, hopping on one leg, one arm useless, throwing grenades," a sergeant recalled. Last week, President Johnson presented Donlon with the first Congressional Medal of Honor of the Vietnamese war for "conspicuous gallantry, extraordinary heroism and intrepidity at the risk of his own life above and beyond the call of duty."

Newsweek

and USAF efforts mounted up to 35 sorties per day. The intent was to enable Saigon's forces to function more effectively in the bush, and it worked.

Winding down?

Apparently, in the belief that the war was being won, the 19th Tactical Air Support Squadron equipped with Cessna O-1F Bird Dogs was deactivated in August 1964. It was one of many signals to the airmen that the war was almost over. That same month, the Vietnamese attacked US ships and retaliatory air strikes were flown, but for participants of the "in-country war", it felt as if things were winding down. When the 19th Squadron was reactivated a few months later, everybody assumed that this was just another of the many changes that kept occurring. Everybody said the VC were being licked and the guys would soon be able to go home.

LBJ Replaces B-57s

Destroyed by Reds

President Johnson sought means Sunday to tighten defenses against mortar attacks such as raked a U.S. air base in South Vietnam Saturday, and he immediately replaced the jet bombers destroyed in that strike.

The attack on Bien Hoa airfield near Saigon killed four Americans and destroyed five B-57 twin-engine jet bombers.

The President's moves were announced by the White House after a 75-minute Sunday afternoon meeting between Johnson and top aides including Secretary of State Dean Rusk, Defense Secretary Robert S. McNamara, international security affairs adviser McGeorge Bundy, Under Secretary of State George W. Ball and William P. Bundy, assistant secretary of state for Far Eastern affairs.

The Administration tended to regard the affair as serious

Wrecked B-57 bombers attest that air superiority is no guarantee against a ground mortar attack

because of the loss of life and planes, but not as a major development in the war against the communist insurgents. It was seen as an episode of a type difficult to prevent in such a war where the enemy has many opportunities for such hit-and-run surprise attacks.

Stars and Stripes

Viet Cong Provocations

Nobody ever claimed that the Brink Hotel in Saigon was any great shakes. The old, colonial style building had been taken over as a US Army officers' billet and was replete with all the little pleasures that we brought with us to war, including a shoeshine stand, a small PX selling nylons, makeup and cosmetics to our all-male force, and a dining area

A smashed Jeep is seen after a Viet Cong bomb attack in the streets of Saigon

nicknamed "the Pit". Prices being low everywhere, most of the men preferred to eat up the street where several joints offered hamburgers and other amenities.

On the afternoon of 24 December, tinsel hung from the ceiling in the dining area and a plastic Christmas tree was alight in a corner. With Army officer advisors preparing to celebrate Christmas Eve, a Viet Cong sapper on a bicycle hurled a 250 lb (113 kg) *plastique* charge into the place and the Brink Hotel ex-

ploded, throwing flames and debris out into the street and collapsing upon itself. Two Americans and 51 South Vietnamese were killed.

How to Hit Back?

We didn't know it then, of course, but following Lyndon Johnson's re-election the previous month, Ambassador Maxwell Taylor had urged that there be swift and powerful retaliation against North Vietnam for any such VC provocation.

1965

JANUARY 1965

2nd Two companies of ARVN Rangers are ambushed within 40 miles of Saigon. 200 South Vietnamese troops and five US advisers are killed.

3rd Anti-government rioting in Saigon.

13th US government admits that two aircraft have been shot down over Laos.

23rd A mob of 3000 Buddhists storms the United States Information Service in the old imperial capital, Hue, and burns more than 5000 books. The US vice-consul is stoned by the mob.

28th After a coup in which there are no casualties, the Army takes over in Saigon, ending a short-lived interlude of civilian rule.

Vietnamese Marines await a helicopter lift into an assault. These are amongst the most effective of ARVN troops

Vietnamese paratroopers celebrate Airborne Day in Saigon. Winning the support of such elite troops was essential in the many coups which took place in South Vietnam in the mid-1960s

A Home from Home

The streets of Saigon are wide and pleasantly arced over by tall, graceful tamarind trees, reminiscent of a city in southern France or parts of New Orleans.

Bustling City

The noise and bustle of the city are scented with the pungent, exotic smells of the Orient; joss sticks burn at the ancestor shrines of the pagodas and smells and color combine in sensuous riot at the wholesale produce market. Though the Viet Cong control much of the countryside, fruits, vegetables and rice still flow into Saigon by truck and cart; the Viet Cong tax all this produce and, in any case, don't want to alienate the farmers.

On the streets the children smile at you and urge you to pay an old man to run an ancient outdoor movie projector mounted on a bicycle. But though most of the children are very friendly, one youth stared at me contemptuously and spat on the ground.

Diversions

For unmarried US military personnel or those who don't have their families with them, Saigon offers plenty of diversion; there are the downtown bars where B-girls in Western costume idly toss dice while waiting for customers, and there is the Rex Hotel for officers where a Filipino dance band blares until late into the night. There is the American school which runs from kindergarten through high school, there are bridge games, dinner parties, and trips to the commissary, and there is adequate housing – though rents run as high as $400 a month for a two-bedroom home. "I sometimes think things

Korean Move Approved

Seoul, South Korea, Tuesday, Jan. 26 – National Assembly approved today Government plans to send about 2,000 noncombat troops to South Vietnam. The vote was 106 to 11 with 8 abstentions.

NY Times

Viets Sack U.S. Library

A mob of 3,000 young buddhists stormed the United States Information Service (USIS) library in the old imperial capital of Hue Saturday night and burned more than 5,000 books.

The U.S. vice consul in Hue, Anthony Lake, was stoned by the mob when he tried to enter the Library to put out the fires. He was not hurt.

U.S. authorities placed Hue off limits to American soldiers stationed in and around the city.

The mob appeared to be led by a core of about 100 young agitators. They first demonstrated and shouted slogans at a billet occupied by American servicemen and at the U.S. Consulate.

Their leaders then turned them toward the library building.

Until then the demonstrations had been peaceful.

Suddenly, rocks were thrown smashing ground floor windows of the library. The mob surged forward and into the building.

Stars and Stripes

Saigon, where French colonialism meets the Orient, and where most creature comforts are available to the rapidly growing American community

here must look worse from New York," Mrs Joseph Luman, the 29-year-old wife of a US Embassy official, remarked to me.

A pretty brunette, Mrs Luman lives on the ground floor of a spacious French-style villa. "I've been here a year and a half," says Mrs Luman. "Sometimes it's bad and sometimes it's good. You read about things that happen in the countryside but still you try to live normally. At times, though, you get discouraged. Last night we heard artillery fire – what the servants call boom-boom. But yet I really like Saigon. True, it's called a city, but it's more like a small town. After a trip to Bangkok I was really glad to get back – even though the Kindo movie theater had just been bombed."

Newsweek

Help for Civilians, Too

PLEI DO LIM – Many American soldiers sent to South Vietnam as military advisers have found their greatest satisfaction in setting up a kind of peace corps in the villages.

"Every time we have to kill," one West Point graduate said, "it's failure for us. It means we haven't been able to get across to the people in the area."

At another post, the officers talked matter-of-factly about two Viet Cong guerrillas their patrol killed last week. But they became enthusiastic as they told of a windmill they would soon receive from Saigon to provide power for 700 villagers around the post.

An American major near Danang spends his free moments working on a mold for hollow bricks. "It will save material and give better insulation than the solid ones they're using," he explained. "If I don't do anything else while here I'm going to get them making the right kind of bricks."

Because of a lack of contact with the enemy, the camp was scheduled for closing last year.

The present team would have been sent to an area with more military action.

But the camp has been kept open and the team is charged with safeguarding more than 10,000 villagers who have moved to near the camp for protection.

Babies and Bombers

Despite nightly patrols, security sometimes fails. Last fall the Viet Cong slipped in by night and set fire to three of the villages. "The families rebuilt right away without complaining," Specialist 5 Thor Johnston recalled. "They seemed used to it."

Specialist Johnston, a strapping demolitions crewman from Eureka, Calif., stood in the sun watching Djaraf tribesmen cutting and weaving bamboo to repair their neat huts. "Someday these people are going to make an atom bomb out of bamboo," he said.

At the camp's dispensary, two American medical corpsmen and their Vietnamese helpers treat 1,500 to 2,000 soldiers and villagers each month.

One of them, Sgt. Billie Johnson of New Town, Mo., said his team baulked only at delivering babies. "It can become a status symbol for the women to have their babies delivered by an American. Pretty soon you're doing nothing else."

The medics have interpreters on hand as they make preliminary exmainations. The Americans will ask "daud?" which means "hurt?" or "pain?"

But they put no stock in the answer.

"Ask any of them if they have a pain and they'll say yes just to oblige you," Sergeant Johnson said.

New York Times

An American Lieutenant Colonel gets acquainted with local children as he distributes CARE packages sent as aid from the United States

FEBRUARY 1965

4th McGeorge Bundy, American Special Assistant for National Security, arrives in Saigon for talks with US ambassador General Maxwell Taylor.

6th Soviet premier Alexei Kosygin arrives in Hanoi. He pledges support for forces working towards the unification of Vietnam and condemns American policy.

7th Viet Cong make combined attacks on US bases, the most effective of which are against Pleiku in the Central Highlands where eight Americans are killed and 126 wounded. Losses in material include 10 aircraft destroyed and 15 damaged.

7th Retaliation for the Viet Cong attacks includes air strikes into North Vietnam.

13th President Johnson decides to give the go-ahead for the sustained bombing campaign against North Vietnam – Operation Rolling Thunder.

19th Beginning of a coup attempt in South Vietnam that ends with the removal of the head of state, General Khanh.

22nd General William Westmoreland requests US Marines to protect the base at Da Nang.

26th The first South Korean troops arrive in Vietnam.

Only 20 to 25% of US Troops in Vietnam Receive Combat Pay

WASHINGTON – Not every United States military man in Vietnam gets special combat pay, officials pointed out today. Only about 20 to 25 per cent of the 23,000 American military men there receive such pay.

The extra pay for exposure to hostile fire is $55 a month regardless of grade or rank. The term "combat pay" is only a colloquialism and is avoided in official terminology because the United States is not regarded as engaged in combat in Vietnam.

The New York Times

Three GIs Killed by Viet Cong After Home Guard Unit Fled

SAIGON – A company of South Vietnamese home guardsmen deserted four United States military advisers and five of their own men during a Viet Cong attack Wednesday, United States military informants said yesterday.

The home guard threw down their weapons and left a hill fortification as the Communist guerrillas approached in the dark with loudspeakers, calling: "We only want to kill the Americans. All the rest can go free if they leave their weapons."

Day of Attack on Billet

The next morning the three Americans and five tribesmen were found dead on the hilltop at Ducphong.

The New York Times

Jerseyan's Ordeal: 35 Hours in Rubble of Quinhon Billet

QUINHON – The roof fell in on Specialist 4 Arthur G. Abendschein at 8.05 pm on Wednesday as he frantically reloaded his carbine.

Specialist Abendschein, a 30-year-old resident of Almonesson, NJ, south of Camden, had stood on a second floor balcony and had fired a magazine of bullets at a squad of Viet Cong attackers. For 35 hours he did not stand again.

Three explosive charges collapsed the four-storey barracks around him and 42 other soldiers.

The specialist, known as the jokester of the 140th Maintenance Detachment, which works on the planes at Quinhon, had only "20 days to zero" – 20 days left before he was to go home.

He found himself flat on his back in a splintered cavern measuring about 6 feet by 2 by 2. Broken masonry was stacked for 15 feet above him and to a greater distance on each side. There was a three-inch gash in his head.

For hours, no one knew he was caught in the wreckage. Trapped and maimed men nearer the rim were helped first. The cries of the wounded drowned out Specialist Abendschein's calls, but a voice contact was finally established.

3-Hour Task Seen

Recuers started tunnelling for him yesterday at 3.30 pm. They were confident that he would be pulled out of the hole by 6 pm, but they soon struck trouble.

A slight Hawaiian, Specialist 5 Pedreno Ebos, volunteered to burrow through the debris. He accidentally started a small landslide, which cascaded rubble on the entombed man's bare back.

"Get the hell out of here and leave me," Specialist Abendschein called. "Don't get caught." But Specialist Ebos stayed.

The trapped man called out, "Send me down a hammer and chisel and I'll dig my own way out." The rescuers obliged, and he started picking at the concrete, swinging in short thrusts over his head.

At one point, the specialist fell asleep. An officer dashed coffee in his face through the widening hole.

Finally, two young mountain tribesmen from a Vietnamese Special Forces company guarding the wreckage came to the rescue. Peeling off their fatigues, they climbed into the tunnel at 5.30 am and began digging. They were Siu Alam and Ksor Gong, members from the Jerai tribe. They emerged with Specialist Abendschein at 7.40 am.

The specialist smiled and did a dance.

The New York Times

Not all South Vietnamese irregulars are as reliable as these Junk Force members

American-Piloted
U.S. Jets in
Viet Combat for 1st Time

An F-100 drops its deadly cargo on to an unsuspecting enemy beneath the jungle canopy. For the first time, **US** pilots are officially flying such operations over **South Vietnam**

SAIGON – The United States disclosed Wednesday that U.S. jets piloted by Americans have gone into combat action inside the Republic of Vietnam for the first time to give "maximum assistance" to the Vietnamese in the war against the communists.

A U.S. spokesman said twin-jet B-57 bombers first went into action last week against communist Viet Cong forces in Phoue Tuy Province, about 40 miles southeast of Saigon.

The B-57s and American F-100 jet aircraft from two jet bomber bases in South Vietnam blasted the communists anew Wednesday to help rescue Vietnamese troops trapped by a Viet Cong offensive 240 miles north of Saigon.

Stars and Stripes

USAF Martin B-57 bombers are being used operationally in Vietnam for the first time. They are supporting South Vietnamese ground troops

Under Cover on Night

It was 2 am on the morning of Feb. 7, only hours after Kosygin had assured a cheering crowd in Hanoi that Russia would "not remain indifferent" if "acts of war" were carried out against North Vietnam, that Sp/5 Jesse A. Pyle of Marina, Calif., noticed dark shadows moving near the perimeter wire 100 yards from the US advisers' barracks in a Vietnamese Army headquarters at Pleiku in Vietnam's central highlands. Pyle opened fire. It was the last act of his life. The shadows, materializing into Communist Viet Cong guerrillas, fatally wounded Pyle with their grenades. But his quick action had awakened the men located inside the compound. As a result, the Viet Cong were forced to set off their explosive charges – which were improvised from beer cans wrapped in bamboo cord – prematurely or not at all.

Four miles away at Camp Holloway, a US helicopter base, the Viet Cong had better luck. A handful of demolition experts, again penetrating an outer perimeter guarded by American sentries, audaciously attached demolition charges to helicopters parked on the 4,500-foot air strip. The moment the first charge exploded, mortar shells rained in from the outskirts of a "friendly" village. (To add to the irony, the mortars and shells were captured US equipment.)

Newsweek

17

MARCH 1965

2nd The first of the Rolling Thunder raids against North Vietnam takes place.

3rd US aircraft strike at the Ho Chi Minh Trail in Laos.

8th Three US vessels land two Marine battalions, totalling 3500 men, under Brigadier General Frederick Karch, to help defend Da Nang.

9th The first US tanks, M48A3s of the 3rd Marine Tank Battalion, come ashore at Da Nang.

10th Marines make first contact with communist forces.

14th US and South Vietnamese aircraft use napalm over North Vietnam for the first time.

22nd US government embarrassed by revelation that "non-lethal gas that disables temporarily" has been supplied to South Vietnamese forces for use in the field.

30th A car bomb explodes outside the US embassy in Saigon causing over 200 casualties, of whom 22 die.

A Welcome for the Marines

Under slate-grey skies, US Marine landing craft plowed through 5 ft waves in the Bay of Danang, came to a halt with gravelly crunches and dropped their ramps. Out poured hundreds of US Marines in full battle dress, with M-14 rifles held at high port. They were the vanguard of a 3,500-man force, the first Marines since Korea to hit the beaches in a combat zone and the first US combat troops to arrive in South Vietnam.

The Marines were shot at once during the landing operation, when a Viet Cong rifleman hit the wing of a C-130 hercules transport as it approached Danang with a load of Marines from camps on Okinawa, but no real damage was done.

First to hit the beach was Corporal Garry Parsons, who splashed onto the wet sand and sprinted 50 yards into a stand of pine trees – and a platoon of photographers. Parsons' comment was candid if not immortal. Cried he, "I'm glad to get off that damned ship!"

Girls and Frogmen

Marines are indoctrinated in boot camp that there is no such thing as a "friendly" beach, and as they dashed ashore, they were ready for anything – except perhaps the winsome welcoming committee of Vietnamese girls bearing garlands of yellow dahlias and red gladioli.

It took just 65 minutes to put 1,400 Marines ashore with rifles, machine guns, rocket and grenade launchers. At Danang, the brigade's other battalion came in the easy way – by air from Okinawa. Both battalions came prepared for heavy combat: they had 105 mm howitzers, M-48 medium tanks, 106 mm recoilless rifles.

However, in one of their first joint patrols with Vietnamese rangers, the Marines were slightly unnerved. "The Vietnamese seemed to know their business all right," said Lieut.

Arms in Vietnam Criticized by GIs

SAIGON – There was a flurry of new complaints today from United States servicemen in South Vietnam who said they were fighting with shoddy weapons, were often short of ammunition and often lacked equipment – although, they said, some items were for sale on the black market.

One American adviser stationed in central Vietnam said that although the war was getting serious the most up-to-date weapons had not come to all units.

"The Armalite automatic rifle would fill the bill nicely with its proved effectiveness," the adviser said. "But only the Special Forces and some privileged units get these. The best we get is the automatic carbine. As things get worse here, we need the best weapon for personal protection."

Another adviser said the ammunition magazines for the carbines were too lightly constructed and jammed easily under hard usage.

"I read somewhere that the Defense Department says the Americans in Vietnam are the best equipped fighting men ever to go overseas," he added. "They still have to show that."

The New York Times

Two 'Grunts' here are armed with the new lightweight M16 rifle, while one has an older M14

Donald H. Hering, "but we were a little shook up when they started lighting cigarettes and listening to jazz on their transistors while we were patrolling."

Time

Three Marines patrol through a paddy field shortly after arriving at Da Nang. Even without the enemy, such terrain and the humid climate is enough to exhaust the strongest man

Water Wings

US Air Force 1st Lieut. James A. Cullen of Winchester, Mass., could hardly have been in a tighter spot. Hit by Viet Minh gunners during a bombing run over Quangkhe during last week's raids, Cullen bailed out of his F-100 Super Sabre into the Gulf of Tonkin – and practically into the midst of a flotilla of armed Communist junks and torpedo boats. Muzzles flashing, the Red vessels sped toward Cullen as he desperately sought cover behind his life raft. Said he: "I thought I was finished."

He very well might have been, but seven US Navy Skyraiders from a nearby Seventh Fleet carrier suddenly swooped in almost low enough to get their bellies wet and buzzed the Red vessels. Meanwhile, an amphibious Air Force HU-16 "Albatross" that had been circling off Quangkhe in case of just such an emergency, zeroed in on a radio homing beacon built into Cullen's life belt and sighted a brilliant orange marker dye that the downed pilot had released into the water. Defying 5 ft waves, the Albatross set down without mishap in the choppy gulf, taxied up to Cullen, and was flying him back to South Vietnam only 30 minutes after he hit the water.

On the way, it joined another Huskie and an escort of American fighters that had picked up yet another urgent distress call – from a US captain whose Thunderchief jet was shot down over the tangled jungle near Quangkhe. Sighting a signal fire that the captain had resourcefully lighted on the bank of a stream, one Huskie descended to 100 ft, hauled the captain into the chopper with a steel cable and winch. As he scrambled gratefully aboard, the rescued pilot cried to the crew, "I love you, I love you."

Time

Victory at Kannack

The Viet Cong waited until a thick layer of rain cloud covered the mountain crests around Kannack. Insured against US jet attacks, they struck, nearly 1,000 strong, at the camp's north, south and east flanks. Dozens of assault squads in black shorts and green kerchiefs of parachute silk slipped up to the barbed-wire perimeter carrying Bangalore torpedoes. There followed bangs galore.

Then shock troops dragged wicker baskets full of grenades and ammo through holes blown in the wire, knocked out a sandbagged bunker on Kannack's northeast corner with one shot from a 57-mm recoilless rifle, then blasted through the camp's bloody southeast angle to carry a string of defensive bunkers. All told, Kannack's defenders lost 33 dead and 27 wounded – most of them in the first assault.

Wives and Desperation

But the mountain men – a mixture of Hrey, Bahnar, Rhade and Muong tribals – dug in and held. As they turned their mortars on their own overrun positions, their women carted ammunition into the trenches and fed belts into the clattering machine guns. "I think the montagnards fought well because most had their families with them," said an American adviser. "These people are ruthless when it comes to life or death. One guy was in a bunker, completely cut off, and the VC called on him to surrender. He

DANANG – Gunnery Sgt. Raymond Charles Benfatti stopped for a moment this morning to catch his breath and find his company commander.

The sergeant, who has spent 18 years in the Marine Corps, had just reached the top of Hill 327, which dominates the western approaches to the Danang airfield.

"We are plenty glad to be here even if that might sound funny to some people," he said. "We had been aboard ship in the Seventh Fleet for so long it was like sitting on the bench. It was time the coach sent us in."

"I never had any doubts about what I wanted to do when I finished school," he said. "My brother Victor was a marine, killed in Guam. He was my idol as a youngster and I believed the Marine Corps was the best life I could pick."

"We are quite ready for this job," the sergeant declared. "It's only a protective one but we can handle anything that may get in our way, have no doubt about that."

When Sergeant Benfatti is not engaged in protecting airfields, his principal interests are swimming, boxing and his eight children.

He has not seen them or his wife for nine months and it will be considerably longer before he leaves Danang and gets back to Oceanside, Calif., where they are living.

"That's the only thing wrong with this duty," he said. "But my wife understands. She is married to a marine. Her brother is a marine and her sister is married to one, too. As for me, I am quite satisfied to be a marine. I am hoping to go right on past 20 years and make it 30 if I can."

The New York Times

told them to go to hell and ran down the hill."

End of the Trail

Demoralized, the Viet Cong drew back. In the morning light, more than 100 Communist dead dangled on the wire, some clutching grenades and belts of unburnt ammunition.

Time

1st President Johnson secretly agrees to send more US forces to Vietnam, and to allow them to be used for offensive action against communist forces.

3rd Air strikes over North Vietnam concentrate on general strategic targets, as well as strictly military ones, for the first time.

7th President Johnson offers unconditional discussions on the future of Vietnam. He says that any peace "demands an independent South Vietnam – securely guaranteed . . ."

7th Viet Cong threaten to kill a captured US civilian official if the South Vietnamese execute a prominent Viet Cong captive.

10th Further Marine units arrive at Da Nang.

15th Biggest air raid of war so far takes place in Tay Ninh Province.

17th 15,000 students stage an anti-war rally in Washington.

20th Marines are permitted to extend operations outside the previous eight-mile perimeter around Da Nang.

26th 20,000 Cambodian students attack the US embassy in Phnom Penh, and tear up the US flag.

"Hanoi Hannah"

Taunts GIs in South Vietnam

Hanoi Hattie and Hanoi Hannah are broadcasting to United States troops in South Vietnam, warning them in accented English that "there is no safety for you Americans anywhere in the country".

In the tradition of Axis Sally, Tokyo Rose and Seoul City Sue – Americans who broadcast for the enemy in earlier wars – the Hanoi radio has been beaming daily programs to American servicemen since last October, attempting to impair their morale and to persuade them to demand to be sent home from Vietnam.

Hanoi Hattie and Hanoi Hannah are Vietnamese, according to information available here. Their names, as given in the broadcasts, are Thu Huong and Thu Mai, but the troops quickly affixed nicknames to them.

The New York Times

Coast Guard Units Going to Vietnam

WASHINGTON, April 29 – Units of the United States Coast Guard have been ordered to South Vietnam to join in coastal patrols to block infiltration of Communist guerillas and arms.

A Coast Guard spokesman said 17 high-speed cutters and 200 men would be sent to Vietnam for operations under the control of United States Navy forces.

NY Times

The Adviser

Major Lane Rogers, 36, a lean, dry-humoured US Marine Corps regular, has been in Viet Nam for 10½ months as adviser to a Vietnamese marine battalion. He has no command capacity whatever. All he can do is offer suggestions, when and if they are solicited by his Vietnamese "counterpart." To perform effectively, the adviser must earn the trust and friendship of his Vietnamese opposite number – a process that often takes weeks, and sometimes is never achieved.

Rogers worked with that same commander for weeks without really gaining his confidence. Finally, Rogers recalls, "there was a Viet Cong sniper who seemed to nip away at us every evening after supper. I used to sneak down to a dike just behind him and try to catch him. Then I went to Saigon for a couple of days. When I got back, I noticed

Being an adviser can be dangerous, especially when your greater height makes you an easy mark for snipers

my counterpart grinning widely. that evening he told me that that VC wasn't going 'Bang! Bang!' any more. He had shot him during my absence. He showed me the brand new Russian carbine he had taken off the sniper. I had it chromed and polished in Saigon and presented it to him. That's when we first became really close friends."

"These Vietnamese are brave people," he says. "You go out on operation and – well – maybe things aren't done quite the way you want them to be. But then, in the middle of a battle, one of these little characters comes grinning up to you and hands you a hot cup of coffee."

Time

Mac the Fac's Last Mission

Short (5 ft 7 ins) and powerfully built, with a bow-legged, gangling walk, the blue-eyed "Mac the Fac" – Air Force Major William W. McAllister, 36, a "forward air controller" looked like the all-American Butch.

Clad in grey coveralls, with a .38 revolver on his hip and a knife strapped to his leg, McAllister was in the air so much of the time that he began counting "missions" by the day instead of by the flight. He was so expert at detecting guerrilla camouflage that he could spot a Viet Cong position within seconds. He flew in low, marked enemy positions with smoke bombs, called in hot fighter bombers, and then got the hell out of the way. The whole business scared him almost stiff. But he went in lower, more often and took more hits than any other US pilot so far in the Vietnam war.

As renowned as his daring was Mac's ever-bubbling, extroversive ebullience. Buzzing along over the jungle, he would sing a raucous couplet into his radio for the benefit of ground walkie-talkies in the area:

Throw a nickel on the grass,
Save a fighter pilot's ****.

Then his familiar voice would crackle through loudspeakers: "Hello you marines down there. Here's your air power."

"Home Next Week"

Last week McAllister seemed even more cheerful than usual. The reason for his special good humor was that this week, after a year in Vietnam, he was scheduled to go home to his wife Gail and a nine-year-old son and seven-year-old daughter in Victorville, Calif. Last Thursday afternoon, some US Marine friends ran into him at Phucat.

"I'll see you over a beer in

An O-1 Bird Dog light observation plane swoops low through the trees in the dangerous search for Viet Cong troops

Quinhon after I finish this last flight. I've got plenty to celebrate. I'm going home next week, and this is my last mission."

It was. At 5 pm, McAllister took off in his single-engine L-19, climbing steeply as always. The plane reached approximately 300 ft of altitude. Then – possibly as a result of damage from antiaircraft fire – it went out of control and crashed. Mac the Fac was instantly killed.

Time

Johnson Proposes $1 bil. S.E. Asia Aid

President Johnson said Wednesday that the United States is ready for "unconditional discussions" to bring peace to the Republic of Vietnam as a first step toward a $1 billion aid program to develop Southeast Asia.

In an address at Johns Hopkins University which was broadcast to the world, Johnson said that any such peace "demands an independent South Vietnam – securely guaranteed and able to shape its own relationships to all others – free from outside interference – tied to no alliance – a military base for no other country."

Until then, he added, the United States will not be defeated, not grow tired, and will not withdraw, "either openly or under the cloak of a meaningless agreement."

Stars and Stripes

MAY 1965

3rd Men of the 173rd Airborne Brigade, the first US Army combat unit committed, begin to deploy to Bien Hoa Air Base, near Saigon.

7th Congress approves a further $700 million for the war.

10th Viet Cong overrun provincial capital of Phuo Clong Province and are only forced out by heavy air attacks.

13th US suspends bombing of North Vietnam, hoping for reciprocal gesture from the communists.

13th Viet Cong attack installations just five miles from Saigon.

16th Forty aircraft are destroyed and 27 Americans are killed in an accidental series of explosions at Bien Hoa Air Base.

19th Bombing of the North resumes.

26th First Australian troops set out for Vietnam.

27th Bombardment from US Navy vessels of Viet Cong positions in central Vietnam for the first time.

29th ARVN battalion cut to pieces by Viet Cong near Bagia.

Arms Haul

KIENHOA – Vietnamese troops, exploring a swamp that the Viet Cong had held for two years, have come across crates of some of the most advanced weapons in South Vietnam.

The large scale cache has yielded flamethrowers never before found in the country, large-gauge rockets and 70 mm howitzer shells.

Except for 240 American Springfield rifles, the bulk of the equipment appeared to have been manufactured by the Chinese Communists.

Arms Hidden in Huts

The weapons had been hidden in thatch-roofed huts built so low that thick jungle foliage obscured them from view from the air.

Troops of the Vietnamese Seventh Division have found about 20 of the huts so far.

Military officers from Saigon said the Viet Cong cache was the largest ever uncovered as a result of a battle. Bigger depots, such as the one at Vungro Bay, had been located through intelligence reports.

The New York Times

The Cock Crows

In the face of heavy ground fire, Lieut. Colonel James Robinson Risner, 40, led his Fighting Cock squadron and 90 other jets into North Vietnam early last month, and hammered at the critical rail and highway bridge near Thanhhoa until finally it was destroyed. His F-105 was heavily damaged by antiaircraft fire, but he refused to be diverted from his mission. For such "extraordinary herosim," Air Force

"Find Viet Cong"

Returning from an inspection tour of the Da Nang base, Gen. Wallace M. Greene, 58-year-old commandant of the Marine Corps, seemed undisturbed by reports that the Viet Cong are poised for a major offensive against the base. "Just let 'em try it," said Greene. "The Marine mission is to kill Viet Cong. They can't do it by sitting on their ditty boxes. I told them to find the Viet Cong and kill 'em. That's the way to carry out their mission."

One night last week, the sky was suddenly lit up by flares, and Gunnery Sgt. Sam Pierce said hopefully: "Maybe they've decided to mix it up with us a little." But Sergeant Robinson, a battle-tested veteran of Guadalcanal, was less optimistic. "It's probably those damned monkeys playing around with the trip flares again," he said. He was right.

Newsweek

Above: Vietnamese troops gather round a small supply cache, possibly indicating more communist material nearby

Items discovered in a large VC cache include automatic rifles, machine guns, and rocket-propelled-grenade launchers

Chief of Staff General J. P. McConnell last week brought Robbie Risner back from Vietnam, awarded him the Air Force Cross, second in rank only to the nation's highest decoration, the Congressional Medal of Honor.

Time

F-105 Thunderchiefs at Takhli RYAB makes an impressive display

The Grenade Ripped into His Arm

SONGBE – S. Sgt. Horace E. Young was lying wounded in the mess hall at 3 am yesterday when a grenade rolled through the door.

He had been struck in the leg an hour earlier by fragments from the mortar rounds the Viet Cong had used before overrunning this provincial capital.

He could hardly move. But he tried to shove the grenade outside with the barrel of his empty rifle. The grenade exploded and ripped into his arm.

In the darkness, Young, in unbearable pain, grabbed at a silhouette. "It's a friend" whispered Specialist 4th Gige E. Kelso of Alton, Ill.

"Let's try to get us a weapon," Young said.

Kelso wiped Young's blood off his face and neck.

Young pulled out a short knife and dragged himself through the mess hall, which had become a temporary aid station.

In the storeroom he struggled weakly with a youthful Viet Cong who had broken into the small mess building.

Then Sergeant Young, 34 years old, of Moline, Ill., collapsed amid cans of tomato juice and bled to death.

His body was shipped to Saigon yesterday with the knife in his hand. No one had been able to pry it loose.

Getting Intimate

As in every war the US fights, the PX has followed the flag in Vietnam. Store Keeper I/C Charles Gray, 28, of Birmingham, Alabama, runs the huge new Navy exchange in Cholon – Saigon's Chinese sister city – and he sells everything from handkerchiefs to hi-fi sets, including stamps, bras, and golf clubs. But the biggest seller of all, according to Gray, is hair spray, which GIs buy up at the rate of some 500 cans per week as presents for their Vietnamese girl friends. "Revlon Intimate is one item we just can't keep enough of in stock," laments Gray.

Newsweek

Navy Guns Open Fire

U.S. ships have entered the Republic of Vietnam ground war by firing at land targets in coastal provinces along the South China Sea, a U.S. spokesman said Thursday.

Four U.S. destroyers have fired shells on six missions against Viet Cong targets in the coastal areas of Binh Dinh, Binh Tuan and Phu Yen provinces since May 20, the spokesman said.

They have been credited with thwarting at least one Viet Cong attack on a Vietnamese district headquarters, the U.S. spokesman said.

Stars and Stripes

The US Navy has patrolled Vietnamese waters for years, but not until now has it provided gunfire support to South Vietnamese troops on shore

2nd US Marines and ARVN forces combine in operations around Chu Lai air base.

3rd A further battalion of ARVN forces is destroyed by Viet Cong ambushes.

7th General Westmoreland requests more troops, asking for US involvement to go up to over 200,000 men.

10th A district capital 60 miles from Saigon is attacked and then falls temporarily to the Viet Cong. US paratroopers are held in readiness to help the ARVN during this fighting.

16th Secretary of Defense Robert McNamara announces that 21,000 more troops are to be sent to Vietnam.

18th Head of the South Vietnamese Air Force Air Vice Marshal Nguyen Cao Ky, becomes new prime minister of South Vietnam after the previous incumbent resigns because of protests from Catholics.

22nd The deepest raids into North Vietnam so far lead to attacks on targets just 80 miles from the Chinese border.

28th US forces are used in an aggressive role for the first time, when members of the 173rd Airborne, together with Australian and ARVN troops, sweep through areas north of Saigon.

Air Vice Marshal Nguyen Cao Ky, seen here with Deputy Ambassador Alexis Johnson, is the new premier of South Vietnam

Hilltop Massacre

The Viet Cong offensive began on Saturday, May 29, when hard-core guerrilla units ambushed the First Battalion of the Vietnamese 51st Regiment west of the provincial capital of Quang Ngai. In short order, the First Battalion was badly mauled, and when other elements of the 51st – including three US advisers, First Lt. Donald R. Robison, Platoon Sgt. Henry A. Musa and Marine Gunnery Sgt. Louis Roundtree – tried to come to its aid, they too were ambushed and surrounded.

With his unit's radio out, Robison could not call for help and soon the Viet Cong broke through the defense perimeter. Robison advised the Vietnamese to try for a breakout and when the Vietnamese commander refused, the three Americans made a break for it on their own. Crawling through paddy fields and irrigation ditches, under fire by their Viet Cong pursuers, the Americans heard one last intense volley back at the ambush site, and then silence. When they managed to work their way back to Quang Ngai, they could only report grimly that the entire unit had been wiped out.

Next day, fresh government forces moved out of Quang Ngai in a counter attack, and at first, Capt. Christopher O'Sullivan, 29, of New York, adviser to the 39th Vietnamese Rangers, radioed back that they had met little resistance. But then, all along the nearby ridges, Viet Cong popped out of tunnels and poured murderous rifle fire into the South Vietnamese ranks. With machine-gun bullets rattling and men falling on all sides, O'Sullivan and Marine Corps Staff Sgt. Willie D. Tyrone charged up one hill with their South Vietnamese unit. The hill was taken temporarily, but in the assault O'Sullivan was killed. Big Willie Tyrone, a 32-year-old Texan, carried the captain's body to the top of the hill and radioed the bad news to headquarters.

Last to Die

"Everything is quiet," reported Tyrone. "I've got a slight crease on my left arm ... it's nothing serious." The reply came back: "We'll try to get in there at first light and pull you out." "Roger," answered Tyrone. It was the last word ever heard from him. In the morning, when the US helicopters whirled in, the hilltop was strewn with the bodies of Viet Cong and of government troops. Some of the Rangers, grotesquely mangled, had been hit by mortar bursts. Other died with arms folded over their gaping wounds, as if to hold in their life's blood. in their midst lay Willie Tyrone who must have been one of the last men on the hill to die.

Newsweek

Terror Bombs Rip Saigon Restaurant

SAIGON – Two terrorist bombs ripped through a floating restaurant on the Saigon River Friday night, killing 25 and wounding dozens of diners.

Of the dead, nine were Americans, five of them U.S. servicemen. Eleven Americans were among the wounded.

U.S. military authorities listed 25 persons killed and 33 wounded. They added that they

The streets of Saigon are littered with the detritus of a terrorist bomb

expected these figures to change as more casualties were found in hospitals and clinics scattered throughout the city.

Unofficial sources said the death toll probably will be 30 or more and that the wounded were expected to exceed 100.

Stars and Stripes

US Troops Move In

American paratroopers were rushed to a major airstrip near embattled Dong Xoai Sunday after a Vietnamese paratroop battalion was decimated in a Viet Cong ambush Saturday night.

The Americans, numbering about 600 combat troops and 300 artillerymen, flew into Phuoc Vinh, 40 miles north of Saigon, in big U.S. Air Force C-123s.

They immediately began digging in around the airport which is the main supply point for military installations throughout the special Phuoc Binh Thanh zone.

The U.S. paratroopers began arriving at Phuoc Vinh early Sunday afternoon.

The movement of the U.S. unit came when the enormity of the Saturday ambush against the Vietnamese 7th Paratrooper Bn. became known.

The ambush was the latest in a series of major Viet Cong thrusts against government units around Dong Xoai. The Viet Cong destroyed the 1st Bn. of the 7th Regt. Thursday, mauled the 2nd Ranger Bn. Thursday night and continued harassing government posts and units Friday.

Latest reports indicate that 250 men from the 400 strong Vietnamese paratroop battalion are missing, believed killed or captured. From the Saturday action only 150 men, 20 of them wounded, have returned to Dong Xoai from the ambush point.

Stars and Stripes

U.S. Steps Up Combat Role

President Johnson has authorized U.S. troops in the Republic of Vietnam to drop their advisory role under certain conditions and battle the communist Viet Cong in direct combat.

The decision was revealed Tuesday by the State Department, which said the troops would go into action only upon request by South Vietnam military leaders, and only in conjunction with South Vietnam troops.

Senate minority leader Everett M. Dirksen (R-Ill.) said he feared the move would "transform this into a conventional war." He added, however, "I'm afraid circumstances may compel it."

Military scources in Washington applauded the move as the only way communist guerrilla units can be destroyed "where they live."

Stars and Stripes

Above: Many Marines patrol with powerful M14 rifles, the new M16 not yet being in large scale service. However, actual combat is teaching that helmets are safer than fatigue caps

Mid-air Meeting

"It was a real World War II type of tangle." Lieut. Comdr. Edwin A. Greathouse, leader of the Navy fighters said in describing the aerial battle in which his propeller-driven A-1H Skyraiders, of a 1947 class, brought down a North Vietnamese MIG yesterday.

It was 45 minutes before sunset when the MIG's headed for the Skyraiders at about 650 miles an hour and fired two rockets, apparently of a ballistic type. The rockets missed by a wide margin.

The American fighters dived toward the forest and levelled off at almost treetop altitude, a tactic the Skyraider pilots had been taught to evade enemy jets. At low altitudes the MIG's are not as manoeuvrable as propeller aircraft.

The American pilots succeeded by their tactics in separating the two MIG's. Lieutenants Johnson and Hartman, in a 90-degree bank, came at one of the MIG's, which was on Commander Greathouse's tail.

The MIG, Lieutenant Johnson said, "was a little over optimum range and I had him in my sights." He continued: "I figured that I might hit him, and I did."

The MIG, bearing the red and orange markings of the North Vietnamese Air Force, crashed into the forest and exploded. The other MIG fled.

Lieutenant Johnson, asked how he felt about shooting down a MIG, replied: "I did not feel much at all. He made a couple of mistakes, and that's the way it is."

The New York Times

JULY 1965

1st Viet Cong teams manage to get through perimeter defences at Da Nang air base, and destroy three aircraft.

8th Maxwell Taylor resigns as US Ambassador to South Vietnam. His successor is to be Henry Cabot Lodge.

10th The Viet Cong free 60 ARVN prisoners.

12th Marine Lieutenant Frank Reasoner dies helping his injured radio officer during a Viet Cong ambush. He will be the first Marine in Vietnam to be awarded the Congressional Medal of Honor.

15th Premier Ky is quoted as saying that Adolf Hitler is one of his heroes.

15th The first contingent of New Zealand troops arrives in South Vietnam.

20th Ho Chi Minh claims that his people are willing to fight for 20 years or more until they win.

28th President Johnson announces that US troop levels will go up to 125,000 men, and that the monthly draft call will increase from 17,000 to 35,000.

31st Men of the 101st Airborne Division move into South Vietnam. They will be based near Cam Ranh Bay.

Pilots Describe Downing of MIG's

"I grinned and said, 'Hot Damn'." That, said Capt. Thomas S. Roberts of La Grange, Ga.; was how he reacted yesterday over North Vietnam after a missile from his United States Air Force jet caught a Communist MIG-17 on the tail and sent it into a sharp, smoking dive.

In a second supersonic Phantom jet, Capt. Kenneth E. Holcombe of Detroit fired four missiles at another MIG. Captain Holcombe's flying partners said that they saw a missile zip into the MIG's tailpipe and that the enemy plane "blew completely apart."

The fight took place 25 to 35 miles northwest of Hanoi as the planes picked up the MIGs heading toward United States Air Force F-105 jets hammering a target near the area.

The MIGs swept past the first two-plane element led by Major Hall in a head-on approach. They then started to turn in behind them when they spotted the second element about four miles behind the aircraft piloted by Major Hall and Capt. Harold Anderson of Yuealpa. Calif.

The MIG pilots then tried to turn behind the second group of United States jets. The attackers found themselves outmaneuvered with eight rockets coming at them.

Captain Roberts said: "The MIG obviously lost sight of me. It was simple from then on."

The New York Times

Right: Jubilant fliers from the 45th Tactical Fighter Squadron celebrate the destruction of two enemy MiGs by F-4C Phantoms flown by Captain Thomas S. Roberts and Captain Kenneth E. Holcombe

Martin Marlin flying boats dot the surface of Cam Ranh Bay. The boats are used to patrol the coast, checking out vessels in the South China Sea

Wary US Crews Prowl China Sea

Aboard USS *Currituck*, in the South China Sea. At least 18 American warships and 15 seaplanes have been patrolling the coast of South Vietnam to block infiltration by Viet Cong troops and supplies.

"Maybe the Coast Guard cutters will catch something," Admiral Fowler said. "They've had experience against smugglers but then, these junk skippers have had 2,000 years of experience in what they're doing."

"This is like antisubmarine warfare in one basic respect," said Lieut. Comdr. Gilbert F. Murphy, a 37-year-old officer from Laurel, Md. "It's carried on as much to prevent hostile movements as to sink hostile ships."

"And all we can do," he added, "is guess either that the Viet Cong are eluding us or they are not there."

"We are not picking up much," said Admiral Fowler. "It's like highway patrolling: The speeders must be scared, or maybe there are no speeders."

But just to make sure, the surface patrols pick out junks and other vessels at random and send boarding parties.

"We try not to offend anyone," Admiral Fowler said, "but by now these people, including legitimate shipping, are accustomed to being boarded."

The New York Times

The crews of Coast Guard cutters in Vietnam make use of anti-smuggling experience in their interdiction of VC contraband

High Flyers Grounded

A military investigation was under way in Danang today into the episode of two drunken American marines who climbed into a B-57 jet and threatened to bomb Hanoi. The two men, neither of them a pilot, were taken into custody when they called to guards on the airstrip to ask them how to start the plane.

"Neither of the Marines were pilots," a spokesman said. "The plane didn't move a darned inch."

"I do not know for sure," he said. "But I cannot rule out the possibility that they intended to bomb Hanoi."

The New York Times

3,700 Paratroops Arrive in Vietnam

American troops of the 101st Airborne Div. began landing Thursday at Cam Ranh Bay, 180 miles northeast of Saigon, to bolster U.S. combat forces in Vietnam.

The troop transport *General* *Le Roy Eltinge* brought the 3,700 paratroopers into the deep-water bay where the U.S. is building a major base. The men were transferred to landing craft for the trip ashore.

Stars and Stripes

Shipping Them Out

The exodus for the West Coast and then Vietnam was set to begin, but the inhabitants of Junction City seemed singularly unimpressed. The reason was soon apparent. "This has been going on for 113 years," said John Montgomery, 62, publisher of The Junction City Union. "Fort Riley sent troops to chase the Indians, to the Spanish-American War, to World War I, to Europe in World War II and to Korea just fifteen years ago."

Near Beer

At Inkey's Bar, a stocky barmaid said: "This all started last month, when the orders came in. The boys were told before they went home on their last leave. Sure they talked about it. They all wonder how bad it will be."

Down the street, at JC Cafe, Mildred Morgan presided at the counter. "They've been coming all week to say good-by," she said. "I've been here a long time, and I say these soldiers are better men than they were fifteen years ago."

At a Washington Street liquor store, the woman owner said: "They know they might not come back. I've known some of these boys for three years. They're too young to go. They talk to me about it."

Last Fling

There is a motel half a mile down the highway. The manager said: "A lot of the soldiers have been coming out for a last fling. They feel they might not make it back, so might as well have some fun. People aren't grim. But they aren't happy either."

Newsweek

AUGUST 1965

2nd Viet Cong strike in force at a South Vietnamese Special Forces camp near the Cambodian border. The camp is relieved by men of the 173rd Airborne.

3rd TV news shows US soldiers setting light to village huts with Zippo lighters.

5th Viet Cong sappers again penetrate US defences and blow up oil storage tanks near Da Nang. Two million gallons of fuel are destroyed.

16th Two car bombs explode in the National Police Headquarters in Saigon.

16th Viet Cong attack Marine Supply Column 21, causing losses among the vehicles.

18th The Marines begin Operation Starlite, marking a new escalation in the war as they take on Viet Cong in the Van Tuong peninsula. They claim over 600 enemy dead for the loss of 45 Marine casualties.

26th Viet Cong forces take a government position less than 10 miles from Saigon

31st In order to curb black marketeering in South Vietnam, it is decided to pay foreign troops in a new scrip.

31st A law comes into effect making it illegal to mutilate a US draft card.

A Bird Dog on Song

Riding in a small plane like the Cessna "Bird Dog" at 90 miles an hour and at about 1,200 feet above a guerrilla stronghold can make you feel pretty vulnerable. Crammed into a corset-like flak-vest, I sat on a seat padded by a thick piece of steel-protection against bullets from below. But Capt. Robert A. Norman, Bird Dog's pilot and a veteran of 300 missions of this sort, was completely cool. Pointing down to two small clearings ringed by bunkers and trenches, he said: "We're going to bust these bunkers and the three huts hidden under the trees."

First he checked with headquarters to make certain no friendly ground patrols were in the neighborhood. Then, over the intercom, I heard him calling to the jets which were cruising at 9,000 feet. "Oxlip Six, please come down to 4,000 feet; I'm ready to mark the target." In case of trouble, Norman told the F-100 pilots to bail out to the southwest where, with luck, they would be over friendly territory.

Norman then sent his Bird Dog into a steep dive, heading right for the bunkers. Using a grease-pencil marking on the Plexiglas of his cockpit as a sight, he fired his first white phosphorous rocket. It zoomed toward the ground with a tearing sound, jerking the small plane like a kite. Where the rocket hit the ground, a column of white smoke arose from the trees. By then, however, Bird Dog was beginning to draw machine-gun fire, so Norman climbed steeply out of range.

Engulfed

When the F-100s reported they could see the smoke clearly, Norman told them to drop their bombs slightly to the left where the huts were barely visible. The bombing was amazingly accurate and the clearing soon became engulfed in a billowing cloud of smoke and flames from the napalm. If any guerrillas were in those bunkers and trenches, it was certain death for them. *Newsweek*

Arrival of the Volunteers

The gray bulk of the troopship *General Le Roy Eltinge*, nineteen days out of Oakland, lay upon the green waters of Cam Ranh Bay in South Vietnam. Aboard were 3,900 paratroopers of the 101st Airborne Division, jubilant or depressed, laughing or cursing in the mercurial manner of soldiers since Hannibal's time. From the railing one newcomer shouted down at soldiers at the pier, "Take a break, men, the 101st is here." Ashore, a veteran armored officer shrugged: "I don't care what kind of outfits they send, as long as they're infantry who can go slogging through the boonies."

While the 15,787-man division packed up and kept on training at Fort Benning, Ga., its equipment – including 428 helicopters – was already moving out through the ports of Mobile and Jacksonville.

Inside one barracks a husky, 21-year-old Pfc. quietly munched cookies sent by his sister from Oregon. In the bunk next to him a tall Alabama Negro ruminated: "I don't care about goin'. I care about comin' back. If I see him (the enemy) before he sees me, he's hurtin'." And a Pfc. from Massachusetts, his fingers stained with shoe polish, said somebody had to fight the Communists, but didn't look overjoyed at the prospect. Why, then, was he in this dangerous, volunteer outfit? "When I came into the Army," he said, "I wanted to be in the best."
Newsweek

Secretary of Defense MacNamara is accompanied on his tour of I Corps by General Westmoreland, the US commander in Vietnam

The Whirlybird Catches a Worm

Capt. Howard Henry of the Marines was believed to have made aviation history today by using a helicopter to capture a guerrilla suspect.

Captain Henry of Chickasaw, Ala., and Baltimore, ran down the suspected sniper near Danang and chased him until he threw up his hands to indicate surrender. Then Sgt James Maynard of Cyclone, W. Va, leaped out of the helicopter and bundled the breathless prisoner into the aircraft.

The 32-year-old captain has been in Vietnam only three weeks. Today's exploit was his first combat mission.

The New York Times

Nerves of steel are needed to fly Forward Air Control. Flying their unarmed Cessna O-1 Bird Dogs, they get closer to the enemy than any other fixed wing pilots, as they spot and mark targets for the 'Fast Movers', or jet bombers

Marine Assault Kills 552 VC

CHU LAI, Vietnam – The U.S. Marines reported Thursday they had smashed a big Viet Cong concentration on the Van Tuong Peninsula, inflicting bloody losses on the communist forces.

Marine spokesman said 552 Viet Cong bodies had been counted. Marine casualties were officially called "light," but a U.S. military spokesman in Saigon said the Americans had suffered their heaviest loss of any single engagement of the Vietnamese war.

Security rules prohibit the disclosure of American losses.

Stars and Stripes

Marines smash a major communist concentration near Chu Lai, but take casualties in the process

SEPTEMBER 1965

3rd 532 air missions are flown over Vietnam, the highest figure so far.

7th Marines follow up Operation Starlite with Operation Piranha and claim over 200 enemy dead.

9th US warplanes hit a bridge just 17 miles from the North Vietnamese border with China.

11th The 1st Cavalry Division (Airmobile) begins to arrive in South Vietnam.

16th B-52s bomb targets in the Mekong Delta for the first time.

23rd The South Vietnamese government executes two Viet Cong agents held at Da Nang.

26th Viet Cong radio announces that two US prisoners have been killed in retaliation for the execution of their agents.

29th Hanoi publishes the text of a letter it has written to the Red Cross claiming that as there is no formal state of war, US pilots shot down over the North will not receive the rights of prisoners of war, and will be treated as war criminals.

General William C. Westmoreland welcomes troops from the First Cavalry Division. This new air assault formation is the Army's first division to be deployed in its entirety to Southeast Asia

Hunting Skunks

Darting through the starless night at 1,500 feet, the 197th Aviation Company "Raiders Platoon" – composed of five helicopters heavy-laden with grenade launchers, machine guns and rockets – approached the serpentine Vai Co River some 23 miles west of Saigon. "We are going sampan hunting tonight," said platoon commander Capt. Duane R. Brofer, 35, from Fort Dodge, Iowa. "This river has been one of our best hunting grounds and we should bag a few."

At Brofer's command, Specialist 5 Bill Beasley, 35, of Hinton, W. Va., swung his searchlight in the direction of the Bo Bo Canal in the Plain of Reeds. The makeshift searchlight – a cluster of seven aircraft-landing lights mounted on a maneuverable pod – is the only one of its kind in operation in Vietnam. Suddenly, a sampan scurried across the beam of light. Captain Brofer radioed the US duty officer back with the South Vietnamese Army's 25th Division headquarters that he had spotted a possible target. Immediately the reply came back: "This is Good Nature Control. We don't have anybody there. Let them have it!"

Direct Hit

While Brofer hovered above the sampan, keeping it squarely in the searchlight's beam, the other helicopters swooped down in turn, letting loose with everything they had. Tracer bullets leapt across the darkling water like sparks from a welder's torch, and a thick hail of grenades exploded into the side of the boat. The sampan sank without a trace.

For the next 45 minutes, Captain Brofer's "Skunk Hunters" continued to explore the maze of canals and waterways. But by now, the guerrillas were apparently alerted and had taken cover in the clusters of water lilies and reeds along the river banks.

At dawn, the choppers roared back to their Tan Son Nhut air base. Though on this mission they had managed to destroy only one presumed Viet Cong sampan, a recent raid netted no

fewer than twenty guerrilla barges carrying tons of vital war material. Perhaps even more important, the missions have deprived the Viet Cong of the certainty that they can move men and supplies unhindered under cover of darkness. Says the 197th's commander, Maj. James W. Booth, 35: "This unit

Down in Thanh Hoa

As a 22-year Air Force veteran and an eight-MIG jet ace in Korea, Lieut. Colonel James Robinson Risner, 40, was the archetype of the professional who until recently has borne the brunt of the US military effort in Vietnam.

Last week Robbie's wife and five sons on Okinawa learned that he was missing. Risner's flight of six F-105 Thunderchiefs, said the official report, had streaked off on a late morning mission against a "military target" near Phu De Van Chan mountain range, 80 miles northwest of Hanoi. The weather was clear, visibility good, and the jets dumped three tons of bombs on the site. But the airmen had to brave a murderous curtain of ground fire from mounted .50-cal. machine guns and 37-mm cannon. Risner's jet and that of

another pilot were hit. Desperately, they headed southeast, hoping to reach the South China Sea, where Risner had bailed out last spring.

Last week he almost made it again. Nursing their crippled craft, the two pilots kept airborne for 170 miles – then had to eject near the town of Thanh Hoa, within sight of the water but still over Ho Chi Minh's real estate. Risner landed in a paddyfield, his buddy several miles away. Their squadron mates, circling them, saw both flyers on the ground with no signs of injuries. But by the time rescue aircraft from the carrier *Independence* reached the area, Risner and his buddy had disappeared, and the beeps from Risner's emergency transmitter had ceased.

Time

G.I.s Paid in Scrip to Curb Black Market

SAIGON, South Vietnam, Aug. 31 – United States authorities have announced that effective today, all American and foreign military and civilian personnel serving in Vietnam will be paid in United States military scrip instead of American dollars.

Besides the estimated total of

Scrip has been introduced for Allied military payments

90,000 American troops and the large number of civilian officials here, the measure jointly agreed upon by the South Vietnamese and United States Governments will also affect South Korean, New Zealand, Australian and Filipino military and civilian contingents in Vietnam.

The chief purposes of the introduction of scrip were to curb the dangerous inflation of the Vietnamese economy that is being brought about by the millions of dollars spent by the expanding American military forces here and to wipe out or drastically reduce the black market in American dollars.

New York Times

Ship Impresses Ky,
but That Salad Dressing . . . !

ABOARD U.S.S. INDEPENDENCE, off South Vietnam, Sept. 9 – The United States Navy taught Nguyen Cao Ky something about aircraft carriers today, and he taught it something about French dressing.

Premier Ky, who is a air vice marshal in the South Vietnamese Air Force, spent the day aboard this immense ship as she steamed in the South China Sea about 150 miles east of Saigon.

He seemed to be impressed by what he saw – plane-storage bays as big as baseball diamonds, jet fighters hurled into the air like pebbles from a slingshot, the five-and-a-half-acre flight deck.

Thank you for giving me the opportunity to visit your city," he told the crew of the Independence over the ship's loudspeaker system. "What you are

doing here our people will remember for 100 years to come."

But the premier – reared in a country where Gallic culinary finesse is taken for granted – was unimpressed by one item on the luncheon menu in the private mess of Vice Adm. James R. Reedy, commander of all the carriers in this area.

In front of him was a salad, covered with an orange goo familiar to every American who has ever ordered a blue-plate special.

Premier Ky looked at the salad, disbelieving, then looked at the printed menu beside his plate. "Carrot and lettuce salad," it said, "with French dressing." He shook his head.

"That isn't French dressing," the premier said. "French dressing is made of oil and vinegar."

New York Times

has written history for Army aviation. It has pioneered new tactics and brought a new concept to warfare by using helicopters at night."

Newsweek

Above: Helicopters are often the quickest way of following the Viet Cong into his bolt holes among the myriad waterways of the Mekong Delta

OCTOBER 1965

5th US troops are permitted to use tear gas on operations in Vietnam.

7th Communist Chinese claim to have shot down a US plane over their territory.

8th President Johnson undergoes surgery to remove his gall bladder.

10th 1st Cavalry moves against communist concentrations in the Central Highlands.

15th The first public burning of a draft card takes place in the US. The culprit is arrested.

19th The Special Forces camp at Plei Me is attacked by Viet Cong, who besiege the camp.

23rd 1st Air Cavalry units move into Pleiku Province, taking the fight to North Vietnamese Army concentrations and attempting to relieve Plei Me.

25th Relief forces reach Plei Me.

27th Viet Cong sappers destroy aircraft at Da Nang and Chu Lei.

30th In New York military veterans lead a parade in support of government policy in Vietnam.

The 1st Air Cavalry Division's tent city in the An Khe Valley covers 32 square miles, that bare months ago was covered in heavy vegetation. With its newly developed helicopter assault tactics the Cav will be aiming to control huge tracts of country

Marines Smash Raider Unit in First Fight

DANANG – Three young United States Marines, who had never before fired a rifle in combat, all but annihilated a Viet Cong commando unit this morning.

Just before last midnight, violence erupted as they were getting ready to go to sleep in a van on a lick of sand at the helicopter installation. They were partly undressed.

"We heard three explosions," Corporal Brule said. "They sounded like mortars, so we grabbed our rifles and headed for a hole. It took us about a minute to get there. We didn't even bother to put on our boots."

"We had been in the hole for 30 seconds, maybe, when we saw some people running toward us," Corporal O'Shannon said. "They were about 30 or 40 feet away. When they got within 15 feet of us, we opened fire.

"We dropped them all in about 10 seconds."

The guerrillas were carrying satchel charges – canvas bags filled with dynamite and hand grenades. The charges on the back of one guerrilla exploded, killing him.

Of the 11 men intercepted by Corporals O'Shannon, Mortimer and Brule, 9 were killed and 2 were gravely wounded. Although a grenade had exploded five feet from them, the marines were not hit by even a sliver of shrapnel.

Corporal Brule, a lean young man with deeply etched lines in his forehead, said of his brief taste of close combat: "Lord, did I feel lonely!"

The New York Times

Between Professionals

When the "Screaming Eagles" of the 101st Airborne Division set out on "Operation Gibraltar" in the central highlands of South Vietnam, they expected just another routine search-and-destroy mission. But minutes after giant Huey helicopters began landing a strike force from the 101st in an abandoned paddy near the village of An Ninh, the paratroopers found themselves fighting for their lives against a superior force of Viet Cong regulars.

The trouble started when, in a case of mutual surprise, the troopers landed literally in the midst of a Viet Cong battalion. The paddy was, in fact, right next to VC battalion headquarters, and, as the helicopters came in for a landing, the Viet Cong dove into prepared positions and began pouring deadly fire into the paratroopers. "I jumped into a hole with two of our troops who were firing up a storm," recalled Pfc. Steve Van Meter, a 19-year-old combat photographer. "Next thing I knew the guy beside me had been hit right above the left eye. It almost tore his head off and killed him instantly. Before I recovered from that, the guy on my left yelled. He'd been hit in the arm."

Don't Pull Back!
Unable to land any more men, the helicopters had no choice but to leave the 260 they had already unloaded pinned down in an area about the size of a soccer field. The most damaging Viet Cong fire came from a 50-foot knoll at one end of this area. "About 30 of our men charged the knoll, yelling and screaming," Van Meter said. Almost at once, the officer leading the charge, Maj. Herbert J. Dexter, was hit in the leg. "As soon as he fell," Meter recounted, "a couple of VC came out of their holes less than 10 feet from him. They just stood there pumping him full of holes. The major's last words before he died were: 'Don't pull back! Don't pull back!'"

Then Second Lt. George H. Carter, 24, promptly took over the command. Said Van Meter: "They took that hill almost by hand-to-hand combat. The men just grabbed the VC and threw them off the hill. One man went to a mortar and actually ripped the sight off with his bare hands."

What finally kept the paratroopers from being overrun, though, was the Air Force. "They started bombing around our perimeter," Van Meter said. "At times they were so close that shrapnel was hitting everybody. We had two men killed because of Air Force bombs dropping so close. But we can't complain. They really saved us, I think."
Newsweek

Siege Broken by Viet, 1st Cav Troops

A Vietnamese regiment led by armor reached the beleaguered outpost of Plei Me Monday night without encountering any significant Viet Cong opposition, a U.S. military spokesman said.

He said the relief column was just outside the Special Forces compound and the only reason elements of the column did not enter the camp was because there was no room.

The spokesman said that on the basis of incomplete reports the Viet Cong apparently offered no opposition from its dozen or more machine gun emplacements around the camp.

Stars and Stripes

Into the Valley of Death

Near An Khe, a patrol from the US 101st Airborne "Screaming Eagles" nabbed a Viet Cong, who fingered his home base in a nearby, boxlike valley. The 101st promptly ringed the Viet Cong on three sides of the valley, while 2nd Battalion Commander Colonel Wilfred Smith flew his three companies into the valley's portal by helicopter to close the trap. Trouble was, the dried-up quilt of rice paddies chosen for landing was hard by the VC camp. So the Screaming Eagles got the hot welcome of a Viet Cong battalion. "I've hit a buzz saw," Smith shouted into his radio as two choppers crashed. Smith lost all three of his company commanders, had 24 of his 28 helicopters hit or disabled, got only half his troops on the ground and into battle. But reinforcements tried again, and in two days of short, brutal clashes, the Eagles rammed the Viet Cong backward into a holocaust of bombs and napalm from US planes and finally turned the field over to the incoming 1st Cavalry Airmobile, somewhat bloody but purged of the VC. For all the hail of lead, US losses were surprisingly light. The Viet Cong left 226 dead, many of them elite troops with red stars on their belts and buckles.

Time

The Army of the Republic of Vietnam used US-supplied armor to come to the aid of the Special Forces camp at Plei Me

Charleston, Vietnam

Fifteen miles long, five miles wide, deep enough for any ocean vessel, rimmed by smooth, sun-blanched beaches. Cam Ranh Bay was probably the world's most under-developed great natural harbor. Until, that is, four months ago – when the 4,000 men of the 35th Engineer Group went to work.

With bulldozers and dynamite, they have moved mountains of sand, built some 40 miles of road and helped construct a 10,000-ft runway from which the first jets will blast off against the enemy next month. Ammo depots, a ten-tank fuel dump with a capacity of 230,000 gal., and a T-pier are all under construction; next month a floating 350-ft De Long pier will be towed in from Charleston, S.C.

When finished early next year at a cost that may run as high as $100 million, Cam Ranh will be a port the size of Charleston, easing the pressure on Saigon's chockablock facilities. It will need all the dock space the engineers can clear: one measure of the US commitment in Vietnam is that last January only 65,000 tons of military equipment were fed into the nation by sea; during November more than 750,000 tons will arrive – a tenfold increase. Eventually, Cam Ranh's facilities will be able to store 45 days' supply for all the US forces in Central Vietnam.

Time

Flying Cranes Haul Anything

They sit like enormous grasshoppers on the top of a knoll, four of them, lined up along the edge of the largest heliport in the world.

Of the 434 aircraft of the First Cavalry Division (Airmobile), these are the favorites – four CH-54A Flying Cranes, the United States Army's entire operational fleet of heavy helicopters. They are the conversation piece of the division.

The flying Cranes can do astonishing things, and in the few weeks they have been here they have impressed everyone. In a single trip, one lifted enough C-rations to feed a battalion for three days. Another hauled a 105-millimeter howitzer, its crew and ammunition into battle.

Thirty yards long, with gigantic six-bladed rotors 72 feet in diameter, they look so gawky that they seem rooted to the ground. It seems impossible that such a contraption – a spindly boom, a rotor and a bubble of a cockpit – could pick up 10 tons and speed across the jungle at 120 miles an hour. But it can.

New York Times

The CH-54 Skycrane performed a wide variety of tasks in Vietnam, from retrieving downed aircraft as seen here, to carrying a specially designed portable surgical theater

Viet Cong Hide Behind Children, Then Shoot Them

The Viet Cong used a group of children as shields Friday during a military operation. Then another group of Viet Cong opened fire on the children.

Marine Maj. B. H. Mann reported Tuesday that he witnessed the incident, which occurred Friday during a Marine amphibious and helicopter assault against the Viet Cong near the coastal city of Qui Mhon, 260 miles north of here.

Mann, flying a copter from the helicopter assault ship Iwo Jima, was asked by a forward air controller to check a group of 18 people near a stream.

As Mann neared the group he saw children among them and ordered the forward air controller to hold fire. The group then got into a boat to cross the stream. The men in the group sat in the boat and held the children on their laps as two persons poled the boat to the other side, Mann said.

As they approached shallow water on the other shore the men threw the children into the water and ran ashore.

As soon as the men had cleared the area, guerrillas on the peninsula opened fire on the children.

Stars and Stripes

Battle of the Bunker

Near Bien Hoa, a Viet Cong deserter was captured by a company of the lst Infantry Division – the "Big Red One" – and led it straight to his buddies' bunker. Some bunker. The first US charge was turned back by anti-personnel mines set off electrically. A second, then a third US attack was driven back by withering rifle and machine-gun fire. Finally, the GIs called for a flamethrower. It was brought up by helicopter and Private Wayne Beck of Rolla, Mol, strapped it on his back for a fourth assault. Beck got within 60ft of the bunker before a mine and a bullet cut him down. Even as he fell, he sprayed the bunker with fire. Still the VC refused to surrender, so the troops called for Air Force Skyraiders, which again and again dive-bombed the cave-like compartments with 750lb bombs, napalm and machine-gun fire. With that, the Viet Cong slunk off into the jungle, leaving 14 of their dead in the big bunker.

Time

Student Is Arrested

PHILADELPHIA, Oct. 20 – Jeremiah T. Dickinson, a freshman at Haverford College, was arrested on the campus today by agents of the Federal Bureau of Investigation on charges of refusing to register for the draft. He was released by United States Commissioner William Bruno in $500 bail.

New York Times

The Big Guns Arrive

SAIGON, South Vietnam, Oct. 23 – Four battalions of heavy artillery began landing in South Vietnam today to protect areas around American bases, roads and other lines of communications, a United States military spokesman said.

Two of the battalions are 175-mm. howitzer units, while the other two are armed with eight-inch howitzers. Each battalion has 12 cannon.

The spokesman said the guns would be stationed at United States military bases in the Central Highlands and along the coast north of Saigon.

The eight-inch howitzer fires a 190-pound shell a maximum distance of almost 10 miles. The 175-mm. howitzer can hurl a 147-pound shell over 18 miles.

The United States is also increasing the strength of its medium artillery here, the spokesman said. Four more battalions of 105-mm. howitzers and 155-mm. howitzers will arrive soon to increase the defenses of United States military bases. Each battalion is armed with 18 howitzers.

New York Times

The M107 175mm self-propelled gun has given the army a superb long-range weapon, a single battery providing fire-support over a huge area of country

Words From On High

Tucked away in their hammocks beneath the dripping rain-forest canopy, the Viet Cong guerrillas could hardly believe their ears. Out of the night sky came an ominous, warbling whine, like bagpipes punctuated with cymbals. It was Buddhist funeral music – a dissonant dirge cascading from the darkness. Then a snatch of dialogue between a mother and child: "Mother, where's Daddy?" "Don't ask me questions. I'm very worried about him." "But I miss Daddy very much. Why is he gone so long?" Then the music and voices faded slowly into the distance, and the platoon settled back to a restless sleep.

Litterbugs

It was, of course, only one of the many sights and sounds that the Viet Cong are treated to every day, courtesy of JUSPAO – the Joint United States Public Affairs Office, which handles psychological warfare in South Vietnam. During daylight hours, JUSPAO's eight aircraft dump tons of leaflets on the enemy – 3,500,000 a week, ranging from safe-conduct passes to maps showing the best way out of Red territory. Says one of JUSPAO's "psywar" adepts: "We're the world's worst litterbugs."

Time

The 'Bullshit Bombers' rain verbal and written propaganda down on the Viet Cong, in a psychological campaign designed to impair communist fighting spirit. Even if nothing happens, the chances are that at least the VC have lost a night's sleep!

NOVEMBER 1965

1st 1st Cavalry begins operations in the Ia Drang Valley, initiating a series of engagements that will become the heaviest fighting in the war so far.

2nd A Quaker anti-war protester burns himself to death in front of the Pentagon.

12th Reporting on the fighting in the Ia Drang Valley, Secretary of Defence McNamara describes how the 1st Cavalry has blunted a communist offensive designed to cut South Vietnam in two.

12th McNamara announces an increase in troop levels, but gives no definite figures, saying he does not want to tip off the enemy.

14th In the Ia Drang Valley, Second Lieutenant Walter Marm leads his men in an assault on a communist position in a display of bravery that wins him the Congressional Medal of Honor.

19th The Chairman of the House Armed Service Committee calls for the bombing of Hanoi and Halphong, which have so far been spared raids.

26th Final Air Cavalry units leave the Ia Drang valley.

27th Military advisors suggest to President Johnson that US troop levels should rise to 400,000 men.

28th President-elect Marcos of the Philippines states that he will send troops to South Vietnam.

The accuracy of US bombing, as seen here where ten tons fall on target without touching a village, has led to Senate calls for military targets in Hanoi and Haiphong to be bombed

Grenade Surgery Repaid by a Hug

A wizened South Vietnamese peasant sat up in bed today and cheerfully exhibited a scar marking the place where a surgeon had cut a live grenade out of his back.

Mr Chinh, who comes from a village in Longan Province in the Mekong Delta, said he had been terrified during the eight-minute operation.

"I kept my eyes open," he said, "but I looked away from the side where the doctor was operating. I could feel something scraping around inside me as they worked. Then, suddenly, I felt very light, and I knew the grenade had been taken out."

General Humphreys and two assistants worked in a hospital outbuilding behind a wall of sandbags, using long-handled surgical tools. When the operation was over, the Air Force surgeon picked up Mr Chinh and carried him into the operating room to close the wound. "Alive," the peasant exclaimed in Vietnamese, tugging at his wispy beard. "I knew before the operation that I could very easily die."

The patient, now something of a celebrity, said he hugged and kissed General Humphreys this morning when the surgeon stopped by to check his progress.

Mr Chinh said South Vietnamese soldiers fired the grenade into his back with a launcher last Sunday morning when he failed to put his hands up promptly.

The New York Times

Cav Kills 869 Reds

SAIGON – Enemy dead littered the battlefield Tuesday as communist troops launched a series of counter-attacks on a brigade of U.S. 1st Cav. Div. (Airmobile) troops near Plei Me.

The latest confirmed body count was 869 enemy killed, with 15 captured, a U.S. military spokesman said here.

Stars and Stripes

Death on the River

Escorted by a larger gunboat, five squat, gray craft bristling with machine guns and 20-mm cannon chugged at a steady 8 knots along the Ham Luong River. Aboard the smaller boats were South Vietnamese Rangers headed for government outposts that had been overrun by guerrillas the previous night.

As the little convoy moved

VC, Viet Toll High in 'Fiercest' battle

Relief troops Sunday carefully picked their way across a devastated rubber plantation littered with scores of Vietnamese dead. A U.S. military spokesman said government casualties were heavy in the action which took place about 45 miles north-northwest of Saigon. An infantry regiment was hit by human waves of Viet Cong in the Michelin rubber plantation early Saturday. The headquarters unit and two battalions were overrun and massacred.

The casulaties could be the highest in any single action of the war.

The Vietnamese regimental commander and his American adviser were killed. Casualties among the Americans also were reported to have been heavy.

The larger Viet Cong formations, leavened in part by North Vietnamese regular soldiers, are well trained and well led. Pitched battles with government and American troops are now becoming more common

A U.S. spokesman said Vietnamese troops reported counting 300 enemy dead.

There was still no full account by late Sunday of what took place during the battle Saturday. A U.S. spokesman said "there is still a lot of understandable confusion up there."

There was little doubt, however, that the communists planned and executed the devastating attack with precision, coordination and fearlessness, the spokesman said.

Stars and Stripes

A Vietnamese patrol-boat with an American adviser aboard probes gingerly down a Mekong canal, seeking out the Viet Cong. Ambushes on these crowded waterways are common

along, its leader, Lt. Cmdr. Nguyen Van Hoa, squinted at the tangled mangroves half a mile away and muttered: "This looks like a good place for a Viet Cong ambush." Prudently, he ordered the gunboat to probe the shoreline with its 3-inch guns.

The response was shattering. From the shore, the guerrillas cut loose with a torrent of heavy-weapons and small-arms fire that churned up the water around the patrol. The fourth boat in line rocked drunkenly as three recoilless rifle rounds tore into it. Its captain, bleeding from shrapnel wounds, yelled into his radio, "Help me, help me. All of us are wounded or killed and we are sinking." As he spoke, his boat swung out of control and ran aground. Those Rangers aboard it who could still move scrambled ashore and disappeared into the underbrush.

Bloody Cargo

Seconds later, a shell from a 75-mm recoilless rifle pierced the armor of another boat and hit a Ranger who was carrying a string of hand grenades around his waist. The grenades exploded, spraying the inside of the vessel with fragments. With at least half the 100 Rangers aboard dead or wounded, the boat turned around and took its demoralized and bloody cargo back to base. In less than ten frantic minutes it was all over. The remaining boats pulled back from the scene of the ambush, and the objective of the mission 10 miles downstream was forgotten for the moment.

Newsweek

U.S. is Changing Face of Vietnam

SAIGON, South Vietnam, Nov. 27 – Navy Seabees, army engineers and four of the largest construction concerns in the world are changing the landscape of South Vietnam over night.

Jet airfields, docks, ports, roads, bridges, military quarters and even a city are being built by thousands of men and women and hundreds of earth moving machines.

At least $350 million in con-tracts have been approved. Tentative plans increase this total to $500 million, and future needs may soon push it much higher.

Never before in any war, according to officers in charge here, has so much construction work been planned for one country in so short a time. By late next summer most of the projects now started or still in the planning stage are expected to be largely finished.

New York Times

After th

BIENHOA – It was an ironically beautiful Vietnamese evening, with the rays of a full moon refracted through broken clouds.

Pfc. William Henry, 19-years-old, of Jackson Heights, Queens, had spent an hour on a barren hilltop Monday, knowing that most of his platoon had pulled out without him. He had sat there, he said later, firing his machine gun, sure he was going to die.

But he had not died, and now he and Pfc. Russell Dennis, also

Above: Massive **US** funded engineering works are changing the face of Vietnam. Everything from airfields to ports are being built, as here at **Qui Nhon**. The work is profitable to the many civilian engineers employed on such projects

Right: The oriental pastoral scenes and the wild jungle landscapes of Vietnam are being changed, interrupted by buildings and structures such as these **Tropospheric Scatter** long range communication aerials at **Nha Trang**

Battle: Seven Empty Bunks

19, were back at the door of their squad tent.

The first thing they noticed as they drew back the tent flap and walked inside was that they heard no music and no shouting. They were to discover later that four of their comrades had been

The major battle in the Ia Drang valley is the first confrontation between large American and NVA regular units. Here the bodies of dead Cavalrymen are removed from the scene of the battle below Chu Pong mountain

killed and three seriously wounded.

By all accounts, the battle had been a famous victory for the Americans. Private Henry listened, his eyes inexpressibly sad.

"It wasn't worth it," he said, twisting his hat in his hands. "I know every guy up there wrapped up in a poncho, and it isn't worth it."

Staff Sgt. John T. White of Jamaica, Queens, spent most of last night in the company orderly room, talking to anyone

who would listen because he could not go to sleep. His squad had been almost wiped out.

"I've done the very best I could," he said. "I haven't shirked. I've tried to make my commander proud of me and my squad. Now all I want to do is get out of here, get away from this place, go home. But I can't take my men with me, because they're most of them dead."

"You can't make friends in times like this; all you can have is associates."

The battalion commander,

Lieut. Col. John E. Tyler of Winona, Miss., slumped in his chair as he talked about the dead officers. He wore two days' growth of beard and a filthy fatigue uniform.

"If anybody should have to pay high life-insurance rates," he said, "It's rifle company platoon leaders. Their life expectancy on the assault is about 12 seconds."

Then he turned to the other officers at the table.

"No reveille tomorrow," he said.

The New York Times

A Reporter's Death

If Dickey Chapelle had had her choice of death, it would have been exactly as it happened last week – in combat with the United States Marines. The 47-year-old photographer war correspondent tripped on a Viet Cong booby trap and died almost instantly of multiple wounds in the head. It was the end of a love affair of many years between Dickey and the US Marines.

A few weeks ago, Dickey began her fifth reportorial stint in Vietnam, this time as correspondent for the National Observer and WOR-RKO Radio. On Wednesday night last week she slept in a foxhole, and early the next morning she and her Marine company moved down a hill from a bivouac area to begin the day's operation. The booby trap exploded at the foot of the hill, triggered by a grenade wired to an 81-mm mortar. Just before she was loaded into a medical evacuation helicopter, a chaplain gave Dickey the last rites of the Roman Catholic Church and minutes later she became the fourth Vietnam correspondent to die in action this year.

Newsweek

Iadrang Fight Enters 6th Day

A United States Army battalion was ambushed and mauled yesterday by several hundred North Vietnamese regulars in the Iadrang River valley, about 200 miles north of Saigon.

The ambush, involving 750 troops of the United States' First Cavalry Division (Airmobile), was the worst suffered so far, by an American combat unit in Vietnam. A company at the center of the battalion was practically wiped out.

For five days the narrow valley, about seven miles from the Cambodian border, has been a scene of ferocious fighting between Airmobile units and the North Vietnamese 66th Regiment, estimated at 2,000 elite troops.

The military spokesman said the bodies of 300 North Vietnamese had been counted. But battlefield witnesses said it was still impossible to make an accurate estimate of Communist losses although it was evident that the North Vietnamese had suffered severely.

New York Times

'Puff the Magic Dragon' Aids Air War Effort

"Puff, the Magic Dragon" is among the many kinds of weapons, old and new, serving in the war against the Viet-cong.

Puff is the soldiers' name for the old C-47 transport, workhorse of World War II, in its present incarnation. The C-47 is the military version of the Douglas DC-3, long familiar on many airline routes.

The Air Force announced today that the Fourth Air Commando Squadron had arrived at Tan Sonn Hut airfield in Saigon. The squadron flies what are

Flame belches, dragon-like, from a mini-gun aboard a 'Spooky'. Circling the enemy, wing tilted towards the ground, the gunship pours a devastating stream of fire towards the target

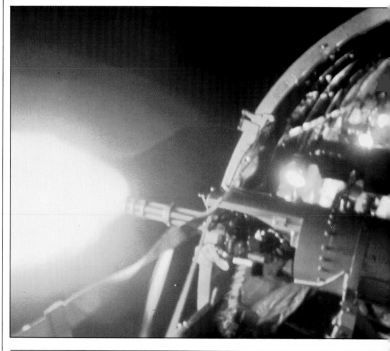

Heroism at Iadrang

"Dawn sure took a long time coming," said Specialist Daniel Torres, 26 years old, of Corpus Christi, Tex.

Specialist Torres is a medical corpsman with Company A of the First Battalion, Fifth Cavalry, United States First Cavalry Division (Airmobile).

The Texas soldier spent the night of Nov 17 lying alone in no man's land with 15 wounded Americans. They had to be left behind when a cavalry battalion of about 500 men was ambushed by a North Vietnamese regular force estimated at 1,000 men.

He said that at about 8.30 pm, a lieutenant from the company said by radio that he had been hit. He said he had a number of other wounded with him.

"The captain asked for 20 volunteers to go out and bring them in," Specialist Torres said. "The first platoon volunteered. The wounded needed a medic so I went, too.

"It took us a long time to find them. When we got there, we found about 25 wounded – a lot more than we could carry. I used up my morphine and bandages. Then I searched around and found the bags of two medics who were dead. I took their mor-phine and bandages and fixed up the rest of the wounded the best I could."

"I picked out five critical cases," he continued, "and put them on some litters I had taken off the med-evac choppers. There were four or five other walking wounded who could make their own way back."

Volunteer Asked For

"The platoon sergeant asked for a volunteer to stay with the other 15 wounded. I didn't see any point in keeping an infantryman up there. He couldn't do anything for the wounded. I was a medic and that was my job, so I figured I'd stay."

"About half an hour after the platoon left," Specialist Torres said, "I started hearing the Viet Cong moving around about 100 meters in front of us."

"Six or seven times," he said, "I heard some GI out there yell, 'Help, help!' or 'No, no, don't!' and then brraap, and the yelling would stop. I figured they were coming back to pick up their own wounded and were shooting our guys whenever they found them."

"I picked up my rifle and collected about ten clips of ammo and crawled off to a trail about 15 meters away," Specialist Torres said. "The trail looked like the way they'd probably come. I figured I'd take some of them with me before they got us."

"Every once in a while," he said, "I'd crawl back and take a look at the wounded. The captain told me over the radio the patrol couldn't come back because it was too dangerous, but the wounded kept asking when the patrol was coming to pick them up. I told them it was on the way."

Specialist Torres and the wounded were finally rescued about two hours later.

"I'm a medic – I figured it was my job to stay," Specialist Torres said. "I wasn't going to leave any of the wounded out there."

The New York Times

called FC-47s – "gooney birds" transformed into fighter planes.

The "F" in the new designation stands for fighter, a title as seemingly inappropriate as "tank" would be for a tricycle.

A war cannot be fought with-out a C-47, one flier says, and the old two-engine, propeller driven aircraft has proved useful in more than its original role as a transport. It has been fitted with machine guns in its door and in the port side of its fuselage.

The guns spew out 6,000 to 10,000 rounds a minute. When a ground unit needs air support, the C-47 circles the action and delivers a tremendous volume of fire.

New York Times

With three miniguns each firing up to 6,000 30-caliber rounds per minute, 'Puff the Magic Dragon' provided as much fire as an Infantry battalion, and in action at night was a highly impressive sight

Left: Troopers from the 1st Cavalry Division advance through the Ia Drang Valley under fire from the enemy. The 'First Team' fought a bitter, three-day battle with NVA regulars.

Dead and wounded cavalrymen lie under a flare crossed sky after the NVA ambush on the night of November 17/18. American casualties were much higher than in any other battle.

DECEMBER 1965

1st US aircraft attack SAM sites five miles from Hanoi.

2nd US Secretary of State Dean Rusk announces that the US would be willing to attend an international conference on Southeast Asia.

4th Viet Cong bomb destroys a Saigon hotel, killing eight servicemen.

8th US and ARVN forces move into the Que Son valley, and meet stiff resistance.

11th US engineers begin expanding base facilities in Thailand.

15th An electricity supplying plant near Haiphong is attacked by US aircraft.

16th General Westmoreland requests a total of 443,000 troops to be deployed within a year.

19th A curfew is imposed on US troops in Saigon.

24th A truce comes into effect – the government undertakes to initiate no offensive action for 30 hours, while the communist forces undertake a 12-hour break.

31st Bombing of North Vietnam resumes after a seven-day break.

Moderation in All

Five months ago the US command in Saigon stopped releasing any day-by-day casualty figures and instead began characterizing the losses suffered in individual actions as "light," "moderate" or "heavy." In practice, the description used has almost invariably been "light" or "moderate". The adjective chosen to describe losses in a particular action is always used in relation to the total force engaged: thus, an entire platoon might be virtually wiped out, but if the battalion to which it belonged lost only 1 or 2 per cent of its overall strength, the casualties would be described as "light". Losses that would be described as "moderate" in a unit on the defensive might be called "light" in a unit on the attack since troops on the offensive are expected to suffer heavier casualties.

When are casualties officially "heavy"? "When the unit involved can no longer fight as a unit," answers a Saigon information officer. Thus a unit might lose 40 per cent of its strength, but if it still had most of its officers and NCOs left, its

Murder at the Metropole

Shortly before dawn, one morning late in the week, a small, gray Peugeot pick-up truck, piled high with fruit and vegetables, pulled up before the Metropole Hotel, US enlisted men's quarters in downtown Saigon. Out of the truck jumped four men clad in civilian clothes who immediately opened up with machine guns on an American MP and Vietnamese policeman standing silhouetted against the lighted entrance.

Wounded in the shoulder, the American, SP/4 William S. Seippel of Pittsburgh, continued firing back until both his shotgun and .45-caliber pistol clicked empty. Then, pointing at the truck, he shouted: "This truck's going to explode!" At that, Seippel and the Vietnamese guard ran inside and took cover behind a pillar in the hotel lobby.

Inside the Metropole, where 211 US servicemen were billeted, Sp/5 Thomas E. Lee, 23, of Fort Worth, Texas, ran to a bal-cony to see what was happening. "There was a big boom and a blinding light," Lee said. "It knocked me flat. I picked myself up and ran down the stairs and started to carry out the dead and wounded."

All told, the explosion killed eight people, including one US Marine and a New Zealand artilleryman, and wounded 137, including 72 Americans.

The toll would have been even higher if the second stage of the terrorist scheme had worked. But, fortunately, a Claymore mine, planted by the Viet Cong nearby and timed to go off as the wounded poured out of the billets into the dark street, was discovered and disarmed shortly after the blast.

Newsweek

"In combat, there's only one color, and that's olive drab." When your life depends on the guy next to you, you don't care about the colour of his skin, only if he can do his job

"Only One Color"

casualties would be called "moderate". Which, to a civilian, might seem an immoderate use of the word "moderate".

Newsweek

The Army's policy of announcing light, moderate or heavy casualties will disguise the cost of such actions as the Cavalry's battle in the Ia Drang Valley

Declares Capt. Henry B. Tucker of the 173rd Airborne Brigade: "I see only one color. And that's olive drab."

No one knows precisely how many Negroes are serving in Vietnam. From the fact that about 8 per cent of the men in the armed forces are Negroes, the Pentagon estimates that Negroes make up about 13,000 of the some 165,000 troops now in Vietnam. Some units, however, are far more heavily Negro than others. Captain Tucker's company, for instance, is 60 per cent Negro, and airborne units in general seem to have a disproportionate number of Negro personnel.

Indeed, the services are far ahead of US business in fair-employment practices. As a result, Negroes have come to re-

It seems that for the moment the racial tensions building up in US cities have been avoided in the Army, which needs teamwork for many tasks. But large numbers of conscripts flooding into the service may change the situation

gard the armed forces as a sort of sanctuary from discrimination. Says Sgt. Sylvester Bryant, 32, of Columbus, Ga.: "I come from the South. When I joined up, it's no secret we were having trouble back there. The Army did a helluva lot for me." And Maj. Roosevelt Wilson, a 35-year-old Negro from Dillwyn, Va., adds: "I've been allowed to compete and I've been given credit for what I've done. In the Army, it doesn't matter if you're blue, green or gray – if you're a captain, you're a captain."

Newsweek

Yule in Vietnam

For the Grunts in the field, Christmas in Vietnam is not Yule logs and snow, but is largely mud, patrols, and danger

TUYEN NHON, Special Forces Camp, Vietnam – Christmas Eve, 1965, in the Mekong Delta. Eight Americans all wearing the green berets of the Army Special Forces, wait, watch and listen through a long, quiet darkness.

Maybe tonight. Maybe not. Only the slow passage of the endless hours will tell whether the cease-fire will last the night.

Eight Americans, each with his own thoughts of Christmas and home. Each far away from snow, silver bells, Christmas carols and Santa Claus. Each wondering if this Christmas Eve is the night Charlie will pick to unleash the death and destruction the soldiers know is waiting out there.

Christmas is something that is far away this year. There isn't much time for it. But each man gives it a thought between rounds of checking the compound, loading weapons, and trying to catch a few hours sleep. It's all the Christmas they'll get tonight.

Christmas Is a Wet Foxhole

CAMNE – For the 123 men of Company K, Third Battalion, Third Marines, Christmas began with the rain.

All morning the drizzle continued. The day's project was a Christmas tree. It was fashioned from a scrawny, barren sapling, propped up with bricks. On it the marines hung two hand grenades, mess kit, spoons, beer cans, wet socks. A C-ration cracker was placed at the top instead of a Star of Bethlehem.

Two huge boxes filled with gifts "from the people of New Jersey" provided by the state American Legion, arrived in mid afternoon. They were the occasion for a denunciation of the "Vietniks" and expressions of thanks to "the good people who understand."

At 2.40 a marine "mule", a four-wheel vehicle more indestructible than the jeep, hove into sight across the rice paddies with a cargo of thermos cans. Inside the cans was Christmas dinner.

The marines sloshed through the mud to the schoolhouse to line up for their turkey, mashed potatoes and bread. The meal had been mass-produced three miles away in a field kitchen, but it bore the stamp of home for the troops.

There was no air of festivity. The men were too lonely and too far away from home to celebrate.

The New York Times

To these men of the 3d Marines, even a wet foxhole is a better prospect at Christmas than fording streams on patrol

Paratroopers from the 173
Airborne Brigade are symbolic of
America's combat commitment in
Vietnam, first expressed in the
year just past

JANUARY 1966

1st Operation Marauder begins – paratroopers drop on to Oriental River area.

1st Strom Thurmond, US Republican senator, states his view that nuclear weapons should be used, if necessary, as a last resort to gain victory in Vietnam.

3rd Cambodia threatens retaliation against South Vietnam if violation of its territory or airspace takes place.

6th First use of 120-mm mortars in Viet Cong attack on Special Forces camp at Khe Sanh in Quang Tri Province.

8th Start of US/Australian/NZ combined Operation Crimp against "Iron Triangle", a Viet Cong stronghold north of Saigon.

8th US Senator Mike Mansfield, the Senate majority leader, observes grimly that the whole of Southeast Asia "cannot be ruled out as a battlefield". Senate minority leader Everett Dirksen urges that North Vietnam be blockaded.

Finding the Ho Chi Minh Trail

The U.S. has long suspected that a branch of the Communist "underground railroad" – the Ho Chi Minh trail – cut through Cambodia. But proof was hard to obtain: so wild and enemy-infested is the Viet Nam side of the Cambodian border that no allied troops had ventured to the border since the French left in 1954.

The 1st Air Cav's mission was to determine if the Communists were indeed using Cambodia as both funnel and sanctuary for troops infiltrating from the north. If so, the First Team hoped to provoke an attack, giving the U.S. a chance to act on last month's warning that pursuit across the Cambodian border would henceforth follow a continuing attack from the other side.

Doubt about the enemy's use of Cambodia was quickly dispelled. Beside one clearly defined crossing point on the riverbank stood a camp with 400 lean-to structures, 200 foxholes and a small hospital – fit for a regiment and freshly evacuated. Tethered on the opposite Cambodian bank of the shallow river, only 55 ft. wide at that point, were ill-concealed sampans loaded with ammunition boxes. At one point, a G.I. patrol even caught sight of twelve uniformed North Vietnamese soldiers hastily paddling across the river into Cambodia. 1st Air Cav Lieut. Colonel Kenneth Mertel took his helicopter down the middle of the narrow stream, hoping to draw fire, which presumably would have justified a U.S. response. None came. But now that the U.S. had penetrated right to the threshold of what had long been the enemy's privileged domain, chances were it would come soon enough.

Time

Tanks in Vietnam

The United States Army has decided to send a battalion of tanks into the war in Vietnam for the first time, informed military sources said today.

The battalion, with 72 tanks, would become the largest concentration of armor in Vietnam. It would be likely to enter action on the firm rolling plains of the Central Highlands.

The sources said the tank designated for use in South Vietnam was the M-48, classified by the Army as a medium tank. It is equipped with a 90-mm. main gun, a .30-caliber machine gun, and a .50-caliber machine gun.

The tank weighs 105,000 pounds and has a cruising range of 70 miles with a recommended top speed of 30 miles an hour.

The Army describes it as "a low-silhouette combat vehicle providing mobile firepower and crew protection for offensive combat."

In most regions of Vietnam, characterized by tangles of swamps and jungles, tanks have been ruled out as impractical. But military authorities have said the Central Highlands are "perfect tank country," comparable to many sections of Europe, where tanks were used extensively in World War II.

New York Times

With tanks now committed on the war, training for amphibious landings takes on importance

Getting Wounded

PFC George J. Pigmtora, a medic with the First Cavalry, had plenty of experience helping other wounded GIs when Charlie got him. It happened on 25 January 1966 during Operation Masher near Bong Song. A few inches to the right, and Pigmtora would have smoked his last Marlboro. He was one of the lucky ones. he was going to walk away from it.

Sometimes you feel nothing at first, or just a faint stinging. The force of a rifle bullet is enough to throw you back and plop you down on your duff, suddenly and unmistakably. It almost never really hurts much, because the trauma comes with the impact and a man in trauma doesn't feel pain. But it only takes a moment to learn whether you're going to walk away from it or spend the rest of your life with tubes and wires attached. In combat, most casualties are caused by shrapnel; most deaths are caused by rifle bullets.

B-52 Raid:
18-Hour Day for 15-Second Bombing

This is how the 18 hours passed for one of the crews, the six men who took a B-52 variously known as 70058, "Susie Q" and "the beat" to South Vietnam and brought it back to Guam.

The crew members of 70058 are as varied in background and temperament as any men could be, although not so neatly "typical" as the players in a Hollywood war film. These are the six men:

Pilot – Capt. William C. Hall, of Davis, W. Va., a 38-year-old sinewy little man who was once a first sergeant and now has only 18 more paydays – 18 months until retirement to Northern California.

Farm-boy Flier

Co-pilot – Capt. Larry W. Sutherland, of Mulvane, Kan., 30, a farm boy who went to West Point and then as he says "defected because I don't like to walk," quiet, crew-cut and professional.

Navigator – First Lieut. Thomas L. Price, of San Francisco, 24, a blond cast in the Tab Hunter mold who wants to make the Air Force his career and also wants to catch a glimpse of Vietnam, the country he visits but never sees.

Electronics systems operator – First Lieut. Theodore Lesher of Ann Arbor, Mich., 26, a mathematics major from the University of Michigan and the acknowledged "brain" of the six, an intense and swarthy bachelor.

Radar navigator – (Bombardier) Capt. Hoover Lee of Honolulu, 37, so gregarious that people in Guam remembered him when he returned here for a second tour after six years' absence, but untalkative and analytical during flight.

Tail gunner – S. Sgt. Bud C. Hyatt, of Tucson, Ariz., 35, a gangling, unpretentious, friendly man who spends each flight cooped up in a cubicle 250 feet from the others, cut off except for the intercom.

Suits and Scarves

The crew lives together in a suite of rooms, Quarters No: 333 in the alert compound and flies together except when one of them is sick.

At midnight they had enormous breakfasts. Captain Hall ordered a three-egg omelet, chipped beef on toast and orange juice. And at 1 o'clock they sat down together in a row of schoolhouse chairs in the briefing room.

Dressed in identical gray suits, they studied elaborately colored slides, listened to several briefing officers and jotted down a string of bewildering numbers and letters.

The meeting ended with an exhortation from the unit commander, Col. W. T. Cumiskey, of Brooklyn, who bounded onto the stage in flying suit and a white silk scarf. "It looks as if we've got a good one going tonight," he said.

At 3 am the crew of 70058 climbed into a bus for the ride to the flight line and began the laborious task of getting the plane ready for the mission. Captain Hall and Captain Sutherland crammed into the plane's tiny cockpit surrounded by hundreds of dials and switches and went through 13 pages of instructions, checking off each item as they finished with it.

By 3.50 the preflight checkout was complete. The crew had a last cigarette, and at 4.40 engine No. 4 accelerated into a whistling whine. At 5.10 Captain Hall inched the throttles forward and the B-52, ungainly on the ground, lurched out onto the taxiway.

Captain Says Little

No order to taxi came from the control tower. This and all the other operations until the return to Guam were carried out at preset times. Captain Hall spoke no more than a dozen words into his radio all day.

At exactly 5.30 the pilot jammed eight throttles forward and the $13.5 million, 22-ton warplane started down the runway. Captain Hall had to fight the wheel to keep 70058 on course because the jetwash of the B-52 only seconds ahead had set up turbulent air currents.

For the next four hours, Pink 2, the plane's code name for today's strike, cruised placidly across the Pacific.

When the gold and blue dawn broke, Pink 1, floating along less than a mile ahead, looked like a model airplane hung from the ceiling of a recreation room.

At 9.15 Captain Hall lowered his electrically-controlled seat and slipped on a pair of leather gloves for the most exacting part of the trip, aerial refueling.

From a base that cannot be identified for security reasons, a KC-135 tanker, similar in design to a Boeing-707 passenger plane, had set out to meet Pink 2 and to pour into her enough fuel to get to Vietnam and back.

Working the throttles with his right hand and manipulating the stick with his left, Captain Hall brought the B-52 to within 18 feet of the tanker and held it there while a man in a cage at the rear of the KC-135 slipped a long boom into a receptacle on top of the bomber's fuselage.

It took 20 minutes to complete the transfer. Once during that period the two planes came unhooked. Bill Hall, a proud man, was irritated.

"I'm not the best in the world at this," he said on the intercom, "but I'm better than that. He had his bloomin' airspeed all over the place when I have to go from full-throttle to idle and I still can't keep up with him. Something's wrong."

At 11.14 the B-52 floated across the Vietnamese coast at more than 20,000 feet and turned north toward Danang.

Computers Put to Work

In a windowless compartment below the cockpit, Lieutenant Price and Captain Lee went to work with their radar sets and computers. They zeroed in a mountain peak and a bridge, then punched into the computer

B-52 Stratofortresses were to mount these marathon long-distance tactical raids right through the Vietnam War.

the distances of these landmarks from the target. The computer did the rest.

At 11.46 Captain Hall began counting: "30-20-10," then more rapidly, "5-4-3-2-1."

No one pressed a button when the count ended. No one said "Bombs away."

But at 11.47, precisely on schedule, the bomb-bay doors swung open and 500-pound bombs cascaded out. At the same instant 750-pounders dropped from their places under the wings.

Above Captain Lee's head, yellow lights winked. In front of Captain Hall and Captain Sutherland an orange light, labeled "Bomb released," a reminder that the B-52 was designed to carry a single nuclear weapon, began blinking frantically.

"One hundred per cent," Captain Lee remarked a few seconds later. "No hangers, all of them away."

"I have the aircraft," Captain Hall said, grasping the controls. As he banked the plane to the right, puffs of black smoke rose from a shadowy hillside where Viet Cong troops were spotted a few days before.

Off to the left "Pink 1" had also unloaded its bombs, but wide of the target, apparently as a result of a radar error. No one on the B-52s knew whether either plane had killed enemy troops or simply plowed furrows in Vietnamese farmland.

No one discussed the question. The bombs were away and the bombers began the long, boring trip home.

The New York Times

AMERICAN EXPANSION

10th Amphibious Operation Double Eagle launched into Quang Ngai Province.

17th A diplomat at the US aid mission, Douglas Ramsey, is seized from his car by the Viet Cong.

19th Opening of Operation Van Buren carried out by US airborne and allied forces in Phu Yen Province.

21st Ceasefire in observance of Vietnamese festival of Tet is violated by the Viet Cong.

24th Joint US/South Vietnamese/South Korean forces search-and-destroy Operation Masher/White Wing/Thang Phong II (Bon Son campaign) commences in Binh Dinh Province.

28th General Westmoreland submits a request for 16,000 troops over and above the 443,000 already asked for.

31st US announces the end of its 37-day break in bombing operations against North Vietnam.

The advent of the helicopter meant the end of traditional airborne assaults, although one combat jump took place during operation Masher/White Wing

Tunnel Rats

When US Infantrymen first encountered the tunnel complex around Cu Chi, they had no idea of their true extent

Operation Crimp, aimed at rooting Charlie out of his Cu Chi stronghold near Saigon, was only hours old. Lt. Col. Robert Haldane saw that his troopers of the 1st Battalion, 28th Infantry – part of the First Infantry Division, the Big Red One – were practically halted at the LZ where they'd emerged from helicopters. Men were being hit by mortar rounds, machine gun bullets, grenade fragments. Whatever Charlie was defending here, he had his mind made up.

After one of his companies launched a probing action, the Viet Cong fire ceased and Haldane's men began to clean up after their wounded. The battalion advanced toward a region of tall rubber trees and began uncovering Viet Cong supply caches – rice, salt, foodstuffs. Haldane's men advanced and sealed off the area, securing a rubber plantation and reaching the banks of the Saigon River. The GIs noticed a number of oddly-shaped ditches but no sign of Charlie. The Viet Cong seemed to have disappeared into thin air.

Sgt. Stewart Green was the first GI to discover a camouflaged wooden door concealing the entrance to a tunnel. Haldane's men went in, uncovered Viet Cong hospital supplies, then foraged into the black depths. A group of GIs came face-to-face with 30 Viet Cong troops deep under the ground but, before the GIs knew what was happening, the Viet Cong had escaped. The battalion commander ordered the use of smoke grenades, certain this would kill or flush out any enemy remaining underfoot. Smoke from the grenades abruptly shot skyward from tunnel exits the GIs hadn't discovered, revealing that the tunnel complex was far larger than suspected. Neither the grenades nor other demolitions uprooted any Viet Cong.

Flashlights and Knives

Lt. Col. Haldane's force, which uncovered its first tunnel on 10 January 1966, was only one of several units – American and Australian – which came upon Viet Cong tunnel entrances in the Cu Chi region. Over time, GI specialists – Tunnel Rats – had to volunteer to fight inside the 200-mile subterranean network. Even then, results were debatable. In a war fought in darkness with flashlights, knives and pistols, the Viet Cong seemed always to maintain the edge.

The 25th "Tropic Lightning" Infantry Division from Hawaii actually built its base camp atop the intricate network of Viet Cong tunnels. The GIs regarded the tunnels as simple passageways beneath the earth and never quite cottoned on to the fact that an entire, vast, city lay under their feet. Each time they succeeded in clearing a section of tunnels, the Viet Cong seemed to open up two more.

Brave men on both sides fought in the tunnels. A man who came squirming out of a tunnel covered with dirt might not be easily identifiable, and more than one American Tunnel Rat was nearly blown away by his pals. The GIs never quite succeeded in eliminating the enemy's firm grip on the world beneath the ground. The Viet Cong remained dug in. The tunnel war, like the rest of the war, was long and no end seemed in sight.

TUNNEL RATS

VC Shatter Truce

Some 400 Viet Cong troops overran a Republic of Korea Marine outpost in a bloody battle early Friday as the Vietnam ceasefire exploded into armed clashes throughout the country.

A U.S. spokesman said 50 VC violations of the ceasefire involving armed attacks had been reported, "and I'm sure there will be others." So far 15 of the assaults have involved Vietnamese units; the others were against other Free World forces.

"There have been U.S. casualties," the spokesman added.

(The Associated Press reported two U.S. Marine sergeants were killed when guerrillas caught a leatherneck platoon on a security patrol in a cross fire as it stuggled through the mud of a flooded rice paddy seven miles south of Da Nang.)

The clash between the VC and the ROK marines took place near Tuy Hoa, on the central coastal plain shortly after 1 a.m. in the rain.

Using local VC troops dressed in black pajamas and native hats as a human shield, the regular VC forces were able to get within about 10 yards of the ROK marine platoon guarding the perimeters of its headquarters area.

The VC opened up from three sides and overran the post, but the marines rallied and staged a counterattack which ended in hand-to-hand fighting, while their artillery opened fire on the enemy.

At daylight the marines counted 46 VC dead and three suspects detained.

Stars and Stripes

Calm Reigns in Battle-Torn Vietnam

The war in Vietnam halted Thursday. Despite the confusion between the various time zones about when cease-fires were to go into effect and the number of countries involved, the fighting stopped.

The only incident involving U.S. troops came about noon Thursday when the cease-fire went into effect. It occurred seven miles west of Tuy Hoa on the central coast when the VC fired on the 1st Brigade of the 101st Airborne. The troopers returned fire and one VC was killed before the enemy fled.

The Vietnamese reported only one clash after the halt in hostilities. It was a minor action lasting less than a half hour.

U.S. planes and troops continued their operations up until midday, then pulled back in keeping with the promise to observe the Vietnamese holiday season of Tet. The cease-fire is supposed to last until 6 p.m. Sunday.

A U.S. spokesman said American forces are maintaining a full alert and planes are making surveillance flights.

Also, operations such as the Market Time blockade of the Vietnamese coast are continuing without interruption.

When asked if the U.S. might extend the cease-fire as was attempted during the Christmas lull, the spokesman said full operations are scheduled to resume Sunday evening, "and this includes offensive action."

Stars and Stripes

Freedom Fighter

The Vietnamese Air Force (VNAF), which had been advised by Americans sinced August 1960, wanted all along to transition into jet aircraft. The inexpensive and lightweight Northrop F-5 Freedom fighter was tried out in Vietnam by US pilots under a program called Operation Sukoshi Tiger. Proven successful, the new jet fighter was then delivered to the VNAF.

Northrop's F-5 was designed to be cheap to build and easy to operate, a handy first-generation jet fighter for America's allies

Trucks Still Roll in Helicopter War

Even in the Airmobile Division, somebody always has to go by truck. The United States' First Cavalry Division (Airmobile) is the unit with 434 helicopters that has changed many patterns of ground combat. The helicopter, not the two-and-a-half-ton truck, is its prime mover.

Assault units of the division's Third Brigade, the outfit that fought the battle of the Iadrang River valley last November, have moved into this area near the South China Sea for Operation Masher, an effort that may last two weeks.

To keep more than 5,000 men on an operation for an extended period, a certain amount of heavy equipment – field kitchens, earth movers, heavy artillery, radio vans – must be moved into forward areas. Roads are still the best means of moving it.

So, at 6.00 this morning, 300 engineers, artillerymen and support troops climbed into jeeps and "deuce-and-a-half" trucks in the division base camp at Ankhe, 45 air miles southwest of Bongson. It was still dark, and the air was cold and damp.

The convoy wound onto Route 19, which leads to a mountain pass toward the seacoast. Dozens of battles have been fought for control of it, by the French against the Communist-led nationalists known as Vietminh, and now by the allies against the Vietcong.

This morning, however, the three-hour ride to the junction with Route 1 was uneventful. The trucks and jeeps crept along at 20 miles an hour, passing First Cavalry and South Korean Army outposts set up to protect the road.

New York Times

FEBRUARY 1966

6-9th US President Johnson meets South Vietnamese Premier Ky in Honolulu, Hawaii. The President declares: "We are determined to win not only military victory but victory over hunger, disease and despair."

7th The South Vietnamese government admits that under its rural pacification plan it would take between five and six years to take control of a province.

7th US aircraft attack a North Vietnamese training centre at Dien Bien Phu.

8th General Gavin warns of possible Chinese entry into the conflict if US troop numbers greatly increase.

10th China accuses USSR of conspiring with the US to force North Vietnam to the negotiating table.

11th President Johnson announces that the American strength of 205,000 troops currently serving in Vietnam will be gradually increased.

14th Mines kill 56 South Vietnamese peasants near Tuy Hoa, 225 miles northeast of Saigon.

17th General Taylor states that the aim of Operation Rolling Thunder, the US air campaign, is "to change the will of the enemy leadership"

23rd According to the allied mission in Saigon, 90,000 South Vietnamese deserted in 1965 – twice the number in 1964.

25th As part of Operation Mastiff, three Viet Cong camps and an arms factory are destroyed in the Boi Loi Woods by US 1st Infantry Division. The division moves on into Long Than district under Operation Mallet.

27th US Marines take on Viet Cong positions northeast of Phubai in Operation New York.

Lambs to the Slaughter

As early as Jan. 26, five Special Forces teams of five men each had been dropped into the An Lao valley to find and "fix" the enemy. Immediately, these teams came under enemy fire and radioed back that they had found at least a battalion – and possibly an entire regiment – of Viet Cong.

The First Cav. allowed itself to be diverted by the Viet Cong's rear-guard action outside Bong Son. By the time the First Cav. finally descended into the valley, nine days had passed, fully half of the Special Forces troops had been wiped out and the enemy had disappeared.

At Special Forces headquarters in Nha Trang, 200 miles northeast of Saigon, Gen. William C. Westmoreland, the commander of US forces in Vietnam, last week personally debriefed the survivors of the An

Fresh Troops Pour In
Allies in Largest Push to Date

The bloody fighting north of Bong Son has developed into the largest military operation of the Vietnam war as thousands of fresh troops poured into the battlefield.

Operation White Wing – previously called Masher – 55 miles north of Qui Nhon in the Bong Son area, "has been reinforced by other elements of the 1st Cav, and is now a multi-brigade operation," a military spokesman said Saturday.

The operation, which involves Vietnamese army units and the Korean Tiger troops, was described as a "continually expanding three-country operation."

With the increase to multi-brigade size, Maj. Gen. Harry W. O. Kinnard, leader of the 1st Air Cav., has assumed command.

When questioned about operation Double Eagle, the marine amphibious landing 20 miles to the north of White Wing, the spokesman explained that there has been no pincer-type movement but that the two units are coordinating their actions. He added the marines are moving toward the 1st Cav. troops as the operation continues.

White Wing had little contact Friday, as the 1st Cav. continued to search for the Viet Cong. They have killed 518 Viet Cong, captured 120 and detained 582 suspects since the operation began Jan. 25.

Stars and Stripes

US Bombs North Ends 37-Day Lull

U.S. Air Force and Navy planes blasted targets in North Vietnam Monday, ending the 37-day halt in

Lao Valley. "Those boys were real bitter, and they didn't pull any punches with the boss," reported one US officer. "They expected heavy casualties, but after finding and fixing the enemy and fighting like lions for several days, the least they expected was that their sacrifice would be exploited. Next time, we'll make damn sure we have our own back-up force."

Newsweek

By the time the 1st Cav got to the An Lao, there was little they could do but sanitise the area

air strikes that began Christmas Eve.

The announcement came at 3 p.m. when a special press briefing was called to release a one paragraph statement:

"The prime minister of Vietnam and the American ambassador to Vietnam announce that U.S. aircraft today attacked targets in designated areas in North Vietnam."

Heavy anti-aircraft fire was reported and one plane was lost as reports came in on the first four targets hit.

Stars and Stripes

Paradise Lost

For four years the pleasant coastal plain of Binh Dinh has been a private Communist demiparadise of palm-topped villages and emerald paddies. That came to an abrupt end early one rainy morning when the first helicopter assault forces of the 1st Air Cav took off from Moore's staging area, called "Dog" and headed for LZ-4, a landing zone nestled between two villages.

Kiss & Fire

The enemy was waiting. Almost at once five choppers were shot down. "We're in a hornets' nest!" radioed Captain John Fesmire. Soon, both his mortar platoon leader and radio operator were killed, his company was scattered to the north of the helidrop zone, and a rescue company sent to his assistance was pinned down by crossfire as well.

The sergeant who had taken over the weapons platoon was trapped near a machine gun nest. He had his mortar tube –

but no base plate, no plotting board, no aiming stakes, no forward observer. With only six rounds of ammunition, he watched five explode harmlessly some distance from the target. Then he lifted his last round, kissed it, and fired. It leveled the machine gunners' hut.

It was nearly 24 hours before the defenders of LZ-4 were relieved and White Wing took flight. Choppers dropped fresh troops to roll up the flank of the Viet Cong firing on LZ-4 from the southwest, while still another battalion was lifted into a blocking position to the north.

Elbows & Helmets

Unable to escape, the Communists, now identified as two regiments – one regular North Vietnamese, one partly Viet Cong – had to fight, to their sorrow. By the third day of White Wing, nearly 400 of the enemy had been killed, against relatively light casualties by the allies. One 1st Air Cav company was mistaken for the enemy by twelve advancing armored personnel carriers full of South Vietnamese. The APCs let loose

The cultivated fields and orderly villages of Binh Dinh held very different dangers from the highland jungles, but no less real

with .50-cal. machine gun fire that set the GIs and news correspondents accompanying them sprawling in the sand, digging for their lives with elbows and helmets. "Jesus Christ! Cease fire! Cease fire!" radioed the US company commander. The guns finally fell silent, but not before New York Timesman R. W. (Johnny) Apple had had his pants neatly laid open by a .50-cal. slug.

Time

Helmets Off to the Men Down Under

The mainspring of the 1,700-man Australian contingent in Vietnam, the "Fighting First" Battalion of the Royal Australian Regiment is currently attached to the US 173rd Airborne Brigade. Since their arrival in Vietnam last summer, the "diggers" of the First Battalion have carried out no fewer than nineteen major operations. During a sweep through the notorious Iron Triangle, they uncovered a vast complex of tunnels, burrowed 60 feet deep in places, which turned out to be the Viet Cong's headquarters for the entire Saigon area. Remarked one US intelligence official of the Australian find: "It will take months for the Viet Cong to repair the damage to their organisation."

Before going to Vietnam, the Fighting First, which saw action in the jungles of Borneo against the Japanese in World War II, spent twelve years helping the British put down Communist in-

surgency in Malaya. And some of the Australian NCOs and officers now serving in Vietnam are veterans of that campaign.

Economizers

As a result, Australian tactics and techniques differ sharply from those used by the Americans. While the American GI, for example, usually carries only one canteen of water, the Australian digger carries four plus enough rations to last two or three days. Eschewing heavy

steel helmets in the steamy jungle, the Aussies wear light bush hats. They carry less ammunition than the Americans and fire an average of only 60 rounds from their rifles for every 100 expended by the US soldier. Most important, when on an operation, the Australians keep on the move in order to throw off the enemy and, unlike Americans, would never dream of taking a break for a telltale cigarette.

Newsweek

The Australians who fought in Vietnam brought with them twenty years of experience of fighting communist guerrillas

MARINES IN DELTA

MARCH 1966

4th US Marines and ARVN take part in air assault to dislodge NVA/Viet Cong forces near Quang Ngai City in an operation codenamed Utah/Lien Ket 26.

7th The heaviest air raids of the war see 200 missions flown by US Navy and Air Force aircraft.

8-11th Ashau Special Forces camp, 60 miles from Da Nang, attacked by the NVA, forcing the allies to withdraw.

9th The US admits the destruction of 20,000 acres of crops in an attempt to deny food to the Viet Cong.

10th Lieutenant General Thi, a leading Buddhist, is sacked from the South Vietnamese National Leadership Committee, giving rise to a wave of Buddhist violence against the Ky regime.

16th US Representative Clement Zablocki, not long returned from a visit to Vietnam, alleges that in recent search-and-destroy operations six civilians died for every success against a Viet Cong guerrilla.

19th South Korea decides to send a further 20,000 troops to Vietnam. Her current commitment is 21,000.

19th Operation Texas launched to repel Viet Cong attack on An Hoa. The force consists of US Marines and ARVN airborne troops.

25th Anti-Ky Buddhists take over radio stations in Hue and Da Nang, demanding the resignation of the premier and his regime.

26th In New York City, 15 World War II and Korean War veterans incinerate their discharge and separation documents.

26th Under Operation Garfield the 3rd Brigade of the 25th Infantry Division patrols the Darlac Plains and the Chu Pong Mountains along the Cambodian border.

Sidearms and full survival kit were essentials for Skyraider pilots. Flying low, slow and in the thick of it, they risked capture every time they flew

US HIKING VIET TROOPS BY 20,000
215,000 Men Already In-Country

Defense Secretary Robert S. McNamara said Wednesday he has authorized an increase in U.S. forces in the Republic of Vietnam to 235,000 men. He said this strength could be boosted to over 350,000 without calling reservists to active duty.

McNamara told a news conference another 20,000 troops have been ordered to Vietnam, on top of the 215,000 now there.

This was the first public disclosure that U.S. armed strength in Vietnam had reached 215,000.

McNamara also said the United States has the capability to send 21 more battalions to Vietnam within the next 90 days, if such action should be required.

The Defense Secretary said, however, that based on his present assessment, such action is not likely.

Stars and Stripes

Overwhelmed, the Green Berets fought until their ammunition was exhausted, but were finally over-run

REDS OVERRUN CAMP
Lone Survivor Radios

The radio operator at the A Shau Special Forces camp reported early Thursday that he was the "lone survivor" – shortly before the camp was apparently overrun by the Viet Cong.

The message was the last received from the camp which was defended by 300 Montagnard soldiers and 12 U.S. Army Special forces advisers, according to AP.

It followed earlier messages which reported the camp, 30 miles southwest of Hue and a scant 1½ miles from the laotian border, was under full attack. The messages told of hand-to-hand fighting along the barbed wire covered walls of the fortress-like camp and a last ditch stand in the camp's communications bunker.

Getting Short

"**M**an, I'm getting so short, I can walk through a door without opening it."

Of course, there *are* no doors here in the bush, in the highlands of South Vietnam. Not out here where we spend half the time fighting leeches, insects, and poisonous snakes. But believe me, when a guy gets short, he talks about being short.

The tour of duty is one year. 365 days. And there isn't a dogface in this entire country who doesn't know *exactly* how many days he has left to go. You hear the guys talking about it all the time.

"Man, you got 230 days left? Man, I can't even *remember* when I had 230 days left. Man, I got 37 days and a wakeup."

"What the heck are you talking about? You're practically a lifer. Me, I only got *seventeen* and a wakeup . . ."

It's considered sacrilege to tamper with anybody's "days left." The military bends over backwards to make sure a man gets out of here when he's supposed to get out, perhaps because it's so important to morale – it's sort of like a contract, you know, and everybody takes that contract very seriously.

Becoming a FIGMO

When you get down to having 70 days left, you officially become FIGMO, which stands for "F . . . it, I got my orders." A guy who is FIGMO is never given the tough jobs, like walking point on a patrol. When you're FIGMO, you're expected to wear a little yellow ribbon in your collar or on your helmet. Most guys use the yellow ribbon which is attached to the neck of a Seagram's 7 whisky bottle. No one seems to know how that custom originated.

On the blessed day when the chopper comes to lift you out for the trip home, you're expected to make a speech to your buddies, telling them how you're going to take care of their wives and girl friends when you get back to "the World." It's customary to give away small, meaningless gifts, like your insect repellant or the FIGMO ribbon itself. Depending on conditions and how close the Viet Cong are, it is preferred that you not get aboard the chopper sober.

All of this ritual overlooks a basic fact, which is that most battlefield deaths occur in the first three weeks of arriving here. Longevity is no guarantee of survival, to be sure. But it's been demonstrated that experience makes a big difference. Once you get past the initial learning barriers, you have a much improved prospect of getting through your tour in Nam.

Scrapbook

MARINES
IN 1ST DELTA ASSAULT
Protecting Saigon's Lifeline

U.S. marines landed only 30 miles southeast of Saigon Saturday to open a drive aimed at Halting Viet Cong sabotage along the major river channel between the South China Sea and the capital.

It was the farthest south U.S. troops have operated in any numbers since the beginning of the Vietnam war.

Some 1,200 Leathernecks poured ashore from Seventh Fleet ships by landing boat and helicopter shortly after daybreak and immediately began sweeping this rugged stretch of delta land, which guards the east side of the entrance to the Long Tau River.

The river is the only waterway into Saigon big enough to handle most of the huge military and commercial deep-draft cargo ships. One source estimated that 60 per cent of all cargo to Vietnam travels up the Long Tao.

Stars and Stripes

United States Marines got a chance to show off their amphibious skills on the Long Tau, south of Saigon

Up until 3 a.m. Thursday the defenders had reported they were in good shape even though they were under small arms and mortar fire.

At 3.25 a.m. the radio operator reported the camp was under full attack.

A half hour later he reported the camp walls had been breached and the camp split in half by the attackers.

The message from the radio operator that he was the "lone survivor" at the camp came at 4.25 a.m. and was the last radio message.

Stars and Stripes

What Price Glory?

When the Special Forces camp at A Shau fell to the Viet Cong two weeks ago, no one denied that this was a defeat. But it was, after all, a glorious defeat made memorable by the fortitude of A Shau's defenders. Or so, at least, said the early reports. Last week, however, when a fuller story began to emerge, it appeared that along with the heroism at A Shau went an ugly tale of desertion, cowardice and treachery.

When the Viet Cong attacked, say the American survivors, many of the South Vietnamese irregulars who made up the bulk of the A Shau force refused to fight. Most of the resistance was mounted by the handful of Americans in the camp and the hundred-odd Nung tribesmen who were flown into A Shau just the day before the attack.

Panic

After it was decided to abandon the camp, plans were laid to remove the wounded in the first helicopters to arrive. When the choppers landed, however, able-bodied irregulars tried to shove aboard, leaving the wounded behind.

The Nungs and the Americans tried to pull and club them from the choppers. When this failed, and two helicopters crashed in the attempt to get airborne, Special Forces sergeants and Marine crewmen turned their guns on the irregulars, killing seven of them.

Newsweek

APRIL 1966

The 1st Infantry Division advances through the Phuoc Tuy Province under Operation Abilene.

The US Navy is charged with preventing the movement of arms and supplies through the Mekong Delta under Operation Game Warden.

The US 25th Infantry Division arrives from Hawaii.

1st The mayor of Da Nang comes out in open support of the Buddhist rebels.

1st The Viet Cong blow up a Saigon hotel used by US troops. Three Americans and four South Vietnamese are killed.

3rd Marshal Ky admits that Da Nang is "held by communists and the government will undertake operations to clear them out".

4th US F-4C Phantom jets strike the main line of supply between North Vietnam and Nanning in China.

5th Premier Ky enters Da Nang at the head of government forces.

9th The prospect of a takeover of South Vietnam by neutralist Buddhist government worries US administration.

11th The US admits that political instability in South Vietnam limits the efficiency of the ARVN.

11th USAF pilots are restricted to 100 combat missions over North Vietnam or a 12-month tour of Vietnam. The Navy and Marines impose no limit.

12th The US introduces B-52 bombers into the attack on North Vietnam, dropping huge quantities of bombs on the Mugia Pass.

12th The Viet Cong assault Tan Son Nhut Air*Base with mortars and smallarms, killing and injuring soldiers and civilians and damaging aircraft.

17th Hampered by waist-deep mud and the threat of disease the 1st Infantry Division carries out search-and-destroy Operation Lexington III in Rung Sat Special Zone. USN and USAF bomb ever closer to Hanoi and Haiphong.

21st Six US pacifists ejected from South Vietnam for trying to hold anti-war protests.

23rd Sixteen North Vietnamese MiGs engage US aircraft for first time.

24th 1st Infantry Division is north of Tay Ninh under Operation Birmingham.

28th A report that 11 missiles had recently been fired in an engagement with North Vietnamese aircraft without a success prompts investigation into weapons efficiency.

A Bugle Sounds as GIs Go Ashore at Vungtau

The men of the 25th Infantry Division needed no urging to check every possible hiding place

"No, I can't say I'm glad to be here," said First Sgt. Harold P. Powers, "but I couldn't have looked in the mirror if I hadn't come."

Sergeant Powers, who is 31 years old and from Chicago, was one of the first soldiers of the United States Army's 25th Infantry Division to land on the beach of this resort city 50 miles southeast of Saigon this morning.

The arrival of 4,000 men who make up the division's First Brigade brought the unit to its full combat strength of about 15,000 and the number of American troops in Vietnam to about 250,000.

Headquarters at Cuchi

The division headquarters has been established at Cuchi, a village on the plains northeast of Saigon, and the men who arrived today are expected to be stationed there with another brigade.

On the way to the beach in one of the gray landing craft that were slowly emptying the United States Navy troop transport ship *General Nelson Walker*, Sergeant Powers spoke proudly of the men directly in his charge, Company B, 4th Battalion, 23rd Infantry.

"They're in good physical condition," he said. "They've trained hard. Most of the NCOs are combat veterans."

As the landing craft neared the shore, one soldier called out "Hey, Sarge, where's the bugle?"

Confusing the Enemy

"Let's have a charge, sarge," the soldier called.

Sergeant Powers sent an amiable command booming the length of the craft: "Blow a charge, Richardson."

Private Richardson fumbled for the horn and pushed out three strange notes. The men around him roared: "Charge." More notes: another "Charge."

"It's something we plan to use to throw confusion into the enemy," Sergeant Powers explained. "I learned a lot of Chinese calls when I was in Korea and I taught them to the boys. We know the North Vietnamese use bugles and they probably use the same calls.

"When they charge us, Richardson will blow assembly. That ought to confuse them. We've got some signals we've made up ourselves, too, like that charge."

The New York Times

Air Force Heroes

Major Gilmore and Lt. Smith – first of a new generation of USAF MiG killers

On 26 April, Maj. Paul J. Gilmore, in the front seat of the lead F-4C, and lst Lt. William T. Smith in the back, downed the first MIG-21 of the war. They were part of a flight of three F-4's flying escort for two RB-66's. Launching from Da Nang, they rendezvoused with the RB-66's and proceeded north to the Red River, where one RB-66 and one F-4 split off for a separate mission. Gilmore, flying the other F-4, and the other RB-66 proceeded northeast of Hanoi. Almost at once they spotted two or three MIGs coming high in the 2 o'clock position and closing rapidly. Gilmore and his wingman jettisoned their external tanks, lit their after burners, and broke into a hard left-descending turn while the RB-66 departed the area.

They pulled up after the MIGs, which were in afterburner, heading northwest at 30,000 feet.

The second MIG was descending very slowly, trailing white vapor toward the east. The F-4 aircrews lost sight of this aircraft as they closed rapidly or the first, which was making gentle clearing turns as he climbed away.

First-time Hit

At a range of 3,000 feet, Gilmore fired one Sidewinder with a good tone; he then manoeuvred to the left to gain more separation and as a result did not see his first missile track.

"My wingman, flying cover for me, told me later that MIG pilot had ejected after I fired the first missile. I didn't realise I'd hit him the first time. My wingman wondered why I kept after him as I had hit him the first time and the pilot ejected." Because of radio difficulties, his wingman could not inform Gilmore of his success.

After his maneuver to gain separation, Gilmore pulled up behind the pilotless MIG-21 again and fired another Sidewinder without effect. He again rolled to the left, pulled up, and fired his third Sidewinder at a range of 3,000 feet. "After missing [he thought] twice," Gilmore later told newsmen, "I was quite disgusted. I started talking to myself. Then I got my gunsights on him and fired a third time. I observed my missile go directly in his tailpipe and explode his tail."

Time

DA NANG CLASH AVERTED
U.S. Pulls Out Advisers

Republic of Vietnam Prime Minister Nguyen Cao Ky and opposition elements in this northernmost I Corps area appeared Tuesday night to have worked out a compromise to avert possible bloodshed in a clash within the South Vietnamese army.

Ky flew here early Tuesday and held day-long talks with Maj. Gen. Nguyen Van Chuan, newly named I Corps commander.

After the talks were over and Ky had taken off to return to Saigon, Chuan told newsmen the Prime Minister had agreed that about 4,000 Vietnamese Marines who landed overnight at Da Nang air base would remain on base and would not seek to enter the city of Da Nang.

He said elements of the 11th Ranger Bn. that he had ordered to Da Nang were sent back to their station at Hoi An, south of Da Nang.

Chuan added that he had pledged to control the anti-government demonstrations that have swept Da Nang and would try to halt expressions of anti-Americanism here.

Chuan said the Vietnamese Marines flown here on orders of the Saigon government would remain at the air base "to provide security." He said he and Ky had agreed they would not be moved into Da Nang.

Last Sunday Ky charged that Da Nang was in control of communist elements and said the government would launch military operations to bring this to an end.

WASHINGTON

American advisers have been pulled out of opposing Republic of Vietnamese forces at Da Nang to avoid U.S. involvement in the internal political conflict, the State Department said Tuesday.

Stars and Stripes

VC
HIT SAIGON AB
7 Killed, 155 Hurt

The Viet Cong attacked Saigon's Tan Son Nhut AB with mortars early Wednesday, killing 7 Americans and wounding 155 other persons.

The American dead included six soldiers and one sailor.

Among the wounded were 20 Air Force men, 77 other U.S. servicemen, and 58 Vietnamese. It was the first mortar attack on the base, where 10,000 U.S. servicemen are stationed and which houses the residence of Prime Minister Nguyen Cao Ky. The base is about four miles from the heart of Saigon.

Five U.S. aircraft were damaged. They included F-100 fighter-bombers and one TVC-121. The latter is the craft that provides television relay to Saigon. The television plane was described as badly damaged.

Two Vietnamese C-47 cargo planes also were damaged and a fuel storage installation was set ablaze.

Stars and Stripes

Even a secure site such as Saigon's Tan Son Nhut Air Base is not safe from guerrilla attack as VC mortars kill seven

War Dance

From his command post high on the navigating bridge, the *Enterprise*'s skipper, an unflappable 44-year-old captain named James L. Holloway Jr., looks down on the carefully choreographed ballet of carrier warfare that unfolds on the flight deck far below.

Every twenty seconds during the launching periods, as regularly as the tick of a metronome, one rocket-laden jet bomber after another is hurled off of the carrier's 4.47-acre deck with a whoosh of steam, the whiplash crack of catapult cables and the never-ending banshee howl from the bombers' tailpipes.

Newsweek

MAY 1966

1st Infantry Division searches Loc Ninh area under Operation El Paso I after captured document indicates possibility of Viet Cong attack.

2nd Defense Secretary McNamara discloses that around 4500 North Vietnamese per month are infiltrating into the South – three times the figure for the previous year.

6th 1st Air Cavalry Division in action over the Bon Son region under Operation Davy Crockett.

7th Operation Hollingsworth, a planned air assault on what was thought to be the Viet Cong HQ abandoned when weather proves too bad for helicopters.

10th 3rd Brigade of the 25th Infantry Division and ARVN forces embark on Operation Paul Revere/Tahn Phong 14 in the Chu Pong-Ia Drang area to block possible NVA attacks on Special Forces camps at Duc Ho and Plei Me.

11th Surface-to-air missile site 10 miles northeast of Haiphong destroyed by US Navy A-4 Skyhawks.

13th US aircraft accused of violating Chinese airspace and shooting down training plane.

15th Further Buddhist agitation follows Premier Ky's decision to send 1500 ARVN troops to Da Nang.

16th Acting on intelligence gathered by Operation Masher/White Wing the 1st Cavalry Division launches Operation Crazy Horse.

18th Government sources reveal that 254,000 US troops are now serving in Vietnam.

22nd Harold Brown, US Air Force Secretary, warns that an expansion of the air war might lead to Chinese intervention.

30th US aircraft carry out the biggest raids of the war so far on the Vinh-Thanh Hoa area, Highway 12 and the Yen Bay arsenal.

NEW VIETCONG WEAPON: Cucumber Boobytrap

United States marines operating near the coastal enclave of Chulai, 350 miles northeast of Saigon, reported today a new Vietcong weapon – exploding cucumbers.

While probing a recently taken village west of Chulai, Corp. S. L. Sherwin of Chicago said he found a pile of cucumbers topped with one that had been cut in half, hollowed out and filled with explosive powder.

The corporal said he and others of his squad rigged hand grenades to "blow cucumbers over several acres."

Chinese MiG Kill

Controversy erupted from the USAF MIG kill on 12 May, when Communist China charged that U.S. fighters had intruded into Chinese airspace and shot down a Chinese aircraft. China's report placed the air battle in Yunnan province, 25 miles north of the border.

Involved in this aerial victory was an F-4C crewed by Maj. Wilbur R. Dudley and 1st Lt. Impants Kringelis, the third aircraft of a flight of three Phantoms escorting an EB-66 on an ECM mission in the Red River Valley. Four MIG-17s jumped the flight about 105 to 115 miles northwest of Hanoi, more than 20 miles south of China's frontier.

"The enemy flier seemed to be a pretty good pilot, but he made one mistake," Dudley later reported. "He apparently had a case of tunnel vision when he bore in on the EB-66 and never knew we were behind him. That was his mistake. And one mistake is all you're allowed in this game."

Dudley missed with his first Sidewinder, fired just as the MIG began descending in what appeared to be a Split-S maneuver designed to regain an offensive position. When the MIG rolled out behind the EB-66, Dudley fired a second missile. It guided up the MIG's tailpipe and the aircraft disintegrated. It spun out of control and crashed. The pilot was apparently unable to eject, for no parachute was observed. The battle continued a little longer without any further losses on either side, and the two forces then disengaged.

USAF in Vietnam

NAVY PATROLLING VIETNAM'S RIVERS
Newly Organized Command Is Part of Expanded Role

The Navy has recently organized a new river patrol force in Vietnam to operate eventually in all the major rivers and canals of the Mekong Delta.

The river patrol force is part of a major expansion and re-organization of United States naval activities in Vietnam.

The river patrol force, designated Task Force 116 and called by the Navy Operation Game Warden, is just being organized, and so far is using only 16 high-speed, shallow-draft boats that have plastic hulls and are propelled by water jet-propulsion nozzles. These boats are based at Catlo and operate from an LSD (Landing Ship, Dock) "mother" ship.

Operations at present are around the so-called Rungsat Special Zone, which covers the river approaches to Saigon.

Last week, the Navy added to its Rungsat Zone fleet three patrol Air Cushion Vehicles, known to civilians as hovercraft. The vehicle, which travels above the ground or water on a cushion of air produced by a fan in its underside, is to go into operation this week.

New York Times

Hovercraft bring a new dimension to riverine warfare

Diary
of a North Vietnamese Soldier

May 1. Today is farewell day. Departure takes place in a few hours. Meanwhile, Ngoan sews a book bag for me. Since my return, there have been constant visitors. The village people are indeed very kind. In the dark of the night or under pelting rain like tonight, they come to see us in large numbers. I find our people highly aware of the situation and they feel a deep anti-Americanism.

May 11. It's hard to sleep tonight. I don't mind who has to go to South Vietnam first. All my worry centers around the day of reunification and whether I will come back unscathed. How will the family be then? ...

Relying on mobility more than firepower, the North Vietnamese Army rarely carried anything heavier than RPG-7 rocket launchers

Such thoughts assault my mind, and I toss and toss, spending a wakeful night.

Le finally gets his orders to proceed to the town of Thanh Hoa, 60 miles south of Hanoi in North Vietnam's Military Zone IV.

June 11. Things look different in the war zone; troops are more appreciated here. At the bus station, our troops chat with the girls in high spirits. The war is felt more acutely in this zone. People work at night. Cars run without headlights and are heavily camouflaged. Even the bicycles are camouflaged.

June 13. Today we enjoyed only one meal because of the shortage of rice. We feel dog tired as we walk in the night. The pine forest is charred by US rockets. The bridges are blasted by US bombs, the railroads melted and the houses burned. This fans the flames of hate in everyone.

June 19. We depart at 6 pm. When we reach Ky Tan village, we ask to be put up for the night at a house, but the lady refuses because, she says, her house is too small. Her two daughters argue with her and finally she gives in.

July 23. The situation is always tense because of the activities of the enemy air force above us. Not a night is slept without my thinking of the family, and Ngoan is always present in my dreams.

July 27. It is clear Truong Minh Chau [one of Le's section members] has deserted. I worry over his fate. He may get drowned or killed on the way.

Aug. 1. Tonight ... I am washing rice when US planes come and strafe above.

Toward the middle of August, Le prepares for the final stage of his journey into South Vietnam. He is inoculated against various diseases and gets his hair cut. In late September the move begins in earnest and Le has little time to write in his diary except to list the names of the towns his unit passes through. The months of November and December are left a blank as Le makes the dangerous crossing of the 17th parallel into the Ben Hai River Delta area near the town of Quang Tri.

Feb. 6. I stay awake all night because of the cursed boil on my shoulder.

Feb. 20. After lunch my section heads for Kb [an abbreviation for a place name]. We get lost. No liaison agents show us the way. Yet I feel happy, particularly when at nightfall troops pour out from the forest like so many ants. After 3 am, the first unit opens fire. I will stay awake all night.

Feb. 21. The building of installations goes on in preparation for fighting.

Newsweek

JUNE 1966

2nd 1st Infantry Division and ARVN 5th Regiment move into War Zone C in the Binh Long Province under Operation El Paso II in an attempt to prevent the Viet Cong attacking Saigon during the rainy season.

2nd 1st Brigade, 101st Airborne Division is sent into Kontum Province under Operation Hawthorne/Dan Tang 61 to pull the Tou Morong Regional Force outpost back to Dak To.

4th The Ad Hoc Universities Committee for the Statement on Vietnam puts a three-page anti-war advertisement in *The New York Times* signed by 6400 academics.

9th Captain W. S. Carpenter of the 101st Airborne Division will be recommended for the Congressional Medal of Honor for calling down air strikes on his own positions, enabling his company to escape the NVA.

9th The commander of the 101st Airborne Division, General Sternberg, states the need for 500,000 more troops to guard the South Vietnam border against enemy penetration.

11th Private Adam R. Weber, a pacifist black soldier serving with the 25th Infantry Division receives a sentence of one year's hard labour for his refusal to carry a rifle.

11th Defense Secretary McNamara reveals that US troop numbers in Vietnam are to be increased by 18,000 to 285,000.

18th General Westmoreland puts his 1967 manpower requirements at 542,588 – an increase of 111,588 troops.

20th 101st Airborne and 1st Cavalry Division carry out Operation Nathan Hale around the US Special Forces camp at Dong Tri.

21st North Vietnam repeats its demand for a cessation of bombing as a precondition to peace talks.

21st US aircraft strike at North Vietnamese fuel stores.

29th An estimated 50 per cent of the North's fuel is destroyed in air raids near Hanoi and Haiphong.

30th Reaction in the US to air raids is mixed. China regards them as a major escalation.

First Blood

In June, Ranch Hand lost its first aircraft during a combat mission. The UC-123 was hit by ground fire over Quang Tin province in I Corps. The two aircraft flying this mission had received sporadic ground fire over the target. On their fifth pass, one of the aircraft lost an engine, crashed, and burned on a hedge row near a rice paddy. Six US Marine Corps helicopters responded to the distress call. Two landed at the crash site, in spite of ground fire, and rescued all three members of the crew. The pilot of the downed UC-123 was seriously injured, but the others received only minor cuts and bruises.

USAF in SE Asia

US Bombs Area of 2-Day Battle

The battle began Thursday afternoon when Company C, Second Battalion, 502d Regiment of the 101st Airborne Division was almost overrun in a bamboo thicket near here, 295 miles northeast of Saigon.

The company commander, Capt. William S. Carpenter Jr., 28 years old, of Monroe, NY, a former West Point football star, has been recommended for the Congressional Medal of Honor for his action in ordering aircraft to drop napalm and cannon fire on his own position to stop the North Vietnamese assault.

Captain Carpenter stood today near a bomb crater on a scarred ridge as medical helicopters took out his dead and wounded and said: "I can't tell you how I arrived at the decision to call the air strike in on our position."

"I didn't really think about it," he said. "They were all around us and getting into our position."

"Put it right on top of me." Captain Carpenter had shouted into his radio. "We might as well take some of them with us."

Grenades Called Worse

The captain's radio operator, who was next to him, was killed by the air strike, as were a handful of other men in the company.

"The air strike that the captain called in got some of us, but it really helped us. It is what saved us."

Captain Carpenter saluted his battalion commander, Lieut. Col. Henry Emerson of Milford, Pa., and the First Brigade Commander, Brig. Gen. Willard Pearson, and had high praise for his men, particularly the wounded who had spent almost 44 hours in the jungle sleeping in the rain.

"There was not a complaint, sir," said Captain Carpenter. "Not one word."

Another major figure in the battle had been Captain Brown, a short, stocky man with a heavy black beard.

Captain Brown has already been recommended for two Silver stars for previous battles and was proposed for another after he fought his way to Captain Carpenter's side at midnight Thursday.

"Bill Carpenter can have the Congressional Medal of Honor," Captain Brown joked to Colonel Emerson, "just give me a razor, a bath and a Silver Star."

The New York Times

MARINES IN BATTLE Stand at Chu Lai

The US Marines fought off the VC with bullets, grenades, bayonets and finally rocks

As the moon rose over the sprawling U.S. base at Chu Lai one night last week, a patrol of eighteen marines settled down in an observation post on a barren hilltop 25 miles to the northwest. The platoon's mission – to watch the movements of Viet Cong units – promised to be a dull one, for the Viet Cong (unlike the North Vietnamese regulars) have been relatively quiescent in the last few weeks. But shortly after midnight, tedium abruptly gave way to stark drama and high heroism.

Surrounding the Marine position in the dark, a Viet Cong force estimated at 250 men first laid a murderous barrage of 60-mm. mortar shells onto the platoon and then proceeded to sweep it with a searing fusillade of machine-gun and small-arms fire. "From then on," said the platoon leader, S/Sgt. James Howard of San Diego, Calif., "It was Katie-bar-the-door." Wave after wave of Viet Cong surged up the rugged hillside, and each time Howard's men fought them off – with bullets, grenades, bayonets and finally with rocks.

Jets and helicopters from Da Nang and Chu Lai did their best to assist the defenders by strafing and napalming the guerrillas. Nonetheless, by the time a Marine relief force made its way to the hilltop five hours after the attack began, Howard's platoon scarcely existed as a fighting force: five of its members were dead, eleven were wounded and the two unwounded men had only eight rounds of ammunition left. But the marines still held the hilltop, and around them lay 45 Viet Cong bodies.

Newsweek

THUNDERCHIEF VICTORY First Kill for F-105

A flight of four F-105s was flying an Iron Hand (SAM suppression) mission during the afternoon of 29 June when it encountered four MIG-17's about 25 miles north-northwest of Hanoi. The F-105s had just left their target when they detected the MIGs closing at 7 o'clock.

The first MIG fired, but missed tghe third Thunderchief which along with number 4 was breaking and diving. The first and second MIGs then pursued the lead element. The third and fourth MIGs followed, but did not take an active part in the engagement. The F-105 flight leader and his wingman had begun a left turn when the MIGs were sighted. The American aircraft went to afterburners and jettisoned their ordnance as they commenced a dive to the left.

The lead MIG fired at Tracy, in aircraft 2, and made several hits. One 23-mm slug entered the cockpit and knocked Tracy's hand off the throttle, putting him out of afterburner and damaging his instruments, including his gun sight and oxygen equipment. The MIG overshot the Thunderchief and ended up at Tracy's 12 o'clock position.

Tracy fired 200 rounds of 20-mm, observing about 10 hits. The MIG rolled over and did a Split-S into clouds at an altitude of 2,000 feet. Because of the damage to this aircraft, Tracy then left the battle area, with aircraft 3 providing cover.

Cannon fire from the second MIG, meanwhile, hit and damaged the lead F-105. Aircraft 4 engaged the fourth MIG, which had joined in the battle. The lead Thunderchief pilot fired about 200 rounds of 20-mm, but scored no hits. Before departing the area, he fired a burst at the departing MIGs, and again he apparently missed.

USAF in SE Asia

A "Thud" with external bombload sets out to kill SAMs

BOMBING STEP-UP

JULY 1966

1st US steps up bombing of North Vietnamese fuel installations around Hanoi and Haiphong. China calls these raids "barbarous and wanton acts that have further freed us from any bounds of restrictions in helping North Vietnam".

6th According to the Pentagon 55 per cent of North Vietnam's fuel has now been destroyed.

6th Reports appear on Hanoi Radio of captured US servicemen paraded through the streets of the North's capital in front of hostile crowds.

7th A government motion is adopted in the British House of Commons giving support to the US policy in Vietnam but not to the recent round of air strikes on Hanoi and Haiphong.

8th Premier Ky expresses his desire for a full-scale invasion of North Vietnam.

9th USSR complains to the US that the raids on Haiphong put Soviet shipping in the port in danger. The US rejects this charge.

11th The US steps up its bombing of the Ho Chi Minh Trail in Laos, flying over 100 missions a day. A Harris survey indicates that 62 per cent of those asked approve of the air strikes and that 86 per cent thought they would bring the war to a swifter close.

12th US prisoners of war are to go on trial according to North Vietnamese diplomats, but Hanoi insists that they will be treated humanely.

15th In the largest combined operation so far – Operation Hastings/Deckhouse II – six battalions of Marines and five ARVN battalions engage the NVA in the Ngan Valley (nicknamed Helicopter Valley) in Quang Tri Province.

29th Pacifist Terry Sullivan receives a one-year prison sentence. He was one of a large number of Americans who registered their objection to the war by destroying their draft cards.

30th A report that the NVA is crossing the Demilitarized Zone leads to the area being bombed for the first time by US aircraft.

31st US admits bombing targets in Cambodia but insists that "maps available to us show the two targets are in South Vietnam".

Operation Hastings saw eleven battalions committed to the fight, the combined firepower of the US Marines and the Army of the Republic of Viet Nam being brought down on the NVA troops trying to occupy the Ngan Valley

US Rejects Ky Call to Invade China

The United States disassociated itself Tuesday from a call by Republic of Vietnam Premier Nguyen Cao Ky for a military confrontation now with communist China.

A State Department spokesman declared: "Our position of not seeking any wider war has been repeatedly made clear and remains our position."

Ky had proposed in an interview that "it is better to face them (the communist Chinese) right now than in 5 or 10 years." He also suggested an allied invasion of north Vietnam to smash the source of communist aggression against South Vietnam.

Ky's remarks brought a storm of objection in the Senate Tuesday. Senate majority Leader Mike Mansfield (D-Mont.) called on the Johnson Administration to disassociate itself from the Ky declarations.

Stars and Stripes

Blood All The Way

Just one out of 146 . . . The Australians don't count KIAs unless they can walk up and put their foot on the body

The Australian approach to the tactics of the Vietnam war was honed in jungle warfare against the Japanese in World War II and the Communists in Malaya. "Fortunately, we've trained and equipped ourselves for such a war as this in southeast Asia for years," says Brigadier O. D. Jackson, commander of the First Australian Task Force in Vietnam. Whereas US commanders resupply their units every other day in the field, the Aussies slide into "the deep green" prepared to go it alone for a week at a time – and manage to pack ten pounds less per man than the GIs.

In their 14-month stint in force in Vietnam, the Aussies count 146 killed and 192 wounded Viet Cong, to 24 killed and 132 wounded Australians. The total of enemy casualties is probably far too low for the damage the Aussies have done, because of their own stiff accounting standards. No enemy dead is ever claimed unless an Aussie can walk up and put his foot on the body; no wounded counts unless he can be trailed 300 yards, with blood seen all the way.

The Aussies allow no Vietnamese inside their compounds, an inhospitality justified, they feel, on security grounds. Going into the jungle, they rarely wear helmets, and strip the insignia from their uniforms. The average Viet Cong, they snort, is really "no jungle fighter; he uses trails, paths and villages. We don't. But you have to go out into the jungle to trap him. That's when we meet him on our terms instead of his."

Time

FAST RECONNAISSANCE A Key to Air War

On a recent night in North Vietnam a column of 20 tarpaulin-covered trucks rolled down Highway 1 loaded with supplies destined for North Vietnamese soldiers fighting in South Vietnam.

Several thousand feet above the trucks, a United States Air Force reconnaissance jet cut through the sky, its set of especially equipped cameras photographing the column despite the darkness.

His mission completed, the reconnaissance pilot turned back toward South Vietnam and, an hour and a half after the photographs were taken, two Air Force fighter-bombers attacked the convoy.

The F-101 Voodoo was well named – it operated as if by magic, taking photographs even in the dark

It was a typical operation on a typical night in North Vietnam.
New York Times

Lead Poisoning

One recent night, South Korean 1st Lieut. Lee Young Woong looked into a peasant cottage as a woman and her two children were eating their evening rice. He noticed at once what a Westerner might easily have missed: there was too much rice for three people. Company was expected, he concluded. Lee and his squad of ten Koreans rounded up the villagers and placed them under guard in three houses. Then his men moved out to set up an ambush. Two hours later, three Viet Cong came to dinner – and died of lead poisoning. *Time*

U.S. Jets Down MIG Over North

Four U.S. Navy jets tangled with six communist MIG-17s over north Vietnam Wednesday and shot down one of the MIGs, the U.S. announced.

The dogfights took place 23 miles southeast of Hanoi, a spokesman said.

The F4B Phantoms, from the aircraft carrier Constellation were flying cover for other planes attacking rail and highway bridges. All four Navy planes returned to the Constellation without damage.
Stars and Stripes

King of Cumshaw

Plump and puckish, a shy grin on his broad leg-of-mutton face, a shoulder holster sagging from the armpit of his sweat-blotched, green T shirt, a drinker of nothing more stimulating than cream soda. Senior Chief Petty Officer Bernard G. Feddersen, 35, of the Seabees, is renowned from Danang to the Delta as the sharpest cumshaw artist in all Southeast Asia.

Today's scrounger can be an Air Cav supply sergeant or an Air Force crew chief, but Vietnam's Feddersen outdoes them all – both in Yankee horse-trading skill and sheer inventiveness. In a scant 14 months, he unplugged the logistical bottleneck that had plagued the development of the Chu Lai enclave, and in the process set up his outfit as the most efficient unit in the area. "Over here it is a self-help program," says Feddersen, "where you're the self doing the helping."

Deal or Die
When Feddersen's Mobile Construction Battalion 10 arrived at Chu Lai a year ago last May, Saigon's harbor was clogged with ships unable to unload their cargoes, and airstrips elsewhere were glutted with traffic. Morale at Chu Lai itself was desperately low due to an overabundance of sandflies and a dearth of comfort. It was a perfect situation for cumshaw, and fortunately Bernie Feddersen was on hand.

Within 23 days of Feddersen's arrival, he had shaken loose 2,600 lbs of spare parts for failing trucks and bulldozers, procured vitally needed aluminum sections for the airstrip's 8,000 ft jet runway and made MCB 10 the only outfit on the base with a perpetual supply of beer, steaks, lettuce, tomatoes and lumber.

Next week Feddersen leaves Vietnam for the Naval Station at Great Lakes, 200 miles from his home town of Shelbyville, Ill. Officially, he will not be remembered – unless by the parsimonious accountants of the Pentagon. "There's an unwritten law in the outfit," says one Seabee officer at Chu Lai. "We don't ask Feddersen what he's doing or how he's doing it. We only talk about what we want and the weather." Thanks to Cumshaw King Bernie Feddersen and his kind throughout Vietnam, the weather is a lot finer than it might be.
Time

AUGUST 1966

1st 1st Cavalry Division and ARVN forces carry out Operation Paul Revere II in Pleiku Province.

3rd Start of Operation Prairie just south of the DMZ. This is the sequel to Operation Hastings.

6th The 25th anniversary of the bombing of Hiroshima is marked by anti-war demonstrations. The current US commitment in Vietnam is 286,000 troops.

8th Major James A. Kasler, considered the war's top flyer, is shot down and captured.

9th Two South Vietnamese villages, Truong Trung and Truong Tay, 80 miles south of Saigon, are attacked in error by US warplanes. Sixty-three are killed and 100 injured.

13th The Cambodian ruler, Prince Sihanouk, criticizes the US over the attack on Thlock Track, a Cambodian village close to the South Vietnamese border.

16th The House Un-American Activities Committee investigates Americans who have given aid to the Viet Cong with a view to introducing legislation to make this illegal.

23rd The American cargo ship *Baton Rouge Victory* hits a mine laid by the Viet Cong and sinks in the Long Tao River, 22 miles south of Saigon, thus blocking the route from the South Vietnamese capital to the sea.

28th It is reported in three Soviet newspapers that North Vietnamese pilots are undergoing training in a secret Soviet air base.

29th US planes are accused of sinking and damaging Chinese ships in raids on the Gulf of Tonkin.

30th The signature of an economic and technical aid agreement between North Vietnam and China is reported on Hanoi Radio.

Draftees Bolster US Brigade Over Half Were Called to Duty

After a thirty-day sea voyage from Boston, the men of the 196th Light Infantry Brigade were glad to be on dry land again – though few expected to be quite so close to it, quite so soon!

The commanding general of the 25th Infantry Division remarked today that something was "very unusual" about his newly arrived brigade.

What is unusual is that draftees make up more than half of the unit's 3,800 men. The unit, the 196th Light Infantry Brigade, landed this morning on the beach outside Vungtau, a resort 40 miles south of Saigon. In the past, draftees have made up only about 20 per cent of similar units in South Vietnam.

The high number of draftees reflected the build-up of the military to meet the growing United States commitment in Vietnam.

The new arrivals, pale and perspiring after a 30-day troopship voyage from Boston, brought to 291,000 the number of United States troops here. Military planners hope to have 375,000 by the end of the year.

New York Times

"Lying there, under the palm trees, listening to the birds . . . Not this time, Buddy!"

"We Want You"

On the rosters, it is called the 2nd Battalion of the 7th Cavalry of the 1st Cavalry (Airmobile) Division. But to Vietnam veterans who keep up on their casualty rates, it is the "hard-luck" battalion. And the hardest-luck platoon in the hard-luck battalion is the 3rd Platoon of A Company. Last January all of its men were killed when their C-123 crashed near An Khe before Operation Masher. Last week the unlucky 3rd got it again.

One afternoon the 26-man platoon was airlifted to a tiny landing zone in the northern Ia Drang Valley near the Cambodian border, where a North Vietnamese regiment had been spotted. No sooner had four of the six choppers unloaded than an enemy ambush opened up from the surrounding jungle. Most of the men were cut down in their tracks. Three overran one enemy machine-gun nest, only to be chopped up by another. "Sergeant Shockey," the platoon's first sergeant called out, "the commander's dead, and I'm dying. Take over the platoon." Moments later, Sergeant Leroy Shockey himself was felled.

Playing Dead

Then as suddenly as it started, the shooting stopped. As the North Vietnamese moved among the bodies lifting wallets, ammunition and weapons, Shockey played dead – through no fewer than six searches. Other North Vietnamese fanned out through the jungle, looking for the five men who had slipped through the fire. "Come out, GIs," they shouted, "we want you." As a heavy rain swept down and the shouts drew closer, the five made a pact. "We won't surrender, right?" whispered Sergeant Willie Glaspie. "To the finish," agreed Sergeant Francisco Pablo. But the North Vietnamese gave up the search and cleared out.

The next morning, the rest of A Company arrived after an all-night march. "I cried when I saw them," Glaspie recalls. "And I cried when I saw our dead." Of the 26 platoon members, only Shockey and seven others survived. A few hours later, a chaplain arrived for a special Mass. "The smell of death was still in the air," Pablo recalls. "Spent shells were all around. And the blood had been rain-washed pink." Two days later, Pablo and Glaspie volunteered for another helicopter infantry assault. "We ain't unlucky," Glaspie shrugged. "This is just war."

Time

One for the Diggers

Sweeping through a French-run rubber plantation called Binh Ba, 42 miles southeast of Saigon, looking for an enemy force that had mortared the Aussies' main headquarters, a 150-man company of the Royal Australian Regiment's 6th Battalion stumbled on to an estimated two Viet Cong battalions. In the first withering exchange of gunfire, all twelve men of the Australian leading group were killed or wounded. As a torrential rain began to fall, the Communists sought to tighten a noose around the Aussie company, charged in human-wave attacks that were repeatedly beaten back. The fighting was so intense that the Aussies almost ran out of ammunition, and their helicopters braved heavy ground fire and blinding rain to airlift more into the front line.

Death in the Downpour

Muffled by the deafening downpour, a company of Australian reinforcements in armored personnel carriers crept over surrounding hills undetected by the Viet Cong, and opened up with .50-cal. machine guns, cutting down 25 Reds with the first volley. Then Australian, New Zealand and US artillery found the range. When the smoke cleared, the Communists were in full flight, and 220 Viet Cong dead littered the ground. Under a rubber tree, guarding the body of his slain platoon leader, was Private B. C. Miller of Brisbane. Wounded in the face, shoulder and leg, Miller had lapsed into unconsciousness only to be awakened by a Viet Cong trying to tug off his boots. "Bug off!" Miller shouted at the startled Red, who promptly complied.

In four hours, the Aussies had killed more of the enemy than they had in their entire preceding 14 months.

Time

Ambassador Lodge Worried Over Behaviour of GIs

Ambassador Henry Cabot Lodge has told the State Department of his "continuing concern and worry" about the conduct of American soldiers in their contacts with the people of Saigon.

The Ambassador's message, informed sources said, was conveyed in one of several messages on the subject sent to Washington recently by the American Embassy. The sources said the behaviour of United States troops here was "a very, very tough problem."

Unconfirmed reports said high-ranking officials of the South Vietnamese Government had spoken sharply to Mr. Lodge about the need for stricter dicipline among the servicemen.

New York Times

"Work hard, play hard" has always been an American fighting man's motto, but the Government started to wonder if GIs know just which was which

LIGHT INFANTRY IN ACTION

SEPTEMBER 1966

Following up Operation John Paul Jones, 1st Brigade, 101st Airborne Division protects the rice harvest around Tuy Hoa under Operation Seward.

1st In a speech in Phnom Penh, Cambodia, President de Gaulle of France denounces US policy, and urges the US government to pull its troops out of Southeast Asia.

6th At the court martial in New Jersey of three US private soldiers who refused to serve in Vietnam, their defence, that the war is illegal and immoral, is dismissed.

9th It is revealed in Saigon that the US intends to greatly step up its destruction of crops in Viet Cong-occupied areas.

11th A constituent assembly is elected in South Vietnam. Around 81 per cent of registered voters take part despite Viet Cong intimidation and a widespread boycott by Buddhists.

12th In the heaviest air raid of the war to date, approximately 500 USAF aircraft strike at a mixture of targets in the North.

14th Start of Operation Attleboro against Viet Cong by 196th Light Infantry Brigade near the Cambodian border. Attleboro becomes the largest US operation to date, resulting in 1106 known enemy casualties. Journalists report that the South Vietnamese village of Lien Hoa is razed to the ground by US troops of the 1st Cavalry Division.

16-19th China accuses US aircraft of violations of airspace and attacks against villages and border crossings. US admits some violations may have taken place.

19th A group of eminent US scientists call for the use of chemical weapons to be discontinued.

19-23rd Extensive bombing raids by US B-52s against a mixture of targets in the DMZ.

23rd The US announces that its planes are defoliating the jungle south of the DMZ to prevent the North Vietnamese using it as cover.

In jungle like this, there's little chance of even spotting the enemy, so the decision was taken to clear it out, using defoliants delivered from the air

27th Village of Hombe attacked in error by US planes. At least 35 civilians die.

Navy helicopters snatched many an airman from death

Copter
Saves US Pilot at Haiphong

A United States Navy helicopter crew told today how it had rescued a downed American pilot from the harbour of Haiphong. The rescued pilot, Lieut. Comdr Thomas Tucker of Long Prairie, Minn., told the helicopter crew:

"If you guys ever need a favor, come to Tom Tucker and I will do anything. I owe you my life."

The incident began late Wednesday morning when Commander Tucker's RF-8 reconnaissance jet was struck by heavy ground fire while on a mission near Haiphong.

He headed for the sea and radioed that he was "losing control." By the time he was able to eject, the plane was in a steep dive.

After momentarily blacking out, Commander Tucker found that ground fire was being directed against him as he dangled under his parachute.

"I just could not believe they were really shooting at me," he said later.

Landing under Fire

Commander Tucker landed only 100 to 150 yards from the shore, and soon came under new fire from the bank. His efforts to swim out so exhausted him that he inflated his life raft and got aboard it despite the shooting.

Sampans that normally ply the harbor waters set out to capture the American. Some were about 150 yards away when his wingman, Lieut. Comdr Foster Teague, strafed them. They turned and began to flee.

Meantime, a United States Navy air-rescue helicopter had been hovering, as usual, in the Gulf of Tonkin off Haiphong, which is the port city for Hanoi. The helicopter, piloted by Comdr Robert S. Vermilya of Chula Vista, Calif., heard Commander Tucker's distress signal and headed for the area.

Normally he would have waited for fighter planes to give him cover before attempting a rescue. But the wingman, still circling over the downed pilot, radioed: "If you wait he will never make it."

US BIDS FOR PEACE
Would Halt Raids UN Told

The United States formally offered Thursday to end the bombing of north Vietnam and withdraw its forces from the Republic of Vietnam if the communists take corresponding action.

Furthermore, U.S. Ambassador Arthur J. Goldberg said in a speech to the General Assembly, the question of Viet Cong participation in Vietnam peace talks would not be "an insurmountable problem."

Goldberg said the United States still was ready to negotiate a Vietnam settlement on the basis of the 1954 and 1962 Geneva accords, "and we will support a recovening of the Geneva conference, or an Asian conference, or any other general acceptable forum."

Stars and Stripes

GIs
in Vietnam Get
a TV Station

Gen. William C. Westmoreland cut a ribbon of television tape today, formally opening the first armed services television station in a combat zone in Vietnam.

The station, a compactly equipped truck sitting atop Vungvhau Mountain, will beam music, news and American television programs to 24,000 United States troops in the vicinity of Quinhon, a coastal city in central Vietnam.

The programs, donated by the networks, include "Bonanza", "The Beverley Hillbillies" and "Combat".

The 11-ton TV van, costing nearly $200,000, was hauled to the top of the 1,800-foot mountain by bulldozers. Its 5,000- watt beam is transmitted from a 132-foot tower beside the truck.

The station, operating on Channel 11, went on the air Wednesday night for three hours. Eventually it will operate 56 hours a week.

"We might even have our own version of 'Combat' one of these nights," a station technician said. "We have an alert about once a week because of the Viet Cong."

The 12 men assigned to the station live on top of the mountain in armed bunkers.

The New York Times

"So, without much further thought, we decided to go in right away and give it a try," said Commander Vermilya today.

Smiling, he said: "We came in very low – we helicopter pilots don't wear parachutes so we feel better down low."

Copter Under Fire, Too

Machine-gun and antiaircraft fire reached up at, but failed to hit, the four-man helicopter as it flew up the river toward Haiphong looking for Commander Tucker, who had fired an orange flare.

"We almost missed him when we saw him to the starboard and behind us about 100 yards off the beach," the helicopter pilot related. "There was rifle fire splashing all around him."

The pilot, who joked that he was "about to end up in downtown Haiphong," made a sharp turn back and came in over Commander Tucker's life raft dangling a steel cable.

In a stroke of luck, the horseshoe collar at the cable's end fell right on Commander Tucker and Commander Vermilya was able to pull away after only about 10 seconds of dangerous hovering.

The helicopter crew related that Commander Tucker was furious because the North Vietnamese gunners had fired at him while he was descending in his parachute – something he felt was "dirty pool."

Commander Vermilya, who has rescued 13 downed Americans in only two months of duty off North Vietnam, said, "You feel grateful after you get out of a situation like that."

The New York Times

U.S. to Buy
280 Extra
Warplanes

Defense Secretary Robert S. McNamara announced Thursday the United States will increase its planned production of warplanes by approximately 280 aircraft at a cost of $700 million.

McNamara said the additional order for fighter and attack aircraft was prudent, in view of the long lead time – between design and production – involved in getting planes off the production line for war use.

The defense chief said: "I have come to the conclusion that it is wise to place on order aircraft that may be required to support operations beyond June 30, 1967."

This is the end of the current fiscal year, the arbitrary time point MacNamara has used in military planning.

The announcement thus placed American war planning into fiscal 1968, at least on a procurement basis.

McNamara will not announce what types of planes would be added to the purchase order until the manufacturers themselves are told.

He did say, however, that most would be for the Navy.

Pentagon spokesmen indicated, however, that a large number of the extra planes might be the Navy's new A7, a subsonic aircraft used for low-level bombing. The other aircraft, they said, quite likely would be the F4 Phantom, a fighter-bomber which escorts the slower A7 bombing craft.

Stars and Stripes

Carrier-borne attack aircraft such as the A-7 bomber complements the USAF's efforts throughout the war

ARMY
LIGHT INFANTRY
BRIGADE
A Steamlined
Unit in Vietnam

Light infantry brigades, units of a type new to the United States Army, are entering combat in South Vietnam.

The units are the first major tactical organizations sent there that have been specially organized and equipped for the conditions of combat and terrain that characterize the Vietnamese war.

The 196th Light Infantry Brigade from Fort Devens, Mass., recently arrived in Vietnam by ship from Boston, and one other light brigade is in training in this country. The units are streamlined with plenty of manpower and with special attachments, but they are stripped of much of their heavy equipment, trucks and tracked vehicles.

Fighting Force Listed

The 199th Light Infantry Brigade at Fort Benning, Ga., which was activated last June and is scheduled to complete its training about the middle of October, typifies the organization of these new units.

The 199th totals about 4,000 men. its fighting cadre is three rifle battalions, each composed of three rifle companies (which may later be increased to four), one combat support company for heavier weapons and a headquarters company, a total of about 780 men per battalion.

In addition to the infantry battalions, the brigade includes one artillery battalion of 18 towed 105-mm howitzers; one support battalion, including a medical company, a maintenance and supply company and an administration company; and a separate engineer company, cavalry troop and brigade headquarters and headquarters company. *New York Times*

OCTOBER 1966

1st The US bombing of the North Vietnamese city of Phu Ly, 35 miles south of Hanoi, results in the destruction of all the homes and buildings and around 40 civilian casualties.

2-24th 1st Cavalry Division attempts to sweep the 610th NVA Division out of the Phu Cat Mountain area of the Binh Dinh Province under search-and-destroy Operation Irving. There are 681 known enemy casualties by the end of the operation.

2-3rd It is stated in the Soviet press that Russian military advisers have been training North Vietnamese missile teams and have been present during US bombing raids against missile sites.

Vietnamese anti-aircraft defences became more and more complex as the war drew on

3rd Economic and military aid agreement settled between USSR and North Vietnam.

4th US B-52s strike against targets in the DMZ.

10-14th Defense Secretary McNamara goes on his eighth fact-finding visit to South Vietnam. A record 173 sorties are flown over North Vietnam on the 13th.

18th Start of Operation Paul Revere IV by mixed US infantry and cavalry forces close to the Cambodian border in Pleiku Province. There are 977 enemy casualties by the end of the operation.

21st A landmine explosion in the centre of Traon, 75 miles southeast of Saigon, kills 11 and injures 54.

24th Fifteen Vietnamese civilians die and a further 19 are injured when a bus triggers a landmine 18 miles north of Hue.

24-25th At a meeting of the allied leaders in Manila an agreement is signed which states that if "North Vietnam withdraws its forces to the North and ceases infiltration of South Vietnam" the allies will pull out within six months.

25th 1st Cavalry Division gets Operation Thayer II under way in Binh Dinh Province. There are 1757 enemy casualties by the end of the operation.

25th The US Navy launches a campaign against communist shipping in the Dong Hoi area. During the next four weeks 230 craft are sunk.

26th A fire on board the US aircraft carrier *Oriskany* results in 43 crew dead and a further 16 injured. 300 bombs are thrown overboard and four bombers and two helicopters lost.

27th China denounces Manila pull-out pledge as "out and out blackmail and shameless humbug".

31st US Navy engages Viet Cong vessels, sinking 35 junks and sampans.

Sailors Saved Carrier by Throwing Bombs in Sea

The aircraft carrier *Oriskany* came close to being blown out of the Gulf of Tonkin by her own bombs when she caught fire two days ago.

Capt. John H. Iarrobino of Newton, Mass., the skipper, credited his crewmen with a "fantastic feat" in getting rid of 500-pound, 1,000-pound and 2,000-pound bombs that lay within reach of flames darting through the hangar deck.

Lieut. (jg.) Ron Thurman, 32 years old, of Mascot, Tenn., said today in an interview, "If those bombs had gone off, we'd have lost the ship."

To the notes of the Taps, the bodies of 43 of the crew – 35 officers and eight enlisted men – were sent home for burial, their coffins draped with American flags.

The carrier *Coral Sea* has taken *Oriskany*'s station off Vietnam.

Brushes with death and acts of heroism were commonplace during the hours after magnesium flares broke into flames in a storage locker.

One sailor who saw the danger of a possible bomb blast was Aviation Ordinanceman Gregg Blackwell, 18, of Indianapolis.

"I knew it was a magnesium fire," he said. "You can't put it out. All you can do is cool the bulkheads with water."

"I looked around and I saw 1,000-pound bombs sitting close to where the fire was belching out," the sailor said. "I grabbed one bomb and pulled it away from the fire. Then I went up again. I got three-quarters of the way up the bay when there was an explosion. It knocked me down."

He and two buddies, Aviation Ordinanceman 1c Fred H. Arnett, 35, of Gosport, Ind., and Aviation Machinist's Mate 3 c Robert Murphy, 19, of Kansas City, Kan., agreed that the urgency had enabled them to do things they hadn't known they were capable of.

"I took the front end of a 500-pound bomb and one of the other guys took the back and we heaved it over the side," Ordinanceman Blackwell said. He recalled that it normally took four men to lift such a load.

The New York Times

The Magic Dragon

Among the most deadly weapons used in the Vietnamese war is an improbable looking contraption called Puff, the Magic Dragon. A reconditioned US Air Force C-47 cargo plane, Puff owes its name to the fact that its three Gatling style machine guns lined up on one side of the plane can spit tracer bullets into the night sky at the incredible rate of 450 rounds a second. Firing together, they can put a bullet into every square foot of an area the size of a football field in three seconds. Recently NEWSWEEK's John Berthelson went along on a Puff mission in support of a besieged Special Forces camp near Danang. His report:

"Lt. James D. Goodman, the 26-year-old co-pilot, rolled his lumbering, old gooney bird over on its left side, peered into the sight of one of the Gatling mini-guns mounted on steel pods and pulled the trigger. What resulted was an ear-shattering shriek as thousands of 30-caliber shells ripped from the six barrels of the gun and – seconds later – slammed into a group of Viet Cong 2,000 feet below us. Over the plane's radio came the

Properly known as the AC-47 "Spooky", the first generation of fixed-wing gunships were equipped with three six-barrelled 7.62mm machine guns. Later versions were more potent

jubilant message from the Special Forces camp: 'Spooky One Two, this is Nathan Scalp. You were right on target.'

"In the next seat to Lieutenant Goodman, Maj. John C. Haller, the pilot, reached up to turn on his landing lights in an effort to attract fire from the enemy. 'When we first came to Vietnam,' he said, 'the VC gave us a kind of response. They would stand up and fight. But it didn't take them long to learn that wasn't such a good idea. If they shoot at us and miss, they've signed their death warrant.'"

Newsweek

Johnson Signs L.B.J. on Casts of Wounded

Wounded men in an Air Force hospital joked with President Johnson today as he pinned Purple Hearts on their pajamas.

At the 12th Tactical Fighter Wing hospital, the President presented the award to a dozen or more patients.

Outside the white-walled, brightly lit hospital wards, Mr Johnson walked among patients and staff on plank sidewalks laid over the sand.

He was kept busy signing L.B.J. on casts, currency, scraps of paper and the caps of fatigue uniforms.

Finally the President declared, "I'll do two more now, I've gotta go."

More caps and pieces of paper were thrust at him.

"I'll do three more," he said.

The New York Times

GI Busy at War, Asks Draft Board to Wait

Sgt. Custer Watts of the United States Army's First Cavalry Division (Airmobile) a veteran of the D-Day landing at Normandy who wears two Silver Stars and three Purple Hearts and now serves as a combat platoon sergeant, said today that he had received a stiff letter from his draft board in New Tazewell, Tenn.

The board asked why Sergeant Watts had not registered for the draft.

The sergeant said he planned to ask the board to postpone his case until he returned from Vietnam.

The New York Times

Allies Offer Hanoi 6-Point Peace Plan

The Vietnam Allies offered north Vietnam a six-point plan for peace Tuesday night, including a pledge to withdraw all foreign troops from south Vietnam within six months after the communists withdraw.

President Johnson and the six other national leaders insisted, however, that any peace arrangements and subsequent Allied withdrawals would depend on "effective international guarantees" and supervision to insure that the communists live up to their side of the deal.

Stars and Stripes

NOVEMBER 1966

1st South Vietnam's National Day is marked by two Viet Cong terrorist incidents in Saigon. At least eight die.

1st A US minesweeper is sunk by a mine in the Longatao River.

2nd Richard Nixon takes issue with the Manila agreement as not being stern enough.

3rd The US learns that its campaign against oil installations has not succeeded in impeding the flow of supplies and arms into the South. A step-up in air raids is planned.

5th Defense Secretary McNamara discloses that US manning levels in Vietnam will be increased in 1967.

5-6th Having suffered heavy casualties, the 196th Infantry Brigade is taken out of action in III Corps.

7th On a visit to Harvard University, Defense Secretary McNamara encounters student protests.

12th The *New York Times* runs an article which alleges that Saigon corruption swallows up 40 per cent of US aid to Vietnam.

14th A secret report to the President from Defense Secretary McNamara states that the results of a heavier presence of US troops have not been good enough to warrant further large-scale reinforcement.

18th The US "presence in Vietnam is justified" according to the National Conference of Catholic Bishops.

18th North Vietnamese radar installation and cargo ships are bombarded by USN destroyers in the Dong Hoi area.

US Navy destroyers provide safe and secure gun platforms for the bombardment of targets inland. Their gunnery computers ensure that, as soon as one round hits the target, all the rest follow

23rd USN destroyers shell 60 communist supply barges off south coast of North Vietnam. Forty-seven are damaged or sunk.

30th China accuses US planes of sinking five Chinese fishing boats in the Gulf of Tonkin. Fourteen seamen are alleged to have died and a further 20 are reported injured.

Navy's River Patrol Operation Stings Enemy

Throughout the war, the hard-working **US Navy** found itself operating in muddy rivers and creeks as well as out in the blue waters of the **South China Sea**. With **Landing Ships** to act as motherships, **Patrol Boats, River** were able to control the canals and waterways that lace the countryside south of Saigon, as well as the considerable junk traffic up and down the coast

The Navy's unique river patrol craft in Vietnam are beginning to interrupt the Vietcong lines of communication and supply in the Mekong delta's maze of waterways.

What the Navy calls a PBR (Patrol Boat, River) was the hero Monday night in the latest engagement in the river and canal operations in South Vietnam. The boat is the backbone of Operation Game Warden, the Navy's river patrol, established in South Vietnam last spring.

The patrol force, also called Task Force 116, commanded by Capt. Burton B. Witham Jr., supplements the work of the Navy's Coastal Surveillance Force. Both are under Rear Adm. Norvell G. Ward, commander of U.S. Naval forces.

GI War Menu:

Turkey for All, Sooner or Later

Most American servicemen in Vietnam will have Thanksgiving dinners tomorrow starting off with shrimp cocktail and going on through turkey and giblet gravy, dressing, candied sweet potatoes, mixed vegetables and cranberry sauce.

While there is turkey for all, some men on long-range patrols or on isolated outpost duty will have to wait awhile. They can expect to dine on C rations.

For the 62,000 United States Marines in the northern part of the country, the preparations included 25 tons of turkey and 10 tons of ham. *The New York Times*

100 Soldiers Fight 300 Foe G.I. Platoon is Overrun

North Vietnamese Army regulars badly mauled outnumbered American infantrymen in a five-hour battle yesterday in the Central Highlands, a United States military spokesman said tonight.

The spokesman described the casualties suffered by three platoons of the First Cavalry Division (Airmobile) as heavy, indicating that the units were no longer effective fighting forces.

Originally, military spokesmen in Saigon reported that the North Vietnamese had nearly wiped out a platoon of 30 to 35 Airmobile soldiers. But as the fog of war cleared, they were able to piece together that, in fact, a company minus one of its four platoons – or about 100 men – had run into an enemy battalion of 300 to 500 soldiers.

The first reports apparently referred to the middle platoon in a column of three moving southward on patrol through dense jungle about 230 miles northeast of Saigon.

That unit was pinned down by heavy automatic weapons fire and eventually overrun by an estimated 150 to 200 charging North Vietnamese.

The spokesman tonight refused to confirm that only "a few" men survived the overwhelming charge, but he said there had been reports of several wounded Americans being killed by the attackers.

Of the 102 enemy dead, 40 were ringing the middle platoon's position.

New York Times

Capture of Enemy Officer Helps Save GI's Leave

Specialist 4 Richard E. Ladd was beaming as he scrambled aboard a helicopter at 6.15 am today in a tiny forest clearing 10 miles north of this rubber plantation town in Tayninh Province.

A few minutes later, guarding an important prisoner – a North Vietnamese captain – he arrived at divisional headquarters here. Now he had a fair chance to get back to Saigon in time to make his plane connection to Bangkok, Thailand, where he was scheduled to spend a week's rest and recuperation leave. He was looking forward to "the lobster dinner I've promised myself since I arrived in Vietnam 10 months ago."

Yesterday, the 23-year-old soldier from Williamsport, Pa., along with the rest of the First Battalion of the 16th Regiment of the First Infantry Division – nicknamed the Rangers – walked into the clearing just before dusk, too late for helicopters to land.

Specialist Ladd was downcast – convinced he had missed his chance to get to Bangkok.

But just before 2 am today Capt. Thai Thoc of the 101st North Vietnamese Army Regiment blundered into the Rangers' lines and was captured.

A Lucky Capture

Unaware of the Americans' presence, Captain Thoc ran into the hammock of Pfc. Kenneth Hough of Phoenix, Ariz., and dropped his captured American M-16 rifle.

Sgt. 1st Cl. Theodore Strange of Macon, Ga., heard the clatter of the rifle and Private Hough's shouts.

The sergeant said "I thought Hough had flipped his lid, but when I got there, there was this scared Victor Charlie pointing his flashlight on himself to make sure we wouldn't shoot him. Man, was he scared."

The two Americans took the captain's rifle and his .32 caliber pistol and marched him into the darkened command post.

"Who's that with you?" barked Maj. Anthony Jezior, of Cleveland, the battalion operations officer.

"He's a friendly Vietnamese, sir," said Sergeant Strange.

"What do you mean, friendly?" asked the major.

"Well, he's been friendly for the last 10 minutes," said the sergeant.

Minutes later, Captain Thoc was on the radio – telling the Vietnamese interpreter in the American division headquarters here in Dautieng the exact location of his 300-man unit.

Half an hour later, 105-mm, 155-mm and 175-mm guns were firing the first of more than 1,000 rounds. *The New York Times*

Four-Man Crews

The job of the river patrol force is to prevent the Vietcong from using the waterways as supply routes and lines of communication. United States Navy forces supplement the work of the South Vietnamese navy, the maritime branch of the Vietnamese national police force and the Vietnamese customs service.

Each boat is manned by a junior officer and three enlisted men and mounts two heavy machine guns and one light one. The boats have been supported in their river patrols by helicopter gun ships, which base on the LSD (Landing Ship, Dock), or LST (Landing Ship, Tanks) mother ships.

New York Times

DECEMBER 1966

US 9th Infantry Division arrives in Vietnam from Fort Lewis, Washington, to join III Corps.

8th USAF Tactical Fighter Wing arrives in South East Asia.

1st Start of Operation Ala Moana in which the 25th Infantry Division is employed to prevent the Viet Cong entering the rice-growing areas near the Ho Bo and Boi Loi Woods.

2nd Aircraft of the US Navy attack targets five miles from Hanoi. Fuel installations are hit elsewhere in North Vietnam. Eight US planes are shot down, more than in any other single day, bringing the tally so far to 435.

4th Viet Cong guerrillas succeed in penetrating Tan Son Nhut airport, causing damage to one aircraft before getting away.

American airbase defense was punished both by **VC** mortar teams, and by sappers who physically penetrated the bases, destroying aircraft – such as this **C-47** – and materiel and stores with well-placed satchel charges

5th An exchange of fire with North Vietnamese coastal artillery results in the US destroyer *Ingersoll* sustaining some damage.

7th Viet Cong terrorists assassinate Tran Van Van, a member of the South Vietnamese Constituent Assembly, in Saigon.

8-9th North Vietnam, speaking through the International Red Cross, turns down the US President's call for discussions on prisoners of war.

10th Governor-elect of California Ronald Reagan states himself to be in favour of "an all-out total effort" in Vietnam.

13-14th US planes bomb within two miles of Hanoi in an internationally denounced raid. A French newsman reports the village of Caudat to be "completely destroyed by bombs and fire".

14-16th The State Department puts forward that "There is no fixed geographical definition which can be called the city limits of Hanoi." General Westmoreland states that "all ordnance expended by US air-strike aircraft was in the military target areas. None fell in the city of Hanoi."

18-20th US Guam-based B-52s hit targets south of the DMZ where reports put the North Vietnamese 324-B Division preparing to attack.

20th The Chinese press accuses the USSR of, "in collusion with the United States", "resorting to the dirty tricks of forcing peace-talks by coercion, inducement or persuasion."

25th A report by the assistant managing editor of *The New York Times* details the destruction wrought by US bombing raids over North Vietnam.

26th A Defense Department spokesman insists that bombing raids are carried out only against military targets, but that "It is sometimes impossible to avoid all damage to civilian areas."

27-31st A combined US/ARVN joint-service operation takes place against a Viet Cong stronghold in the U Minh Forest in the Mekong Delta. The forest is bombed and napalmed in preparation for the assault by ARVN troops. The US Navy also takes part. There are 104 Viet Cong reported dead and a further 18 taken prisoner.

29th US student organizations warn President Johnson that many might rather go to jail than serve in Vietnam.

Viet Cong Digs Own Grave

It was after midnight on a moonless night last month when a 25th Infantry Division sentry on road watch north of Saigon thought he saw movement up the road. He crouched and began scanning the area with the starlight scope attached to his rifle; through the scope, an image intensifier so sensitive that it can collect and amplify even the faint reflections of starlight from an object, he saw a black-clad figure digging in the road. The GI watched until the hole was dug, then he squeezed off a single shot, detonating the mine that the Viet Cong was about to plant. The sentry paced off the distance – it was 200 yards.

The incident itself made no headlines, but such individual episodes multiplied a hundred or a thousand times illustrate how modern technology is finally being brought to bear by American troops in the jungles and rice fields of Vietnam.

Newsweek

The 16,000-ton Long Beach, one of the US Navy's most powerful surface ships, was the first of a new generation to experience real war when she was detached for patrol duties in the Gulf of Tonkin

U.S. Atomic-Powered Cruiser Off North Vietnam
Vessel Replaces Destroyer in the Gulf of Tonkin

The United States Navy has sent its only nuclear-powered cruiser into the Gulf of Tonkin for patrol duty off the coast of North Vietnam, an American military spokesman said tonight.

The spokesman said the cruiser Long Beach steamed into the South China Sea Nov. 30 to relieve the destroyer *King*.

It was not clear what the duties of the *Long Beach* would be, but in addition to five guns and torpedoes, armament also carried by the King, the nuclear vessel is equipped with intermediate and long-range surface-to-air missiles.

New York Times

Hanoi Again Vows Fight to Victory Insists on Protracted Resistance Against US

North Vietnam has reaffirmed its determination to "carry out a protracted war of resistance" against the United States and to continue the fight until "complete victory," the North Vietnam press agency reported today.

The North Vietnamese statements followed militant but equivocal expressions of support from Communist China. The Chinese said, "We are ready to march to the front any time the Vietnamese people require."

The North Vietnamese and Chinese statements followed accusations by the Communist bloc that American planes attacked residential areas of Hanoi, including the legation quarter, last week.

New York Times

Part-time
Troops, US Led, Aid Saigon

It was an odd-looking squad that set out on patrol today from this village 12 miles inland from Danang.

There were three brawny American marines and nine wiry little Vietnamese whose gold teeth flashed in the sun when they smiled. Together, they form part of Hoaphu's combined action company, one of 50 operating in villages within the three Marine Corps perimeters in South Vietnam.

The combined companies are trying to rid the villages of Vietcong guerrillas and develop local defense forces so that United States marines can be freed for operations against enemy main-force units.

There are those who think that organizations of Americans and South Vietnamese, living and working and fighting side by side produce the best possible hope of uprooting the Vietcong in this nation's thousands of villages.

Called Underrated

The marines in Hoaphu and those in the other combined action companies are volunteers, men with outstanding records and with at least six months of combat experience.

Not so the South Vietnamese. They are ordinary members of the so-called Popular Forces – part-time soldiers who in the past have gained no particular reputation for bravery or skill.

But Sgt. Carrol P. Soape of Dallas, the commander of the Hoaphu company, thinks they have been underrated.

"Training and leadership are what have been missing," he said.

"When people say these P.F.s (Popular Forces) are no good, I've got to disagree with them," the sergeant said. If you're patient, if you're willing to take the trouble to try to see things from their point of view, they'll show you what they can do. And then you see that you've got to think a lot of them.

New York Times

CIDG volunteers like this – later they were known officially as RF/PFs and called Ruff-Puffs – played an important role in the fight for their own country. Fighting alongside American servicemen, they proved very good at their best

JANUARY 1967

1st The US troop figure rises to 380,000 with the arrival of 5000 men of the 9th Infantry Division in Vung Tau.

1st Operation Sam Houston gets under way with the 4th Infantry Division continuing its border surveillance in Kontum and Pleiku Provinces. There are 733 enemy casualties by the end of the operation.

2nd The biggest air engagement of the war to date is marked by the shooting down of seven MiG 21s by US F-4 Phantoms.

3rd North Vietnamese Premier Dong causes a flurry of speculation when he is interpreted as softening his line regarding conditions for ending the conflict.

4-5th The North turns down Britain's proposed peace conference because it excludes the NLF.

5th Two search-and-destroy missions, Fitchburg and Niagara Falls, are used as a front to deploy the 1st and 25th Infantry Divisions to the flanks of the Iron Triangle.

5-16th A combined force of US and South Vietnamese Marines lands in the Mekong Delta to begin Operation Deckhouse V against the communist centre known as the Thanhphu Secret Zone.

8-26th Operation Cedar Falls is carried out in the Iron Triangle by the 1st and 25th Infantry Divisions, 173rd Airborne Brigade, 11th Armored Cavalry Regiment and ARVN forces. There are an estimated 750 enemy casualties by the end of the operation and many documents are captured.

Vietcong Village to be Bulldozed

For years this quiet, ill-kept village, hugging an elbow of the Saigon River 30 miles northwest of the capital, has been a haven for the Viet Cong.

This morning 600 allied soldiers – mostly Americans – descended on the village and began 'solving' the problem.

Within two weeks the more than 3,800 residents of Bensuc will be living in a new refugee settlement 20 miles to the southeast and it is likely that the tattered huts and small shops here will be flattened by bulldozers.

"This is probably the only military or political solution for this place," said an American colonel.

Allied officers in Bensuc acknowledged that the residents might be reluctant to leave their property and the revered graves of their ancestors, but they said that new land would be given to them along with frame, tin-roofed homes that will be "a lot better than what they have now."

"Do What They're Told"
The colonel said "I imagine there will be a lot of wailing and gnashing of teeth, but they'll do what they're told."

Sixty helicopters landed the troops in seven clearings within the village walls this morning.

Shortly afterward, a helicopter equipped with loudspeak-ers began broadcasting this message:

"Attention people of Bensuc! You are surrounded by Republic of South Vietnam and allied forces. Do not run away or you will be shot as Viet Cong. Stay in your homes and wait for further instructions from the air and on the ground. You will not be hurt if you follow instructions."

Then came a second message telling men, women and children: "Go immediately to the schoolhouse. Anyone who does not go to the schoolhouse will be considered a Viet Cong and treated accordingly."

Most Follow Instructions
Most of the residents considered to be passive Viet Cong followed the instructions. Forty-one did not and during the day they were tracked down and killed. There was little question that the men fleeing on bicycles, crawling through rice paddies and thrashing in the murky river were Viet Cong. Some carried rifles, others wore packs. Three were discovered at the mouth of a cave with an assortment of surgical instruments and commercially produced drugs.

At the schoolhouse the people were separated into groups according to age and sex, interrogated, given a warm meal and were seen by an army doctor. One hundred males 15 to 45

Less than 30 miles from Saigon, the so-called Iron Triangle was a permanent thorn in the flesh of the US Army. Left: Men of the 1st Inf. Div. in the bush

At other times, the operation took on the appearance of a turkey shoot. With armor to provide a sanitary cordon, US infantrymen sweep through easier terrain

Ace Describes Epic MIG Battle

"To make a long story extremely short, they lost." With this sentence Col. Robin Olds, a Seventh Air Force fighter wing commander, summed up the swirling air battle in which Air Force Phantom jets knocked seven MIG-21s out of the sky Monday northwest of Hanoi.

Olds, 44, gave details of the war's biggest aerial battle at Tan Son Nhut AB.

The battle raised to 34 the total of MIGs down by U.S. pilots in the Vietnam War.

No U.S. planes were lost, to the MIGs' missile and cannon fire.

Olds said his flight was attacked "very aggressively" by an unknown number of MIGs while making the sweep over north Vietnam.

The seven downed MIG-21s were shot down by air-to-air missiles.

Olds downed his first MIG during the battle. The kills bring his total of enemy planes to 25. He flew P-38s and P-51s in World War II.

Olds said one MIG got up behind him. "It wasn't the first time I have had someone behind me who was angry," he said. "I didn't worry too much, though, knowing that my flight was there providing protection."

At one point he had two MIGs in front and another on his left.

It's a long way from P-38 Lightnings to F-4 Phantoms. Ask Robin Olds!

He rolled up behind the MIG on his left, flying upside down until he lined up the enemy jet.

He fired a missile and saw a tremendous orange flash. One wing of the MIG flew off. The plane went out of control and plunged to earth.

Stars and Stripes

---

years old, unable to prove their identity, were taken away as Viet Cong suspects. Eleven men were judged on the spot to be Viet Cong.

Belongings Go With Them
The villagers were allowed to file home this evening, but tomorrow they will be ordered back to the school, their homes will be searched and in a day or so more, the troops will begin loading them into barges for the trip downstream. Part of their houses, their furniture and their livestock will go with them.

"It takes time and it's troublesome, but I think you find a little less resentment if you take everything they've got and move it with them," said Brig. Gen. James F. Hollingworth, an assistant commander of the United States First Infantry Division.
The New York Times

In IV Corps

In IV Corps a significant incident took place in the area of Camp Thuong Thoi, A-425, Kien Phong Province, on 6 January 1967. A company-size search and destroy patrol engaged an estimated Viet Cong company in fortified positions. A-425 requested assistance from the mobile strike force to hold the Viet Cong in position and destroy them before they could slip across the Cambodian border. A U.S. Air Force forward air controller adjusted artillery fire and called for an immediate air strike while the mobile

Vungtau Landing Brings U.S. Force to 380,000

United States troop strength in South Vietnam rose to 380,000 today with the arrival at Vungtau, 40 miles southeast of Saigon, of 5,000 more members of the Ninth Infantry Division from Fort Riley, Kan.

A military spokesman said the landing was an administrative movement and hence not a hostile action under the terms of the cease-fire marking the new year.

First elements of the division arrived at Vungtau two weeks ago. The division, or some parts of it, is expected to be sent into the Mekong Delta after training in other areas.
New York Times

---

strike force was being committed. Within three hours of the request, enough helicopters had been assembled at Can Tho, and the mobile strike force company had been lifted from there into position, but not before the Viet

Cong company was able to withdraw into Cambodia under cover of darkness and carry away the dead and wounded. All indications were that the Viet Cong suffered heavy casualties.
U.S. Army

10th UN Secretary General U Thant states that he is at variance with the US over Vietnam on three counts and urges an immediate cessation of bombing.

13th The US calls a temporary halt to its bombing raids on the Yen Vien railway yard because of outcries over civilian deaths.

18-26th Premier Ky's goodwill visit to Australia and New Zealand encounters violent protests. The Labour leader of the New Zealand opposition labels him a "murderer" and "a miserable little butcher".

23rd In his book *The Arrogance of Power* Senator William Fulbright urges direct talks between South Vietnam and the Viet Cong.

25th US pilots are forbidden to bomb within a five-mile radius of the centre of Hanoi by order of the Joint Chiefs of Staff.

27th Operation Desoto begins in Duc Pho. By the end of the operation the Marines will be in control of around 43 square kilometres of the area.

G-Eye View of Vietnam

Viet Cong – The Joke's On You. Stumbling down the hint of a path through Laos, Pvt. Nguyen Van Can felt the coolness of Hanoi disappear. He was sick with dysentery and fever. Every step was pain; but he pressed on.

After three months, Private Can crossed over into South Vietnam. It was night, but his instincts were good, and by early morning he had located the 113th Mortar Squad near Pleime.

"We have been waiting for you," whispered the Viet Cong mortar squad sergeant.

The words made Private Can feel proud, and he drew himself up to his full 5 feet 4 inches. Carefully the sergeant took two shells from Private Can's back and dropped them into a mortar. As they whistled toward the American Special Forces camp, he patted the private's shoulder.

"Good work, son," he said. "Now go get two more."

The Language of Love
"Hey you. You No. 1 [the best]. Come here, sit down," the bar girl begins as she spies a GI.

"How long you come Vietnam? How long you stay? Where you work? Work Bien Hoa, huh?

You kill beaucoup VC. You No. 1. You buy me one Saigon tea? I love you too much."

If the soldier agrees to buy a few drinks, the enchanting conversation can go on for hours. He will tell her about his vital job at base ops (the office where flight plans are filed), the zoomies (pilots) he deals with and the three-quarter (small truck) he drives around the base.

She drinks in his words, along with the tea, and tells him how mamasan (the woman in charge of the bar girls) is No. 10 (the worst) and that, while she considers herself lucky to be talking with such a fine person as the soldier, she works in the bar only because her money is fini (finished).

The soldier is understanding. "Same-same with girls in the States," he tells her. "No have money, must work." He has a solution though.

"I have beaucoup money," he says. "You have hootch [house]? Maybe I come you hootch, give you money. Same-same you be happy."

The girl has heard the line before, but she bats her dark eyes like a schoolgirl and replies nervously: "How much you pay?"

The Language of War
In Vietnamese, a girl is a "co," and an old woman is a "ba." The American adviser is a "co van my," with the "my" pronounced "me." ("Co" can mean many things in Vietnamese. Perhaps the best translation for the phrase used here is "old helper, American.") If the adviser is a captain he is a "dai uy" (pronounced "die we"); if a first lieutenant, a "trung uy." Beer is loosely "ba muoi ba" (pronounced "bom-me-bah") or "33," the most available local brand. The Vietnamese like to drink "coka," which is the way they say Coca-Cola. "Troi oi" (pronounced "choi oi") means "Oh my God!" and is used by Americans as a universal exclamation. "Di di" ("dee dee") means "go," and sometimes becomes "di di it up" for "hurry it up."

A soldier on the battlefield is "zapped" or "waxed" but never killed. He is "dinged," not wounded. An infantryman is a "grunt" and, unless he is also a paratrooper, a "leg." Pilots are either "Steve Canyons" or "zoomies." "Round-eyes" are the dreamed-of, but seldom seen, Western girls; "slant-eyes," their Asian counterparts. A

Patrols in country such as this could reduce a thinking infantryman to a very sorry state. With no trails to speak of, the "boonies" were no-one's idea of a fun place to fight

"short-timer" is a man whose tour of duty is about to end, and a "lifer" is the draftee's name for a career soldier.

The most famous initials, VC, for Viet Cong, become Victor Charlie when translated into the international alphabet used in conversations on military radios, and the troops reduce it to "Charlie." (Some men use "Charles" as a variation to produce a mock touch of formality. The use of "Charles" during a briefing will often draw a smile without delaying the business.) FNG designates a "foolish new guy." No one in Vietnam says "yes," or "right" when he can say "Roger" or, better yet, "Rog." And it is fashionable to say "affirmative" and "negative" for "yes" and "no."

The New York Times

Some US servicemen adapted so well to the environment that they became one with it, and much less vulnerable as a result. Navy SEALs were used to living and fighting a long way from anything like assistance or reinforcement

CONTROLLING THE LAND

FEBRUARY 1967

1st The 3rd Marine Division starts search-and-destroy Operation Prairie II in the area south of the DMZ. There are 694 reported NVA losses by the end of the operation.

2nd To disguise preparations for Operation Junction City, troops of the 4th and 25th Infantry Divisions carry out Operation Gadsden in War Zone C.

5th The ARVN commences defoliation of the southern DMZ. Leaders of student bodies get together in Washington and agree to call for voluntary military service and an end to the draft.

8-10th Christians and Jews are involved in a "Fast for Peace" in the US.

8-12th During the Vietnamese festival of Tet US bombing is halted and a ceasefire observed.

11th As the ceasefire ends, 16 operations begin. Among these is Operation Stone, launched by the 1st Marines south of Da Nang, Operation Lam Son 67 carried out by the 1st Infantry Division south of Saigon, and Operation Pershing which involves the 1st Air Cavalry Division in Binh Dinh Province.

13th The 9th Infantry Division and combined South Vietnamese forces conduct Operation Enterprise in Long An Province.

14th Operation Tuscon masks the movement of the 1st Division in preparation for Operation Junction City.

22nd In Tay Ninh Province and surrounding areas Operation Junction City swings into action. Two ARVN and 34 US battalions are involved, backed by a record 575 aircraft sorties. There are 2728 enemy casualties by the end of the operation.

22nd North Vietnam is shelled by land-based artillery for the first time in the war.

22nd The makers of napalm used in Vietnam, the Dow Chemical Company, receive a stormy reception when they hold a recruiting drive at the University of Wisconsin.

22nd A Harris survey indicates that 67 per cent of those polled support continued bombing.

27th The US air base at Da Nang is bombarded by the Viet Cong, killing 12 Americans.

27th The US states that it has sown mines in North Vietnamese rivers.

Men of the United States Army's 9th Infantry Division slogged through the mud of Long An Province during Operation Enterprise. Chewed-up terrain made even patrolling an arduous task, leading to lapses of attention and inviting an ambush or a sniper's bullet

Beyond the Killing

During 1967 the emphasis will shift more and more away from the killing of Communists to the less spectacular – but equally demanding – tasks of land control, population security and nation building.

Pacification is getting to be as big a job as fighting in Vietnam. In several provinces of Vietnam, the Marines have been given the job of entering, securing and pacifying villages and hamlets that have been under Communist influence or control for so long that they were scarcely touched by the French during their long war.

Operating in consort with Saigon's "Revolutionary Development" cadres and "Political Action Teams", the Marines have done much to change the lives of their charges for the better. Corpsmen, doctors and dentists have treated more than 1,250,000 Vietnamese in the five northern provinces. Over the past 22 months, Marines have built everything from markets and roads to schools, dispensaries and meeting halls. They serve as financial counselors, schoolteachers, carpenters, plumbers – even midwives.

At the root of the Marine pacification program are "Combined Action Companies" (CACs). There are now 62 CACs, each composed of one squad of Marines and two of Vietnamese militia. All the Americans are volunteers, and many of them ask to have their tours of duty extended. "If they aren't motivated strongly toward something more than storming enemy positions, then they aren't for CAC," says Colonel Scott Holmgrain, 46, chief civic affairs officer for the Marine Amphibious Force.

Kit Carson Scouts

In what they call their "Kit Carson Program," the Marines often use Viet Cong defectors as scouts, paying them $41 a month. "They point out the guy [Viet Cong guerrilla] we'd been walking right past for so long," says Colonel Donald Mallory, 50, commander of the 5,000-man 1st Marine Regiment.

When they are not patrolling, the Marines help the villagers and try to get to know them better. In Phuoc Trach, a fishing village on the populous coastal plain below Danang, CAC protection allowed Navy Seabees to build a bridge connecting the village with the main road to the provincial capital. In the past, villagers had to sail up a Viet Cong-controlled river to reach

In several coastal provinces, it's the **US** Marine Corps that provides security, operating in conjunction with Vietnamese militia, one squad of Bootnecks to two of volunteers

their market – and pay plenty of fish in tribute along the way.

When it comes to civic action, though, the Marines insist that the "gimme and giveaway" days are gone for good. The villagers themselves must participate. If the villagers put three or four months of their own sweat into a project, the Marines figure, they will take better care of it and fight any Viet Cong attempts to take over or destroy it.

Time

Korean Tigers

"Where there are Fierce Tigers, there are no Vietcong," said the South Korean officer, half hissing through his teeth as he managed to light a cigarette despite the bouncing of the jeep.

It was 10 p.m., 30 miles south of Quinhon in the Cumong Valley, a former Vietcong area of rest and recuperation on the coastal plain of Central Vietnam recently occupied by the Koreans.

For more than an hour, the jeep drove north along the darkened road. No lights were visible in the string of huts in the roadside villages. Occasionally, figures pounced from the darkness, weapons at the ready.

After a slight hesitation the men grunted "Meng Ho." "Meng Ho" the officer shouted back. "Meng Ho" is Korean for Fierce Tiger, and the fierce tigers are the 15,000 men of what is more formally called the Capital Division of the South Korean Army.

Cocky, disciplined and tough – some say brutal – the Fierce Tigers operate the only sizable piece of South Vietnamese territory wrested from the Vietcong where it is possible to drive unarmed at night.

The Tigers were assigned to a 500-square-mile operational area when they landed in Central Vietnam in October 1965. They now claim control of twice as much territory, radiating from the port of Quinhon along National Highways 1, the only north-south axis and 19, which runs west to American bases at Ankhe and Pleiku in the Central Highlands.

New York Times

Charlie Come Home!

When Ong Tao, the Spirit of the Hearth, returns home each year after his call on the Heavenly Jade Emperor, all Vietnam takes a holiday from war and erupts in the festival of Tet to welcome the Lunar New Year.

This week, as the Vietnamese greet the Year of the Ram under cover of the four-day truce agreed to by both sides, some 100,000 Viet Cong are expected to take leave of their units and slip back to their native villages and families for a brief reunion.

Many of them will find waiting a small gift from the government of South Vietnam: a compact do-it-yourself defection kit. Wrapped in vinyl, it contains all that a faltering Viet Cong needs to defect, including a safe-conduct pass and a map of the local district showing precisely where – and how – to find the Allied side. The kit will be only one more reminder – along with the Tet songs on the radio, the broadcast planes overhead and millions of leaflets – that the government's *Chieu Hoi* (Open Arms) extend everywhere.

Cut Price Defection

To those of the enemy who come home to stay, Saigon offers amnesty and retraining to aid the Allied side. Last year the joint US and South Vietnamese *Chieu Hoi* program induced a record 20,242 of the enemy to come over. So far this year, the rate has been running double last year's.

In command of *Chieu Hoi* is

Not all the Vietnamese fighters are just volunteers. **Kit Carson Scouts,** like this one, are ex-VC, converted to the Allied cause

Colonel Phan Van Anh, a stocky, spirited veteran who was himself once a member of the Communist Viet Minh. Anh makes quick inspections of the country's 44 *Chieu Hoi* camps, followed by a notary public who dishes out piasters for the rewards and rations that in the past have too often been skimmed off by corrupt administrators. "You know," says Anh, "the enemy of yesterday may be very good men."

They are also a bargain: the average cost per defector is $125, v. an estimated $400,000 expended to kill one enemy soldier, and 70% of those coming over so far have been combat soldiers. For all the success of *Chieu Hoi*, though, it is still far from winning the war. To date there have been only 200 defectors from the North Vietnamese forces, and no matter how many war-weary Viet Cong come over the line, there will be yet more Northerners to replace them. Still, Saigon feels that the defection rate has reached a turning point and expects this year to more than double the number of defectors to 50,000.

Time

North Viet Build Up

The U.S. command Friday reported a massive supply buildup in north Vietnam during the first three days of the Lunar New Year truce and the suspension of American bombing raids.

U.S. officials said the 4-day cease-fire proclaimed by the Republic of Vietnam government remains in effect, but they would not rule out the possibi-lity that air strikes against north Vietnam might be ordered before the truce ends Sunday should the communist buildup reach levels considered "intolerable" by the U.S. command.

The north Vietnamese movement of supplies southward is "not technically a violation of the stand-down," these sources said, but it was obviously long planned and "creates doubts as to north Vietnamese sincerity about the truce."

American sources said in Saigon that "the volume, scope and direction" of the shipments "creates hazards for our military which cannot be overlooked."

During the first three days of the truce, American reconnaissance has counted more than 900 communist cargo boats and barges moving in the gulf or on inland waterways. This is about five times the normal traffic, sources said.

In addition, hundreds of trucks are on the go all over north Vietnam, moving equipment and supplies into the southern area toward the demilitarized zone.

Stars and Stripes

JUNCTION CITY

MARCH 1967

1-4th — 1st Infantry Division and 173rd Airborne Brigade sustain heavy losses in Operation Junction City.

2nd — A three-point plan for bringing about an end to the war proposed by Senator Robert Kennedy is turned down by Secretary of State Rusk.

7th — Operation Oh Jac Kyo I launched by the South Koreans. There are 831 enemy casualties by the end of the operation.

8th — US Congress makes $4.5 billion available for prosecuting the war.

10-12th — In an escalation of the air war US planes attack an industrial target, bombing the Thai Nguyen steelworks, 38 miles north of Hanoi.

18th — With a new constitution, South Vietnam schedules elections for the autumn.

18th — The US aid to the South is increased by $150 million to bring the total for the year to $700 million.

20th — The Special Landing Force of the 1st Battalion, 4th Marines lands near Gio Lanh as part of Operation Prairie III. There are 29 US dead before the force pulls out.

20-21st — US and South Vietnamese leaders meet in Guam. Premier Ky asks President Johnson "How long can Hanoi enjoy the advantage of restricted bombing of military targets?"

21st — The North announces that Ho Chi Minh has turned down a proposal from President Johnson delivered to him in a secret diplomatic communication. The revelation of the exchange of notes causes surprise in the US.

21st — Over 600 Viet Cong are killed in a single engagement during Operation Junction City in War Zone C.

25th — Dr Martin Luther King labels the war "a blasphemy against all that America stands for".

27th — A USAF captain, Dale E. Noyd, applies to become a conscientious objector. He will be unsuccessful.

28th — The Quaker-financed yacht *The Phoenix* carrying $10,000 medical aid for North Vietnam lands at Haiphong.

31st — US forces kill 591 Viet Cong at Ap Gu during Operation Junction City.

The first US Marines to land in Vietnam expected to be met by bullets, and instead were greeted with flowers. They soon discovered that it was not an opposed landing that they had to fear, but the attacks that would follow, as soon as they started to move inland. Because of Vietnam's geography, it was often easier to despatch a force by sea rather than overland

Point-Blank Artillery Kills 423 Reds

The communists suffered their worst defeat of the war in terms of deaths Tuesday when more than 423 Reds were killed during a battle 17 miles northeast of Tay Ninh City.

Troopers of the 3d Bn., 4th Inf. Div. serving under the 25th Div. task force cut down human wave attacks of 200 and 300 men by firing artillery flat out with cannister loads.

(The Americans were running low on ammunition when a column of 113 armored vehicles, including 33 tanks, clanked to the rescue, AP reported.)

Capt. George Shoemaker, company commander, said "as the Reds were cut down, they would fall back and patch up the wounded before launching a fresh assault." Many of the dead were wearing fresh bandages, he reported.

Lt. Col. John A. Bender, battalion commander, said the fighting was more savage than anything he had seen in World War II or Korea.

The fighting broke out in the dense jungle around the 3d Bn., 4th Div., artillery post when a patrol spotted forces of the 272d VC Regt.

A Pilot in Vietnam Takes Plane 'Home' After Day's Work

At dusk Maj. Theodore Cline taxies his plane from the dirt airstrip that runs through this provincial capital, avoids end-of-the-day traffic at an intersection and parks his O-1E Bird Dog in the Government headquarters compound.

There is a new airstrip of portable steel planking a little more than a mile outside Camau. But the headquarters courtyard is next to the American military advisers' compound, which is the safest place in Anxuyen Province.

"Couldn't very well leave the Bird overnight even on the dirt strip," said the graying 40-year-

Artillery, air strikes and armed helicopters took a tremendous toll of the attacking foces, but it was direct fire from artillery at the camp that was credited with turning back the assaults.

(Of 18 howitzers that the enemy attacked with rockets and mortar shells, 11 were knocked out, AP said. Repairs by the artillerymen, however, put all but four of these back in working order after the battle.

(These guns, making up three batteries of the 2d Bn., 27th Arty. Regt., sat in the middle of a half-mile-wide landing zone established about 70 miles northwest of Saigon to support the month-old Operation Junction City.)

U.S. losses in the fierce fighting throughout the day were 30 killed and 109 wounded.

Stars and Stripes

Hard physical work, sometimes in appalling conditions, has always been the artilleryman's lot, but he is usually compensated for that by not having to fight the enemy hand-to-hand. Usually, but not always, as the gunners supporting the 4th Infantry Div. found out.

old Air Force major from Paris, Ill. "Either there'd be nothing left in the morning or it'd take two hours to disarm the booby traps."

The major is the senior forward air controller for Anxuyen, an area considered so expendable that a local saying goes, "The day Camau gets a government priority, we'll know the war is over."

The fighter-bombers Major Cline calls in for air strikes constitute the only effective offensive weapons in Anxuyen.

Since he arrived in Camau in September, his Bird Dog, a Cessna two-seater, has been hit 11 times.

"It's a question of environment," he said. "Here we've got a lot of mean V.C.'s."

Not far from the tip of the Camau Peninsula lies the scene of the major's most satisfying achievement as forward air controller. Months ago he noticed unusual activity along the river bank, which developed into a target worthy of a B-52 strike.

There are tree-shaded canals where Vietcong battalions are known to camp but which are not bombed. "Too many people living in the villages right with the VC," the major explained.

"Sure, it's a temptation to hit them," he said. "But that's why F.A.C.'s should be gray-haired majors like me. Everytime you walk up to a map to plan a strike, you're playing God."

New York Times

Destroying the Haven

The area, 75 miles northwest of Saigon, has for 20 years been Communism's major stronghold in South Vietnam, and is believed to contain the national headquarters of the Viet Cong.

The US sent noisy C-130s over the area to deliver the first American combat parachute jump of the war. Giant trees crumpled as B-52s from Guam, 2,600 miles away, swept in to carpet the forest with high explosives. Screaming Phantoms and Skyraiders plastered the perimeters of jungle clearings with napalm and thermite bombs, setting brush fires that blazed for days. Helicopters thrummed in to deposit entire platoons of infantrymen, and armored personnel carriers rumbled through the mire.

Yet the Viet Cong made themselves scarce. Even before the assault began, most of them apparently fled across the border into Cambodia. As the Americans, aided by South Vietnamese forces, moved cautiously through the area, the ground was still so hot from napalm that the troops were unable to crouch.

In their drive, the Americans destroyed Viet Cong camps, food supplies and enough concrete bunkers to shelter a division.

The great Communist force that was thought to be in the area never materialized. "If we get in there and don't kill anybody and don't find anything, it will be embarrassing," said Lieut. General Jonathan O. Seaman, commander of the operation, "sometimes knowing what isn't there can be valuable, but I hate to spend this many resources for that kind of intelligence." *Time*

The low speed and stamina of the Skyraider made it invaluable when it came to pin-point accurate low-level bombing. Skyraiders have placed bombs within 20 yards of their own troops

APRIL 1967

2nd Viet Cong claim 864 US casualties at Ap Gu.

2nd The elections in South Vietnam are marked by communist terrorist attacks.

5th Operation Francis Marion commences in the western highlands of Pleiku Province with 4th Infantry Division taking part.

6th Quang Tri City attacked by NVA and Viet Cong across the Benhai River bridge. Thieu calls for an invasion of the North "as a natural act of self-defence".

10th B-52s formerly operating out of Guam arrive in Thailand.

11th China is reported as having reached an agreement with the USSR over supplying the North.

12th A mortar attack against Chu Lai air base results in 28 US casualties.

13th The Viet Cong destroy two bridges on Highway 2 between Quang Tri and Da Nang on the major US DMZ supply line.

15th A six-mile-long barrier is to be built south of the DMZ to block penetration of the South.

15th An estimated 195,000 marchers participate in protests in San Francisco and New York.

20th Operation Prairie IV commences.

20th The first bombing raids against Haiphong take place.

21st Start of Operation Union I by the US Marines in the Que Son Basin.

22nd Task Force Oregon, an Army force consisting of 15,000 men, is created in the Quang Tri and Thau Tien Provinces of South Vietnam.

24th General Westmoreland states that his troops "are dismayed and so am I by recent unpatriotic acts at home".

25th The British freighter *Dartford* is hit in Haiphong in error by US planes.

As more and more trained **NVA** troops moved down the multiplicity of tracks known as the **Ho Chi Minh Trail**, so it became necessary for **MACV** to mount operations such as Francis Marion directed

Outnumbered GIs Cut Down 581 VC

Outnumbered U.S. troops cut down waves of Viet Cong attackers Saturday in a battle that killed at least 581 communists and left only nine Americans dead.

The one-day toll was the highest ever suffered by the VC. Bodies of fallen VC soldiers were still being counted at dusk Saturday, even as the battered enemy force struck again at U.S. defenses.

Thirty-two Americans were wounded.

The communists were overrun after they tried to trap a battalion of the 1st Inf. Div. 6 miles from the Cambodian border in Tay Minh Province.

Stars and Stripes

Hamlet Near Saigon "Pacified" for 5th Time in 10 Years

Last night two battalions of South Vietnamese infantry surrounded Khanh-van. At dawn the troops moved in. Loudspeakers summoned the 2,000 villagers to the market place. The men came slowly from their thatched huts. Their wives and children tagged along.

Major Gian asked the villagers how they felt about having the army back.

One man rose, "We feel good and we feel bad," he said. "We feel good because we will have protection. But we feel bad because the Viet Cong told us that if we let you stay here, they would attack us with mortars and machine guns."

"Until last December, when we began patrolling in here, laying the groundwork for today's operation, Khanhvan has been solidly in Viet Cong hands," said Colonel Schweitzer.

Why, the colonel was asked, did he think pacification would work now, after four failures.

"This time we will leave a battalion of Vietnamese troops with American advisers. They will stay for at least a year and it won't be behind walls."

"And most important," he added, "the villagers have seen what Viet Cong government is like, they don't like it. And there's no longer a feeling of hopelessness among the Government troops and officials. For once they think they're going to win."

The New York Times

Jewish Servicemen in Vietnam Mark Passover

Jewish servicemen in Vietnam sat down to Seder feasts tonight to mark the start of Passover.

The largest of the celebrations was held at the United Service Organisations clubhouse here. It was attended by more than 500 men, ranging in rank from private to colonel.

Many, wearing their green combat fatigue uniforms, arrived on special passes from their division defending the capital. Other observances were held in Nhatrang and Danang.

The armed forces shipped 18 tons of "Kosher for Passover" delicacies, including sacramental wine, gefilte fish, matzoh and boiled chicken, to Vietnam for the celebrations. New kitchen utensils were provided for their preparation.

The New York Times

Raid at Haiphong

Navy jet raiders in two waves Thursday flew through missiles, antiaircraft fire and aerial mines to bomb only a little over a mile from the port city of Haiphong for the first time.

The strike, with the reported personal approval of President Johnson, knocked out both of the city's power plants and plunged the vital port into darkness.

The jets, from the Seventh Fleet carriers Kitty Hawk and Ticonderoga, slashed through the heaviest ground defenses the communists had to offer. But they hit the targets and returned without a loss.

Only one plane was damaged. It had nine holes in it from one of the flurry of Russian-built surface to air (SAM) missiles hurled at the attacking Navy jets.

Stars and Stripes

The port of Haiphong, and its railyards and power stations had long been attractive targets, but it was May, 1967 before the US finally hit it. As a result its air defenses were stiffened up considerably

Why They "Confess" US POW's Brainwashed

It seemed like Korea all over again – only this time the confessional was in Hanoi. A US Navy pilot, screened from the visiting journalists' view, was speaking flatly into a microphone. "I sincerely acknowledge my crimes," said a voice identified as that of Lt. Comdr. Richard A. Stratton, "and repent at having committed them."

When the denunciation of American air strikes against North Vietnam ended, the husky Stratton stepped through a curtained doorway. He was wearing striped pajamas. Suddenly, a North Vietnamese officer snapped a command and Stratton bowed from the waist. Then he straightened, made a quarter turn to the left, bowed again, turned to the right, bowed, straightened. Free-lance photographer Lee Lockwood tried to catch Stratton's eyes. But the eyes of the airman were empty and unfocused. As Lock-

They call it re-education; we call it brainwashing, but whatever the name for this inhuman trial, the Asian communists are some of its most skillful practitioners

wood described it later in an article for *Life*, Stratton was "like a puppet" throughout the entire four-minute "tableau."

Despite assurances from Hanoi that US prisoners of war are being treated humanely, Pentagon and State Department officials have suspected for some time that the North Vietnamese are practising the old Communist art of exacting involuntary "confessions."

To bring Stratton to the confessional the North Vietnamese may well have used the same methods that were employed to break US POWs in North Korea, the techniques made familiar in such books as *The Manchurian Candidate* and *The Ipcress File*.

Newsweek

GI Visitors Change Asian City Life

"I picked Singapore for R and R," an American soldier said,"because I heard it was quiet and not too many Americans come here."

Wearing sports shirts and draped in cameras, the visiting Americans are conspicuous evidence of the United States presence in Asia.

The impact of urban Asia, with its relentless, crowding bustle, its pungent odors and brilliant colors, on the soldiers often seems minuscule. Many spend much of their time drinking with each other in the bars of American R and R hotels or sitting together on a bus headed for a Philippine waterfall.

"Hey, Baby, I Love You"
Their impact on Asia seems greater than Asia's imprint on them. They have helped spread pop music and bowling, the latest American dances and the grating Saigon pidgin English in which bar girls call out, "Hey, Baby, I love you too much."

"I never want to come back to this part of the world," a young army truck mechanic said, "but while I'm here I want to see it. Everything seems interesting to

me – even those people driving on the wrong side of the street."

In Bangkok's Petchburi Street, scores of bars, steam baths and disreputable hotels have sprung up since rest and rehabilitation trips began in 1965.

One mortar gunner visiting Bangkok said, "It's just like paradise." An infantryman friend added, "Bangkok is the friendliest place I've ever seen."

The New York Times

HANOI STEPS-UP THE WAR

MAY 1967

1st Secretary of State Rusk accuses North Vietnam of refusing at least 28 peace talk proposals.

1st Ellsworth Bunker takes over from Henry Cabot Lodge as US Ambassador to Saigon.

2-10th In Stockholm a self-styled war crimes tribunal denounces US activities in Vietnam.

4th The US Special Forces base at Lang Vei near Khe Sanh is attacked and over 100 casualties inflicted.

8th The NVA assault on the Marine base at Con Thien, south of the DMZ, leads to US troops being permitted to fight in the southern part of the DMZ.

10th An anti-war teach-in takes place in 80 colleges across the US.

11th Operation Malheur I and II involving the III Marine Amphibious Task Force begins. Operation Crockett also starts in the Khe Sanh area.

11th U Thant, UN Secretary General, warns of possibility of "direct confrontation" between China and the US.

13th A New York City Fire Department captain organizes a march backing US Southeast Asia policy. 70,000 people turn out.

18th US and South Vietnamese troops make their first move into the DMZ under Operation Practice Line. This operation is split into three prongs codenamed Beau Charger, Lam Son 54 and Hickory.

19th US Naval aircraft carry out the first bombing raids on central Hanoi.

26th Start of Operation Union II with a heliborne assault by elements of 1st Marine Division. There are 701 enemy casualties by the end of the operation.

Propeller Holds Its Own in Jet Age

"We tell people that we grease the body and wings to make them go faster," Maj. Ed Maxson was saying, as he climbed into his cockpit, "but the plain truth is that the engine sprays off over everything."

He was talking about the 20-year-old Douglas A-1E Skyraider.

The Skyraider is the only propeller-driven warplane being used in Vietnam. For as long as the Skyraiders fly at 140 knots, the men who fly them will argue that their planes can still do some jobs better than the jets.

"Hell," said Major Maxson, "we can put our ordnance within 50-foot tolerances. We can stay in the air for five or six hours at a time. We can operate when the weather isn't good enough for jets."

"Big Hog With the Fan"

"To me it's a chance to do some unusual flying that I'll never get a chance to do again."

"The way I see it, jets are every day, but this big hog with the fan out front, why, that's unique."

Swimming Trouble

It is dangerous work, both north and south of the border. The Air Commando Squadron has lost nine planes and four pilots. Major Maxson, shot down by ground fire last March, bailed out at 300 feet. His parachute only partly opened, but he landed in a lake.

"I pulled the tab to inflate my Mae West," he said. "The only trouble was that the soldier who came out to rescue me didn't swim very well, and I had to pull him to shore while he was trying to drown me."

The New York Times

They call it The Spad, after a famous World War I fighter aircraft, and many see it as an anachronism, but there are jobs the A-1 Skyraider does that no other aircraft on the inventory could even look at

VC Attack Saigon Airfields

Viet Cong guerrillas early Friday launched coordinated attacks on two U.S. airfields north of Saigon, military spokesmen said.

They hit the Bien Hoa airfield with heavy mortar, rocket and recoilless rifle attacks 16 miles north of the city and about an hour later struck at Phuoc Vinh 18 miles further north.

U.S. spokesmen said the attack on Bien Hoa, the sprawling air base where more than half of all U.S. and Vietnamese air strikes in South Vietnam are flown from, came at 1 a.m.

Guerrillas lobbed in about 125 rounds of 140mm rockets along with mortars and recoilless rifle fire.

Stars and Stripes

It was Hanoi's turn, too, to come under air attack from the carrier-based bombers. Just as they had at Haiphong, the NVA reinforced the city with large-calibre anti-aircraft artillery and Surface-to-Air Missiles

Escalation from Hanoi

Scarcely three miles south of the DMZ, the Communists attempted to overrun the camp of Con Thien, defended by two companies of Marines and three companies of Vietnamese irregular forces advised by a US Special Forces team. The entire 4th Battalion of the North Vietnamese 821st Regiment attacked, led by two companies of sappers who cut their way through the Marines' barbed wire perimeter by thrusting ahead of them satchel charges and bangalore torpedoes mounted on the tips of bamboo poles. The Marines hit back with rapid M-16 rifle fire and grenades, plus twin 40-mm guns mounted on M-42 "duster" tracked vehicles.

Suddenly an ugly belch of flame lit up the night. "My Christ," yelled an astonished Marine, "they're using flame-throwers!" A column rumbling up with fresh ammunition for

Unconscious TV Star

Mrs A Landon Morrow Sr. was watching a late news program on television, and a film report on fighting in Vietnam caught her attention. Suddenly there was a familiar face in battle gear.

She looked, then shouted: "Come quick, Landon. Here's our son."

The camera had focused briefly on Spec. 4th Cl. Landon Morrow Jr., a radio operator, as the television newsman described fighting in Operation Manhattan.

As the La Grange couple listened and watched, the newsman described an explosion that had wounded a captain and a radio operator. Then there was a film close-up of a soldier lying on the ground.

"We knew then that was our son," said Mrs Morrow. "We didn't see the explosion but the next time they put the camera on him he was lying on the ground. There were two or three working on him. We could tell he was wounded."

Telegrams Follow

The next day the Morrows and their daughter-in-law, Mary, received telegrams explaining that the 20-year-old soldier had been wounded but would survive.

"I'll never forget the night I saw that," said Mrs Morrow. "It was on WSB, Channel 3, on April 30th at 11 p.m."

Mrs Morrow said she would not have recognized her son so quickly if the name of the soldier's unit had not been described. "He said 'Company B, Second Battalion' and I knew that was Landon's outfit," she said.

The New York Times

the Marines ran right into the hose of fire. Six vehicles went up with a roar, and the ammunition began exploding, nicely silhouetting the attackers as targets for the Marines. "I kept on telling my men, just hang on until dawn and we'll be all right," said Sergeant Richard Anderson, a squad leader. They did, and the dawn came up with the welcome thunder of US fighter-bombers. The North Vietnamese fled back out through the wire, leaving behind 196 dead. The outnumbered Marines held the camp, but at the cost of 44 dead and 140 wounded.

Swishing Tail

Many of the enemy dead wore tiger-striped uniforms and had gone into battle barefoot, their shoes tied around their necks. They had been so certain of victory that several carried English-Vietnamese phrase books. Marine Commander Lieut. General Lewis Walt arrived a few hours later to inspect the battlefield. He had barely begun when the cry "Incoming!" went up and three mortar rounds boomed in. Walt and his staff dived for foxholes for the third time in ten days – and the closest call. One round hit only 15 feet from the general. Walt was unhurt, but two of his staff were injured.

Time

One Mile Below the DMZ

One mile below the DMZ, Vietnam – U.S. Marines and South Vietnamese troops launched a massive assault on the DMZ Thursday.

It was the first time Allied forces had crossed into the buffer zone created when Vietnam was divided 13 years ago.

The three-pronged drive, by a multi-battalion force, is named Operation Hickory Nut. It is an attack against North Vietnamese "who have been violating the rules and using the DMZ as a sanctuary," a Marine commander said.

"They have been hitting our bases with rockets, mortars and artillery and then going back into the DMZ. We got sick of it, and we're going in to get them."

A Marine spokesman said at least two North Vietnamese regiments are being tracked down by the allied troops sweeping a 20-mile strip along the southern half of the zone.

U.S. aircraft hammered North Vietnamese artillery positions Thursday, destroying at least 10 guns able to fire into South Vietnam.

Seven of the gun sites were along the northern boundary of the DMZ.

At least 23 North Vietnamese guns have been knocked out near the DMZ since Tuesday, U.S. sources said.

Stars and Stripes

"This used to be the end of the road . . ." **US commanders had been begging for years for permission to go at least into the De-Militarized Zone that separating North from South Vietnam**

JUNE 1967

1st Marines launch Operation Cimarron close to the DMZ.

2-3rd The USSR accuses the US of injuring two Soviet merchant seamen aboard the *Turkestan* which was in Cam Pha port during a bombing raid.

10th Twenty-seven are killed in a mortar attack on Pleiku.

12th The Chinese allege that they have shot down a pilotless US drone reconnaissance aircraft over their territory.

12-17th 1st Infantry Division moves into War Zone D after Viet Cong units.

16th The Viet Cong threaten to kill American prisoners if "three Vietnamese patriots" are executed in Saigon.

17th Two battalions of the 173rd Airborne Brigade are airlifted into Dak To as Operation Greeley begins.

20th The US sends an apology to the USSR over the *Turkestan* incident.

22nd Eighty out of a company of 130 US airborne soldiers are killed at Dak To.

23rd President Johnson and Soviet Premier Kosygin meet in New Jersey.

30th It is announced that Thieu will run for the presidency of South Vietnam in September with Ky as his partner.

Operation Greely involved two battalions of the 173rd Airborne Brigade. Seen here making a helicopter assault, the 173rd were notable for making one of the few combat parachute assaults of the war

VIPs Harry Saigon Officials

Anyone trying to see Gen. William Westmoreland, the American military chief in Vietnam, was out of luck for 90 minutes one recent morning.

The general was busy briefing Ann Landers, whose syndicated column provides guidance for newspaper readers on their personal problems.

Miss Landers' audience with the general was in line with United States Government policy. Convinced that the com-plexities of the war in Vietnam are poorly understood in the United States, Washington has encouraged official and private visitors to come here and see for themselves.

About half of these important visitors want to see General Westmoreland, who normally receives two of them every day. The general is the most sought-after official in Vietnam, followed closely by Ambassador Ellsworth Bunker and the leaders of the South Vietnamese

An M16 armed Marine squad leader screams orders to his men. Early problems were nothing to do with the rifle's design, but more to do with bad training, but the M16s bad reputation lasted a while

M-16 Under Fire

No one in Viet Nam doubts that the stubby, black-stocked M-16 is a dangerous weapon. Of late, however, newsmen, fighting men and Congressmen alike have suggested that the wicked little (7 lbs., 39 in.) automatic rifle can be as dangerous to friend as it is to foe. Though – at the urging of General William Westmoreland – it has become the standard weapon for U.S. combat troops in Viet Nam, its critics charge that the M-16 tends to jam during the intensive firing for which it was designed, leaving many an infantryman helpless in close-up combat.

The M-16 itself came under heavy fire at home after last month's battle for Hills 881 and 861 below the DMZ. "We left with 72 men in our platoon and came back with 19," wrote a Marine Corps rifleman to his family after the battle. "Believe it or not, you know what killed most of us? Our own rifle. Practically every one of our dead was found with his [M-16] torn down next to him where he had been trying to fix it." TV newsmen, in particular, took up the cry that U.S. troops were being betrayed by their own weapons. Last week two congressional subcommittees were studying the "M-16 controversy."

Though the M-16's predecessor rifle, the 11¼-lb. M-14, has a longer range and fires a heavier bullet, it cannot match the M-16s maximum sustained rate of fire (up to 200 rounds a

Government.

The most important visitors, such as Congressmen, cause little trouble during the five days – on the average – that they spend in Vietnam, sources in the protocol office said. The same is not always true for staff members, who usually insist on the same rights and privileges – such as hard-to-come-by air-conditioned quarters and automobiles – as their superiors.

Other less-than-welcome visitors, informed sources said, are military officers who schedule short visits to Vietnam at the end of one month and the beginning of another. In this way they are entitled to collect two full months of combat pay and other allowances given for service in a war theater.

"In one 11-day period, I spent nine and a half days tied up with visitors," said a high American official who works seven days a week and ends up doing all his administrative tasks from 8 p.m. to midnight.

Another high American official maintains three offices in Saigon and leaves instructions that all visitors are to be told he is out of town. "After all," he said, "someone in Vietnam has to do the work."

New York Times

minute v. 60 for the M-14). Many Marines – as well as the South Korean troops in Viet Nam – are still armed with the slower-firing M-14, and as a result the Pentagon has also been faulted for failure to supply all the M-16s that the Allies in Viet Nam demanded.

Like any automatic weapon, the M-16 requires assiduous cleaning and care to keep it from jamming. But not as much as the .30-caliber M-14. "I could troubleshoot an M-16 much faster than I could an M-14," says Lieut. Colonel Henry Miller, chief of Army heavy maintenance in Saigon. Many Marines in the battle above Khe Sanh had been issued their M-16s only a few days before the fight, and were probably unfamiliar with the weapon's demands: constant lubrication, thorough wirebrush reaming of the barrel to prevent leading, "fire discipline" that limits bursts to two or three rounds at a crack.

Time

Secret Weapons

"I'd rather be over on the Cambodian border fighting North Vietnamese regulars than taking my chances with Viet Cong booby traps."

Crudely fashioned and cunningly camouflaged, the booby traps come in all shapes and forms – old-fashioned tiger traps, hollowed-out coconut shells packed with TNT, rat traps which trigger a single bullet, punji boards studded with needle-sharp bamboo stakes capable of piercing a man's leg to the bone. Communist demolition squads are so ingenious that fresh US troops must be cautioned by their officers not to disturb innocent-looking rocks – or even Coke cans – that may explode at the lightest touch. And some US medics have become frankly skittish about handling the bodies of dead comrades – a number of which have been found to be rigged with grenades.

As one convalescing victim of a Viet Cong booby trap remarked: "There's just no school that can tell you how to hunt for booby traps. You only do it by experience, by some kind of sixth sense. My sixth sense stopped working for me the other day."

Newsweek

The Punji trap is one of the simplest and most effective weapons of the war, accounting for a large number of US and allied casualties

JULY 1967

2nd After General Westmoreland requests a further 200,000 troops Defense Secretary McNamara visits South Vietnam to discuss the matter. They agree on a figure of 55,000.

2-14th Start of Operation Buffalo in the southern DMZ involving the 3rd Marine Division. There are 1281 enemy casualties by the end of the operation.

10th ARVN base at An Loc fends off an NVA attack.

11th It emerges that out of 464,000 troops in South Vietnam only 50,000 can at present be used for attacking ground operations.

12th China accuses US of firing guided missiles at a Chinese border post.

16th The 3rd Marine Division gets Operation Kingfisher under way.

19th Start of the South Vietnamese presidential election campaign.

23rd The US 4th Infantry Division engages an NVA company south of Ducco in the Central Highlands, killing at least 148 communists.

29th A fire aboard the US aircraft carrier *Forrestal* kills 134 and injures 62. Twenty planes are destroyed and 42 damaged.

30th A Gallup survey indicates that 52 per cent of those asked do not like the way the President is handling the war and 41 per cent are of the opinion that troops should never have been sent.

Complicated and Crazy

As the war slogged on, many US troops were becoming pessimistic and cynical. This could be seen in the comment of one GI last week.

The GI had just finished shaving in a barrack in Ankhe, an American base. "What do you think of this war?" he suddenly asked a visitor who had begun shaving at a mirror nearby.

The sleepy visitor shrugged. "It's complicated."

"Yeah, it's complicated," the soldier said heatedly. "On March 24th I killed seven good men and I want to know why. It was my buddy's first wedding anniversary and he got killed and I want to know why. *Why?*"

A Moral Obligation

What strikes some observers in the battle zone is the bluntness and almost total cynicism of some soldiers, the confusion of others, and the genuine gung-ho attitude of still others.

"It's our moral obligation to be in this country," said Pfc Michael Ganger, a 20-year-old from Deerfield, Ill., who volunteered for Vietnam. "We've got to back our government in this war."

In a company in the fourth Division, however, the comments were bitter and harsh. "If you put it up to a vote among the GIs, we would all vote to chuck this whole place," said a young infantryman from Brooklyn, who had been a bank clerk in New York. "They say we're stopping Communism here, but that's just politics, just words. That doesn't mean anything to guys who go out every day to shoot some gooks and get shot at."

A radio-telephone operator, also from Brooklyn, grinned wearily. "We're fighting this war over terrain we fought over six months ago and we'll fight for the same terrain six months from now and we'll probably fight for it six years from now," he said with a sigh. "And we still won't win it or lose it. It's crazy."

The New York Times

US Marines on Operation Kingfisher receive covering fire from the twin 40-mm cannon of an Army M42 Duster, along Route 9 between Khe Sanh and Dong Ha.

Ambush at Con Thien

The area had been quiet for weeks, but in the midst of a routine sweep early one morning, two companies of marines of the First Battalion, Ninth Regiment, Third Division, were suddenly hit by intense mortar fire. Then, as the marines sought cover, the North Vietnamese, perhaps a thousand strong, came charging out of the jungle on all sides. Alpha Company managed to form itself into a tight defensive perimeter, but Bravo Company was caught strung out along a narrow dirt road and was quickly cut off under heavy fire. A captain who had recently taken over as commander of Bravo Company tried to rally his men. "He was all up and down that line, shooting his .45," Sgt. Richard Huff recalled later. "He told me to get the mortars firing. Then he ran back up front and that was the last I saw of him alive."

In the enemy onslaught, one platoon was wiped out almost immediately. The rest of Bravo Company, firing back furiously, tried to dig in. "All you could do," said Cpl. Mike Pitts later, "was to protect your buddy's back and hope he was doing the same for you." Added Cpl. Mike Hughes: "We were all wounded, and the men were just lying there, firing. I shouted, 'get up and move back,' and somebody said, 'We can't.' I said: 'You want to live, you got to move.'"

Newsweek

A C-130 provides the backdrop to a rocket hole in the temporary runway at a Marine Corps logistic base. Many such facilities are targets for the NVA during the second half of 1967

New Soviet Weapon Aids North Vietnam

The North Vietnamese are using a new Soviet-made weapon, the RPG7 antitank gun, in their effort to wrest northern territory of South Vietnam from the hands of United States Marines.

A Marine intelligence officer said today that RPG7 shells knocked out two Marine tanks that sought to relieve two Marine companies in a bloody battle Sunday just below the demilitarized zone against elements of North Vietnam's 90th Regiment.

"Those weapons can do the job on any tank we have," he declared. "They can penetrate 11 inches of steel."

The officer said one of the antitank guns had previously been captured "on a special operation in Laos." The Ho Chi Minh supply trail winds south through the Communist-controlled eastern section of Laos.

New York Times

Action at Con Thien

During the second half of 1967, the enemy offensive south of the DMZ was a bloody repetition of the previous year's effort. With more courage than good sense, the NVA streamed across the DMZ throughout the summer only to be met and systematically chewed up in one engagement after another. In July, the enemy, supported by his long-range artillery along the Ben Hai, mounted a major thrust against the 9th Marines near the strongpoint of Con Thien. Reinforced by SLFs Alpha and Bravo, the 9th Marines countered with Operation BUFFALO and, between the 2d and 14th of July, killed 1,290 NVA. Marine losses were 159 dead and 345 wounded.

After this crushing defeat, the NVA shifted its emphasis from direct infantry assaults to attacks by fire. Utilizing long-range rockets and artillery pieces tucked away in caves and treelines along the DMZ, the enemy regularly shelled Marine fire support and logistical bases from Cam Lo to Cua Viet. One of the most destructive attacks was against Dong Ha where, on 3 September, 41 enemy artillery rounds hit the base and touched off a series of spectacular explosions which lasted for over four hours. Several helicopters were damaged but, more important, a fuel farm and a huge stockpile of ammunition went up in smoke. Thousands of gallons of fuel and tons of ammunition were destroyed. The enormous column of smoke from the exploding dumps rose above 12,000 feet and was visible as far south as Hue-Phu Bai.

U.S. Marine Corps History

Civilian Casualties are said to be High

Civilians wounded in Vietnam outnumber military casualties by substantial margins, an official of the American Friends Service Committee reported here today.

Various estimates have placed the ratio at between 3 to 1, all the way up to 8 to 1, according to David Stickney, director of a Quaker program for refugees at Quangngai.

Mr. Stickney, who is on leave of absence from his job as associate director of the Illinois Hospital Association, has just returned to this country after 18 months in South Vietnam.

He reported that between 80 and 85 per cent of the surgical patients at Quangngai hospital were civilian war casualties. Of those, almost all are burn and orthopedic cases, and almost half of them require physical therapy.

The figures, Mr. Stickney said, are based on a survey he made during one representative week last November.

New York Times

AUGUST 1967

8th President Johnson authorizes the bombing of previously prohibited North Vietnamese targets under Operation Rolling Thunder.

9th 1st Marine Division launches Operation Cochise in Que Son valley. Operation Byrd, the pacification of Binh Tzuan Province by the 1st Air Cavalry Division continues.

11th US pilots are authorized to bomb within 25 miles of the Chinese frontier and to engage targets with rockets and cannon within 10 miles. US aircraft attack targets formerly on the prohibited list.

13-19th B-52s bomb the DMZ. A record 203 sorties are flown on the 19th.

18th Governor Reagan of California calls for the US to pull out of Vietnam.

25th Defense Secretary McNamara concedes that the US bombing campaign has had little effect on the North's "war-making capability".

26th South Vietnamese presidential candidate Thieu states that if he is elected he will suspend bombing for a week as a "good-will gesture".

27th Opinions are voiced that some North Vietnamese aircraft are flown from bases in China.

27th Around 355 people die in a series of Viet Cong raids across the South.

30th The monitoring station at the Phubai Marine helicopter base is the target of a Viet Cong attack. Ten Marines are killed and 30 wounded. South Vietnamese losses are 55 killed and 61 wounded.

31st The Senate Preparedness Investigating Committee issues a call to step up bombing against the North and close the port of Haiphong.

A long-range patroller makes his cautious way through thick vegetation. Known as LVRPs, these unconventional warriors seek out the enemy in his own bastions

"The Army's Hippies"

Clad in tiger-striped camouflage suits, their faces smeared black and green with Helena Rubinstein cosmetics, small Army and marine patrols are now prowling through the Viet Cong's backyard, hitting the enemy where once he thought he was safe.

These operations are known as long-range reconnaissance patrols. Originally, their mission was simply to gather intelligence without revealing their presence. Now, however, some patrols call in air or artillery strikes or even attack the unsuspecting enemy on their own.

One hot spot for the "recon" men is "Happy Valley", 15 miles west of the Danang air base. Late last month, a CH-46 helicopter settled into the elephant grass of Happy Valley and out hopped First Lt. Andrew R. Finlayson with a six-man recon team, codenamed "Killer Kane".

The next morning, as they moved up the hill, the marines spotted a North Vietnamese patrol and formed a fighting perimeter. "There, ten feet away, crawling through the grass, came their point man," Finlayson recalled later. Lance Cpl. John Slowick was looking right into the man's eyes as he opened up with his M-16 rifle, killing two North Vietnamese instantly.

The Gas Trick

Enemy reinforcements poured in, and after a 30-minute firefight, Finlayson decided it was time to try the marines' newest evacuation technique. The Americans donned gas masks and saturated the area with tear gas. Then they ran to a clearing, where a helicopter swooped in to the rescue.

"A lot of these guys are juvenile delinquents, beach bums, high school dropouts," Finlayson says affectionately. "You could call them the Army's hippies," adds First Lt. Robert Walden, leader of a recon platoon in the Army's Fourth Infantry Division. "They're nonconformists. They don't go for the strait-laced Army atmosphere."

"What we are trying to do," says the Army's Lieutenant Walden, "is something the enemy has been doing to us for a long time: deny your opponent freedom of movement. If Charlie can move at will, he has a tremendous advantage. But if we can let him know that wherever he is – in base camp, on a high-speed trail or out in the boonies – he's in danger, too, then we've neutralized his advantage."

Newsweek

Arrival of the Arvins

On July 27, a hastily assembled force of 7,500 US infantrymen and 6,000 South Vietnamese marines swept into the area. Helicopters plunked the marines squarely atop the command post of the Viet Cong's tough 263rd Battalion. Ignoring American advice to withdraw in favor of an air strike, the Vietnamese chewed up the Viet Cong unit and captured its deputy commander. In five days the joint operation killed 285 Communists, and most of its success was credited to the gutsy Vietnamese marines.

The marines' aggressive performance was a welcome change of pace. All too often, the Arvins (a nickname for Vietnamese troops, drawn from the title Army of the Republic of Vietnam) have displayed stupendous ineptitude, as well as a distressing reluctance to fight.

"All the good things you hear about Arvins are true, and so are the bad things," said one US officer. "They're like any soldiers – they'll fight if you give them a reason to fight and leaders they can believe in. So far, they are not sure they have either."

Newsweek

U.S. Discloses Laos Bombing

The Air Force revealed officially Sunday for the first time that American warplanes are bombing communist targets in Laos, Vietnam's neighbor to the west.

The U.S. fighter-bombers are conducting air raids "at the request of the Royal Laotian government," a spokesman for the Air Force in Saigon said Sunday.

The Air Force confirmed that American warplanes have been running "armed reconnaissance" missions over Laos, and have been for more than three years. "We are looking for targets and we bomb at the request of the Royal Laotian government," the spokesman said.

The spokesman was unable to list the exact targets, nor would he say how many American planes had been shot down over Laos.

It was reported the main target is the so-called "Ho Chi Minh Trail" that runs from North Vietnam through Laos into South Vietnam.

Stars and Stripes

A USAF Super Sabre fires rockets at a target on the Laotian border. US planes have been active over Laos for 3 years

71 Dead, 112 Missing on Forrestal

The burned and battered carrier Forrestal sailed out of the Tonkin Gulf Sunday for Subic Bay in the Philippines with 71 of her crew known dead, 78 injured and 112 missing.

A search was still going on in the ripped and seared fantail compartments between flight and hangar decks, where exploding bombs and burning fuel from launch-ready jets Saturday trapped most of the missing. Officials said there was little hope of finding any survivors.

Anyone caught in the area, they said, would almost certainly have died in the fire or been asphyxiated.

A freak chain of events apparently touched off Saturday's disastrous fire.

According to eyewitnesses, an A4 Skyhawk near the center of the flight deck started "hot" just before launch and shot a long tongue of flame toward 16 planes parked in a horseshoe on the aft deck.

The hot start apparently was caused by excess fuel in the jet's engine, which creates a burst of flame much like an overfilled cigarette lighter.

The flame ignited a Sidwinder missile under the wing of an F4 Phantom on the starboard side.

The missile streaked across the deck and blew up a 400-gallon belly tank on a parked Skyhawk. Aviation gas spilled from the tank, spreading the fire to other planes.

Capt. John K. Beling, the Forrestal's skipper, said Sunday "no human error was involved. This is one of those things that happen in a war."

Stars and Stripes

The wreckage littering the deck of USS *Forrestal* is ample evidence of the destructive power of modern weaponry, even when it is unleashed by accident as happened here

SEPTEMBER 1967

2nd On the same day as Thieu vaunts his country's attitude to free speech, two newspapers are closed.

2nd The NVA carries out attacks at Con Thien and Dong Ha.

4th Thieu is elected president, with Ky as his deputy, though there are allegations of corruption.

4th Operation Swift commences in the Quang Nam and Quang Tri Provinces involving the 1st Marine Division. There are 517 enemy casualties.

5th Start of Operation Dragon Fire in Quang Ngai Province involving the 2nd South Korean Marine Brigade.

7th Defense Secretary McNamara announces that a barrier, the McNamara Line, is to be built to block communist penetration at the eastern end of the DMZ. The barrier is to be provided with hi-tech listening devices.

10th In the first air raid on North Vietnamese docks, the port area of Cam Pha comes under attack by US aircraft.

13-16th Operation Coronado V commences in the Mekong Delta involving the 9th Infantry Division. There are 213 Viet Cong casualties by the end of the operation.

14th Reports, one of French and the other of Canadian origin, suggest that North Vietnam could be persuaded to come to the negotiating table. The former report holds that the suspension of bombing is still a precondition.

15-16th The Viet Cong attack the US Navy's River Assault Task Force on the Rachba River in the Mekong Delta.

17th US aircraft carry out bombing raid within seven miles of the Chinese border.

19th Operation Bolling begins in Phu Yen Province involving the 173rd Airborne Brigade and the 1st Air Cavalry Division. There are 715 enemy casualties by the end of the operation.

19th Nationalist Chinese embassy in Saigon is blown up.

21st 1200 Thai troops arrive in Saigon.

27th Operation Shenandoah II is launched by the 1st Infantry Division in Binh Duong Province. There are 956 enemy casualties by the end of the operation.

28th US Navy pilots attack and partially destroy the last remaining bridge out of Haiphong.

Cat and Mouse Games Aboard USS Boston

A silvery, gauze-like haze still shrouded the early morning sun when "The Red Baron" – as the *Boston*'s junior officers call their red-headed skipper, Capt. Leon Smith Jr., behind his back – stepped on to the bridge for the start of a firing mission. The ship was steaming off Cap Falaise, just north of the city of Vinh – a dangerous area because of artillery emplacements on the cape and on an island called Hon Me.

This morning's target – a group of enemy "wiblies" (from the initials WBLC, which stand for waterborne logistics craft) loading supplies from trucks at the mouth of a small river – had been spotted moments earlier by one of the carrier pilots who regularly patrols the coast. On order, the *Boston*'s 8-inch guns began to fire. Thick yellow

Village Vote Mixes Fun and Cynicism

Manquang, South Vietnam. Shortly before 6 a.m., the Mayor of this tiny coastal village awoke with a start.

Quickly he pulled on his clothes, including a new pair of sneakers, gulped a glass of tea and rushed to the village square.

"There was a commotion," said the Mayor, Nguyen Van Tu, a 48-year-old farmer. "They were talking and making noise and crowding in front of the polling booth an hour before it opened."

Like thousands of other villagers in South Vietnam, the voters of Manquang went early to cast their ballots in a national election that has aroused world interest. For the voters – mostly farmers, fishermen and carpenters – the day evoked a curious mixture of excitement and melancholy.

Standing in the morning heat, they opened umbrellas, mopped their brows and waited for the clerks to hand them a brown envelope and 11 pieces of paper, each designating one of the presidential slates.

Then the voters stepped into a burlap-curtained booth and placed one ballot in the envelope. The other ballots – the remaining 10 pieces of paper – were dropped into a cardboard carton on the floor of the booth.

By noon the polls were nearly empty and the village was deserted. Government clerks and poll-watchers yawned and drowsed in their seats, Mayor Tu and two friends, a pig trader and a fisherman, drove to a restaurant in a Government truck and picked up plates of steaming rice and meat for the policemen, poll-watchers and soldiers.

By late afternoon voters began drifting toward the polls again. One woman argued heatedly with a Government clerk who refused to let her vote in place of her dying father.

Several elderly women, bewildered by the numerous paper ballots, were instructed by Mayor Tu, who called each of them "Grandma."

"I have no idea about this election and what I'm voting for," said one of the women with a tight, gnarled smile. "I just want peace."

New York Times

Nguyen Van Thieu casts his vote in the election which will make him President of South Vietnam

smoke burst from the bores, its acrid fumes engulfing the bridge. When all six guns fired together, the ship's whole superstructure trembled with the shock.

Going in Close
A few minutes later the spotter plane reported that salvos from the *Boston* and a nearby destroyer had destroyed five of the barges. At that moment, a second plane reported another concentration of barges in the mouth of a river just south of the *Boston*'s position. Smith snapped out an order to the helm and the 17,000-ton guided-missile cruiser heeled over and headed for the new target. "We've got guns all around us now," Smith said as he peered through binoculars at the ominously quiet coastline.

Then the *Boston*'s own guns opened up once more. "The first salvo lifted a barge right out of the river, captain," the gun boss said, relaying a report from a plane. "The second was short." Smith turned to the navigator. "How much more time have I got before we have to reverse course?" "Five minutes." "Well, hell, let's keep going as long as we can," the captain said. The decision was not a trivial one. The longer the *Boston* stuck to its southerly course, the closer it came to the guns of Hon Me island.

Under Enemy Fire
"The gunner says he has plenty of time and wants a gun adjustment," the gun boss said. The captain exploded. "Dammit, I don't have plenty of time. Tell him to go, fire now." The guns roared. "Go again, before we have to turn," Smith ordered. Three more salvos rang out. Suddenly a plume of geysers shot up in the water off the starboard bow. The *Boston* had come under enemy fire. Smith reacted like a coiled spring. "All ahead flank," the skipper shouted instantly. "Let's get out of here.

Get the suppression fire going."

Within seconds the *Boston*'s giant screws were biting into the water and churning up a great white foam as the ship raced out of range of the North Vietnamese coastal batteries. "We were shot at three times last week," Smith explained when the flat coastline was comfortably behind him. "So far we've been lucky. The only thing we've received is a little shrapnel on our decks." Smith paused, then shook his head and said: "But I keep telling myself, I am not going to get away with this much longer."

Newsweek

Detecting Mines In Vietnam Is Harrowing

At dawn five marines slipped quietly out of the camp and trudged in silence toward a muddy road.

One of them, Cpl. Miles N. Smith, of Richfield, N.C., began waving a two-foot metallic detector like a wand. An eerie whistle split the silence. As Corporal Smith walked, the whistle grew shriller. Finally he stopped and gazed at the ground, frowning.

"It ain't what we're looking for," the lanky 21-year-old marine said, picking up a chunk of metal stuck in the mud. "Let's keep going."

As members of an engineer platoon based three miles south of the demilitarized zone, the marines were engaged in finding mines planted almost nightly by enemy soldiers, probing the mines to see how deeply imbedded they were in the soil and then detonating them.

"These mines don't kill as much as they maim," said one Marine captain. "They take a man's leg or arm and cause some horrible wounds."

"I'm a typical farm boy." Corporal Smith said, sitting in front of his tent after a miles-long search for mines. "I was kind of tired of doing the same thing and I volunteered for this. I was wounded only once. But, you know, that can happen to anyone in wartime."

The men usually work in five-man teams. As soon as a mine is discovered, one man probes with his bayonet to see how far beneath the ground the mine is buried – generally six inches to a foot. Others then detonate the mine.

"You can get it in lots of ways," said Cpl. Roger Carmody, 21, of Rockville, Conn.

"When you're probing you can hit the pressure point too hard on the top of the mine or you can try to detonate it and it won't go off, so you get up, start walking toward the mine and then – Boom."

The New York Times

The VC are masters of improvised weapons. Here, a stolen 155mm artillery shell is used as a mine

Electronic 'Wall' to Span Vietnam

Defense Secretary Robert S. McNamara Thursday ordered a barbed wire and electronic barrier laid across South Vietnam to cut the infiltration of North Vietnamese soldiers and supplies across the Demilitarized Zone.

Experts indicated it would be an early warning system rather than a solid barrier, although barbed wire and other obstacles might make the crossing tougher and possibly slow it down.

OCTOBER 1967

3rd Start of Operation Wallowa in which the 1st Air Cavalry Division goes to the aid of Marines in combat on the DMZ.

4th Concerted air strikes bring the communist bombardment of Con Thien to a close.

5th The North Vietnamese Education Minister accuses the US of bombing a school.

10th A document captured from the Viet Cong indicates that in the event of a coalition with its political arm, the NLF, the latter would be in control.

11th 3rd Marine Division, ARVN and the Marine Special Landing Force begin Operation Medina/Bastion Hill/Lam Son 138.

12th Operation Francis Marion and Operation Greeley come together in Operation MacArthur, the battle for Dak To. Two days late Dean Rusk is charged by Senator William J.Fulbright with carrying on a "McCarthy-type crusade" against those who do not agree with the war.

21st 150,000 take part in an anti-war march in Washington which ends in 686 people, including novelist Norman Mailer, being arrested. In London there is a violent demonstration outside the US embassy.

24-25th The first air strike on the Phuc Yen airfield, 18 miles northwest of Hanoi, is carried out by 65 US aircraft over two days.

29th The NVA and Viet Cong launch heavy attacks in the area of the town of Loc Ninh, north of Saigon. House-to-house fighting ensues and the attackers are beaten off. Enemy casualties are put at 900.

31st The North calls on world governments to exert their influence on the US and bring the bombing to an end.

31st The swearing-in of President Thieu and Vice-President Ky takes place in Saigon.

March on Pentagon

Thousands of youthful anti-war demonstrators, some waving Viet Cong flags, tried to storm the Pentagon Saturday but were thrown back by soldiers and U.S. marshals.

At least one round of tear gas was fired during one melee in the driveway leading to the Pentagon mall.

The violence broke out after demonstrators marched on the U.S. military nerve center following a mass rally at the Lincoln Memorial where Dr. Benjamin Spock, baby specialist, author and outspoken war critic, charged President Johnson is "the enemy."

Stars and Stripes

A gunner disposes of a 105mm shell case during Operation MacArthur, during which the 4th Infantry Division battled for Dak To. MacArthur lasted for 478 days and caused over 5,000 known communist casualties

Attack on Loc Ninh

For four and a half hours under cover of darkness, an estimated battalion of the 273d Viet Cong Regiment supported by a battalion from the 84A North Vietnamese Army Artillery Regiment attacked Camp Loc Ninh with mortar, rocket, heavy machine gun, and small arms fire.

The camp went on full alert at 0115. Forward air controllers, Spooky (C-47 aircraft), light fire teams, and tactical air support were at their stations within fifteen minutes and gave continuous support to Loc Ninh throughout the night until the enemy broke contact at 0520.

After the attack ceased at 0530 on 29 October the Loc Ninh Special Forces Camp immediately began to improve its defensive position. On 31 October at 0050 the camp was again attacked by an estimated two battalions of the 273d Viet Cong Regiment, supported by a battalion from the 84A North Vietnamese Army Artillery

Marines cross a flooded river during the interconnected series of Operations Medina/Bastion Hill/Lam Son 138. Such joint operations would often have names assigned for constituent parts

Regiment. At the first sign of light the enemy withdrew to the north, northeast, and northwest. At 0200 on 1 November 1967 Camp Loc Ninh received approximately ten 82-mm. mortar rounds, believed to have been fired in order to allow the enemy to gather his dead and wounded from the battlefield. Contact with the enemy was light and sporadic until the following day at 0050 when the enemy again massed a battalion for an obvious last-ditch effort to overrun the camp. Once again the attack was repelled by the camp's withering defensive fire and especially well-placed air

strikes. After the final air sortie, the enemy became disorganized and fled. Sporadic contact was maintained until dawn.

The enemy employed no tactical innovations in his attacks on Loc Ninh. An attack usually commenced with heavy mortar bombardments, followed in quick succession by ground assaults that were preceded by squad-size sapper units coming from several directions. A larger attack consisted of several assault waves; during the height of battle Loc Ninh withstood at least three such full-scale ground assaults. Usually, the enemy's last offensive oper-

ation was a ruse for body recovery.

The U.S. Special Forces detachment commander was in the communications bunker at first; after forwarding the required reports to higher headquarters, he took his position on the perimeter and directed the defense of the camp. The executive officer served at the point of greatest impact, assisted in resupplying the perimeter with ammunition, gave first aid, and helped with evacuation of the wounded and dead. The team sergeant was everywhere: he moved from position to position on the perimeter, offering en-

couragement and reassurance to the troops and forwarding necessary reports to the detachment commander. The team medic not only treated the wounded on the defensive perimeter but also in the medical bunker. Weapons men divided their time between the mortar crews and the perimeter. Team members were all periodically active and were exceptionally effective in keeping the camp defenses organized. Individual acts of heroism were too numerous to mention; suffice it to say that every U.S. team member was recommended for an award of valor.

Special Forces History

Thunder From a Distant Hill Action at Con Thien

caked body. "This just must be the worst place in the world."

It is Con Thien, South Vietnam, in the autumn of 1967. The artillery bombardments have left the three red hills of Con Thien a crater-pocked moonscape. Monsoon rains, a month ahead of their normal mid-October arrival, have churned the outpost into a quagmire reminiscent of Ypres in World War I.

The Marines at Con Thien live

on C-rations. Because water is scarce, they shave only every other day and can seldom wash.

They live in crude, sandbagged underground bunkers where often the only light comes from an improvised candle with a rag as a wick. Often the only signs of life are a horde of bold rats and a few cats. "The men think they keep the rats down," grumbled one officer. "I suspect they share the garbage."

Time

Crawling out of his sandbagged bunker, the helmeted Marine blinks in the afternoon light, cocks his head for a moment, listening intently, and then starts jogtrotting down the hill. With frayed trousers flapping and a cumbersome flak jacket jiggling against his bare chest, he makes his way through the debris of cartridge boxes and C-ration cans. Deep, viscous red mud sucks at his boots and oozes up to his knees as he struggles down the slope. Suddenly, from high above, comes a familiar, chilling whine. "Incoming!" someone yells, and the leatherneck flattens himself in the mud. The artillery shell bursts 50 yards from him, gouging out a small crater through the slime. A breeze wafts away the cloud of smoke and detritus, the rifleman listens for a moment and then stands up. "Man!" he exclaims, scraping mud from his

Towards the end of 1967, Con Thien near the DMZ became the scene of bitter fighting between the Marines and the NVA. But even in the hardest battles there is usually time for a smoke

BATTLES AT DAK TO

NOVEMBER 1967

1st 3rd Marine Division instigates Operation Scotland in the Khe Sanh area of Quang Tri Province. There are 1561 enemy casualties by the end of the operation. In the Con Thien area the same formation starts Operation Kentucky, the follow-on from Operation Kingfisher. There are 3921 enemy casualties by the end of this operation.

2nd The US consents to the NLF taking part in talks at the UN.

3-22nd Heavy casualties are sustained by both sides in bloody battles around Dak To in the Central Highlands. 1400 NVA and 300 US troops die.

6th Evidence that the Dak To operation is a diversion to draw US forces to the north of the country is found on a dead NVA soldier.

11th Operation Wheeler/Wallowa is begun by the Americal Division in Quang Nam and Quang Tin Provinces. There are 10,000 enemy casualties by the end of the operation.

11th Three US prisoners, two of them black, are released by the Viet Cong in Cambodia. The Viet Cong state that it is a gesture towards the black struggle in the US and a response to anti-war protests.

13th 7th Marine Regiment and Marine Special Landing Force carry out Operation Foster/Badger Hunt in the Dai Loc and An Hoa areas. There are 125 enemy casualties by the end of the operation and 11,500 evacuees from territory under communist control.

14th Major General Bruno Hochmuth, commander of the 3rd Marine Division, is killed when the helicopter in which he is travelling is shot down. He is the most senior US officer to be killed in action in the war to date.

A Marine Corps 106mm recoilless rifle shells communist positions during the opening stages of Operation Scotland, around the Khe Sanh Combat Base in Quang Tri Province

17th President Johnson declares on television that "We are inflicting greater losses than we're taking . . . We are making progress."

19-24th Prince Sihanouk of Cambodia bars US journalists from entering his country after articles are published in which reporters claim to have been to a Viet Cong camp in Cambodia.

21st General Westmoreland tells US newsmen "I am absolutely certain that whereas in 1965 the enemy was winning, today he is certainly losing."

29th Defense Secretary McNamara resigns to take up the post of president of the World Bank.

30th Democrat Senator Eugene J. McCarthy, an advocate of a negotiated end to the war, declares that he intends to enter several Democratic Presidential primaries in 1968.

Trainer with Teeth
A-37 in Action

The A-37 light attack aircraft is a modified version of the Air Force's T-37 trainer. Not suited for full-scale conventional warfare, the A-37 is nonetheless effective in counter-insurgency action, where its simplicity and low cost means that it can maintain a high rate of use against lightly armed ground opposition

From the fighter-bomber, the suspected Vietcong base camp appeared deserted – a flat, tawny field with scorched patches where artillery shells had fallen.

In the next five minutes, the jet whirled repeatedly toward the target and the bombs fell. The pilot and a passenger

watched with a blend of terror and morbid fascination. As black smoke curled from the target – later found to be eight bunkers – the jet streaked back to the Bienhoa air base, 25 miles northeast of Saigon.

The jet that attacked the camp was one of the dozens of A-37 fighter-bombers that have been used since mid-August in an Air Force test program designed to bring a relatively lightweight, inexpensive training plane into battle. The plane, manufactured by the Cessna Aircraft Company, is a modified version of the T-37, which has been used extensively in the United States to train pilots.

The 12,000-pound plane – with a maximum speed of 478 miles an hour – has a limited mission. Because of its weight, size and power, it can only be used in close air support for ground forces.

While none of the planes have been downed by enemy machine gunners, several have been shot at.

"Usually you never know that you've been hit until you get back to base," Colonel Weber said after stepping off the A-37. "When you realize you've been hit while you're up there, then you're in bad, bad trouble."

New York Times

GIs Take Hill
875
Battle of Dak To

A US Army M60 gunner hunkers down behind a fallen tree, his plentiful supply of ammunition ready for use in the five days of bitter fighting for Hill 875 near Dak To

Battle-weary U.S. paratroopers captured Hill 875 Thursday – Thanksgiving Day – after five days of bitter fighting. The victorious American commander claimed Allied forces had killed at least 2,500 to 3,000 enemy in the 21-day Dak To campaign.

Maj. Gen. William R. Peers, commander of the U.S. forces in the Dak To battle, said the combined toll of North Vietnamese troops killed by U.S. and South Vietnamese forces was 1,250 by actual body count.

"And we probably killed at least 2,500 or 3,000, and maybe far more," Peers added. The U.S. Command in Saigon had given the 1,250 figure earlier Thursday.

Stars and Stripes

Thanksgiving

Most of the half-million American troops in Vietnam enjoyed a traditional Thanksgiving Day turkey feast Thursday. But the band of weary soldiers who captured the summit of Hill 875 mostly gave thanks just to be alive.

The men who took the hill Thursday in the central highlands also had a turkey dinner. It was airlifted in by helicopters and eaten in the abandoned ruins of a North Vietnamese command post.

It was their first hot meal in 12 days.

Stars and Stripes

Release From Reality

Pot is easy to come by in Vietnam. At Danang or Bien Hoa, it is sold ready-rolled into filter cigarettes, disguised in sealed Kent packs. At Cam Lo, just south of the Demilitarized Zone, marines buy the stuff from little girls who live in a nearby refugee camp. And marijuana is cheap in Vietnam.

In Danang, a serviceman can swap a $2 bottle of PX whisky for 5 ounces and bulk purchasing can reduce the cost of "roll-you-own" reefers to as little as 3 cents each.

Potheads all over the world love to argue the merits of their favorite leaf – "Acapulco Gold," "Panama Black," "Mex." In this part of Asia, "Cambodian Red" is probably most popular, although the discerning smoker may lean toward the heavy, resinous product of Vietnam's central highlands. Whatever the preference, there is none of the cautious skimping that exists in other, less well-supplied places – the watchful sharing of a thinly rolled "stick", the careful saving of the "roach", or butt, to be mixed with tobacco in a "sandwich" reefer.

Newsweek

UNCHARITABLE CHRISTMAS

DECEMBER 1967

3rd Battalion, 1st Marines involved in Operation Badger Tooth is ambushed at Tham Khe in Quang Tri Province.

1st A Viet Cong official, Nguyen Van Huan, is arrested apparently on his way to a CIA-arranged meeting with the US ambassador.

4th In a combined action with South Vietnamese troops in the Mekong Delta, 9th Infantry Division's riverine force engages and kills 235 Viet Cong.

4-8th "Stop the Draft Week" protests in US.

7th Vice-President Humphrey suggests that there might be non-communist members in the NLF who would agree to talk to the South Vietnamese.

8th 25th Infantry Division opens Operation Yellowstone in War Zone C (Tay Ninh Province). There are 1254 enemy casualties by the end of the operation.

14th The NLF's projected reforms are greeted in a hostile fashion by the US when they are placed before the UN.

17th Start of Operation Uniontown involving 199th Infantry Brigade in Binh Hoa Province. South Korean Capital Division launches Operation Maeng Ho 9 in the same area. There are 749 enemy casualties as a result of the latter operation.

19th 1st Brigade, 101st Airborne Division carries out search-and-destroy Operation Klamath Falls in Binh Thuan and Lam Dong Provinces. Operation Muscatine begins in Quang Ngai Province involving the Americal Division. There are 1129 enemy casualties by the end of this operation.

20th After being applauded by President Johnson for consenting to talk to members of the NLF, President Thieu asserts his non-recognition of the organization, and that discussions would take place with its members as only individuals, not as representatives.

26th The Vientiane government reports engagements with North Vietnamese troops in Laos.

They call it the Thud: F-105 Strikes North

The pilots call it the Thud ("that's what it must sound like when it crashes," one of them says), and they will be sorry when it is no longer here for them to fly.

The Thud is the F-105 Thunderchief – a single-engine jet bomber, shaped like a stiletto, that has proved to be one of the hardest-working planes of the Vietnam war. But, like the British Spitfire of World War II, it will disappear one day soon, because no more are being built and more are lost each month to enemy ground fire and through accidents.

About 90 of these planes are based in Thailand in two wings whose daily work is bombing North Vietnam: the 388th at Korat and the 355th at Takhli.

About five Thunderchiefs a

Bob Hope is one entertainer who can be relied upon to give lonesome GI's far from home a taste of America at Christmas

Spell "Pizzeria" in Vietnamese

Is "pizzeria" translatable? Can "Big Boy Hamburgers" be turned into Vietnamese? What about the "Golden Hands Massage Parlor?" Or the "Miami Bar"? Or the "Crazy Cow Restaurant?"

In a move that amused many Americans and South Vietnamese, the Saigon city hall has ordered all "foreign" signs in Saigon rewritten into Vietnamese. Americans wondered how the profusion of English signs – "Astor Hotel," for instance, or "Copacabana" – could be trans-lated.

The Vietnamese were dismayed. "No. 10," said one young woman in the Princess Bar on Tu Do, using G.I. slang for simply terrible.

"You kidding me," said a woman in the Butterfly Bar.

"The Vietnamese – especially the authorities – don't want to admit publicly that people are scrambling for the American dollar. They want to feel that we are keeping our sovereignty."

The city hall order also attempts to erase the garish quality of many of the streets in Saigon.

"Restaurants, hotels, bars, snack and steambath houses are not allowed to use colored neon lights on their signboards but only white lights," the announcement said.

In the announcement, the word "American" is never used. All non-Vietnamese are referred to as "foreigners."

New York Times

A New Enemy – Tigers

A military spokesman today disclosed a new hazard for servicemen near the demilitarized zone – tigers.

The spokesman said a tiger seized an unidentified marine by the arm last night a few miles south of the buffer zone – which extends for three miles on either side of the border between North and South Vietnam – and dragged him 400 yards to a creek bed.

With his free hand the marine hit the tiger on the head, the spokesman related, whereupon the tiger released the marine and bounded off into the night.

The spokesman said the marine was evacuated for medical treatment.

New York Times

month are currently being lost to enemy fire and a smaller, undisclosed number to "non-combat causes." At that rate, officers here calculate, most if not all of the Thunderchief squadrons will be gone by the early part of 1969. The Thuds will be replaced by F-4C Phantoms or the new, trouble-plagued F-111's, which are due next spring.

Below 10,000 feet, where many of the bomb runs over the North are made, the jet can manage more than 650 miles an hour, whereas the more advanced Phantom reaches its peak efficiency at high altitudes.

The Thunderchiefs don't always run. Although the Phantoms have the primary responsibility for dog-fighting, Thunderchiefs have shot down, according to a recent count, 25 of the 75 enemy planes destroyed by Air Force planes over the North. Their main air-to-air weapon is a 20-mm. gun on the Gatling, or multibarreled principle, which can, if need be, fire 1,000 armor-piercing cannon shells in 10 seconds.

New York Times

It's big, fast, and it has borne the brunt of the air war over North Vietnam. Called the 'Thud' with backhanded affection by the men who fly it, the F-105 is a Vietnam classic

---

Foe's Use of Trail Growing

Informed military sources reported today that North Vietnam was making greater use of the Ho Chi Minh Trail to send supplies to Communist forces in South Vietnam.

Traffic along the trail has increased to a bit more than normal for this time of year, according to the same sources. Some of Hanoi's troop reinforcements, which once were routed over the trail, are now cutting around the corner of the demilitarized zone between North and South Vietnam, then moving along a series of mountain footpaths into the central provinces of South Vietnam, the sources said.

Meanwhile, trucks are moving down the Ho Chi Minh Trail carrying supplies that, in previous years, went by sea or through Cambodia.

The sources based their reports on air reconnaissance and information from ground forces in Laos.

The trail, a complex of roads and paths, is "practically an all-weather road now," qualified sources said.

10,000 Workers Reported

North Vietnam is reported to have used more than 10,000 coolies in constructing the trail from the Nape and Mujia passes into Laos and to the route's southern point in South Vietnam, west of Dakto.

New York Times

The Profits of War

"Look, I didn't start this war ... I'm just trying to put it on a business-like basis." Thus spoke Lt. Milo Minderbinder, the wheeler-dealer mess officer in Joseph Heller's satirical novel *Catch 22*, and his apologia for his light-fingered ways has a familiar ring to anyone who has ever served in any war.

Despite Saigon's bright lights and easy vice, there really isn't much to do in most of Vietnam, especially at night. To fill in the gap, most rear-echelon units operate clubs for officers, NCOs and the men in the ranks. The club managers administer small fortunes. They import shiploads of slot machines, beer and Mother Goose Potato Snax, and somehow or other mess funds are converted into record players and television sets. Invariably, the clubs make plenty of money; a 20-cent beer returns a dime in profit, and there is virtually no overhead, since maintenance personnel are furnished gratis by the local commander. Under military regulations, however, a club's annual net profit cannot exceed $1, so the managers customarily blow their excess funds on what the GIs want most – a real, live band and real, live girls.

The Midwest Chanteuse

There are about 50 civilian show troupes catering to the 1,000 or

so service clubs in Vietnam and most of them are fairly scruffy. One more or less typical group is headed by a skinny, middle-aged comedian from Texas who readily admits to being a mediocre entertainer. His act includes a breathless 18-year-old chanteuse from the Midwest, a sinuous Israeli go-go dancer and a tinny four-piece Filipino band. The act isn't very good, but, for want of anything better, the GIs eat it up, and the Texan grosses as much as $500 on a single weekend night.

Most of the civilian show troupes are represented by agents, and there is a widespread assumption that club managers often take kick-backs from the agents for booking acts into their clubs. "You book for 500 and slip 100 back to the manager," says the leader of one troupe. "Some of them want to stay honest, but if one plays, everyone has to play. Their records are audited by a govern-

Unlike previous wars, the men who fight in Vietnam usually have a chance to see something vaguely entertaining when they get back to the rear areas after a stint in the boonies

ment agency, so if one club gets a show for $400, someone sooner or later is going to wonder why another club pays $500 for the same show. Each manager knows that if he bucks the system, his friends at the other clubs will go to jail."

The Saigon rumor mill has it that the US command is planning a crackdown on crooked club managers and their agent accomplices in the near future. But petty graft is deeply imbedded in the mystique of war and it is unlikely to prove easier to eliminate in Vietnam than it has been anywhere else. The depressing prospect is that wherever men fight, other men will always be on hand chiseling.

Newsweek

JANUARY 1968

2nd US journalist, Everett Morton, is deported from South Vietnam for criticizing the ARVN.

4th Cambodia reveals military aid from China.

8th 100 South Vietnamese peasants are arrested in Da Nang for protesting US presence. South Vietnamese authorities claim demonstration is the work of the Viet Cong.

9th Seven US troops killed and 25 wounded as Viet Cong attack US airfield in Kontum.

13th It is disclosed that 100 South Vietnamese pilots are to be trained in Louisiana.

13th Severe defeat for Laotian troops at the hands of a joint NVA-Pathet Lao force at Nam Bac.

14th US joint-service Operation Niagara is launched to support the heavily attacked base at Khe Sanh. In excess of 5000 aircraft sorties will be flown before the end of the operation.

17th President Johnson restates that talks must precede a halt to bombing.

19th Start of Operation McLain in the Binh Thuan Province. It will claim 1042 enemy casualties.

War Defoliation Studied in Report

The Pentagon will receive this week a study that is understood to say there have been no long-term changes to the balance of nature from the defoliation program in Vietnam.

The study was carried out by the Midwest Research Institute in Kansas City, Mo., at the request of the Defense Depart-

Heavy
Enemy Flow to South is Doubted

An informed source said today that there were no indications of unusually heavy movements of North Vietnamese troops to South Vietnam.

The source had been asked to comment on Washington reports that officials there were not prepared to accept North Vietnamese peace feelers at face value because of indications of a major build-up of enemy strength in the South in the last month.

The Washington sources put the size of the month's buildup at 30,000 to 40,000 men.

Intelligence estimates here put the monthly infiltration rate at 5,000 to 6,000. No fresh North Vietnamese units have been identified in the South in addition to seven divisions known to be there, the source said.

Movements along the Ho Chi Minh Trail have probably been heavier than usual in recent months, the source said, but the increase is seasonal and has been observed in past years.

It reflects the annual step-up in enemy activity that begins with the coming of the dry season in the south in mid-autumn and continues until the following spring.

New York Times

The start of the Ho-Chi Minh Trail: goods flowing from North Vietnam cross the Mu Gia Pass into Laos on the start of the long journey to the communists in the south. Keeping an eye on movements down the trail gives an indication of potential enemy activity on the battlefield, although the start of 1968 and the 'surprise' Tet offensive will see a major miscalculation by incountry intelligence analysts

ment. In view of expected criticism from the scientific community, it was then submitted to the National Academy of Sciences for comment.

The academy review is virtually complete and Pentagon sources say they hope to have the report and commentary by Friday. The Midwest Research

Ranch Hand C-123s lay down pesticides while an F-4 Phantom flies interference

Institute is said to have identified only a few special cases where substantial damage was done to the ecology, or balance of nature, during the program.

New York Times

Not a Moment Too Soon

In late January, Lieutenant Colonel Harry T. Hagaman, Commanding Officer of Marine Fighter Attack Squadron 323, and his Radar Intercept Officer, Captain Dennis F. Brandon, were leading a flight of F-4B Phantoms against what the TAC(A) described as a "suspected" antiaircraft position. The enemy gunners confirmed their presence during the first pass. As Lieutenant Colonel Hagaman's F-4B, armed with napalm and 250lb Snakeyes, skimmed low over the treetops, the North Vietnamese cut loose and laced the belly of his plane with a stitch of 50 caliber shells. The aircraft shuddered under the impact and burst into flames. Captain Brandon, a backseat veteran with over 300 combat missions, knew instantly when he heard the series of ominous "thuds" that the Phantom had been mortally wounded; he quickly pulled his face curtain and ejected. Lieutenant Colonel Hagaman stayed with the bucking Phantom momentarily in a vain effort to stabilize the aircraft by using his rudders. The delay almost cost the pilot his life because the-4B began to tumble end-over-end barely 100 feet above the ground. Suddenly the world outside became a spinning blur of blue and green. The second time that he saw green – indicating that the aircraft was inverted – Lieutenant Colonel Hagaman started to pull his alternate ejection handle which was located between his knees. In the second that it took the escape mechanism to function, the Phantom flipped upright and the ejection cartridges blasted the pilot from the flaming cockpit. Seconds later, the plane cartwheeled into the ground and exploded. The pilot was so low when he "punched out" that the chute had scarcely deployed when his feet touched the ground. Both crewmen hid in the tall elephant grass within earshot of the North Vietnamese who were searching for them. Within minutes, rescue helicopters lumbered on the scene and, while the downed crew's wingman made dummy passes to discourage the enemy soldiers, the choppers darted in and plucked the shaken, but otherwise uninjured, Marines to safety.

Marine Corps History

302,000 Men Face Draft During '68, A 72,000 Increase

A total of 302,000 men will be drafted into the Army in 1968, an increase of 72,000 over last year, in order to replace servicemen who were drafted during the initial military buildup in Vietnam and are now being discharged, defense officials said today.

But total draft needs this year will still be below those in the buildup year of 1966, when 383,000 men were called, because the Army now has a training base established in order to support its current strength of nearly 1.5 million men.

The Army is the only service which accepts draftees.

Draft calls in 1968 will thus average about 25,200 men a month. The calls fluctuate, however, according to the ability of the training camps to absorb men. The March draft call has been set for 39,000 men, while February is for 23,000. The January call was 34,000.

Total strength of the armed forces is scheduled to reach a plateau at midyear of 3,488,000 men, officials said, because of the planned leveling-off in the number of American troops in South Vietnam.

The current Vietnam troop ceiling of 525,000 men will probably be reached sometime this fall, officials said.

New York Times

20th Battle of Khe Sanh commences. After taking the town of Khe Sanh, the NVA bombards the US base mercilessly, the defenders unable to move. The 5000 US bombs dropped each day during the battle add up to five times the power of the bomb which destroyed Hiroshima. The siege eventually ends on 6 April, but the battle continues until the 14th.

21st Start of Operation Lancaster II.

22nd Operation Jeb Stuart begins. 3268 enemy casualties will result.

23rd US spy ship *Pueblo* captured in Sea of Japan by North Koreans.

24th Australians commence Operation Coburg.

26th Head of the pacification programme resigns because of corruption and lack of support.

29th President Johnson requests $26.3 billion be put aside in the budget for the prosecution of the war.

30th Start of the Tet Offensive. Viet Cong and NVA seize many major towns and cities and a suicide squad takes US embassy in Saigon. Although it is eventually a military success for the US, confidence in the government, reflected in the Saigon price for black-market dollars, is low.

Marines Kill 162 Near Buffer Zone

United States marines killed 162 enemy troops in a fierce six-hour fight near the demilitarized zone yesterday, a United States spokesman said today.

Eight marines of the Fourth Marine Regiment were killed and 39 wounded in the fight two miles northeast of Conthien, he said.

Military officers here have expressed concern recently that enemy forces were being built up in that area and in nearby Laos for a major offensive. Yesterday's battle broke out in the morning when a company of the Fourth Regiment making a routine sweep bumped into an enemy force, said to have been North Vietnamese, a mile and a half south of the demilitarized zone, at the border between North Vietnam and South Vietnam.

While a fight raged, a second company of marines nearby joined the battle with what was estimated as a reinforced enemy company of about 150 men.

New York Times

Ships in the Sky

There is no doubt that the quick reaction of the armed helicopters saved Tan Son Nhut and Bien Hoa from serious danger of being overrun. In the first few hours they were the only airborne firepower since the Air Force aircraft could not get clearance to even take off. An Air Force sergeant describing the action on a tape recorder at Tan Son Nhut kept repeating over and over, "Oh, those beautiful Huey gunships!" One of the men in those gunships, Captain Chad C. Payne, a fire team leader, said, "I received fire everywhere I turned. My ships received seven hits, but this was nothing considering the amount of ground fire directed toward us. There were hundreds of Viet Cong bodies everywhere in the vicinity of the Tan Son Nhut perimeter. I've never seen anything like it."

"Those Beautiful Gunships . . ."

Another tribute to the effectiveness of the gunships came from a member of Advisory Team 100 at Tan Son Nhut. When he received word that Tan Son Nhut was under attack, he assembled a patrol of 30 men. "And we ran head-on into one of the attack forces. There were approximately 350 men against my 30. We were certainly outnumbered," he said. "Then those beautiful gunships came in and started circling the area. I threw up a pocket flare to mark the position, and the gunship radioed that we were too close to the enemy force and to pull back some, if possible. We pulled back and then he went in. He was

Army troops move towards the Cambodian border in an attempt to interdict NVA troops and supplies flowing south during Tet

Marines move out into the DMZ after the fierce fight between the 4th Marine Regiment and North Vietnamese regulars northeast of Con Thien

ARVN:
Toward Fighting Trim

The U.S. had a Christmas gift for each of the men in South Viet Nam's 1st Regiment of the 1st Division, based just south of the Demilitarized Zone. It was the lightweight, fast-firing M-16 rifle, which packs far more punch than the older and heavier weapons that the ARVN (for Army of the Republic of Viet Nam) troopers had been carrying. The 1st Regiment soon had a chance to use them. During the Christmas truce, its scouts spotted a large North Vietnamese force moving into the Quang Tri coastal flats. As soon as the truce had ended, the ARVN moved to the attack, boxing the Communists into a four-sided trap with the help of a U.S. Marine blocking force. In a fierce day-long battle, the ARVN soldiers, using their new M-16s, killed at least 100 of the North Vietnamese *v.* only 15 ARVN dead, while allied air, artillery and helicopters killed another 100. A day later, another ARVN battalion flushed a Viet Cong unit in Quang Ngai province to the south and killed 40.

For the ARVN, such victories are quite a change. It was not so many months ago that General William Westmoreland felt obliged to pass the word down the U.S. chain of command: if you can't say something good about the ARVN, don't say anything at all. The resulting silence was almost as damaging to the ARVN as the heavy shellfire of criticism it replaced. Of late, however, the ARVN has been doing some pretty effective firing of its own on the battlefield. Its performance has enabled U.S. officers to talk about the ARVN again, this time in terms of results and performances from the DMZ to the Delta, including victories in 37 of the ARVN's last 45 major contacts with the Communists.

Time

ARVN troops in Saigon. The South Vietnamese could fight quite effectively when well led

right on target, placing rockets right in the middle of Charlie's position. We killed over 200 enemy, and I'd estimate that 80-85 percent was attributable to the helicopters. The morning of the 31st, if I had met that pilot, I'd have kissed him."

Another area of heavy activity was at the US Embassy in downtown Saigon. Chief Warrant Officer Richard Inskeep of the 191st Assault Helicopter Company was the first to land a chopper on the embassy during the heavy fight, bringing ammunition and evacuating one wounded man. "We were receiving fire from all sides," said Mr Inskeep. "But we couldn't see anybody around so we lifted off. My gunner then spotted someone in a hole of the roof, so we made a tight turn and came back on to the pad. The fire was so intense that the gunner and crew chief had to pull the ammunition out of the ship and crawl across the roof as they pushed it in front of them. They pushed the ammunition down the hole and helped bring the wounded man back across the roof to the ship."

Watching from below was Mr George Jacobson, Mission Coordinator of the US Embassy. Commenting on the helicopter's approach, Mr Jacobson said, "He came in low and I thought for a minute he was going to hit the building, but at the last minute he pulled up and made a beautiful landing on the roof. Afterwards I realized that he did it on purpose to avoid the enemy fire. It was a tremendous piece of airmanship." Mr Jacobson, a retired Army colonel, was to finish off the last guerrilla inside the embassy. As troopers of the 101st were landed on the Embassy's helipad, the enemy guerrilla tried to escape the troopers, spotted Mr Jacobson, and fired three shots. He missed and Jacobson shot him with a .45 that had quickly been tossed up to his second floor window by troops below. This was the finale to the six and one-half hour battle within the embassy.

Larger in Life

She was about to perform on an outdoor stage that seemed to be surrounded by the Vietnamese hills of Danang. "I looked at this big green mountain," Raquel Welch said afterward, "and suddenly it began to move. That's when I realized the mountain was all men." In case the well-stacked superstarlet had any lingering doubts, the whistles and shouts from more than 10,000 GIs probably convinced her. One Marine company had bivouacked in front of the stage for two days to be sure of a ringside view of Raquel and other beauties appearing with Bob Hope on his seventeenth Christmas visit to US troops – and his fourth straight year in South Vietnam. "It's just great to be here with the boys," beamed Raquel in response to the war whoops that greeted her mini-clad 37-22½-35½ figure. "They might have been boys before you came out here, Raquel," cracked Hope, "but now they're men."

Newsweek

Hanoi Says It Shot Down 1,063 U.S. Planes in 1967

Assault on a City

North Vietnam reported today that it shot down 1,063 American planes in 1967.

The North Vietnamese press agency also said that the number of United States pilots seized in North Vietnam last year was "higher than in 1965 and 1966." It did not say how many were captured.

In another dispatch, the agency said that "nearly 365,000 enemy troops," including 170,000 American and allied troops, were killed in South Vietnam last year.

The enemy figures for United States deaths and plane losses in 1967 exceed American figures for the whole war. As of Dec. 23, the official United States total of

American dead since 1961 was 15,812, with 99,305 listed as wounded.

The United States said 767 planes were lost over the North by that date.

New York Times

A 57-mm AA battery, part of Hanoi's anti-air ring of steel around the Northern capital

Into Saigon, in the days just before Tet, slipped more than 3,000 Communist soldiers armed with weapons ranging up to machine-gun and bazooka size. Some came openly into the open city, weapons concealed in luggage or under baskets of food, riding buses, taxis and motor scooters, or walking. Others came furtively; some of the Viet Cong who attacked the US embassy had ridden into town concealed in a truckload of flowers. Once in town, they hid their weapons. Only after the attack did Vietnamese intelligence realize that the unusual number of funerals the previous week was no accident: the Viet Cong had buried their weapons in the funeral coffins, dug them up on the night of the assault.

Firecrackers or Smallarms?
They even test-fired their guns during the peak of the Tet celebrations, the sound of shots mingling with that of the firecrackers going off . . . An enemy force of at least 700 men tackled the city's most vital military target: Tan Son Nhut airstrip and its adjoining MACV compound, housing Westmoreland's headquarters and the 7th Air Force Command Center, the nerve centers of US command in the war. The Communists breached the immediate base perimeter, slipping past some 150 outposts without a shot being fired, and got within 1,000 feet of the runways before they were halted in eight hours of bloody hand-to-hand combat. All told, the Communists attacked from 18 different points around Tan Son Nhut, getting close enough to MACV to put bullets through Westy's windows. Westmoreland's staff officers were issued weapons and sent out to help sandbag the compound, and Westmoreland moved into his windowless command room in the center of MACV's first floor.

Other Communist units raced through the city shooting at US

Vietcong
Attack Two U.S. Outposts

The Vietcong attacked two United States headquarters last night and this morning with rockets and mortars.

A United States spokesman said the headquarters for the II Corps at Pleiku and the surrounding area, including the new Pleiku airfield, were attacked early this morning in a 50-minute rocket barrage.

The base camp of the United States 25th Infantry Division at Cuchi, 21 miles northwest of Saigon, was struck with 50 rounds of mortar fire earlier.

The spokesman said 14 Americans had been wounded in the Pleiku attack and 45 in the battle at Cuchi. Thirteen of them were hurt seriously enough to require hospitalization. Damage at both posts was described as light.

New York Times

Above: Air Force Security Police move out to the perimeter of Tan Son Nhut after Saigon's airport comes under Viet Cong attack

US Army photographers watch a base chapel burn after a Viet Cong rocket attack

officers' and enlisted men's billets, Ambassador Ellsworth Bunker's home, Westmoreland's home, the radio and TV stations. Wearing ARVN clothes, raiders seized part of the Vietnamese Joint General Staff Headquarters, and turned the defenders' machine guns against helicopters diving in to dislodge them.

Time

FEBRUARY 1968

1st Television cameras record the execution of a Viet Cong captive by Saigon's police chief.

3rd Kontum falls to the NVA.

4th Operation Tran Hung Dao commences around Saigon.

7th NVA troops using Soviet-built light tanks take US camp at Lang Vei, killing 300 including eight US personnel.

11th Saigon government is to mobilize a further 65,000 men in the light of the Tet Offensive.

13th Fear of a second offensive leads to authorization of US reinforcements.

16th US sends the AC-130 gunship to Vietnam.

16th Hanoi releases three POWs.

16th It is disclosed that the Tet Offensive has created 350,000 more refugees.

20th Senate hearings discuss what went on between Congress and the White House at the time of the Tonkin Gulf resolution.

21st Total US troop commitment is now 495,000.

23rd Argument rages between US command and South Vietnamese over the true aim of the Tet Offensive.

24th Imperial Palace in Hue is recaptured by ARVN troops.

26th Opening of Operation Houston in the Thua Thien and Quang Nam areas. 702 enemy casualties are reported by the end of the operation.

28th 206,756 more men are asked for by General Westmoreland, which would bring the total committed to 731,756.

29th Start of Operation Napoleon/Saline on the Cua Viet River. There are 3495 enemy casualties reported by the end of the operation.

Special Warplane Sent to Vietnam

The United States is rushing a specially modified plane to Vietnam to bolster the defenses around Khesanh.

The heavily armed craft can fly over enemy lines for hours and is equipped with sensing devices to locate the enemy despite darkness, fog, heavy clouds or jungle cover.

The plane, the AC-130, is a modified version of a four-engine military cargo craft. Eight automatic weapons, when fired simultaneously from their mountings on one side of the plane, can turn out 48,000 rounds a minute.

In the expected battle at Khesanh, in which American strategists are counting on superior firepower to defeat massed enemy manpower, the addition of even a single new item such as the AC-130 could make a difference, military men contend.

Only One at Present

The AC-130 is the only one of its kind at present although an unspecified number of additional transports are being modified in Greenville, Tex., with the necessary armor, sensors and machine guns.

The plane was quietly tested for three months in Vietnam late last year. It had only recently returned to Wright-Patterson Air Force Base at Dayton, Ohio, for further evaluation when it was ordered to return to Vietnam, sources here say.

"People out there [in Vietnam] say it's the only weapon system they know that's more accurate in bad weather than in clear skies," according to Gen. Bruce K. Holloway, Vice Chief of Staff of the Air Force. "Furthermore its firepower really is pretty awesome."

The plane is mounted with four 7.62-mm. guns and four 20£mm. cannons each capable of firing 6,000 rounds in 60 seconds. By comparison, an armed version of the C-47 transport of World War II vintage, which has been employed widely in Vietnam, carries only three 7.62-mm. guns.

Unaffected by Weather

And while the AC-47, nicknamed "Puff the Magic Dragon" by soldiers in Vietnam, requires visual sighting, the AC-130 is said to be able to direct fire accurately under the worst weather conditions.

New York Times

The AC-130 is a potent new weapon being deployed to support the beleaguered outpost at Khe Sanh

Frantic Battle Saves U.S. Embassy

For the handful of Americans inside the glossy white U.S. Embassy, the fight that began at 2.54 a.m. Wednesday was one of survival.

The 19 Viet Cong commandos who blasted their way through the embassy's ornate concrete wall with explosive charges made it clear early that they intended to stay until they were killed, and to take as many Americans with them as they could.

For the young soldiers of the 716th Military Police Bn., crawling along the exposed gutters and sidewalks toward the besieged embassy, the mission was to clean out the enemy before he could get inside the building.

The Viet Cong planned the embassy attack well.

They dressed some of their commandos in the black pajamas of the Vietnamese peasant, others in the white shirts of the Saigon white collar worker. All carried perfectly forged curfew passes.

When the attack began, those in white shirts fastened the top button as a mark of identification. Those in peasant garb pulled red armbands up their sleeves.

At the designated time, enemy mortars and rockets began crashing down on the capital.

The Communist commandos sprinted down the wide tree-lined boulevard, dodging from trunk to trunk. The Vietnamese guards outside the embassy were crouched down to avoid the incoming shells. The Viet Cong laid the charge in an instant. The loud explosion blew in the northern corner of the embassy outer wall and they were inside.

Stars and Stripes

A dead Viet Cong and a hole in the wall are relics of the communist attack on the US Embassy in Saigon

Co-ordinated Attack on S. Viet Cities

Enemy mortar and rocket crews lashed out at 37 cities including Saigon this morning in concerted bombardment.

Shells struck the central part of the capital, within two blocks of the United States Embassy, wounded 39 United States servicemen at Tan Sonn Hut Airfield on the city's outskirts, and fell on the headquarters of the national police.

But unlike the shelling that preceded the recent Lunar New Year offensive, the bombardment was not accompanied by heavy ground attacks. Thus it fell short of constituting the "second wave" that had been feared by many Americans and South Vietnamese.

Co-ordination Unusual

Enemy infantrymen struck in force at only two cities – both in the Central Highlands – and threatened Cailay, 45 miles southwest of Saigon in the Mekong Delta.

New York Times

The Fight for Life

The captain saw one of his men come face to face with a North Vietnamese in the inky darkness; the young American all but decapitated his adversary with a crushing, round-house right to the face, then leaped on the flattened soldier and finished the job with a knife. Another man was jumped from behind by a North Vietnamese who grabbed him around the neck and was just about to slit his throat when one of the Marine's buddies jabbed the muzzle of his M-16 between the two combatants. With his selector on full automatic, he fired off a full magazine; the burst tore huge chunks from the back of the embattled Marine's flak jacket but it also cut the North Vietnamese in half.

Two New Copters Going Into Action

The long, thin helicopter shaped like a jet fighter swooped over a nearby hill, then dived at the "enemy" bunker.

High overhead, an oval-shaped reconnaissance helicopter circled. It had called in the attack ship and had marked the target with a smoke rocket.

The "enemy" bunker on the edge of the United States Army's Longbinh post was only simulated today, as a number of high-ranking military officers watched a special demonstration of the two newest helicopters being put into combat in South Vietnam.

The new attack helicopter, the AH-1G Huey Cobra, looks more like a sleek fighter plane than a helicopter. Just 36 inches wide – 40 per cent of the conventional armed helicopter's frontal width – it seats two pilots in airplane-type cockpits.

Man in Rear is Pilot

The man in the rear flies the helicopter and fires the rockets and Gatling-type six-barreled machine guns fixed on stubby wings on each side. The forward man fires a six-barreled minigun in a movable chin turret under the nose.

"This is what we call a professional gunship," said Col. J. Elmore Swenson of Columbus, Ga. "It can dive at a 60-degree angle while the old Huey dived at 15 degrees. And it can cruise at 160 miles an hour, compared to 90 for the old models.

"The gunships frequently must escort the troop carriers, which are also Hueys. The old Huey, once it fell behind, could never catch up. This new Cobra can fly rings around the carriers. That's the prime reason for the Cobra."

Copter is Faster

Compared with the 54-foot Huey Cobra, the 27-foot OH-6A light observation helicopter looks like a toy. But it can fly faster than present observation helicopters and carries a minigun on the left side.

Both helicopters arrived in Vietnam early in the year in small numbers.

New York Times

Reds
Open Up on Khe Sanh

Communist forces pushed their seven-day offensive Monday with heavy artillery and ground attacks on the U.S. Marine bastion at Khe Sanh. U.S. headquarters disclosed it had moved 3,500 crack Army paratroopers to the critical northern sector "to be prepared for any contingency."

Some of the 3,500 paratroopers, a brigade from the U.S. 101st Airborne Div., are currently on an operation against Communist forces in the northern sector.

The new fighting at Khe Sanh came as the week-long Communist offensive on South Vietnamese cities continued in many areas, including Saigon and the old imperial capital of Hue far to the north.

The ground attack at Khe Sanh by an estimated 200 to 300 North Vietnamese troops armed with Bangalore torpedoes, explosive charges and bazooka-

type rockets was directed at a company of Marines defending Hill 861A.

The hill is a bald patch of scarred earth that dominates the combat base's northwestern approaches 3 miles away.
Stars and Stripes

Khe Sanh was a dangerous place. US artillery on the Combat Base worked day and night replying to the communist fire which made the airstrip a perilous location (below)

Airmobile Division
Short of Copters and Supplies

When the United States First Cavalry Division (Airmobile) was ordered into the northern part of South Vietnam last month, there was widespread speculation that its troops would reinforce the Marine base at Khesanh if it was attacked.

But today there is growing evidence that the division is not prepared for such an assignment.

Maj. Gen, John J. Tolson has said he believes his division could serve as a reaction force "anywhere up here."

But he also said: "I hope for

the time being we don't have to go to Khesanh."

Supply Level at Minimum
Major elements of the division have been committed in the vicinity of Hue and Quangtri, the capitals of the northernmost provinces of Quantri and Thuathien. Also, the division is faced with a shortage of supplies and a reduction on the number of helicopters available for combat missions.

While minimum supply levels have been regained, adequate reserves for sustained heavy fighting appear to be lacking.

At the weekend, only about half of the division's 425 helicopters were in flying condition and several of them were still in the division's old operating area, 125 miles to the south.
New York Times

Foe Hurled Back from Key Village

An enemy force of more than 300 seized a village within easy mortar range of Tan Son Nhut air base and Gen. William C. Westmoreland's headquarters yesterday and held it for eight hours before being driven back.

Striking at midmorning, the Vietcong troops quickly overran the police station and the market place in the village of Tanthoi. United States armored vehicles and South Vietnamese troops rushed to the village and fought the enemy with machine guns and mobile cannons.

It was the key battle in a day of renewed fighting on the out-

skirts of Saigon. At another point, eight miles northwest of the city, an enemy force opened fire on a United States patrol column.

Six Americans Killed
At least six United States infantrymen were killed and 29 wounded in the clashes. Enemy casualties were undetermined.

The attacks came as the Hanoi radio asserted that offensives against South Vietnamese centers had diverted allied attention from the rural areas and given Vietcong and North Vietnamese forces "masterly over extremely large areas of the countryside."

Although a spokesman for the United States Mission said that the Hanoi radio had greatly overstated the situation, several officials in the pacification program said it was true that many allied military units had been sent into the cities as a result of the recent offensives.
New York Times

Flagpole Raising and Knicker Waving

"Attention to Colors." The order having been given, Captain William H. Dabney, a product of the Virginia Military Institute, snapped to attention, faced the jerry-rigged flagpole and saluted, as did every other man in Company 1, 3rd Battalion, 26th Marines.

The parade ground was a battle-scarred hilltop to the west of Khe Sanh and the men in the formation stood half submerged in trenches or foxholes. Instead of crisply starched utilities, razor sharp creases, and gleam-ing brass, these Marines sported scraggly beards, ragged trousers, and rotted helmet liner straps. The only man in the company who could play a bugle, Second Lieutenant Owen S. Matthews, lifted the pock-marked instrument to his lips and spat out a choppy version of "To the Colors" while two enlisted men raced to the RC-292 radio antenna which served as the flagpole and gingerly attached the Stars and Stripes. As the mast, with its shredded banner, came upright, the Marines could hear the ominous "thunk, thunk, thunk," to the southwest of their position which meant that North Vietnamese 120mm mortar rounds had left their tubes.

When Lieutenant Matthews sharply cut off the last note of his piece, Company 1 disappeared; men dropped into trenches, dived headlong into foxholes, or scrambled into bunkers. The area which moments before had been bristling with humanity was suddenly a ghost town. Seconds later explosions walked across the hilltop, spewing black smoke, dirt and debris into the air. Rocks, splinters and spent shell fragments rained on the flattened Marines but, as usual, no-one was hurt. As quickly as the attack came, it was over. While the smoke lazily drifted away, a much smaller banner rose from the Marines' positions. A pole adorned with a pair of red, silk panties – Maggie's Drawers – was waved back and forth above one trenchline to inform the enemy that he had missed again. A few men stood up and jeered or cursed at the distant gunners; others simply saluted with an appropriately obscene gesture.

The War Around the Corner

Like the South Vietnamese and the American command, Saigon's 450-man press corps suspected the Viet Cong would mount an attack on the capital city. Photographer David Douglas Duncan, who has covered wars for 25 years, was about to take a flight to Danang when he jumped off and decided to stay in Saigon instead. Still, no one was prepared for the force and the fury of the Viet Cong onslaught that ripped Saigon and other South Vietnamese cities last week. "We thought they had a capability the US hadn't counted on, but we never dreamed we were so right."

Reporters scrambled into the streets in the predawn darkness to follow the troops to the action and like the troops they hid behind walls and trees to escape sniper fire. Associated Press photographer Horst Faas was awakened at 3 am and rushed to Independence Palace, which was under rocket attack. AP newsmen Peter Arnett, John Nance and John Holloway were pinned down by gunfire and had to dive under parked cars as they shot pictures of Vietnam police and American MPs closing in on the palace. NBC's Howard Tuckner dashed through the gate of the US Embassy with the first squad of MPs who were fighting to recapture it from the Viet Cong. It was still too dark to film, but he 'talked' the story on to tape.

Hitching into Hue
UPI's Robert Kaylor was the only newsman in Nha Trang when Viet Cong assaulted the town; he phoned out exclusive reports for days. CBS cameraman John Schneider was in Danang when the Viet Cong overran most of Hue. No one was able to get into the besieged city and so Schneider hitched a ride with a forward air controller on his way to direct air strikes. Since the Viet Cong held the Hue airfield, the plane had to land at Phu Bai, also under attack. Hitchhiking and walking, Schneider reached Hue in time to shoot 900 feet of exclusive film showing ARVN troops starting their counterattack.

Narrow escapes were commonplace as ARVN soldiers – and American MPs – often fired off a round to halt anyone mov-ing down a street. The police also made gunpoint searches of cars, including those of newsmen. UPI's Kate Webb rushed to the American Embassy. "Suddenly the wall I had my back to seemed to be the wall of an executioner's yard," she reported. "My military clothes stood out green against the whiteness."

Some reporters were wounded at the opening of the siege, although none was killed. UPI photographer William Hall was shot five times when he ran into a Vietnamese Army checkpoint outside of Saigon. Jean-Yves Gautron, a French free-lance photographer on assignment for the AP, was shot when he bent over to help a wounded soldier; Nguyen Thanh Long, a Vietnamese sound technician for ABC, was wounded in the groin; CBS correspondent Igor Oganesoff was wounded while covering the Marine defense of Khe Sanh; CBS cameraman Alex Brauer was struck in the stomach by a fragment of a machine-gun bullet outside Danang.

AP photographer Eddie Adams and NBC cameraman Vo Suu shot perhaps the most shocking film sequence since Jack Ruby murdered Lee Harvey Oswald before millions of television viewers: the execution of a captured Viet Cong officer by Brig. Gen Nguyen Ngoc Loan, chief of the national police. "Loan gave no indication that he was going to shoot the man until he did it. I was about 5 feet away when it happened. As Loan's hand holding the revolver came up, so did my camera – but I didn't expect what was going to happen. I just shot by instinct."

"How long," asked New York Times columnist James Reston, "can this unspeakable slaughter go on?"

Newsweek

Vietnamese Rangers patrol through Saigon's Cholon racecourse while hunting for nearby Viet Cong

Marine Corps M48 tanks rumble through the outskirts of Hue, the old imperial capital of Vietnam

Foe Still Clings to Hue Positions

Enemy forces withstood the third successive day of heavy bombing and a thick fog of tear gas yesterday to continue their tight hold on large sections of the walls of Hue's historic Citadel.

United States Marines took advantage of the bombardment to bring another block and a half of territory under the control near the Citadel, which was built as the capital of the Annamese empire in the 19th century. But at nightfall they were still two blocks from a major enemy strongpoint at the southeastern corner of the wall.

Foe's Tanks Sighted
This morning, marines near the demilitarized zone reported that enemy tanks had been sighted near Conthien, a fortress that the North Vietnamese shelled repeatedly last fall.

This was the third time tanks had been sighted near the border of North Vietnam. "Marine tank and artillery crews fired at long range on the enemy tanks," the United States military command said. "The North Vietnamese tanks did not return the fire and immediately disappeared."

New York Times

Johnson Denies
Atom Use is Considered

President Johnson said today that no recommendation had been made to him for the possible use of nuclear weapons in the Vietnam war and indicated that no such step was being considered by the Administration.

In emphatic, almost emotional terms, the President sought at a White House news conference to end the growing speculation in Congressional circles that nuclear weapons were being considered in Vietnam, particularly for the defense of the Marine outpost at Khesanh.

Such speculation, he said, is "against the national interest" and has no foundation in fact.

"It is reasonably apparent and known to all that it is very much against the national interest to carry on discussions about the deployment of nuclear weapons," he said.

Strongest Denial Yet
"So far as I am aware, they [the Secretaries of State and the Joint Chiefs of Staff] have at no time even considered or made a recommendation in any respect to the employment of nuclear weapons.

"They are on our planes on training missions from time to time."

The President's statements represented the strongest denial yet on the matter.

New York Times

Above: A Marine corps rifleman with a buddy acting as spotter returns NVA sniper fire at the Khe Sanh Combat Base

Below: 82nd Airborne troopers move out towards Hue, having been sent as emergency reinforcements to Vietnam

The Man Who Planned the Offensive

It is one of those little ironies of fate that General Vo Nguyen Giap's name contains the Vietnamese words for force (Vo) and armor (Giap). The commander of North Vietnam's armed forces and the overlord of the Viet Cong, he is a dangerous and wily foe who has become something of a legend in both Vietnams for his stunning defeat of the French at Dienbienphu. He is one of the principal developers – along with Mao Tse-tung and Cuba's late Che Guevara – of the art of guerrilla warfare, a tactician of such talents that US military experts have compared him with German Field Marshal Erwin Rommel. "You know when he's in charge," said a top Pentagon official last week. "You can feel him there." Yet Giap had no formal training as a soldier. "The only military academy I have been to," he boasted after Dienbienphu, "is that of the bush."

Time

Central Highland Pacification Program Set Back

The impact of the Vietcong attack is perhaps best manifested by what occurred in the villages and hamlets around Quinhon, in the Central Highlands province. American officials in this strategically important region now maintain that a major aim of the Vietcong attack was upheaval in hamlets that had been considered sympathetic to the Government or pacified.

"What the Vietcong did was occupy the hamlets we pacified just for the purpose of having the allies move in and bomb them out," one American official said. "By their presence, the hamlets were destroyed."

"We'll overcome the physical damage, no problem about that, but the psychological effect on the people is something else," added the official, who is close to the pacification effort. "It's all pretty nebulous at this point."

Because the Vietcong moved into hamlets considered pacified or under Government control, the entire 1968 program for the province has now been shelved.

"We were going to expand our whole plan," another official commented. "Now we're going right back to where we were and, in some cases, going back to the hamlets in the 1966 plan. The program is now set back anywhere from 14 to 18 months."

Six
Hours of Viet Cong Terror

It was late on the first night of Tet, the Vietnamese lunar new year, and most of Saigon's three million inhabitants were fast asleep, groggy after a day of feasting on squid and sugar cane and endless bottles of La Rue beer. Along broad, brightly lit Thong Nhut Boulevard, a slender man named Nguyen Van Muoi slowly guided his black Citroen sedan past a gleaming white building. In the back seat of the car, Muoi carried an elaborately carved samurai sword as a good luck charm. Shortly before 3 a.m., as he approached the building once again, Muoi glanced at his watch and then shouted out of the car window. "Tien!" (forward) he yelled, "Tien!" And with that signal, 19 young Communist commandos – all members of the Viet Cong's elite C-10 Sapper Battalion – bounded from their hiding places in the shadows of trees and dashed down the street toward the Embassy of the United States of America.

Into the Compound
Two US Military Policemen standing guard by a side gate were killed in the first moments of the attack. Simultaneously, some of the raiders blew a gaping hole through the embassy's reinforced-concrete outer wall with a 3.5-inch bazooka and clambered through it.

Once inside the landscaped embassy garden, the lead commandos blew the lock off the side gate on Mac Dinh Chi Street and let their comrades in. Then, the full complement of heavily armed men fanned out through the 4-acre compound. Within seconds, each man was crouching at the precise position that he had been taught to take during long and arduous months of secret training for the attack.

Inside the main chancellery building, six American civilians – trapped in the communications and code rooms on the fourth floor – reported by telephone that the embassy was under siege. Soon after that, the phone lines were cut. Downstairs, two Marine guards ran across the floodlit marble floor of the lobby toward the solid teakwood doors at the front entrance. "Explosions, bangs and thumps crashed all around me," recalled 20-year-old Sgt. Ronald W. Harper of Cambridge, Minn., the senior Marine guard. "I figured the Viet Cong were coming in. I slammed the embassy doors shut and as I did so a rocket hit the window and the side of the door. It wounded my buddy in the arms, face and legs and threw me to the ground."

Death in a Jeep
Not quite 20 minutes after the attack began, a "reaction force" of six Marines from the 716th Police Battalion arrived outside the embassy – only to be pinned down in the gutters by enemy fire. Two more MPs, careering around a corner in a jeep, drove directly into the blistering crossfire and were killed.

With first light, Army Maj. Hillel Schwartz, 39, received orders over his field radio to lead his first helicopter assault of the war – against his own embassy. Twice, the Huey helicopters carrying Schwartz and two platoons of "Screaming Eagle" paratroopers from the 101st Air-

A swathe of destruction through residential areas of Saigon is mute evidence of VC occupation

borne Division fluttered within yards of the embassy's rooftop landing pad – and twice they were driven away by a fusillade of heavy fire directed by the Viet Cong from their entrenched positions.

The Grenade Didn't Go Off
Finally, at a few minutes past seven, the small force of MPs in front of the embassy charged directly into the enemy's line of fire. Leading the way through the exploding grenades and whistling machine-gun bullets was a young Marine private first class from Holbrook, Mass., named Paul Healey. "It was just getting light," Healey said later. "Lieutenant Case, my platoon commander, shot the lock off the front gate. It took six rounds. I ran up to the front door of the building and I could see the Marine guard moving around inside. I heard a movement to my left and turned and a Viet Cong threw a grenade at me. I killed him – and I thought I was dead too. But the grenade never went off, so I shot two more who were behind him."

Newsweek's John Donnelly reported:

"By the time I reached the embassy compound, dead Viet Cong were sprawled on the manicured lawn and in the gravel by the flowerpots, their blood slowly seeping into the earth.

They had all been equipped with brand-new AK-47 submachine guns and were carrying at least three B-40 rocket launchers. Some of the terrorists had web gear with ammo pouches and pockets of food and medicine – an almost certain sign that they were members of a main-force Viet Cong unit.

"The Military Police had a Viet Cong trapped in a two-storey white stucco villa at the rear of the compound which served as the residence of the mission co-ordinator, retired Col. George Jacobson. Crouched behind the ornamental flower-pots on the compound lawn, the MPS fired at the lower windows of the house. It was impossible to see exactly where the Viet Cong was hiding out, but now and then he would return a few rounds and everyone would hit the deck. Finally, an embassy security officer tossed a pistol and several tear-gas grenades up to Jacobson on the second floor. The gas drove the Viet Cong up the staircase where he saw Jacobson and got off three shots that missed. Jacobson then took aim with his .45 caliber automatic and killed him."

Newsweek

Tonkin Incident Provoked by Navy?

The Senate Foreign Relations Committee said Thursday it has a secret U.S. Navy message supporting Sen. Wayne Morse's contention that the American destroyers involved in the 1964 Gulf of Tonkin incident provoked and enemy attack.

Morse told the Senate Wednesday that the destroyer Maddox was "a spy ship" that incited a North Vietnamese attack on it and a sister destroyer, the Turner Joy, Aug. 4, 1964. He disputed Defense Secretary Robert S. McNamara's statement that the ships were on a routine, non-hostile patrol.

A spokesman for the committee said its staff report includes a classified Navy cable suggesting that the destroyers were trying electronically to lure Communist naval vessels away from a South Vietnamese bombardment mission in the gulf.

Stars and Stripes

5,000 Reds Die in Raids

Nearly 5,000 Communists have been killed in 54 hours of savage fighting that has swept across South Vietnam, the U.S. Military Command said Thursday.

The soaring casualty toll was announced as sharp firefights erupted again Thursday in outlying sections of Saigon and heavy action was reported in other areas of the country.

Command spokesmen said 4,959 enemy were killed in action during the period from 6 p.m. Monday to midnight Wednesday. Another 1,862 persons were seized as Viet Cong suspects.

U.S. casualties for the period were listed at 232 killed and 929 wounded. South Vietnamese government casualties were 300 killed and 747 wounded, spokesmen said. *Stars and Stripes*

Made in China!

One Marine had an extremely close call during the fight but lived to tell about it. On the northern side of the perimeter, Private First Class Michael A. Barry of the 1st Squad was engaged in a furious hand grenade duel with the NVA soldiers when a ChiCom grenade hit him on top of the helmet and landed at the young Marine's feet. Pfc. Barry quickly picked it up and drew back to throw but the grenade went off in his hand. Had it been an American M-26 grenade, the private would undoubtedly have been blown to bits but ChiCom grenades frequently produced an uneven frag pattern. In this case, the bulk of the blast went down and away from the Marine's body; Barry had the back of his right arm, his back, and his right leg peppered with metal fragments but he did not lose any fingers and continued to function for the rest of the battle.

Up Tight at Khe Sanh

Since the enemy started shelling Khe Sanh on January 21, more than 30 marines have been killed there and 180 wounded badly enough to require evacuation.

The Marine bastion, a porkchop shaped camp about one-half mile long and one-quarter mile wide, is criss-crossed with ditches and chock-a-block with sandbag-covered bunkers. The bunkers aren't very comfortable and they aren't very deep. But to the 6,000 marines at Khe Sanh, their bunkers are the nearest thing to home. Most bunkers, in fact, even have pet rats. "I haven't given mine a name yet," one young leatherneck said last week. "I'll wait and see if he survives another week."

Dropping the Tailgates
Disembarking at Khe Sanh is like jumping off a slow-moving freight train. The giant Air Force C-130 and C-123 transports that shuttle back and forth to the encampment twelve or fifteen times a day never do come to a full stop. If they did, they would be sitting ducks for the North Vietnamese gunners who periodically lob shells into the base. To avoid that, the C-130s drop their tailgates and spew out men and supplies while they are still taxiing. Three minutes after landing, the pilots gun their engines, and take off at a 45-degree angle to avoid the enemy machine guns dug in a little more than a mile from the end of the runway.

The first thing a visitor to Khe Sanh learns is that two is a crowd anywhere above ground. A captured enemy soldier told interrogators that the North

Long-range **US Army** artillery shells **NVA** positions around the cut-off Marine base at Khe Sanh, some 20 miles away

Scenes from the streets of Hue are eloquent testimony to the ferocity of the fighting in that once beautiful old city. It is a block-by-block, house-by-house affair. Urban fighting on this scale is new to Vietnam, and is probably the Marine Corp's most bitterly fought battle since the end of World War II

Allies Mopping Up in Hue

Allied forces slugged away at remaining pockets of resistance in the Hue citadel late Saturday, while other units moved outside the city to cut off Communist approach routes.

South Vietnamese troops took over the old imperial palace grounds in the citadel early in the day. Commanders termed the remaining action in the citadel a process of "mopping up."

Stars and Stripes

Vietnamese forward observers perched in the hills around the base were specifically looking for bunches of marines as targets for their mortars and rockets.

The Wrinkles Vanish

The men who live in Khe Sanh have developed split personalities under the pounding of enemy shells. For at least a half hour after a barrage, everyone is what the marines call "up tight." Nobody walks. Instead, everyone moves at a run, keeping one eye peeled for possible cover. Even men driving vehicles keep only one hand on the wheel; the other they keep on the vehicle's half open door, so they can jump out at the first hint of trouble. Only after the shock has worn off does the camp return to normal. Then the marines slow down and even the wrinkles of fear on their faces seem to vanish.

I got a taste of what it was like to be "up tight" at Khe Sanh the

morning after I arrived. As I was talking to the troops of Bravo Company along the southern edge of the airstrip there was a terrific whoosh overhead. An instant later, the shell hit with a roar somewhere behind me. When the sound of the explosion died down, I could hear the painfully familiar cry of "Corpsman! Corpsman!" At the same moment, a marine crouching in a slit trench to my right began to yell: "Don't bunch up, you people. That's just what they want you monkeys to do." The cry was echoed across the camp. "Don't bunch up, spread out ..."

When It's Got Your Name on It ...

But for some marines, the warning came too late. The rockets, it turned out, had scored a direct hit on the bunker of Khe Sanh's commander, Col. David Lownds of Plantation, Fla. Luckily, Colonel Lownds was not there when the shell landed. But in the road in front of the bunker

lay a Marine officer, his flak jacket torn half off, a pool of blood forming around his body. Corpsmen loaded him gently into a litter and rushed off toward the aid station, but the look in their eyes had already pronounced him dead. He was a first lieutenant who had arrived at Khe Sanh only 24 hours earlier to take over as regimental adjutant.

I dodged over to a young unshaven marine who was surveying the shambles that had been a small building only moments earlier. He looked up with a half-smile and muttered "You never know when it's got your name on it, you won't know what hit you anyway."

Thirty minutes later, before the "up tight" feeling could wear off, another explosion shook the ground. Brownish red smoke billowed up from the ammunition dump at the east end of the camp and three smaller explosions followed. Then a marine hollered: "Get the damage truck down

there. The explosives are cooking off."

Up Tight and on Edge

Within minutes, an absurd little red fire truck rumbled past me toward the ammo dump. Then a bare-headed junior officer half stumbled, half ran up the road toward me. His left arm was bleeding and his clothes were covered with soot and red dust. He moved past the bunker I was in and fell to his knees. A major raced over and knelt beside him. The wounded man looked up and yelled "Jesus Christ, sir, I told them not to put any more ammo down there. They've got that place zeroed in and it cost me a good man, a good man ..."

Being "up tight" half the time seems to put a special edge on life at Khe Sanh. Perhaps this feeling was best summed up by a sign in Bravo Company's orderly room. It read: "For those who fight for it, life has a flavor the protected never know."

Newsweek

MARCH 1968

2nd Ambush near Tan Son Nhut kills 48 US troops.

6th The totals of casualties for the Tet Offensive are given as 50,000 communists, 11,000 ARVN, 2000 US and 7500 civilians.

11th Largest operation of the war to date – Operation Quyet Thang – commences around Saigon.

13th The US refuses to allow a South Vietnamese "volunteer" invasion of the North.

17th 300 arrested in demonstrations outside the US embassy in London. 50 others are injured.

17th The combined US/ARVN Operation Duong Can Dan opens. There are over 1250 enemy casualties by the end.

22nd It is announced that General Westmoreland will become Army Chief of Staff. He will be replaced in Vietnam by his deputy there, General Creighton W. Abrams.

29th The US lets out three NVA POWs.

30th Operation Cochise Green starts in Binh Dinh Province. It will result in 929 enemy casualties.

31st President Johnson halts bombing of the North (with the exception of the northern sector of the DMZ) and announces that he will not run for President.

Fight for a Citadel

The Citadel of Hue resembled nothing so much as the ruins of Monte Cassino after allied bombs had reduced it to rubble. An avalanche of bricks littered the streets and open spaces, and loose piles of masonry provided cover for both sides in the battle for the fortress. With every explosion of bomb or shell, the air turned red with choking brick dust. Having fought through Hue block by block, house by house, then yard by yard, the US Marines were now engaged in what a company commander called a "brick-by-brick fight" to drive the North Vietnamese forces from the Citadel. Finally, when allied troops had shrunk the Communists' ground to three fortified pockets, South Vietnamese soldiers, flanked by a company of Black Panther Rangers, shelled a hole in the wall guarding the most important redoubt – the Imperial City - and swarmed in. They found only a handful of defenders left.

Behind Jagged Battlements
Thus came the allies' all-but-decisive blow to recapture the scene of the fiercest and most costly battle of the Vietnamese war to date, a battle so unlike any that had gone before it in the war that allied forces had to learn by doing. During the four weeks that they had clutched the city, over 2,000 North Vietnamese soldiers and Viet Cong had holed up hard – behind the foundations of crumbled buildings, among the jagged battlement of the Citadel's six-mile wall, in darkened houses and inside the secondary wall of the imperial city. Enemy sharpshooters trained their scopes on the allies from Hue's highest spots; machine-gunners picked wide-angle vantage points; and mortar fire struck everywhere like an infernal rain.

Against this strong opposition, the allies waged a relentless two-prong attack – US Marines southbound on the east, ARVN Marines headed the same way on the west. Clearing the way through the city's debris-covered avenues came US tanks, their turret guns swivelling from side to side as if to sniff the air, then belching fire at the Citadel walls. Overhead, helicopters sprayed napalm across the ponds and courtyards of the Imperial Palace, and fighter-bombers blasted away at three main enemy positions. From below, out to sea, a US cruiser kept shelling the Communists.

Khe Sanh Marines on Guard for Enemy Tunnels

The United States marine put on a steel helmet and a flak vest and stepped across the red-clay slope of the company perimeter, his hands holding two thin brass rods in front of him and parallel to the ground.

The divining rod, which many regard as worthless, has entered the inventory of the embattled marines at the Khesanh outpost.

None of his buddies in the nearby bunkers laughed as Lance Cpl. D. E. Isgris, 20 years old, of Bonne Terre, Mo., followed his brass rods up and down the slopes. He was waiting for the twist of the rods that might indicate a tunnel.

The possibility that the North Vietnamese who surround Khe-sanh might tunnel under this two-square-mile plateau has been a constant worry. The surface enemy trenches are now within 50 yards of the perimeter in some places.

'We Use It'
Late last week, an enemy rocket struck the wire at the northwest perimeter of Khesanh, opening a newly dug tunnel six feet below the surface. Now every possible device is being used to locate more enemy digging.

"No matter how stupid anything is, and I don't say the brass rods are stupid, we use it," said the base commander, Col. David E. Lownds of Plantation, Fla.

"If some country boy from the Kentucky hills says he has a gadget that he used to hunt

foxes with, and wants to try to find tunnels, I say go ahead. I try everything."

New York Times

Marines dug into the rich red soil of Khe Sanh have to take care that the communists don't dig deeper, right underfoot!

Praying to the Gods of War

For the weary battalions of Marines bellying through the chunks of rubble, progress was slow and costly in lives. Time after time, whole companies were pinned down against their rubble shields by a single, well-placed machine-gunner. A persistent drizzle socked in their air cover for most of the week. Even when air support came in, Communist artillery made the most of the low-flying weather: in 446 sorties by US helicopters, Communist guns scored strikes against no fewer than 60. Said Lieut. General Robert E. Cushman Jr., commander of I Corps forces: "The gods of war were in their favor."

From a crescent-shaped position along the west wall, the enemy was able to keep a steady stream of supplies and reinforcements flowing into the Citadel. At week's end this position was threatened by allied forces advancing on the Citadel from the west. For mobility within the city, the Communist troops found a second, more cunning conduit. They crawled through sewer lines beneath the city that led up to street level behind allied lines. Time and again, Communist mortar and rocket fire slammed into the advancing US armor. Sometimes a tank lurched, then treaded wildly through brick walls at streetside, where its crew, one or two of them wounded, would jump from the hatch; another crew would be immediately called in.

The Citadel recaptured

US Leathernecks, taking grim note of each setback, only pressed the enemy harder. Sharpshooters with high-powered scopes hunkered down behind battlements in "secure" sections of the Citadel wall, squeezing off occasional rounds at moving targets. As they waited out the weather for air cover or rested for their next push, the unshaven, dust-covered Marines sipped endless cups of powdered coffee, occasionally breaking out a liberated magnum of French champagne to accompany their C-rations.

By week's end, they had gained nearly 500 precious yards inside the Citadel, pinning an enemy force of about 350 men to three small strongholds. The most important advance came when low-crouching US

Marines pushing into the Citadel of Hue respond to a die-hard nest of Viet Cong fighters, holding out after the city has fallen

Marines swept on to the long south wall overlooking the Perfume riverbank, a position that finally gave the allies sturdy positions on each wall of the Citadel. The Marines celebrated by triumphantly running up the Stars and Stripes in full view of modern Hue, across the river. The death toll was among the most expensive of the war; nearly 450 allied dead, including some 100 US Marines, and so many casualties that the 5th Battalion's 1st Regiment was finally left at half strength.

Still, the allies moved on toward the imperial city, the seat of Vietnam's government and a center of its learning during the 19th century. There stood the palace complex, with its graceful red and gold buildings and pagoda roofing, its grounds of tall shade trees and frangipani, and its collections of *bleu d'Hue* porcelain. It was still standing. It was also an eerie place to die, and its Communist defenders evidently decided to get out while they could. They left behind an unexploded shell near the fragile imperial throne, a cache of rifles and ammunition, and the carcasses of a horse and a dog, which they had slaughtered for food.

Time

48 Americans Die in Ambush

Forty-eight Americans have been killed and 28 wounded in the ambush of a United States infantry company four miles north of Tan Son Nhut Air Base in Saigon. Twenty enemy soldiers were killed.

Fewer than half of the company's 150 soldiers escaped unscathed, a United States military spokesman reported yesterday.

The ambush, one of the worst in the war, occurred Saturday. Most of the American casualties were sustained during the first burst of fire from machine guns, automatic rifles, mortars and rocket launchers. Mines were also detonated.

Estimate of Strength

Allied intelligence officers believe that 8,000 to 10,000 enemy troops have moved within 15 miles of Saigon. There is growing speculation that these troops intend to make a second major assault on the south Vietnamese capital.

New York Times

McNamara Goes

The President of the United States and the man he came to honor got stuck in an elevator for 12 minutes. Rain, sleet and a grim, low overcast forced cancellation of a ceremonial flypast by Navy and Air Force jets. And the speeches of dignified farewell could not be heard because the public address system failed. For Robert S. McNamara, who served as Secretary of Defense for seven years and one month with dedication and efficiency, today was a decidedly untidy last day at the Pentagon.

New York Times

The Death of Hue

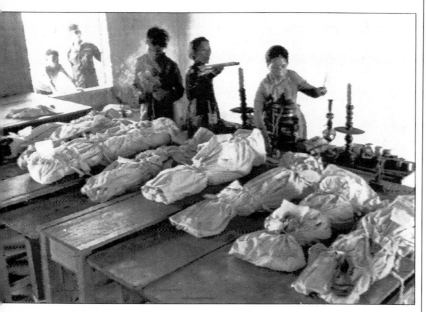

Air Drops are Khe Sanh's Lifeline

The nose of the big transport plane pitched upward violently and more than 13 tons of howitzer ammunition tumbled out of the tail door to the enemy-surrounded United States Marine Corps outposts below at Khesanh.

Clinging to the frame on the sharply angled plane, Airman 1st Cl. Rocco Damelio, the loadmaster, watched 14 green mottled parachutes blossom and called to the pilot "Load clear!"

With that, Maj. Arthur L. Wright pushed forward on the controls with all his weight. As the nose of the four-engine C-130 dropped, Major Wright banked smartly to the left, then climbed away from the mountains ahead and the North Vietnamese gunners hiding in the bomb-scarred ridges around the outpost.

Because of the growing intensity of groundfire, more than 90 per cent of the supplies going into the Khesanh outpost are

For 25 days, the huge red and blue Viet Cong flag fluttered over the once picturesque city of Hue. But last week, as US and Vietnamese troops occupied the city after some of the bitterest fighting of the war and hauled down the enemy banner, there were no smiles, no kisses, no tossed flowers for the conquerors. Americans walking the streets of Hue drew impassive, sometimes hatefilled stares. "We understand why you had to do it but we can never forgive you for it – for all the destruction and death you caused."

Hue, once the glory of South Vietnam's cities, now evokes memories of burned-out, gutted European cities of World War II. Our mud-spattered convoy churned its way past block after block where dust and rubble were all that were left. Bands of young children, five and six years old, played with empty C-ration cans, smoked American cigarettes and yelled "Hey, you, GI." Others walked around the rubble in the oversized helmets and boots of dead US marines.

No Triumphal Parade

Down the street we passed a column of marines. In taking the city they had sustained terrific casualties – some of the highest of the war – and now they looked blank and weary. One marine, his clothing muddy and wet, had written "condemned" on his hel-

Bodies from a mass grave in Hue are testimony to the brutal 15 day Viet Cong occupation

met. Another had glued a small silver crucifix to his. And at the rear of the tattered column, still another battered-looking marine proudly carried a shredded American flag tied to a long tree branch.

It was not a triumphal parade. On all sides, as the marines marched along, all they could see was destruction. No one knows how many bombs, how much napalm was dropped on Hue. But it was enough. "We used everything but nuclear weapons on this town," recalled a marine. And what the bombs did not destroy, the soldiers and marines – both US and Vietnamese- finished off in a weeklong binge of looting. "There ain't much left of Hue," said another US marine.

When the battle began, the US and South Vietnamese commanders hoped to spare Hue's many treasures: the gilded temples, the Purple Forbidden City, the priceless collections in the museum. But in the end everything had to go. As one US officer told me: "At first, the Vietnamese said we couldn't bomb this temple or that house. But when both of us started to take such heavy casualties, there were no arguments. We knocked down everything we wanted to."

Newsweek

being dropped. Nearly every aircraft that has flown over the outpost has been shot at. At least 25 per cent have been hit.

Someone in the crew of six said he thought he had felt a jolt as the parcels left the plane.

"You won't feel anything," said Major Wright, who has been flying in Vietnam for nine months.

"In the daytime it's very difficult to see if they are shooting at you," he continued. "But it's a 90 per cent certainty that we were shot at back there. Give a guy a rifle and when he sees an airplane, even if he is 10 miles away, he'll shoot at it."

On radar drops, the planes approach Khesanh as if they were making an instrument landing. When they pass a mark, a known number of seconds from the drop zone, a ground controller notifies the navigator, who clicks on a stop watch. At the moment when the plane should be over the drop zone, the navigator says: "Green light."

At that signal, Major Wright's co-pilot, Capt. Anthony G. Borra of Queens, punched a black button labeled "chute release."

At the same time, Major Wright pulled back on the controls, pitching the nose of the plane up sharply. That started the cargo on its way.

From the ground came word that the cargo had landed 75 yards from the center.

The C-130s are based at Saigon and Camranh Bay, which are two hours and an hour and a half flying time from Khesanh. But with a stop at Bienhoa to take on the ammunition, the trip from Saigon took Major Wright four and a half hours.

New York Times

Khe Sanh could have been a catastrophe like Dien Bien Phu 14 years before, but US airpower is more than equal to the task of supplying the base even after communist fire makes the airstrip all but unusable

Highland Troops See Little of Foe

Allied forces in the Central Highlands are engaged in the kind of action that were typical of the war in South Vietnam more than a year ago.

They are searching diligently with helicopters, radar and riflemen – sometimes catching a trace of the enemy but seldom drawing him into large-scale battle.

Intelligence officers have no doubt that North Vietnamese regulars and Vietcong guerrillas are present in force, but the enemy is clearly avoiding battle.

Instead, he has turned to harassment. Mortar shells and rockets have been dropped into military installations and cities. Ambushes and mining incidents have increased on Highways 14 and 19, the main overland supply links.

The situation in the Highlands reflects the military picture in most of the country. The exception, of course, is in the northern provinces.

New York Times

Troops in the quiet Central Highlands are in a very different war to those in the north

Rusk Talks of A-to-Z Review of War

The Senate Foreign Relations Committee pressed Secretary of State Dean rusk today to disclose whether the Administration was planning to expand the war in Vietnam.

The Secretary, however, would go no further than the statement that the Administration was re-examining its policy from "A to Z" and considering "all alternatives."

Among the alternative, Mr. Rusk indicated, is an increase in the American military strength in Vietnam.

In a day-long, nationally televised defense of Administration policy, Mr. Rusk acknowledged that the United States and South Vietnam had suffered some "serious setbacks" in the recent enemy offensive.

He contended, however, that the military picture was becoming more encouraging because the United States and its allies were "returning to the initiative."

New York Times

A Day at Dong Ha

The afternoon I arrived at Delta Med, the workload had been relatively light. "Things will probably pick up," said one American doctor, and a short time later – at 4.30 p.m. – he was proven painfully correct. A huge Marine helicopter landed, and medical corpsmen rushed three wounded marines from Khe Sanh into the receiving room on stretchers. One of them – his face hidden in dusty red bandages – was obviously in serious condition.

The previously vacant receiving room was now packed with doctors and corpsmen. As they pulled the heavy blanket away from the badly wounded marine's body, a jagged hole in the stomach received instant attention. Another smaller wound in the throat was still bleeding. "Bring some blood," one of the doctors cried out.

Litter Cases

The other two marines were less badly wounded. "These two are OK," said another doctor. "Let's get them out of here." Soon, all three of them, including the marine with the gaping stomach, were piled aboard a waiting C-130 and flown out to a better-equipped hospital at Danang. "He'll make it to Danang, said a doctor hopefully.

Once again, the waiting room was empty. The three wounded marines had been treated and shuttled back to the airstrip within fifteen minutes. Then, at 5.40 p.m., I heard the clatter of landing helicopters and headed back to the receiving room. This time seven marines were rushed through the door. Five were litter cases. The other two limped in and took seats on a bench a few feet away from the operating tables.

The stretcher case nearest the door was already turning green in the face, and his body shook violently. A corpsman quickly cut away the blood-soaked fatigues and examined two holes in his stomach. Doctors started glucose and plasma injections in both arms. "How do you feel, buddy?" a doctor asked. The marine just shook his head.

Gooks All Over the Place

I felt someone's eyes on me and turned to one of the marines on the bench. "What happened?" I asked. "We were moving up to a village," he said woodenly, his blond hair matted against his head. "They said there was only supposed to be a few snipers in that village. Well, I'll tell you what. They was gooks all over that place and we got our asses kicked."

The marine went silent, and I looked around the room. Another of the men had been shot through the neck, and apparently the bullet had snapped his vocal cords. He scribbled something on a piece of paper, and one corpsman said to another: "He says there are at least ten or fifteen more wounded out there." The foul smell of blood was thick in the air as the corpsmen swept up the bloody bandages. But something seemed to be missing. Then it hit me. There was pain in the face of every marine who was conscious. But not one of them cried out.

At 7.45, three more marines were carried in. One was a Negro, wide awake on a stretcher, calmly answering questions. He didn't realise that his left leg had been torn off just below the knee – or that his right foot was hanging only be tendons and flesh. A doctor nodded to a corpsman standing at the foot of the stretcher. Quickly, the corpsman picked up a pair of surgical scissors and started to cut the mangled foot away from the ankle. "My leg, my leg," screamed the marine. The amputation was finished in seconds and another corpsman carried away the bone and flesh still packed inside the bloody combat boot. The marine, shot full of morphine, was soon quiet.

Newsweek

Helicopters are the easiest way of getting wounded out of Khe Sanh. But NVA shells make the first stage of the trip very dangerous. Nevertheless, casualties are regularly flown out to mobile surgical hospitals at Dong Ha, and on to better equipped facilities at Da Nang and even 'back in the World'.

Marines to Start New Village Plan

Under a new system to be started in a few days, United States marine pacification teams will move from village to village, spending about two weeks in each one, trying to teach the inhabitants how to defend themselves.

Until the Lunar New year offensive, the Marines had pacification teams of 14 men and one medical orderly. They lived permanently in villages, working with South Vietnamese units to pacify and secure the village.

Col. M. Bradly, director here of the Marine pacification program, said the Marines had given up their original pacification plans because of a lack of security.

"Our aim now is to provide a purely military security in the coastal areas where the people are, around our main bases and on Highway 1," the colonel said.

The change from permanent to mobile teams was necessary, he added, because the Marines did not have enough men to put in villages on a permanent basis.

New York Times

President Lyndon B. Johnson, seen here at the roll out of the Air Force's new C-5 Galaxy transport plane, is determined that the communist shall not triumph at Khe Sanh. Yet the battles of Tete, Khe Sanh and Hue have been a blow to his administration

Khe Sanh Raid Fails

Charging through a natural camouflage of predawn fog, more than 500 North Vietnamese infantrymen drove to the barbed-wire ring around the U.S. fortress at Khe Sanh Friday.

South Vietnamese Rangers and giant Air Force B52 bombers crushed the attack, the heaviest mounted yet against the 500 Rangers and 5,000 U.S. Marine defenders.

Associated press correspondent Peter Arnett reported from Khe Sanh that the eight-engine B52 Stratofortresses, flying in direct support of infantrymen at Khe Sanh for the first time in more than 1,000 sorties, rained tons of explosives only 750 yards in front of the Rangers' lines.

Arnett said that the North Vietnamese troops lost 70 dead. Casualties among the Allied defenders in the ground attack and an eaqlier heavy shelling of the fortress were reported as "very light."

Stars and Stripes

Khe Sanh is holding out well against an NVA force 30,000 strong, and the few attacks which reach the perimeter of the combat base are beaten off relatively easily

Mills Says War Could Force Tax Rise

Representative Wilbur D. Mills, the House's chief architect for tax policy, said today that "substantial acceleration" of the war in Vietnam "could force" Congress to enact a general tax increase.

The Arkansas Democrat said, however, that a significant further increase in military spending would create an even greater need for cutbacks elsewhere in the Government's budget of the sort that he has been seeking with relatively little success ever since last summer.

New York Times

APRIL 1968

1st — 1st Air Cavalry launches Operation Pegasus/Lan Som 207 in an attempt to lift the siege at Khe Sanh.

1st — Operation Carentan II starts in Quang Tri and Thua Thien Provinces. It will result in 2100 enemy casualties.

3rd — After ridiculing the bombing restrictions imposed by the US as a "perfidious trick", the North states that it is prepared to discuss a total halt.

6th — Siege of Khe Sanh is lifted.

8th — Start of Operation Toan Thang in the Saigon area. This is the biggest ground-force operation to date and will result in 7645 reported enemy casualties.

8th — Operation Burlington Trail begins in Quang Tri Province. There are 1931 enemy casualties by the end.

10-12th — Lang Vei Special Forces camp is retaken, lost, and taken again.

15th — Operation Scotland II is under way in the Khe Sanh area.

19th — Combined Operation Delaware/Lam Son 216 begins. It is concentrated on the Ashau Valley.

21st — Viet Cong defector discloses plans to attack Saigon.

22nd — Defense Secretary Clifford, who replaced Robert McNamara in January, broaches the idea that will later be implemented as "Vietnamization".

30th — Mass truancy in US colleges as an anti-war protest.

The Big "Easter Egg Hunt"

Ironically, the last engagement took place between Hills 881S and 881N precisely where, on 20 January, the whole affair had begun. The 3rd Battalion, 26th Marines which had started the fight, was also on hand to finish it.

Lieutenant Colonel Studt moved his attacking elements into position the night of the 13th. The assault companies of 3/26 slipped out of the defensive wire under the cover of darkness and moved down the forward slope of the hill along routes which were protected by security patrols. As he watched the Marines file by, the battalion's operations officer, Major Caulfield, could not help but be concerned about them. Most of the men had spent the past two and a half months in a foxhole or trench; they had received minimum rations and a maximum of enemy shelling. All were tired and dirty; some suffered from large body sores because the water received by these men had gone into their bodies and not on them. Even though they were Marines, the major wondered how they would perform the next morning.

The attack, which the troops referred to as their "Easter Egg Hunt," was preceded by a deluge

Khe Sanh Siege Lifted

The 76-day enemy siege of Khe Sanh was lifted Friday and U.S. Marines and Army units struck out through the hills looking for vanishing North Vietnamese.

A 20,000-man allied relief column that approached almost unopposed to within less than a mile of the combat base made no attempt to enter as enemy gunners zeroed in with 110 rounds of artillery and mortar fire.

While the possibility of another battle was not excluded, it appeared the enemy had abandoned any attempt to wipe out the base astride an invasion route from Laos.

U.S. officers said the North Vietnamese force around Khe Sanh, once estimated at 20,000, had been reduced to about 7,000.

Stars and Stripes

A Cavalry firebase is prepared for Operation Pegasus, which will see to the relief of Khe Sanh

of supporting fire. In addition to the artillery of 1/13 at Khe Sanh and the 175mm bases, 15mm and 8-inch batteries of the 1st ACD at LZ Stud were called on to help cave in the enemy bunkers. Strike aircraft worked over the hill with bombs, rockets and napalm.

As the assault troops advanced, the weapons on 881S provided direct overhead fire which sometimes preceded the front ranks by no more than 50 meters. As usual, the recoilless rifles were extremely effective.

Because of the weight and speed of the attack, the enemy was never able to recover. Moving behind a wall of steel, the battalion clawed its way through the defenses between the two hills and prepared for the final push. Major Caulfield, who had worried about the Marines' weakened condition the night before, soon found the opposite was true - he was having trouble holding them back. At one point, a group of NVA soldiers who had been hammered senseless by the prep fires, broke from their positions and fled into the open. An airborne spotter directed the companies to hold up while he called in air and artillery. Scanning the front lines, Major Caulfield noticed that a handful of Marines with fixed bayonets were in hot pursuit of the enemy. The Major contacted the company commander by radio and told him to collar his troops. The reply was, "Sir, I can't stop them . . ."

The men of 3/26 stormed the hill, swarmed over the crest and killed anyone who stood in their way. At 1428, the objective was secured and the men signaled their victory in traditional fashion, as Colonel Meyers later described: "I watched the jungle utility-clad Marine 'shinny-up' a shrapnel torn tree whose limbs had been sheared from the intensive prep fires, and affix the Stars and Stripes."

The hills around Khe Sanh are pounded by artillery and air power, including massive strikes from B-52 bombers

An Efficient Slaughter

On a lovely sunny afternoon in the green valley of Nam Hoa, about ten miles southwest of Hue, I was with Warrant Officer Ostara, an Australian adviser with the South Vietnam army, standing on the sloping sides of a recently dug hole. In the bottom were rush mats over sheets of plastic. Ostara drew them back and I saw two bodies, dead Vietnamese, with their arms tied behind their backs just above the elbows. They had been shot through the back of the head, the bullet coming out through the mouth. The faces would have been difficult to recognize, but the day before, 27 women from the village walked out three miles carrying mattocks to dig for their missing husbands and sons, having heard about this patch of disturbed earth near the roadside. Ostara told me that the enemy had come through on their way to Hue. They had taken 27 men. Some were leaders and some were younger, strong enough to be porters or even ancillary workers.

Shot in the Head

"Men were simply condemned by drumhead courts and executed as enemies of the people," said Bob Kelly, the senior province adviser in Thua Thien province. "These were the leaders, often quite small men. Others were executed when their usefulness ceased, or when they didn't co-operate they were shot for their trouble. Some of my staff were badly mutilated, but I am inclined to believe this was done after they were killed. Their hands were tied and they were shot behind the head. I helped to dig one body out but I have been told by Vietnamese whom I respect that some people were buried alive."

Lieut. Gregory Sharp, an American adviser with the Vietnam 21st Ranger Battalion, told me that his men had come across about 25 new graves in a cemetery five miles east of Hue on March 14. From half a dozen of the graves the heads were sticking up out of the sandy soil and, according to Sharp, "there wasn't much left of them – buzzards and dogs, I suppose. Some had been shot in the head and some hadn't. They had been buried alive, I think. There were sort of scratches in the sand in one place, as if someone had clawed his way out." At Quan Ta Ngan three Australian warrant officers saw seven men in one of three graves they found. The seven, I was told, had been shot one after the other, through the back of the head, hands tied.

Inspecting the Graves

Soon after arriving in Hue, I went in a Jeep with three Vietnam officers to inspect sites where the bodies of executed men were said to have been found. We went first to Gia Hoi high school in District Two, east of the Citadel. Here 22 new graves had been found, each containing between three and seven bodies. It is still a horrifying place. The officers told me that the bodies had been tied and, again, most had been shot through the head, but "some had been buried alive."

There are about 40,000 Roman Catholic Vietnamese in Hue. What happened to them? About three-quarters of the Roman Catholics in Hue live in Phu Cam, on the southern outskirts of the city. They resisted strongly when the enemy came in, and some were executed.

Four Vietnam priests were taken away and three foreign priests were killed. Two French priests were actually given permission by the Viet Cong to return to Phu Cam and help the sisters – and then they were shot on the way back. Another French priest was executed, perhaps because he was chaplain to the Americans.

Summing up all this evidence about the behavior of the Viet Cong and the North Vietnamese army in Hue, one thing is abundantly clear and ought to surprise no-one. They put into practice, with their usual efficiency, the traditional Communist policy of punishing by execution selected leaders who support their enemies. In Hue, as elsewhere, they were unable on the whole to capture and execute the more important officials, because these men were careful to protect themselves in heavily fortified compounds, defended by soldiers and police. In Hue, as elsewhere, the more defenseless "little people" were the victims – the village and hamlet chiefs, the teachers and the policemen.

Already, most of these positions have been filled again, and I find it impossible to write adequately about the courage of men who succeed the executed.

Time

New Scope Helps G.I.s Spot Foe at Night

American troops in Vietnam are using thousands of electronic "starlight scopes" enabling them to see the Vietcong as well at night as during the day, the Army said today.

As the devices become more plentiful, the Army said, the Vietcong will be denied the cover of darkness on which they have long relied.

Unlike the older infrared sniperscope, the compact starlight scope sends out no radiation of its own and hence cannot be detected by the enemy. It picks up the faintest of light – from the stars, the moon or phosphorous in the jungle, regardless of cloud cover and magnifies it 40,000 times. That is enough to turn night virtually into day for someone looking through the scope.

"We're taking the night away from Charlie," said Maj. Gen. W. B. Katta, head of the Army Electronics command, which developed the starlight scope and demonstrated its use today.

"We feel it will have a profound influence on warfare," General Latta said.

New York Times

The Starlight Scope night vision device should help US troops contest 'Charlie's' long-held rule of the Vietnam night

26th Marines Honored by President

On 23 May 1968, several members of the 26th Marines who had fought at Khe Sanh had a reunion of sorts in Washington, D.C. and the surroundings were a far cry from the dirt and grime of the combat base. The "CP" belonged to the President of the United States, Lyndon B. Johnson. In the Cabinet Room of the White House, the Commander in Chief paused to honor the men of the 26th Marines and awarded the Presidential Unit Citation to the regiment. Colonel Lownds, whose large handlebar mustache had been shaved off at the direction of "the highest possible authority" – his wife, and Sergeant Major Agrippa W. Smith, senior enlisted man at the KSCB, were on hand to receive the award. While it was fitting that the 26th Marines be cited as a unit, the President also praised the South Vietnamese, U.S. Army, U.S. Navy, U.S. Air Force, and Marine aviation and support units which contributed so gallantly to the defense of the installation.

Marine Corps History

Members of the 26th Marines find the cabinet room of the White House is a long way from the mud and blood of Khe Sanh (below)

Bangkok Magnet for Vietnam GIs

Each morning a chartered Pan American jet lands at Don Muang Airport here and 163 American servicemen get off. As they come down the ramp squinting in the tropical sun the fatigue of six months or more of fighting in South Vietnam seems to drain from their faces.

From the airport, the soldiers are bussed to the air-conditioned conference room of a Bangkok tourist agency, where Capt. Gary Robbins of the Army briefs them on Bangkok.

All Hotels Have Pools

"All the hotels have swimming pools," he explains, "and all have American-style bars and dining rooms that are open 24 hours a day, air-conditioning in every room and hot and cold running water."

At the mention of hot water, the soldiers who arrived this morning broke into a cheer.

"I thought you'd like that," said the captain.

"There are narcotics pushers working in the city," he said. "If any of you are approached to buy or traffic in narcotics of any type break contact with the individual and call the military police."

Captain Robbins also mentioned "enemy agents" in the city.

"You must be particularly careful about being approached in bars," he said. "Leave the war stories back where you made them up. Do not be drawn into conversation about your unit, its location, operations or casualties."

Finally, the captain warned of the pitfalls of Thai beer. "It is about 18% alcohol and it really sneaks up on you," he said.

So far as female companionship is concerned, Captain Robbins told the soldiers they could expect any bar girl to go back to their hotel with them for about $10 a night but he warned: "Your chances of coming into contact with venereal disease are about 50-50. If you become infected, go to the dispensary during duty hours and get treated."

Bars Popular With GIs

The soldiers on the tours have five days in Bangkok, most of which they spend in the bars and massage parlors that have grown up around the city. A whole new district known as Petchburi Road has sprung up on the edge of the capital to accommodate these businesses.

The relaxing servicemen spend an average of $300 apiece during their stay, according to the Army figures. Some spend as much as $800. Last month this spending totaled $1.7 million.

At the end of their five-day vacations, the soldiers are given a short talk before they head back to the war.

A Marine sergeant who gave it yesterday told the men with obvious irony:

"The Republic of Vietnam asks you not to bring back any flowers, fresh fruit or food – anything that might contaminate their country. After all Vietnam has done for us, I think that's the least we can do."

The New York Times

U.S., Hanoi Agree on Paris for Talks

The United States and North Vietnam agreed Friday to meet in Paris late next week to start discussing conditions for possible Vietnam peace talks.

President Johnson announced at a nationally televised and broadcast news conference: "I have sent a message informing Hanoi that the day of May 10 and the site of Paris are acceptable to the United States."

The President's statement came shortly over an hour after a Hanoi Radio broadcast proposed Paris as "an appropriate venue for the formal bilateral talks." The North Vietnamese broadcast said talks should begin "on May 10 or a few days later."

In Paris, the South Vietnamese consulate said representatives of their government "will sit in on" the talks.

NEW ATTACKS

MAY 1968

3rd It is decided that talks between the US and the North will start in Paris around 10 May.

5th Start of second major communist offensive of 1968 as 119 cities are attacked with Saigon the main target. US air strikes on a Viet Cong headquarters in the city itself, using napalm and high explosive allow ground troops in to bring the battle to a close. 5270 communists die.

9th Thieu reasserts that Saigon government will never recognize NLF.

10th Talks begin in Paris.

11th North Vietnam and the US decide that only they, and not the South Vietnamese government or the NLF, will be involved in the initial talks.

17th Operation Jeb Stuart III under way in Quang Tri and Thua Thien Provinces. 2114 enemy casualties will ensue. Operation Nevada Eagle launched.

18th Start of Operation Mameluke Thrust in Quang Nam Province.

25th Start of third major communist offensive against Saigon.

27th Thailand announces it is to despatch a further 5000 men to Vietnam.

GIs in Delta Use Stealth and Surprise

Almost five and one-half years ago, at a hamlet called Apbac, less than three miles from here, American public opinion suffered its first major shock of the Vietnam war.

On Jan. 2, 1963, a small force of Vietcong at Apbac shot down five American helicopters, fought off several battalions of South Vietnamese troops, killed more than 60 of them and retreated successfully the next day.

It was a realtively big action for the time. Of greater importance were the doubts it raised about official optimism in Saigon and Washington.

After so many subsequent shocks, it may come as no surprise to learn that Apbac and the surrounding hamlets in the Mekong Delta are still controlled by the Vietcong. But the guerrillas today face a serious and determined challenge to their long mastery of this vital area 40 miles southwest of Saigon. The keystone of the challenge is disruption of the enemy's security.

Use of Stealth
Under the command of Col. Henry Emerson, 42 years old, of Milford, Pa., the troops of the First Brigade of the United States Ninth Division are attempting to fight the war in ways some observers of Vietnam have always thought it should be done.

The emphasis in the two battalions currently under Colonel Emerson's command is on "small unit actions," on stealth and surprise, and on night fighting.

The primary assignment of the brigade is to protect 16 miles of strategic Highway 4 – the main roadway in the delta – from the town of Cailay to a point near Mytho.

Rather than a defensive attitude, the method adopted has been offfensive.

Patrols Venture Nightly
Each night more than a score of 12-man ambush patrols fan out into the rice paddies and lines of trees of each side of the east-to-west highway, and smaller

122

groups take up ground nearer the road.

Larger patrols of one of three platoons, totaling as many as 100 men, leave the base camps regularly on two days. The ambush patrols attempt, with varying success, to remain undetected.

New York Times

GI Jeep Patrols Hunt Saigon Foe

The 20-year-old military policeman scanned the knots of men and women in doorways and the lighted windows two and three stories up. Then, for just a moment, fixed his glance on a figure leaning out of one of the windows.

"You don't know who the sniper is until he shoots at you," he said. "You've got to play like everyone's a sniper."

During the dusk-to-dawn curfew, they patrol the city in teams of two jeeps, with two to four men each, looking for signs of enemy activity.

"Looking for Trouble"

"Our patrols are out looking for trouble," said Lieut. Col. Gordon D. Rowe, commander of the 716th Military Police Battalion.

The primary mission of the MPs, Colonel Rowe said, is to protect the 135 American military installations in Saigon. In the process they find themselves involved in the defense of the city.

"All the time you're on duty you've got that queasy feeling," said Specialist 4 Raymond Thundercloud, the driver of one of the jeeps.

Refugees a Problem

"When the refugees move in I think lots of Viet Cong move in with them," Specialist Thundercloud said. "You get a kind of eerie feeling when you find yourself in a closed-in alley with them on all sides. You have to be careful where you shoot, too."

"My men have to hold their fire until they have a definite target," Colonel Rowe said. "I won't let them just fire in a general direction."

"The lone terrorist gets in with innocent people, and if we promiscuously open up with grenade launchers and automatic weapons, we're going to kill a lot of the wrong people. I don't know what that accomplishes."

The men fighting in the cities are faced with the problem of identifying the enemy. They all look alike to the military policeman. The man in the shadowy doorway could be a Viet Cong terrorist or the owner of a shoe shop. These thoughts keep the military policemen tense.

"They're not scared," Colonel Rowe said of his men. "But they know, they know."

The New York Times

Patrolling the cities of Vietnam in jeeps is a high risk occupation, when the Viet Cong sapper or sniper looks exactly the same as the harmless farmer or bar worker next to him

Saigon's People Resigned to Blows of War

When enemy troops moved into her neighborhood last week, Mrs. Nguyen Thi Bai hurried from her home in fright to find a taxi driver willing to take her household goods to safety.

While she was looking for a three-wheeled Lambretta – the cheapest kind of Saigon taxi – rockets smashed into her house and killed her teen-age son.

"Oh, my son, my son," Mrs. Bai said again and again today. "I should have let him go and hire a tri-Lambretta instead of going myself. But I thought he would be safe inside the house."

It was a typical reaction to the suffering and destruction that has been caused over the last 10 days by enemy attacks and allied counterattacks in the Saigon area.

After 25 years of war, most Vietnamese appear to look upon it as an elemental force – like fires and typhoons.

They Don't Blame Enemy

And instead of blaming either the enemy or the allies for killing their relatives or destroying their homes, many victims of this month's fighting in Saigon blame only themselves – for not reacting rapidly enough, for failing to get their children out of danger quickly, or for failing to move their clothing and valuables at the first hint of danger.

New York Times

A quarter of a century of war have made the Vietnamese resigned to, if not accepting of, the latest Viet Cong attacks (right)

ARVN tanks rumbling through the outskirts of Saigon are an everyday sight to the inhabitants of that city

Too Close for Comfort

In the early stages of the conflict, Arc Light strikes were not authorized within a prescribed distance of friendly lines. The NVA had taken advantage of the buffer zone by moving troops and supplies in as close to the Marine base as possible to avoid the bomber raids. When American airborne observers noted enemy bunker complexes cropping up near the KSCB, the no-bomb line was moved in to about half of the original distance. At first the regimental commander was afraid that the resulting concussion would collapse his own bunkers and trenches; as it turned out, the enemy fortifications were the only ones which suffered. The first few B-52 raids inside the old line touched off scores of secondary explosions and undoubtedly snapped the North Vietnamese out of their sense of security. The closer strikes also served as a morale booster for the defenders who flocked from their bunkers to watch, what the Marines called, "Number One on the hit parade."

The unmistakeable signature of a B-52 raid pounds the Viet Cong

Unconventional Commandos

Readers of Cartoonist Roy Crane's comic strip "Buz Sawyer" were introduced back in 1966 to an outfit called the US Navy Seals (for Sea, Air and Land), an elite bunch of commandos with which Buz performed deeds of derring-do in Vietnam. It may have seemed like rousing fantasy to readers, but the fact was that just such an outfit was operating in Vietnam – where its presence was one of the most closely kept secrets of the war. Only now, in fact, when the Communists themselves have learned of the Seals' presence the hard way, has the Navy begun to disclose some of their real adventures and reveal something about how they operate.

Reconnaissance and demolition

In Vietnam, the Seals' primary missions are reconnaissance and demolition, and their principal weapons stealth, surprise – and patience. Last week *Time*'s Glenn Troelstrup became the first newsman in Vietnam permitted to accompany a Seal team on a mission. Dropped by Navy river patrol boats deep into Viet Cong country southeast of Saigon in the swampy mangrove sector of Rung Sat, the Seals set up an ambush beside a small stream. There, for 14 long hours, they froze in position, hip-deep in mud, clad in camouflage suits and bush hats, their faces blackened. Their only communication was by tugs on a string running among them.

Slipping into the Sampan

Finally, two armed Viet Cong slipped into their resupply sampan and moved confidently out into the silent stream. Within five seconds both Viet Cong were dead, cut down by a hail of automatic fire. Quickly, one of the Seals waded out into the water, which was infested by alligators, snakes and manta rays, pulled the riddled sampan to shore and stripped it. Other squad members immediately sent five signal flares aloft. Within 15 minutes a Navy patrol boat, covered by a Navy helicopter, had plucked the little squad of Seals off the shore and was taking them back to secure territory. The Seals had hit again, turning the Viet Cong's own tactics against him, making the hunter suddenly become the hunted.

US Navy SEALS pause during an operation deep in the Mekong Delta. These unconventional soldiers are among the most effective American fighting men in Vietnam, being highly skilled commandos who go after the Viet Cong quietly and without fuss deep within his strongholds

Time

How the Battle for Khe Sanh Was Won

As allied patrols scoured the scorched and battered moonscape of Khe Sanh last week, they found North Vietnamese trenches and bunkers, tons of supplies and ammunition, some 1,300 bodies and hardly a trace of opposition. What loomed as the largest, most decisive and most controversial battle of the Vietnam war would now never be joined.

But a major battle did occur at Khe Sanh – one that prevented the bloody hand-to-hand battle on the ground that many military men had anticipated. It was a battle of the air might of the US against every stratagem that the besieging enemy could muster. Bombing the North Vietnamese with such precision that they were destroyed before they could ever launch their attack, the US could justly claim a considerable victory at Khe Sanh without ever having committed its ground forces to the fray. Khe Sanh was, in fact, a landmark in the use of airpower in warfare – the first time that aerial bombardment has denied an attacker the ability to assault his target.

Zeroeing in on the Marines

From the beginning of the North Vietnamese build-up, the US command was convinced that General Vo Nguyen Giap, intended to try to overrun Khe Sanh as he had stormed Dienbienphu 14 years earlier. As he had done against the French garrison, Giap assembled large numbers of his best-trained assault troops around Khe Sanh, together with huge quantities of weaponry.

In addition, deep in the Lao-tian hillsides Giap placed Russian-made 152mm cannons, their long tubes zeroed in on besieged Marines. Altogether, Hanoi's gunners poured more explosives into Khe Sanh than they had into Dienbienphu. And as in 1954, the North Vietnamese by night tunneled ever closer to the Marine perimeter, drawing the net of fortified attack positions ever tighter. In terms of firepower and supplies, the Communists were better prepared to strike at Khe Sanh than they ever had been at Dienbienphu. During the early days of the six-week siege, they even had the weather - low clouds, fog and mist – in their favor.

The US decided that the only way to defend Khe Sanh was by a massive application of airpower.

A Model Operation

Working over a sandbox model of the Khe Sanh area, two of the US Army's most gifted tacticians – General Creighton Abrams and Lieut. General William B. Rosson – figured out the most logical places for Giap to concentrate men and supplies, then designated those areas as prime targets for US planes.

To co-ordinate all the activities, an ABCCC (Airborne Command and Control Center) was kept in the sky high over Khe Sanh at all times. It was a C-130 Herky Bird packed with the latest electronic gear, which enabled the Air Force colonel on board to talk with Marines on the ground, pilots in the sur-

A fuel dump explodes at Khe Sanh. Air Power ensured that any such loses were quickly made good

rounding sky and his own superiors in Saigon. US airmen enclosed the besieged fortress in a virtual curtain of falling bombs. Though the Marines lost most of their original supply of artillery ammunition when an enemy shell hit their supply dump early in the siege, they were able to call in airpower for the sort of pin-point destruction that is normally associated with howitzers. When the lowering clouds lifted a few hundred feet, dart-like Air Force F-100s, Navy and Marine F-4 fighter-bombers and stubby A-4 light bombers zipped under the overcast to place high explosives on the spreading enemy trenches. Huge, eight-jet B-52s, which bomb by radar, flew over Khe Sanh regardless of the weather.

The Pull-out

Some time around March 12, the day before the 14th anniversary of his victory at Dienbienphu, General Giap seems to have come to the conclusion that he would not be able to repeat his earlier feat, and he stopped sending replacements to Khe Sanh. Then, on March 22, he ordered one of his two battered divisions around Khe Sanh to withdraw. That same day the monsoon began to lift from Khe Sanh, and the better weather brought the fighter-bombers to join with the B-52s in earth-jarring raids. The heavy US bombing only heightened the desire of the remaining North Vietnamese troops to get out. The testimony of captured NVA regulars indicates that the bombing so disrupted the Communist supply lines that Giap's men were nearly starving. The prisoners said that they had been subsisting for weeks on less than half a pound of rice a day; for the last

three days before their capture, they had had no food whatsoever. Relieved to be free of the threat of instant death, the prisoners told of one regiment that had lost 75% of its 2,000 men to US bombs and artillery.

Time

LBJ Won't Run

President Johnson said Sunday, "I shall not seek and I will not accept the nomination for another term as president."

He said he does not believe that with war in Vietnam he should "devote an hour or a day of my time" to any partisan cause.

Johnson made his dramatic withdrawal at the end of a nationally broadcast speech in which he disclosed he is ordering a halt in nearly all air and sea action against North Vietnam in a move to bring peace talks.

Johnson recalled that 52 months and 10 days ago he came into the presidency through the tragic death of President John F. Kennedy.

Now he said there is divisiveness in the country and made an appeal for unity.

"I would ask all Americans to guard against divisiveness and all its ugly consequences."

In announcing the Vietnam moves, Johnson said there will be a pause in air attacks on North Vietnam, except in the area near the demilitarized zone.

He called this "the first step to de-escalate" the war, saying the U.S. will substantially reduce "the present level of hostilities."

Stars and Stripes

THE LONGEST WAR

JUNE 1968

10th General Abrams takes over from General Westmoreland.

14th Four people, including Dr Benjamin Spock, the author of a famous book on child care, are convicted in Boston on charges relating to assisting draft dodgers.

19th President Thieu signs a bill allowing for general mobilization in South Vietnam. South Vietnamese troops eliminate last Viet Cong bastion in Saigon suburbs.

26th South Vietnamese demand a place at Paris talks. North Vietnamese negotiators reiterate insistence on unconditional cessation of bombing.

27th US admits withdrawal from Khe Sanh has begun.

29th South Vietnamese Premier Tran accuses the US of giving too much away at talks.

War Longest US Has Ever Fought

The undeclared war in Vietnam has become, by at least one standard of measurement, the longest the United States has fought.

At midnight last night the war has lasted six years, six months and one day, dated from the death of the first American serviceman killed by the Viet Cong. Specialist 4 James Davis of Livingston, Tenn., was killed on Dec. 22, 1961 and President Johnson said later that the soldier was "the first American to fall in defense of our freedom in Vietnam."

The Revolutionary War lasted six years and six months if its conclusion is considered, as it generally is, the surrender of Cornwallis at Yorktown, Oct. 19, 1781.

The New York Times

N. Viets May Be Using Copters

Unidentified aircraft – believed to be enemy helicopters – have been spotted and fired on by U.S. Navy vessels near the eastern end of the Demilitarized Zone, the U.S. military command in Vietnam said Monday night.

If they are enemy copters, it marks the first time they have been used in the war.

The report comes on the heels of rumors that a Communist copter gunship was responsible for the sinking of a Navy Swift boat, the PCF 19, at 1.30 a.m. Sunday a few miles below the DMZ.

It was the first U.S. gunboat lost in the war. Early reports on the sinking indicated it was the work of Communist shore batteries above the DMZ. The boat went down about a mile offshore, four miles below the DMZ. Five of the seven crewmen were listed as missing. The other two were picked up.

Stars and Stripes

Grief With a Touch of Bitterness

In the barracks and mess halls of this sprawling, dusty camp, American soldiers listened in bitter quiet today to the news from Los Angeles.

The death of Senator Robert F. Kennedy stirred grief and a surprising undertone of anger and confusion.

"Everyone's asking what the hell we're here for when we can't even deal with things back home," said Pfc. Richard Ferling, a telephone lineman from Rockford, Illinois. "Even sergeants are saying it – Let's settle our own problems first."

For many soldiers in Vietnam, the death of Senator Kennedy, the racial violence in the United States and the talks with the North Vietnamese in Paris have stirred bewilderment and for some, explicit doubts about their mission here.

"We want this war to end," said a private from Wisconsin in a comment that was repeated over and over today at Longbinh. "They need us at home more than they do here, don't they?"

A blond, curly-haired military policeman from Pittsburgh, Specialist 4 David Tournay, commented:

"I got so mad I wrote a letter to my wife and told her that when I get discharged I just want to move out of the States."

Broadcast By Radio

The afternoon silence was broken sporadically by the sound of Armed Forces Radio broadcasts from Los Angeles.

"Everyone's listening, everyone cares," said Specialist John Finley, a 21-year-old military policeman from Northport, L.I. "You wanted something done about this war and you wanted the right person to do it, and somehow you felt he would have done it."

"Why, why is there this total lack of responsibility at home?" he asked. "First it was his brother, then Martin Luther King and then him."

A Sultry Day of Talk

"He had the same dreams as us, you know," said Specialist 4 James Sorenson, a jeep driver from Los Angeles. "He was young."

"He was a hippie!" exclaimed Pfc. Bradford Smith, a frail, bespectacled soldier with a solemn smile. "Really, that's why most of us like him."

Perhaps the soldiers who were affected most deeply were Negroes, who stood in small groups listening to transistors, shaking their heads, cursing and shaking their heads again.

"I'm Negro, You're White"

"You're over here in this heat and you try to run Charlie down and you count every God-damn day, in this hellhole, and then look just look at what's back there waiting for me!"

He tapped his finger on his chest. "Look, I'm Negro. You're white," he told a visitor. "If you people can't get together, if you people kill your best how do you expect me and you to get together?"

"And if we can't get along," he added softly, "there's no way in hell that we can teach Vietnam anything."

The New York Times

The Army of the Republic of Vietnam is often portrayed as a bunch of incompetents led by corrupt, venial officers. The truth is, when adequately led the ARVN soldier proved just as committed and dedicated as his communist opponent. Much of the battle in Saigon in 1968 (above and left) was fought by the ARVNs, and they comprehensively beat the Viet Cong

---

Last VC Holdouts Routed in Saigon

Grenade-hurling Vietnamese Special Forces troopers, racing from bunker to bunker, wiped out the last Viet Cong stronghold in Saigon's suburbs in face-to-face fighting that ended at dawn Monday.

The elite soldiers, brought to Saigon specifically to wrench free a hamlet held by the Viet Cong for two weeks, killed 30 guerrillas and drove 100 others fleeing into rice paddies along the Saigon River. Fifteen prisoners were taken.

Stars and Stripes

Marines Leaving Khe Sanh; Red Shift in Tactics Cited

The U.S. Marines are pulling out of the Khe Sanh combat base on the northern frontier, where they weathered a 77-day siege last winter with 2,500 casualties. The U.S. command, announcing the move Thursday, cited mounting enemy pressure as part of the reason.

"There have been two significant changes in the military situation in Vietnam since early this year," the command said. "An increase in friendly strength, mobility and firepower and an increase in the enemy's threat due to both a greater flow of replacements and a change in tactics."

During the long winter siege, senior U.S. officers called the base in South Vietnam's northwest corner indispensable. They said it would be held at any cost.

But the pullout decision apparently had already been made by the time a division-plus relief force arrived at Khe Sanh in April.

Stars and Stripes

Marines are helicoptered into action near the DMZ. The idea of combat bases is abandoned for a strategy of mobile operations less than four months after the epic siege of Khe Sanh

JULY 1968

1st B-52 bomber raids start up again north of the DMZ.

3rd According to figures from Saigon more US personnel died during the first six months of 1968 than in the whole of 1967.

4th A joint NVA/Viet Cong assault at Dau Tieng is thrown back.

14-18th On a visit to South Vietnam Defense Secretary Clifford announces that it is the US intention that all South Vietnamese Army units will get the M16 rifle.

17th Start of Operation Quyet Chien. It will result in 15,593 enemy casualties.

18-20th Remarks made by President Thieu at a meeting with President Johnson in Honolulu, Hawaii suggest that he accepts "Vietnamization".

20th The 14th anniversary of the 1954 Geneva Accords is designated "National Shame Day" in the South.

21st The US is accused by the dead men's widows of the murder of six South Vietnamese supporters of Vice-President Ky. An enquiry upholds the original verdict that the six were killed by a helicopter rocket that malfunctioned.

Son of Patton Leads Tank Regiment

"In World War II these tanks were the spearheads, the ground gainers," said Col. George S. Patton, 3rd, stepping past rows of tanks waiting to move out. "Here it's a hell of a lot different. The helicopter lets the infantry do the exploiting while the armor more or less supports or fills in the gaps."

As the only son of the famous World War II general, George S. Patton Jr., the hefty, cigar-puffing colonel who recently assumed command of the 11th Armored Cavalry Regiment, speaks of his father with a blend of tentativeness and awe.

"A Tremendous Personality"
"He was colorful, yeah," Colonel Patton said. "He was a real student of history, too, and had a tremendous personality."

"Finding Charlie is the whole war," he said. "The problem is finding him and armor has a role in that."

"Armor just doesn't mean steel and tanks," he added. "Armor is a way of thinking, a way of life to me.

"It's a combination of tanks and air cavalry and gunships and reconnaissance. You can't only emphasize armor here because of the terrain. You have jungles, mountains, rice paddies and swamps, and it's damned hard for a tank to move through here."

"Yeah, we've had contact. Small stuff, ankle biters, I call them," he said sipping a cup of coffee. "We've lost some men too, to antipersonnel and antitank mines. Charlie lays the mines so damned skillfully and without any established pattern."

"He's an elusive and quite smart enemy," added the colonel, who was a company commander in the Korean war.

Vietnam is not really tank country, but US armored units made a significant contribution to the war, although in less glamorous roles than was common during World War II

"But I think perhaps he may be overrated."

"I think he's hungry and tired and wet, and I think perhaps he may be losing some of his motivation. But he's got such a hell of a lot of motivation that's the thing. He's got a lot of political motivation and he's quite well organized. But I think we'll get him, we'll do it."

The New York Times

Foe is Friendly At US Hospital

Longbinh. A soft drizzle splattered on the roof of the long tent. An American doctor peered inside and stepped toward the bed of a North Vietnamese who smiled weakly and gripped the casts on his legs.

"How are you today?" asked the doctor, Capt. James W. Hedden, leaning forward and nodding.

"Thank you, thank you," said the patient, pushing himself up on both elbows. "Khong dau, khong dau," which means "no pain."

Captain Hedden turned and walked slowly past the beds of the wounded Viet Cong and North Vietnamese prisoners – young men with shaved heads who grinned at the hefty American or nodded nervously or turned away.

Hanoi-Trained Doctor
"The man with the wound in both legs is a North Vietnamese doctor," said Captain Hedden, stepping outside the steamy tent into the rain. "He's Hanoi-trained and he's quite interested in how we work. He's not too communicative, though."

"He's doing quite well now but he seems to have developed a bleeding ulcer – a typical doctor's disease," Captain Hedden said with a smile. "Even North Vietnamese doctors get ulcers."

As the commanding officer of the 50th Medical Clearing Company in Longbinh, Captain Hedden heads a group of four doctors and 120 enlisted men who treat wounded enemy prisoners in the largest Army hospital facility for Viet Cong and North Vietnamese.

"They're Tough"
"Many of them stay as long as a year here before they go to POW camps," said Captain Hedden, a 33-year-old doctor from Chattanooga. "We get every type of wound – some extremely critical head and chest wounds – and some of these people don't survive."

"But they're relatively stoic, they endure pain very well. They are also very strong. Many of them walk around with low blood levels and intestinal worms and malaria. They're tough."

"Most of these people are friendly," Captain Hedden said. "They joke and laugh. They thank you frequently. There's very little hostility."

In the prison compound, the North Vietnamese and Viet Cong wake shortly after dawn. Thermal canisters with bacon and eggs, cereal and coffee are brought into the tents and the prisoners eat breakfast on plastic trays.

Bowls of Rice Preferred
"Most of them don't like eggs too well," said a 21-year-old hospital attendant, Specialist 5 Daniel McIlwee. "I think they kind of like most of the Army chow, but what they really like is the bowls of rice we give them."

"You can give them a steak and apple pie, but if they don't get that rice, they'll throw a fit," the tall, cheerful Oklahoman added.

"One fellow created the damndest fuss about the wires in his shoulder and kept wanting me to take them out," Captain Hedden said. "I finally told him that if I took the wires out I would lose much face. He understood immediately. He hasn't bothered me since."

Ho Chi Minh
He smiled to a tattooed prisoner in his fifties whom the American enlisted men had nicknamed Ho Chi Minh to the delight of the prisoners, who giggled whenever the name was mentioned.

"Frankly, most of the prisoners seem to like it here," the doctor said. "There's very little talk about the war and they seem quite content. For all of them, I guess, the war is over."

The New York Times

232 Red Boats Bagged as Navy Jets Set Mark

An armada of U.S. Navy warplanes destroyed or damaged 232 Communist supply boats in the largest single day's catch of the war, military spokesmen announced Sunday.

At the same time, other U.S. warplanes maneuvered through Communist surface-to-air missiles and heavy antiaircraft fire to pound the North Vietnamese panhandle with 130 air strikes, heaviest total in two weeks.

The 130 air strikes over the North Saturday were concentrated on the scores of canals and highways that wind through the southern half of North Vietnam below the 19th parallel. Headquarters said nearly 200 Navy fighter-bombers from three carriers off the coast of North Vietnam destroyed or damaged the 232 supply boats in sweeping raids over an area stretching from the 19th parallel 75 miles south to Cape Mui Ron.

A spokesman called it "the largest bag of boats for the war." He said that repeated air strikes on roads, bridges and truck parks had forced the North Vietnamese to switch to the waterways in efforts to push arms and ammunition into the south for an anticipated countrywide offensive.

Stars and Stripes

A burning North Vietnamese gunboat is seen with the shadow of a US reconnaissance plane

MISTAKES

AUGUST 1968

2nd Start of Operation Lam Son 245 in Thua Thien Province. It will account for 636 enemy casualties.

4th Operation Somerset Plain/Lam Son 246 begins in the Ashau Valley.

5-8th As he becomes the Republican candidate for the forthcoming US Presidential election, Richard Nixon promises to "bring an honorable end to the war in Vietnam".

10th A US jet kills eight US troops in error in the Ashau Valley.

15th Heavy fighting in and around the DMZ as ARVN and US troops engage the North Vietnamese Army.

17th Defense Department figures put the number of combat missions flown since February 1965 at 117,000. Over 2.5 million tons of bombs and rockets have been used.

18th Positions throughout the South are assailed by 19 NVA/Viet Cong assaults which are particularly concentrated close to the Cambodian border northwest of Saigon.

19th A Harris survey indicates that 61 per cent of those asked in the US are against calling a halt to the bombing.

24th The ARVN begins Operation Tien Bo in Quang Duc Province. There are 1091 enemy casualties by the end of the operation.

26-29th As the Democratic Convention endorses the administration's platform rather than that of the anti-war grouping, rioting takes place outside the hall.

Radar-guided Sparrow missiles can cause problems, when the targets on radar are not enemy helicopters but allied ships!

Major Deplores Saigon Officers

The major trembles when he speaks. "I have seen too much war," he says. "I have seen 20 years of war."

"I have too much bitterness in my heart now," he says, lighting a cigarette. "Maybe I will leave the army soon. Everything is too late for me. My son will replace me, and maybe his world will be happier."

Leadership Blamed

"Our soldiers are good, as good as the Viet Cong or the North Vietnamese, but the problem is leadership."

"What do you think of generals who have three cars at home and never leave their headquarters?" he asked. "I know generals like that. What do you think of generals who use

Fatal Error

On two successive nights last June, U.S. F-4 Phantom jets scrambled to intercept what they took to be North Vietnamese helicopters, spotted for the first time crossing the Demilitarized Zone between North and South Viet Nam. The sightings were made by U.S. counter-mortar radar teams atop the hills overlooking the South China Sea. Their radar screens showed blips moving low and slowly, as invading helicopters might if hugging the waves for concealment. Once aloft, the Phantoms soon had moving blips on their own radar screens and unleashed Sparrow rockets at the targets. An eager South Vietnamese officer reported that 13 Communist helicopters had been destroyed.

On the same nights, a number of allied ships reported being attacked by enemy aircraft. That, too, had never happened in the war. Seven miles offshore near the DMZ, three shells narrowly missed the U.S.S. *Boston*. A 50-ft. patrol boat was sunk, taking five of her U.S. crew down with her. The Australian destroyer H.M.A.S. *Hobart* was hit by three rockets that killed two of her sailors.

Last week a U.S. board of investigation confirmed the tragic error that had been suspected ever since two survivors of the patrol boat had said that they had been attacked by a U.S. plane and the fragments of rockets that hit the *Hobart* had turned out to be Sparrow parts. What the spotters and pilots had taken for helicopters on their radar was, said the board, the allied ships. The pilots, of course, never saw their actual targets. The Sparrows are guided by radar and computers.

A covey of North Vietnamese helicopters might have triggered the whole chain of disastrous events and escaped before the Phantoms were airborne. But the board said that no evidence has been produced of enemy helicopter action near the DMZ. For the future, the U.S. command in Saigon promised that "action has been taken to provide improved coordination and control" of allied forces to prevent any repetition of June's deadly miscalculations.

Time

aircraft for themselves, for their own pleasure, while soldiers in the field cannot get supplies or ammunition or food?"

"We have officers who spend 15 years in Saigon, and they get medals and get promoted," he said. "We have soldiers who spend 10 years in Dakto, and they get nothing. It is a matter of knowing the right people, of paying the right people."

"In the Viet Cong the commanders are the same as the soldiers," the officer said. "If the Viet Cong commander has sandals, the soldiers have sandals. The commanders eat the same food as the Viet Cong. Everything is the same. With us - too much difference."

"What the Vietnamese soldier worries about is his family," the major went on. "If the mother and wife and children are taken care of, the soldier will fight, like the Viet Cong, for 10 years. But once the soldier leaves home, no-one cares for the family."

The New York Times

Dirges from the Sky Pursue Fleeting Foe

When North Vietnamese forces retreated Monday after an unsuccessful assault on the Ducalp Special Forces camp, psychological warfare pilots were ordered to pursue them.

Instead of using bullets and bombs, the pilots bombarded the enemy troops with leaflets and propaganda broadcasts.

Flying out of the United States Air Force base here, the psychological warfare men try to rattle the enemy by playing Vietnamese funeral music and tape-recorded enemy casualty figures over a loudspeaker system. Then they plead with the enemy soldiers to lay down their arms and rally to the Government's side.

The enemy often answers with a hail of bullets.

"Everyone hears about the kill-ratio," said Lieut. William L. Foust, who runs the Air Force "delivery system" for the psychological warfare program. "But few people realize how much effort we put into trying to get the enemy to surrender peacefully. We'd much rather capture a man or have him surrender, than kill him. If an enemy soldier rallies to the Government's cause, we gain a man and they lose one. If we kill an enemy soldier, their side just loses a man and we don't gain one."

"We can't give our psywar crews enough credit," added Col. Frederick L. Webster Jr., the deputy commander of the 14th Wing. "They go out unarmed and they get four or five times as much ground fire as the crews that are armed."

New York Times

O-2 observation planes are used to broadcast psychological warfare to enemy troops

Green Berets Pleased by Renewed Attention

Although the Green Berets are superb warriors, much of their role demands skill in non-warlike areas like public health

Until two weeks ago, the beret-wearing members of the Special Forces of the United States Army were convinced that everyone had forgotten about them but John Wayne.

Then suddenly, this summer, everything started blossoming again for the Green Berets, who like to fight and like the world to know about it.

First, John Wayne's movie, "The Green Berets," was released. Then, two weeks ago, the enemy began moving against the Special Forces in strength.

Eight times since then, the enemy has attacked Special Forces camps. And the Special Forces, rather than being plunged into gloom by the assaults, seem delighted by the public interest they have stirred.

The Special Forces now operate 61 camps, a decrease of about 20 in the last two years. Three were lost to the enemy and most of the rest were in secure areas and were turned over to the South Vietnamese militia.

The trend in the Special Forces is away from fixed outposts and toward mobile reaction of "Mike" forces as the Green Berets call them.

As many of the Green Berets see it, the United States should have insisted on jointly commanding South Vietnamese troops, sending mostly sergeants and officers into South Vietnam, rather than hundreds of thousands of privates and private first class.

"They should be running the Vietnamese army the way we do the C.I.D.G.'s," said one Special Forces officer. "The Vietnamese need leadership, and we've got it. If we had a Joint Commander ARVN, we could have avoided a lot of the build up and saved a lot of American lives."

One of the Special Forces favorite claims is that it has lost only one American for every 79 enemy killed. Conventional American military forces claim about 15 enemy for each American lost.

New York Times

SEPTEMBER 1968

2nd US steps up bombing raids.

11-16th 1500 NVA/Viet Cong get into Tay Ninh. After a four-day battle they are beaten off by the South Vietnamese Army.

11th Start of Operation Lam Son 261 in Thua Thien and Quang Tri Provinces. There are 724 reported enemy casualties by the end of the operation.

13th Large-scale combined allied joint-service operation in the DMZ begins. It will claim 742 North Vietnamese and 65 American lives.

20th A paper by an Agriculture Department expert suggests that US officials in Saigon underestimate the extent of ecological damage caused in Vietnam by defoliating agents.

28th A battle begins for the Special Forces camp at Thuong Duc, situated between Da Nang and the Laotian border.

30th The battleship USS *New Jersey* begins bombarding the DMZ from her station off the Vietnam coast.

Paris Talks Remain Unreal

You hear very little opposition to the talks in Paris as you move among infantrymen in the country. On the other hand, they have little confidence that the talks will get them home.

They are banking on their "DEROS" – Date of Estimated Return from Overseas.

"My DEROS is the 23rd of February, 1969," Specialist 4 Joseph Hensley of Erie, Pa., said as he guarded a bridge near Tanan, in the Mekong Delta. "That's when I'll be going home."

"The Paris talks are OK, if they work," he added, "but I kind of got my doubts whether they'll work."

"If you start thinking that peace is coming and that maybe you ought to ease up so you won't be the last one killed, then that's when you are going to get it," said Pfc. Louis Vidt, who is 21 and from Pittsburgh. "If you start making wrong moves because you can't think straight, you're sure to get zapped."

Big Enemy Push Forecast

As Private Vidt talked, Pfc. Danny Clairday sprawled on an air mattress in the same bunker on the outskirts of Saigon and nodded in agreement.

"Nobody's laying down on the job," Private Clairday said in a soft drawl he brought to Vietnam from Jerusalem, Ark. "The only protection a soldier has got is to do his job right. You don't do a good job, you ain't gonna make it."

"They slacked up for a while, but now I think they're going to have a big push," said Pfc. Jim Meyers, a 19-year-old native of Rudyard, Mont. "We're setting up ambushes at night and then

Allies Sweep DMZ

U.S. and Vietnamese troops, backed by aircraft, naval gunfire and tanks, went into the Demilitarized Zone Friday after dug-in North Vietnamese troops.

The allied force reported 158 Reds killed in a day-long battle.

Elements of the U.S. Army's 5th Mechanized Div.; the 3rd Marine Div. and the South Vietnamese 1st Inf. Div. attacked the fortified enemy position two miles northeast of Gio Linh in the southern portion of the DMZ.

Backed up by Marine tanks, Air Force jets, naval gunfire and Army artillery, the ground troops drove the Communists from their bunkers.

U.S. casualties were 22 wounded, all Army. No Americans were killed. Vietnamese losses were reported light.

After completing a sweep of the battle area, the Allies returned to their bases in Quang Tri Province.

Near Loc Ninh, 80 miles north of Saigon, 1st Inf. Div. troops

A Marine Corps tank provides the punch to operations to sweep the supposedly 'demilitarized' zone of dug-in enemy troops

killed 38 Communists Friday, bringing to 167 the enemy's losses in a savage series of fights that began early thursday.

Three U.S. troopers were killed and nine wounded in Friday's fighting.

Stars and Stripes

patrolling in the daytime around the edges of Saigon. And we're getting people. A North Vietnamese captain was captured last week and a sergeant this week."

"They were both with reconnaissance units," he added. "They were looking for a weak spot so they could send their troops into Saigon. No, it's not over yet. I'm pretty sure of it."

"Viet Cong Ain't Gonna Quit"
"The Viet Cong ain't gonna quit," said Specialist 4 Wroldon Franks, a 25-year-old oil worker from Winnsboro, La. "I saw one Viet Cong take four 50-caliber machine-gun bullets in him and he was still fighting. Peace talks don't get to those kind of people."

Specialist 4 Jearold Harper, who is 20 and from St. Louis, said: "Those people at the peace talks don't give a damn. They're sitting in a dry seat. We're the ones in the mud. Bring them guys over here for a while where it's rough and then they might start talking serious."

"I hope those guys in Paris settle the war," added Pfc. Goodwin, who is 20 and from Trenton, Ga. "I hope they do it a long time before I leave. I can do without this war."

The New York Times

Spooky the Plane Hailed in Vietnam

NHATRANG – The smell of gun powder filled the airplane and parched the lips of the gun crew. The gunners drank water and coffee in great gulps to cleanse their mouths.

At every free moment they adjusted and readjusted their headset to muffle the sound of the guns. But nothing worked. Even with the headsets on, the guns sounded like a thousand carpenters hammering simultaneously on metal.

Peering out the window, you could see tracer bullets flowing in a fiery arc to the ground, 3,000 feet below. The stream of red seemed unbroken.

This was the scene this week aboard a Spooky as it came to the rescue of the embattled Duclap Special Forces camp near the Cambodian border.

The firepower of the ancient planes, which are converted C-47s, the so-called Goony-birds from the World War II era, continually comforts and amazes American and South Vietnamese ground troops who call for them at the first sign of an enemy attack at night.

"Spooky, Spooky, where the hell are you?" a radio operator shouted from Duclap this week. "Right here and ready to fire!" Col. Frederick J. Webster, the pilot, answered.

An unmistakable sigh of relief came over the radio from Duclap.

The Spookies, which get their name from their ghostly ability to come into a target area quietly, are equipped with three 7.2mm machine guns. Each so-called minigun can fire 6,000 bullets a minute. Thus, according to the Air Force, a Spooky can lay down as much fire power as a full battalion of infantry riflemen.

The Spooky is only used when allied forces are under attack and, a 14th Wing spokesman says, the Spookies have never fired on the wrong target.

"If we aren't sure we don't fire," Colonel Allman said. "We work in such close support of friendly ground troops that we can't afford to make mistakes."

After the siege was broken at Duclap, M. Sgt. Ted Boody of Hollis, Queens, sat bearded and weary in the sun and said that he and the other Duclap defenders would have been "goners" had it not been for the Spookies.

"One time there, they were coming at us right over the barbed wire," he said. "I thought it was all over, but then the Spookies came in and stopped them cold."

The New York Times

The awesome power of the 'Spooky' gunship is apparent when you realize that only one shell in five is a tracer!

No Bomb Halt: LBJ

President Johnson Tuesday again rejected a complete halt to bombing in North Vietnam and said that events in Eastern Europe make it clear "we are still a long way from the kind of peaceful world we all wish to see."

"The message out of Czechoslovakia," Johnson said, "is plain; the independence of nations and the liberty of men are still under challenge. And the free parts of the world will survive only if they are capable of maintaining their strength and building their unity."

Yet Johnson said that the United States will continue in every honorable way open to move toward more normal relations with Russia and other Communist countries.

Stars and Stripes

THE BATTLES CONTINUE

OCTOBER 1968

3rd Twenty-four US personnel die when a helicopter collides with a transport aircraft over Camp Evans near Hue.

9-14th North Vietnamese sound out the US by suggesting that they might agree to allow South Vietnam to the conference table in return for a halt to the bombing.

11th 7000, including serving soldiers, reservists and veterans take part in march in San Francisco; the first of its kind to be organised by servicemen.

14th It is announced that 24,000 servicemen will do obligatory second tours of Vietnam.

16th Start of Operation Lam Son 271 in the Quang Tri Province. There are 603 enemy casualties by the end of the operation.

22nd President Thieu states that he is no longer against a cessation of bombing.

24th Operation Henderson Hill commences in Quang Nam Province. There are 700 enemy casualties by the end of the operation.

26th Communists attack base near Cambodian border.

27th 50,000 demonstrators take part in an anti-war march in London.

31st President Johnson orders a cessation of bombing of North Vietnam. The NLF and the South Vietnamese are allowed to take part in the Paris peace talks.

Help Is Swift, and Another Wounded GI Will Live

The medevac workhorse is the C-141 Starlifter, a four-engine jet transport that carries cargo to Vietnam and patients on the way back. They fly from three bases in Vietnam – Camranh Bay, Danang and Saigon – to the continental United States by way of Japan or the Philippines.

The planes are not hospitals, but they are equipped with respirators and drugs to be used in emergencies. Such emergencies, the nurses say, are quite rare.

A C-141 Starlifter is the workhorse of the Medevac effort, flying soldiers home to the States for treatment within hours of being wounded

Little Complaining
The casualties slept, talked politics and the World Series, read magazines and paperbacks and joked with the nurses and white-shirted medical technicians. There was little complaining but also little enthusiasm for the war they were leaving.

"I may have a lot of pain with this," said Specialist 4 Mark Rambow, 19, of Detroit, patting the bandages that covered the spot where a mine had torn open his abdomen. "But I wouldn't change places with one of those guys back there."

The New York Times

All the assets of a technological culture are brought into play in Vietnam. Radar sets designed to track incoming shells are used to add security to US bases

Incoming!

SUPPORT BASE JULIE A handful of American soldiers heard the unmistakable hollow thump of an enemy shell leaving a mortar tube in the thick jungle undergrowth.

They yelled, "Incoming mortars!" and all of the 400 men at Support Base Julie began racing for their bunkers. By the time the shells landed near the barbed wire perimeter the men were safely under cover and no one was hurt.

"Nervousness is what saved us," said M. Sgt. Myrl Blum of Columbus, Ohio, from the depths of a deep trench that was covered with steel and sandbags. "These kids are so nervous - if somebody belches out there, they'll yell 'incoming!'".

"Everyone Has Shrapnel!"
Sgt. Jeffrey Hicks, 20, of Jefferson City, Mo., leaned against a bunker to relieve the pressure on a sprained ankle, while he scratched gently at shrapnel splinters embedded in his back.

"They're not bad," he said of his back wounds. "About everyone here has got some shrapnel in him. We've been taking a lot of incoming, you see."

The New York Times

The Americans ask, the Vietnamese ask, "Does anybody care?"

Footnotes on the Vietnam Dispatches

Pages from the notebook of a correspondent who has spent 15 months in Vietnam – his impressions of the "red-eyed and grimy" soldiers, the self-important "desk-jobs" in the American mission, the "graceful, lithe, moody" Vietnamese and, above all, "this suffering Vietnam."

The Fourth US Infantry Division unit was called the New York Company since most of it men were from Brooklyn, the Bronx, Manhattan. The company commander, a captain, was from Missouri. A tall and thin West Pointer with an engaging smile.

"They seem to know how to operate well in the dark," says the captain standing outside his tent on a hot, breezeless morning at a landing strip near Pleiku. "They're born jungle-fighters."

"I kid them about their accent," he says, as the soldiers near him start laughing. "I don't understand some of the words they use."

Planning R-and-R

The captain is new and somewhat uneasy with the company. He arrived only weeks earlier, but most of the troops have been in Vietnam 10 to 11 months. The soldiers watch his moves carefully and with some suspicion – they bluntly miss their old captain who has returned home to Flatbush.

Later in the hot afternoon, the captain sits alone in front of his tent and reads a letter on pink stationery from his wife. He shows his first sergeant a picture of his wife and daughter, both smiling and blonde and wearing white dresses, standing in front of a porch that resembles the other porches of so many other similar photographs that are carried in Vietnam.

"I'm going to meet her in Hawaii on my R-and-R," he says quietly. "We're planning it now."

Nearby, the troops sprawl over the dry grass and talk. In civilian life – "the real world," as they say – they were bank clerks, construction workers, students, salesmen and electricians. Their leader is a Brooklyn longshoreman, a 22-year-old sergeant who speaks softly and intensely but not without humor. "Oh baby, like the guys from the South – you give them a good mule and some country music and they're happy," he says. "I mean, New York guys want to hear Tony Bennett. They want to hear Justin Tubbs."

The New York Times
(Magazine)

Reds Still threaten Thuong Duc Camp

Elements of three Communist regiments were still threatening the Thuong Duc Special Forces camp Monday, and a North Vietnamese battle flag was reported still flying from a group of villages a mile from the camp, despite two days of Allied efforts to drive the Reds out.

Fighting broke out around two outposts of the camp early Saturday. A North Vietnamese attacking force was beaten back by government troops who killed 39 enemy troops.

But another Communist force occupied a complex of small villages across a nearby river at the same time and the Special Forces troops battled them through Sunday night.

Many of the villagers fled across the river into the district headquarters which is protected by the Special Forces camp.

About 100 South Vietnamese troops assaulted the village complex from the east Sunday and managed to fight their way inside the hamlets, but heavy enemy fire pinned them down. They slipped out of the complex in the dark and returned to the main camp.

Thuong Duc Camp was still under siege late Monday by large elements of three Communist regiments.

Stars and Stripes

The opponent in Vietnam varied, from ill-trained guerrillas to the trained and equipped NVA professionals seen here

Humphrey Willing to Call Off Bombing

Hubert H. Humphrey said Monday that if elected President he would be willing to stop the bombing of North Vietnam – thus dramatically moving away from the Johnson administration war policy.

Humphrey, in a half-hour speech on foreign policy at a critical time in his presidential campaign, said North Vietnam has contended it would promptly conduct "good faith negotiations if we stop the present limited bombing of the north."

Humphrey told a nationwide television audience: "As President, I would be willing to stop the bombing of the north as an acceptable risk for peace because I believe it could lead to success in the negotiations and a shorter war. This would be the best protection for our troops."

Humphrey repeated, however, an earlier statement that neither he nor anyone else had control over the Vietnam war while President Johnson remained in office.

Stars and Stripes

NOVEMBER 1968

1st As a part of the pacification effort the Le Loi and Phoenix Programs are introduced. The latter draws widespread condemnation for its reported use of torture and assassination.

1st It is announced that bombing is to be stepped up on Ho Chi Minh Trail.

2nd The South Vietnamese government states it will boycott Paris talks because the NLF has been admitted.

6th Richard Nixon elected President of the United States of America.

10th Guns inside the DMZ carry out the first bombardments of US positions since bombing of the North ceased.

11th Start of US joint-service Operation Commando Hunt to interdict communist routes of infiltration through Laos into the South and check sensor systems on the Ho Chi Minh Trail.

23rd US troops encircle and attack communist forces between the La Tho and Ky Lam Rivers, killing 1210.

26th The South Vietnamese government announces that it will take part in the Paris talks.

26th US troops carry out first operation inside the DMZ since bombing ceased.

New Jersey Blasts Away

From the moment *New Jersey* arrived on the gun line there was no doubt in any man's mind that we were going to bash the hell out of some North Vietnamese.

I can tell you, after talking to ground-pounders who saw the ship at work, that no sight of the entire war was as impressive as our battleship letting loose with its main battery of nine 16-inch guns. Each of those guns could fire a shell weighing 1,900 pounds over a distance of 32,500 yards, and there was nothing – *nothing* – which could withstand the penetrating force and the impact. The most heavily fortified North Vietnamese bunkers, even those with solid concrete roofs that were untouchable by Marine artillery, were blown away when our shells came howling down on top of them.

Artificial Sunrise

Life aboard a battleship on the gun line was far from exciting, even when the 16-inch main battery or the ten 5-inch guns were being fired. My life revolved around a narrow bunk, a footlocker, the personal items in one duffle bag, and my compulsion for scurrying down to the ship's bakery at 1 a.m. to sample the fresh-baked new bread at the beginning of the day. On a ship this size, you didn't necessarily see your buddies all that often, unless you passed them on "Broadway" – the long open corridor passing beneath the bridge, connecting turret two and turret three. When the guns were firing, everybody knew it but not everybody had work to do, so, even then, it was possible to catch some shut-eye or record a tape to send home.

One Marine told me that when *New Jersey* was firing, her guns lit up the eastern sky like a sunrise and the shells sounded like an express train going overhead. On a 25 November 1968

The awesome power of USS *New Jersey*'s nine 16-inch guns is on call for American troops fighting near the demilitarized Zone at the end of 1968 and into 1969

firing mission, the big battlewagon was credited with destroying 117 North Vietnamese structures along the DMZ. Most of the time the targets – located by Skyhawk spotter planes – were too far away to see, but there were times when you could watch the 16-inch shells rising from the guns, arching over in their trajectory, and coming down to explode along the shoreline.

Battleship Sailor

Crime Paying

Thievery is rampant. An American businessman complains of the theft of medical supplies – especially lucrative – by his non-Vietnamese workers who open up boxes filled with catheters and medicine, remove them and then seal up the box. Months later, a doctor in a province or military hospital opens up the box, possibly in an emergency, and finds nothing. The contents are on the black market or possibly even in the hands of the Viet Cong.

Some thievery is only exacerbated by the refusal of Americans to create an incident, behave uncoolly. A cashier at the PX is found stealing. An American officer fires her. The Vietnamese threaten to walk out and strike unless the woman is rehired, the American officer is reassigned.

The thievery confuses many Americans, then disillusions, finally embitters.

The New York Times

Fighting Fauna

Animals play a major role on both sides of the conflict. More than 1,000 dogs are in action on the allied side alone, and nearly 100 veterinarians serving in the US Army in Vietnam help care for them. German shepherd scout dogs lead jungle patrols sniffing out ambushes. Often they are more alert than their masters: last week, a US Marine com-

Giving an Arm and a Leg

A chilly rain splashes the Quonset hut hospital in Dongha, south of the demilitarized zone. The helicopters move in through the morning, bounding on to the landing pad in a whirl of dust and noise, while the Navy corpsmen remove the wounded, who stare at the sky and lick the rain from their lips.

That morning in Danang, a Marine general with a swagger stick had told of pinning a Purple Heart on a quadruple amputee who asked if he could remain in the Marines. The general was pleased, "That's patriotism."

Time

pany commander took heavy casualties in an ambush after ignoring a dog's warning. The shepherds have an uncanny knack for avoiding booby traps (apparently, their ears can pick up the tiny sound made by the breeze on a taut trip wire). One handler, Marine Sergeant Roy Jergins, says: "I walk where my dog walks, and I walk right through the booby traps." Mean sentry dogs who attack anyone but their handlers guard key US installations. Tracker dogs, Labrador retrievers trained in Malaysia, are used to sniff out enemy withdrawal routes. After one recent ambush in III Corps, a tracker led a US unit on a 5½

Dogs were for security in Vietnam, as well as sentries and to track the enemy on patrol

hour chase that ended at an abandoned rubber plantation. Sure enough, the Communists were hiding there, and the Americans killed 70 of them.

Time

U.S. Warns Reds on DMZ Attack

North Vietnam has used the Demilitarized Zone five times this week to move troops, equipment and to fire at U.S. reconnaissance planes, the American command said Thursday.

In four of the incidents, occurring Wednesday, U.S. artillery and ships fired back at the Communists, spokesmen said. The fifth incident occurred Monday.

The spotter planes, none of which was reported hit in the exchange of fire, directed U.S. counter-barrages and reported at least 35 secondary explosions and several fires.

A Marine tank battalion sighted the headlights of 10 vehicles moving through the buffer zone northeast of Con Thien, spokesmen said, but the targets were not fired on.

Communist troops also stepped up their attacks against South Vietnamese villages and Allied camps Tuesday. One shelling came possibly from within the Demilitarized Zone.

Twenty settlements or bases had been assaulted in the past 24 hours, military spokesmen said Wednesday, the greatest number since President Johnson called the bombing halt.

It was first reported that a South Vietnamese fire support base had been mortared from North Vietnamese positions within the buffer zone early Tuesday. But officials said later there was a possibility the Red gun sites were within South Vietnam. The incident was being investigated.

The Reds shelled U.S. Marine outposts five times Sunday from the DMZ, the first time since Johnson stopped attacks on the north.

Johnson had demanded the withdrawal of all Communist troops from the buffer strip in exchange for the bombing halt. The U.S. Command here has not commented on either of the attacks.

Stars and Stripes

DECEMBER 1968

1st Start of Operation Speedy Express south of Saigon. There are 10,899 enemy casualties by the end of the operation.

6th Operation Taylor Common launched in Quang Nam Province. It will claim 1299 enemy casualties.

8th ARVN troops commence Operation Le Loi I in Quang Nam Province. There are 695 enemy casualties by the end of the operation.

11th It is alleged that the Le Loi and Phoenix Programs have so far brought a 3.5 per cent rise in the number of South Vietnamese living in government-controlled areas.

12th Paris talks are at a standstill over, among other issues, the seating plan and the shape of the table.

12-13th US B-52 bombers raid targets north of Saigon.

17th Vice-President Ky is labelled a "little tinhorn dictator" by Senator George McGovern.

23rd According to a member of the NLF at the Paris talks, the US and the Viet Cong are "the direct adversaries" in the war and therefore it should be they who settle it.

The Press Conference

The majors and Navy officers answer with bored hesitancy. The ritual, for them, is marked by a single rule. "I will not tell you a damned thing and you know it and I know it so let's not waste each others' time."

And with the ritual are the basic corruptions of language. The dead are KIAs, the wounded are WIAs. An ambush is a "meeting engagement." A fight is a "contact." "The weeklies are on the rack" means that the dead and wounded figures for the past seven days are listed.

The New York Times

Over the 30,000 Mark

In one 24-hour period last week, 31 US fighting men died in Vietnam. Among them were 16 Marines helping to mop up a trapped enemy unit below Danang and one infantryman in a patrol that was ambushed 40 miles north of Saigon. One of the 31, impossible to single out, became the 30,000th American to be killed in action in Vietnam since the grisly log was begun on Jan 1, 1961. Almost half of the total (14,400) died this year, many in

the three major offensives launched by the Communists since the Tet holiday on Jan 30.

Already the longest war ever fought by the US, Vietnam now ranks as its fifth costliest (after World War II, with 291,557 battle deaths; the Civil War, with 220,938; World War I, with 53,402; and Korea, with 33,629). With the killed-in-action rate running at roughly 200 per week, Vietnam should move past Korea into fourth place some time this spring – unless

the negotiators in Paris make dramatic progress. The war has been far more expensive for native combatants. South Vietnam has suffered 73,118 military dead in the past eight years. The Viet Cong and the North Vietnamese, according to an Allied estimate based on sometimes undependable body counts, have lost 422,979 dead since 1961.

Time

Photographers

Sgt Donald L. Shearee

"It's a small section, just me and another man . . . at LZ Stud, commonly known as Vandergrift Combat Base . . . We go out on the operations and cover the operations, shooting historical footage for HQ MC . . . We try to get with one of the attacking forces, either the first force in or the second company or battalion in. The main coverage we want to get are the Marines in action in contact. Before contact, we shoot moving into position, Marines landing, Marines setting up positions and checking out any type of bunkers or trenches or houses they find on their way in . . . Once they get into contact, we try to cover as much as we can of the whole company in contact, any heroic actions that take place."

R. L. Broomfield, Cpl

"Posed shots are not allowed. They've got to be action shots that actually happen. You've gotta be ready all the time."

"You keep low. You get around behind the guy you're trying to get on film. You can't stick your head up so you've gotta be shooting a high-angle level and crawl around the best you can."

Gary A. Muller, Lt Col

"Five photographers in the 3rd Marine Division have been killed and quite a few others have been wounded."

Interviews by Alan I. Isaacs

War Tour is Ending for F111

The controversial F111 fighter-bombers, brought into the war to deliver devastating strikes against Communist targets, are being sent home.

U.S. Air Force officials here announced Wednesday that a detachment of the super-sophisticated planes stationed at Takhli Royal Tha Air Base, Thailand, will be returned to Nellis Air Force Base outside Las Vegas, Nev., within the next two weeks.

F111s flew only slightly more than 50 attacks against Red targets during their deployment to the fighting. The swing-wing, $7 million jets flew their first mission March 26, their last May 1.

Stars and Stripes

The F111, seen here over Takhli, made an inauspicious combat debut, but by 1972 it was to prove a great warplane

The Women

"They twitter and sing," wrote novelist Graham Greene of the women of South Vietnam. In their diaphanous silk *ao dais*, they can readily appear as delicate and inconsequential as so many songbirds. In fact, Vietnamese women are birds of a very different feather. Heiresses of an ancient tradition of matriarchy, they have become, under the pressure of two decades of war, Asia's most emancipated women. They fight, politic, run businesses and their families and, through their husbands, probably control much of South Vietnam's endemic corruption.

Bewitching Beauties

Thus, it is not surprising that women have amassed some of the largest fortunes in South Vietnam. At least a dozen are estimated to be worth more than $5,000,000. The wife of one former port director became rich by charging a fee for every ship that docked at Saigon. Others

As ever, Bob Hope's Christmas Show brings talented entertainers and pretty girls to give the fun-starved GIs a taste of home

Below: Drawn by an F-102 rather than a sleigh, a suitably warlike Santa Claus decorates a rooftop at Da Nang Air Base

make practical use of military information that their husbands bring home. Before a unit is moved, for example, a wife who owns bars or brothels near by will unload the locations on un-suspecting buyers, then pick up land cheaply at the new location. Before the US 9th Division moved out of Nha Be last December, there was a rush of real estate trading around the base in November.

For all their new freedom, power and influence, the women of South Vietnam have lost none of the charm that has captivated generations of Westerners. They can be so bewitching that some 500 GIs have braved the tangles of red tape that the Army purposely puts in their way and brought home South Vietnamese war brides. *Time*

JANUARY 1969

1st Start of Operation Quyet Thang. There are a reported 88,000 enemy casualties by the end of the operation.

5th Former US Ambassador to Saigon, Henry Cabot Lodge, is to take over from senior negotiator Averell Harriman at the Paris peace talks.

6th South Vietnamese Education Minister dies as a result of a car-bomb attack.

11th Cambodia shoots down US helicopter allegedly violating its airspace.

15th The amount of war-funding requested goes down for the first time, in President Johnson's last budget.

18th Start of the four-party Paris peace talks.

20th Richard Nixon is inaugurated President of the United States of America.

22nd Inhabited Viet Cong tunnel network found in Cape Batangan.

22nd Start of Operation Dewey Canyon I in the Da Krong Valley in Quang Tri Province. There are 1335 enemy casualties by the end of the operation.

25th Start of the first plenary session in Paris.

28th In Paris the NLF shuns proposed swap of POWs.

Strike and Counter-strike Advisors in Action

Last November, Capt. Robert F. Olson, 33, took over a US Army five-man Mobile Advisory Team in Anphuc. The Americans live austerely in a Popular Forces (PF) fort (mud, logs, barbed wire and bamboo) and buy most of their food on the local market.

Olson has had some brushes with the Viet Cong. Four months ago, accompanied by a US sergeant carrying an M-60 machine gun, the captain went on patrol with the part-time un-paid People's Defense squad of Thuthan hamlet. They ran into the Viet Cong as the latter were approaching to attack the hamlet's PF outpost.

"We opened up with the M-60," Olson said. "We wounded two water buffalo, four chickens and one duck. But I think we also got some of the VC. They fired back and pulled away."

The hamlet chief promptly led a PF relief force from the outpost to help. But the Viet Cong had set up an ambush. Several of the PF were wounded. One was left behind. He dismantled his rifle and waited in the dark for rescue. Olson carried him out.

Washington Post

Mobile Advisory Team members like these live and work in close proximity to the people they're there to help. Conditions are "austere" – read "primitive" – but the Americans become one with the community, lessening the possibility of surprise attacks and ambush, and they are right on the spot to stop trouble before it even starts

Life with Charlie
A Viet Cong Prisoner Speaks

Last week the crew of an American helicopter operating over a clearing near Ca Mau city spotted a bearded figure clad in black pajamas and waving a mosquito net. It was Major James N. Rowe. He had escaped from his captors with the unenviable distinction of having been a prisoner of the Viet Cong for five years.

In the time since his capture, Rowe had become an almost legendary figure in Viet Nam. The Special Forces refused to give up on him. Occasionally, intelligence reports would drift in indicating that he was not only alive but making life difficult for his jailers. There were recurring tales about a prisoner that the Viet Cong called "Mr Trouble,"

Even after five years in captivity, Major James Rowe never stopped looking for chances to escape.

apparently because he had made several attempts at escape and remained utterly defiant of his captors. Some in Saigon thought that Rowe was Mr. Trouble. In 1967, a Viet Cong defector who had seen Rowe in a prison camp grudgingly characterized him as "stubborn, sneaky and very smart."

The Guard Became Unconscious ...

Rowe's chance for escape finally came on the last day of 1968, when allied troops launched a sweep near the camp and the prisoners were moved out. "I got one guard to separate with me," Rowe recalled. "At that point, the guard became unconscious and I got to the chopper." How did the guard become unconscious? "I'd rather not go into that at this point," said the major with a smile.

Time

Keeping Tea Prices Down

You now get 275 piasters for a dollar. Devaluation. It means you can afford to go into town again and renew those old bar acquaintances. Great. But don't forget the law of economics in Vietnam – and elsewhere. With more guys spending more money in the bars, prices will be under pressure to rise. But they don't have to. And you can help keep them down, not only in the bars, but elsewhere. A lot of GIs who banded together a couple of years ago proved that they could force prices of Saigon Tea to stay down. They formed a movement called STIF. It stood for "Saigon Tea is Fini". The idea was to go in a bar which had doubled its prices, sit there all night with a bottle or two of beer and buy no drinks for the more expensive ladies. It was a concerted effort and there was a lot of intercommunication between units – mimeographed sheets, etc. – to make sure the whole GI front would hold. It did. Bars which

had raised their prices dropped them again. There were a few grunts beat over the ear by irate barmaids, but it passed. Only it didn't last long. The big buildup of troops and mainly civilians jacked prices up again.

More for Tea

With the current devaluation, there will be a similar pressure to up the tea cost. But if enough guys decide that it ain't worth six hundred piasters to converse with a girl while she downs a thimbleful of colored water, then her price drops.

We're not against buying Saigon Teas. It's a long established practice that has survived a lot of crises. But the business of paying through the nose is something that the GIs in concert can stop. Everybody could be happy if nobody gets greedy. So stay alert to those outrageous prices you might run across and buy sensibly. It will get you more in the long run.

Grunt Free Press

Not your idea of a tropical boating holiday? Many a GI serving with the riverine force would agree with you

River Bank Search Viet Cong River Lifeline

TRACU One fairly typical recent morning, two fiberglass patrol boats left Tracu's dock on a 12-hour river bank search mission. Tiny inlets, overhanging canopies of

branches laced with vines, flooded meadows – the river was meant for bass, not caches. Standing beside the helmsman of one boat, Army lst Lt. David C. Wheeler, 23, of Arlington,

VA., pointed out occasional square mud mounds between the trees. These were Vietcong bunkers, deserted by day, frequented by night. The boat passed a crude sign that said:

"You die, GI."
"We'd pull it down," said a sailor, "but they've probably got it booby-trapped."

Washington Post

FEBRUARY 1969

15th	US troop numbers in Vietnam put at 539,000.
22nd	First communist bombardment of Saigon since October 1968.
22nd	US draft dodgers and deserters given refuge in Sweden.
23rd	Start of the so-called "post-Tet" communist offensive on over 100 targets, including Saigon, costs an estimated 100 US lives.
24th	US bodycount from the offensive rises to 200.
24th	Start of Operation Quyet Thang 22 in Quang Ngai Province. There are 777 enemy casualties by the end of the operation.
25th	Thirty-six US personnel die in one incident as a result of a North Vietnamese suicide operation as the offensive continues.
27th	US sources put American losses in the current offensive at between 250 and 300 compared with enemy casualties totalling 5300.
27th	Start of Operation Quang Nam in Quang Nam Province. There are 688 enemy casualties reported by the end of the operation.

Letter to America

When Pfc. Dennis Doame sits himself down behind the lines in Vietnam to comply with his mother's going away instructionsthat he keep her informed, he tells it like it is. Any mother of a 19 year old amateur soldier can see from such a letter that nothing is really happening to her boy out there in the rice paddies – or, at least, hasn't yet. Following, minus only a few personal references, are his New Year's Day assurances that war is nowhere near the hell all mothers seem to think it must be. He's the son of Mr and Mrs L. A. Doame Jr. of Baltimore.

Dear Mom and Dad,

How are you? I'm fine. Today I saw an article on the Colts. It was about their victory over the Browns. It said that Tom Matte was hurt, but not how badly. I hope he can play in the Super

Booby traps were something every Grunt had to watch for. Most were simple devices, such as this trip-wire-activated cross-bow trap.

Bowl. The Las Vegas bookies favor the Colts by 17 points.

t is so hot here. I would love to go swimming. The only trouble is that I don't have any swimming trunks. Please send me some. They don't have any at the PX.

Tonight Radio AFVN is playing the top 30 country and western songs of 1968. I bet Dad would like to listen to that. If I had a tape recorder I could have some great tapes between last night's top 100 and tonight's top 30.

Last month, I got a haircut and massage at the barbershop. It is run by the Vietnamese. That was the last time I will let those gook barbers give me a massage! They beat the hell out of my head, and I left with a headache.

When I was up at Bien Phu, I really got to like our "tiger scout." His name was Vo Van Dang. He was 5ft 2in tall and weighed 97lbs. He was 20 years old. He looked like he was 15 years old. He was strong and fast for his size. I learned that he

used to be a NVA regular. I wonder if he killed any GIs before he came over to our side. He sure was loyal to us. Several times he saved our lives. He could spot a booby trap better than us because he used to make them himself. Sometimes he found out from the villagers if there were any VC in the area.

When our platoon leader sent him on a suicide mission, he went. And when he was thrown to the ground, bleeding pretty badly, he told us to stay back. There were more booby traps all around him. He was really a nice guy. Everyone agreed that he was the best tiger scout in the company.

Washington Post

Suicide Attack Marines Repel Human Waves

SAIGON – North Vietnamese infantrymen, attacking behind suicide volunteers who turned themselves into human bombs, slashed into two U.S. Marine outposts near the Demilitarized Zone early Tuesday but were driven out in vicious hand-to-hand fighting.

As the smoke of battle cleared, the Marines counted their losses – 36 killed and 97 wounded in the biggest of a series of attacks launched by the Communists Sunday.

Fifty-six Communist soldiers were known dead, their bodies sprawled inside the perimeters or on the barb wire. The Marines had yet to make a sweep of the fog-shrouded battlefields.

Sandal-clad Communist sappers carrying tiny flashlights and with explosive satchel charges strapped to their bodies attacked the two outposts, four and nine miles west-northwest of the geographical designation called "The Rockpile" about 4 a.m.

The Communists attacked the bases in two 200-man waves, UPI's David Lamb reported from the scene. Mortar rounds thudded into the outposts as the assaults began, Lamb reported.

The Communists blazed away with automatic weapons fire and tossed their satchel charges into Marine bunkers, penetrating the barb wire perimeter of both camps and forcing the Leathernecks to call in artillery barrages on their own positions.

One Marine killed five Communists with a knife in hand-to-hand combat. Another beat one to death with hand grenade.

The leatherneck commander at Fire Base Russell, just two miles below the DMZ, reported to Marine headquarters in Da Nang that enemy sappers taped 25-pound bundles of TNT on their backs, wrapped the detonating cord around their chests, and then charged to blast lanes through the Marines defenses.

Stars and Stripes

War Begins with Punch Cards

A chartered Boeing 707, flight W2B3, rolled to a stop at the Bienhoa air terminal at 12.10 p.m. the other day, and 165 passengers, all in fatigues and none of them smiling, stepped into their year of war.

"Gentlemen, welcome to Vietnam," someone said into a microphone. Nearby, 165 other soldiers, their year in Vietnam finished, prepared to board the same jet for a 20-hour flight back into "the world." The groups exchanged glances.

The Young Tourists

The new arrivals boarded buses for a six-mile, bouncing ride past Vietnamese shanty towns, rows of bars and massage parlors, a goat sniffing through a dump heap, along miles of barbed wire and sandbags – although they were never more than 25 miles from Saigon – all

to the accompaniment of rock music from the bus's radio, which at one point proclaimed: "From Saigon, ladies and gentlemen, the beat goes on."

Most of the soldiers stared out the windows. Said one: "People actually live in those things huh?" and another, "Some of these places been bombed, or are they just falling apart?" And a third: "Those trees dead, or is that just the way they are here?"

At the 90th Replacement Battalion, which has charge of 80 per cent of the Army's arriving and departing troops – it "celebrated" its one millionth arrival in February – another man with

a microphone said: "Gentlemen, welcome to Vietnam 'in-country' processing."

For the next five hours, the new soldiers filled out forms, collected equipment, exchanged money, listened to lectures and stood in lines.

"Gentlemen, there is a snack bar and an ice-cream shop next to the finance building. These facilities are off limits to you until you have completed your processing. Gentlemen, there will be absolutely no talking while you are processing. Gentlemen, I want you to prepare to process . . ."

The New York Times

MARCH 1969

1st President Thieu labels offensive a "complete failure". Start of Operation Wayne Grey in Kontum Province, resulting in 608 enemy casualties. Operation Oklahoma Hills starts in Quang Nam Province. 596 enemy casualties ensue. Operation Massachusetts Striker gets under way in the Ashau Valley.

5th Rocket attack on Saigon kills 22 civilians.

6th The casualty figures for week one of the post-Tet offensive stand at 453 US personnel, 521 South Vietnamese, 6752 enemy killed. 2593 US personnel are reported wounded.

8th US troops reported as operating inside Laos.

10th Hue undergoes Viet Cong rocket attack.

14th President Nixon states that the communist offensive means that there can be no troop withdrawals for the time being.

15th Start of Operation Maine Crag, the first offensive US operation in the DMZ since 1968.

18th Operation Breakfast (the "Menu" raids), the bombing of Cambodia, begins. The US Congress and public are not informed. The operation is renamed Operation Freedom Deal on 14 May 1970.

18th Start of Operation Atlas Wedge around Saigon.

19th Defense Secretary Laird calls for over $150 million to develop the South Vietnamese Army with a view to its taking over from US personnel.

20th Operation Quyet Thang 25, which results in 592 enemy casualties, is under way in Quang Ngai Province.

22nd A US Gallup Poll indicates that of those asked 32 per cent advocate stepping up the conflict while 26 per cent are for pulling out.

24th Lieutenant General William B. Rosson is to be the new deputy commander of US forces in Vietnam.

Does Your Desk Job Bug You?

In combat, a man has to develop new reflexes in order to survive and live peacefully. For the grunt, this involves reflexes which will help dodge bullets and mortars and booby traps. For the deskbound commando, reflexes also must be sharpened and adapted for comfortable living. For example, killing flies and mosquitoes.

The fly swatter, when available, makes the job easier, but here too, a certain amount of skill is required. Approach the fly from the rear, with swatter at the ready and again, make the thrust toward the fly's rear. An ideal altitude for the strike is three feet, with no backward thrust. Flies watch what's going on so don't telegraph your punches.

Deadlier than the Fly

The mosquito, of course, is much more deadly than the fly, and greater effort and dedication is required in combating these ubiquitous creatures. First of all, the Vietnamese mosquito never telegraphs his punches. He's bitten you and run for cover before you feel the sting. Like the VC, he hits his opponent when the opponent is weakest, namely, in the seconds before dropping off to sleep. Or he may lie low on the floor under a desk and strike quickly at ankles and knees in a massive assault before retreating.

Don't expect too much in the way of results at first. But as your tour in Vietnam lengthens, you will find that you have come a long way toward reacting toward flies and mosquitoes. It's a new reflex in your inventory that might come in handy in civilian life.

Grunt Free Press

Classified Ads

PFC POTTER SKI: Please contact Dispensary reference your missed appointment for penicillin shot. Urgent.

TRAVEL: F4C Phantom pilot, leaving Danang 0530 Hours 4 March, seeks paying passenger to share costs. Ring Hotshot Charlie, Danang 00020.

MEN: Sure fire method guaranteed to improve your virility. Suzy's Bar, Tu-Do, Saigon. 20 attractive hostesses.

WANTED: Affectionate, possibly intimate relationship with pen pal, female. Fire Base Alpha, Highlands, VN.

CHASTE male seeks chaste female for discussions on chastity. Ron. Bien Hoa 98765.

BROADMINDED UNINHIBITED SWINGERS are invited to join our Square Dance group meeting Mondays at Red Cross Club, Danang.

WOMEN suffering from frigidity. Our guaranteed and proven therapy awaits you. Call 3rd Platoon, B Company, 6th Bn., Di An.

LUCY: I hear your voice at night in the jungle. Charlie, 2nd Plt, C Co.

EXHIBITION: Nightly in Bangkok. Watch living statues in action. Tickets sold front of Chao Feeyah Hotel.

USED GRENADES WANTED. Will pay spot cash for quality specimens. Burt's. Fu Kyu Box 1999.

MOM: 364 days to go and it seems like I got here yesterday. Tom.

DOES ANYONE have a home for our company mascot, a Doberman Pinscher who turned out to be gay. Write, B Co, 999th Rgt., Phy Tho.

Grunt Free Press

Armored Warfare

It was at Ben Het in March 1969 that American and North Vietnamese armor clashed for the first and only time.

Both Sergeant First Class Hugh H. Havermale and Staff Sergeant Jerry W. Jones heard the sound of tracks and heavy engines through the noise of the artillery. With no free world tanks to the west, the probability of an enemy tank attack sent everyone into action. High explosive anti-tank (HEAT) ammunition was loaded into tank guns and from battle stations all eyes strained into the darkness.

In his tank, Sergeant Havermale scanned the area with an infrared searchlight, but could not identify targets in the fog. Sergeant Jones, from his tank, could see the area from which the tank sounds were coming but had no searchlight. Tension grew. Suddenly an anti-tank mine exploded 1,100 meters to

the southwest, giving away the location of the enemy; the battle for Ben Het now began in earnest.

Aiming at the Flashes

Although immobilized, the enemy PT76 tank that had hit the mine was still able to fight. Even before the echo of the explosion had died, the PT76 had fired a round that fell short of the defenders' position. The re-

mainder of the enemy force opened fire, and seven other gun flashes could be seen. The US forces returned the fire with HEAT ammunition from the tanks and fire from all other weapons as well. Specialist 4 Frank Hembree was the first American tank gunner to fire, and he remembers: "I only had his muzzle flashes to sight on, but I couldn't wait for a better target because his shells were

Some areas of Vietnam turned out to be pretty good tank country, but it was the Americans who benefitted, not the Vietnamese. Just once did US and NVA armor meet in battle

landing real close to us." The muzzle flashes proved to be enough for Specialist Hembree; his second round turned the enemy tank into a fireball.

US Army
"Mounted Combat in Vietnam"

GIs Hurl Back N. Viet Battalion

A battalion of well-equipped North Vietnamese soldiers – some of them carrying flame-throwers – charged an isolated U.S. landing zone early Saturday but crumbled as the little camp's howitzers were fired at them like rifles.

The attack on the 1st Air Cav. Div.'s Landing Zone Grant, about 45 miles northwest of Saigon, was coupled with two other unsuccessful assaults on American bases along Communist corridors to the capital.

Meanwhile, Communist gunners opened up overnight on some 50 targets scattered throughout Vietnam. Most of the shellings were aimed at small military units, U.S. spokesmen said. Few casualties and only light damage was reported.

Stars and Stripes

After artillery and aerial bombardment, the land around LZ Grant looks like a First World War battlefield in miniature

MORE COSTLY THAN KOREA

APRIL 1969

1st Defense Secretary Laird discloses a projected 10 per cent reduction in B-52 missions over South Vietnam because of defence spending cuts.

3rd Laird insists that the US is trying to Vietnamize the war as quickly as it can, given the current communist offensive.

3rd It is revealed that 33,641 US personnel have died so far in combat during the war. This exceeds by 12 the figure for the Korean War.

5-6th Nationwide anti-war protests take place in the US.

14th US troops beat off a concerted enemy assault against a base northwest of Saigon. 198 communists and 13 US personnel die.

15th Operation Washington Green opens in the An Lao Valley in Binh Dinh Province. There are 1957 enemy casualties by the end of the operation.

16th Prince Sihanouk of Cambodia expresses his willingness to re-establish diplomatic relations with Washington. A fortnight later this is rescinded because of a controversy surrounding a group of offshore islands.

18th Start of Operation Dang Thang 69 in Binh Dinh Province. There are 507 enemy casualties by the end of the operation.

19th The South Vietnamese Air Force takes delivery of the first 20 of a scheduled 60 fighter-bombers.

24-25th In a two-day operation on the border northwest of Saigon, US B-52s reportedly expend nearly 3000 tons of bombs.

26-27th Eleven US soldiers and 313 enemy are reported dead after engagements close to the Cambodian border.

30th US troop numbers in Vietnam reach their peak at 543,000.

A Flagpole in Beallsville

The Beallsville City Council decided this week to erect a flagpole and a granite plaque in the town's tiny cemetery, where four of Beallsville's dead from the Vietnam War are buried.

The former farm center, on a 1,000 foot high plateau in southeastern Ohio in the Alleghany Mountain foothills has a population of about 450.

Six of its young men have been killed in Vietnam in the last three years, about 90 times the national average. Four are buried here, two in other cemeteries.

Fifteen have gone to the Vietnam war from Beallsville. Five have returned alive. Four are still fighting.

New York Times

The Dangers of Defoliation

By April 1969, all Ranch Hand planes had been converted to the jet-equipped UC-123K version. The extra power provided by the jets allowed Ranch Hand to fly some experimental spray runs at an airspeed of 180 knots, about 50 knots greater than the usual speed. This higher speed made the spray planes harder for gunners on the ground to hit, but it reduced the time available for the pilots to make flight path adjustments necessitated by varying terrain and target shapes.

Landing in the Paddies

Ground fire was still a serious problem in early and mid-1969, as a mission on April 7 illustrated. On that date, a formation of seven Ranch Hand aircraft had planned to make three separate passes over their targets in the Delta. On the first pass, all but one were hit by .30- and .50-caliber machine gun fire. Two of the UC-123Ks lost an engine and proceeded at once to Bien Hoa. The five remaining aircraft received ground fire on the second pass, and the last plane in the formation lost effective aileron control as bullets penetrated its left wing and control surfaces. Like the crew of the UC-123 the previous December, the crew maintained limited directional control by using differential power settings on its left and right engines. After flying to the airstrip at Ben Tre for an emergency landing, the crew discovered a C-130 on the dirt runway which could not move clear in time for the damaged Ranch Hand plane to land. Unable to climb away from the field and return for another landing attempt, the crew chose to set the aircraft down in rice paddies 200 yards to the side of the runway. The crew escaped injury, but the UC-123K received extensive damage. In response to this incident, Seventh Air Force again restricted Ranch Hand's activities in IV Corps.

"USAF in Vietnam"

Root Beer and Chicken with Noodles

SAIGON "I love you, I love you," shouted the skinny, dirty soldier to the helicopter pilot as he hugged the gunner.

Spec. 5 Thomas H. Van Putten, 21, of Caledonia, Mich., wandered around the jungle of Tayninh province, some 70 miles northwest of Saigon, for 18 days after escaping from the Vietcong who captured him more than a year ago.

The American helicopter spotted Van Putten Thursday and took him to a hospital at Longbinh, 10 miles north of Saigon, a US spokesman announced today.

The spokesman said Van Putten was in good condition but suffering from malnutrition and

Ranch Hand aircraft – this is a UC-123B Provider – fly low and slow over terrain that could be purpose-built for hiding anti-aircraft units

Blacks Against the War

After the noontime chow on July 27, 1967, at a rifle range in Camp Pendleton, Calif., a dozen or so Negro Marines gathered under a shade tree.

Some dozed, some read newspapers, some talked about girls and their Military Occupational Specialty. Mostly, in that hot summer, they talked of Vietnam and the rioting in the cities.

Much of the talk came from Pfc. George Daniels of Queens, who was then 18, and Lance Cpl. William L. Harvey, also of Queens and then 19.

Their theme, as testimony at their subsequent trials made plain, was simple.

"Vietnam is a white man's war. Black men should not go, only to return and fight whites at home. Let us all ask the company commander for a mast – the Marine procedure that enables an enlisted man to bring a grievance to his commanding officer – and tell him how we feel."

A few weeks later Daniels and Harvey were arrested and in November were tried before a general court martial.

Washington Post

Racial tensions, spilled over from "the world", put extra strain on United States servicemen, especially the infantrymen who stay alive by trusting their squad-mates, irrespective of their color

dehydration. He will be flown home to visit his parents tomorrow.

One of the first things Van Putten reportedly said to the helicopter crew that rescued him was, "I've escaped from the enemy. Give me something to eat."

His first meal after being found consisted of warm root beer, fruit cocktail and chicken with noodles.

"I have never tasted such delicious food in all my life," Van Putten said.

On his first night back he said, "I try to sleep but the bed is too comfortable. I just keep wanting to talk to people."

Washington Post

Reds Bushwhacked on Cambodian Border

One American soldier was wounded early Saturday when 213 Communists died in a battle so lopsided it wasn't worth the name.

U.S. cannons fired into Cambodia to silence Red mortars threatening the defenders of "Frontier City," a tiny circle around some 200 GIs less than a mile from the border.

Machine gun-firing helicopters began picking off Communists about 10 p.m. Friday as the Reds hustled into place. The enemy troops hid in groves of trees and behind sun-baked paddy dikes on the broad plain 35 miles west of Saigon.

The camp's defenders, members of C Co., 4th Bn., 9th Inf. of the 25th Inf. Div. watched on radar scopes or peered through $35,000 telescopes that allowed them to see in the dark while about a battallion of Red troops – most of them North Vietnamese – prepared for a charge.

Stars and Stripes

BETTER CONDITIONS

MAY 1969

	Operation Frederick Hill gets under way in the area of Tam Ky.
1st	Start of Operation Virginia Ridge in Quang Tri Province. There are 560 enemy casualties by the end of the operation.
5th	An assault on a US camp northwest of Saigon ends with 125 enemy and nine US personnel dead.
6th	In what is one of the worst accidents of the war, a US helicopter crashes, killing 34 and bringing the total number of helicopters lost to 2595.
8th	The NLF submits its 10-point peace plan at the Paris talks.
9th	A newspaper report in *The New York Times* on the secret bombing of Cambodia leads to an FBI hunt to find who leaked the information to the press.
10th	Start of Operation Apache Snow in Thau Thien Province. There are 977 enemy casualties by the end of the operation.
10-20th	597 communists and 56 US personnel die in the 10-day battle for Apbia mountain (afterwards known as "Hamburger Hill").
11-12th	159 targets in South Vietnam suffer under communist artillery bombardment.

Stumbling Into Ambush

Brig. Gen. S. L. A. Marshall, USA (Ret.) said yesterday 40 per cent of American combat losses in Vietnam are the result of "our own mistakes."

He blamed these casualties on foolishness, impatience and heroics by US troops, and singled out "lieutenants, captains (and) platoon sergeants" as the weakest cog in the American war machine in Vietnam.

Marshall, a well-known military historian and combat journalist, made the comments in an interview in connection with the publication of his new book "Ambush".

The book depicts small American units stumbling and bumbling into death traps set by the Vietcong. "Ambush" is based upon interviews with survivors of Vietnam battles in the winter of 1966-67.

Washington Post

The New Warfare

SAIGON Battlefield amenities unknown to earlier armies have almost eliminated combat fatigue among United States troops in South Vietnam, according to American medical authorities here.

Official statistics for the 550,000 United States servicemen in the war zone show that fewer than 100 are treated each year for the mental state that results from too much exposure to combat.

By contrast, during World Wars I and II and the Korean war, thousands of men had to be taken out because of combat fatigue, also known as shell-shock or battle exhaustion. Specific figures from previous wars could not be obtained.

Medical officers say today's American soldier is fighting under conditions much less wearing – mentally – than those that faced his predecessors.

Into the Badlands

SAIGON US Marines caught up with a force of North Vietnamese regulars on the banks of the Vugia River near Danang Wednesday and reported killing 60. American jets hit the Communist ranks with napalm and rockets.

US officials said nine Marines were killed and 60 were wounded in the day-long battle 12 miles southwest of Danang, an area the Americans call Arizona Territory because of its resemblance to the badlands of the Old West. Many of the US casualties were inflicted by a mortar shell which crashed into a command post.

Washington Post

A skilled ground-strike pilot can use napalm with almost surgical precision, giving hard-pressed infantry time to re-group

Points Made by Officers

The officers made the following points:

"Most of the operations in which the US soldier in South Vietnam takes part last only a few days and often involve little fighting. When he returns to his base camp, he has access to hot showers, movies and post exchanges . . . "

"Whenever there is fighting, he goes into it convinced his training, equipment and leadership are among the best in the world. A phone call will bring him devastating aircraft and artillery support. Conversely, he need not worry about enemy air attacks . . . "

"If he is wounded, evacuation usually is within 20 minutes and medical care is so intense and expert that survival odds are better than 95 to 1 . . . "

"He is guaranteed a week's leave – out of Vietnam – during a duty tour that never exceeds 13 months. One of his cliches is 'I guess I can stand anything for a year.'"

The New York Times

"Ah, Gee, it's so good to relax after a hard day at the plant . . ." Not quite, but at least GIs know that after action there will be a chance to clean up

Back in War Zone C

TAYNINH Once again, North Vietnamese and Vietcong troops have withdrawn into the sanctuary of the dense jungle and bamboo forest that stretches north and east of here to the Cambodian border.

The area – designated on both allied and enemy maps as War Zone C – has served for years as a haven for enemy troops. Whenever it has suited their purpose, North Vietnamese and Vietcong units have pulled back into the relative safety of the network of underground bunkers, supply depots and jungle-protected staging camps that they have built over the years in War Zone C.

Allied intelligence estimates that 15,000 to 20,000 North Vietnamese regulars are there now, resting from their recent offensive.

The New York Times

There is just no substitute for vigilance, especially when the terrain in which you're fighting is littered with secondary jungle and bamboo forests so thick that you may never see more than ten yards

14th President Nixon gives his reply to the NLF 10-point program.

14th Da Nang comes under communist artillery fire.

Part of the massive US facility at Da Nang burns after a communist artillery attack. Major air bases are prime Viet Cong and NVA targets. Their large size means that they have long perimeters for saboteurs to penetrate, and they are crammed with explosive targets like ordnance depots and fuel farms

15th Operation Dan Quyen 38-A commences in the Ben Het/Dak To area. There are 945 enemy casualties by the end of the operation.

16th Start of Operation Lamar Plain in Quang Tin Province. There are 524 enemy casualties by the end of the operation.

18th US and South Vietnamese troops beat off communist attacks on camps near Xuan Loc, east of Saigon.

20th As US troops capture Hamburger Hill, Senator Edward Kennedy labels the battle "senseless and irresponsible".

28th US forces leave Apbia mountain (Hamburger Hill), "continuing their reconnaissance-in-force mission throughout the Ashau valley".

Battle for Tayninh

TAYNINH Since last August, when the enemy fought his way into the heart of this handsome provincial capital, Tayninh has been the focal point of some of the bitterest fighting in Vietnam.

A series of savage battles has been fought in the jungle that surrounds the city. Night-time shelling by the enemy has become routine.

Sounds of Night

Despite the destruction, the explosion caused no hysteria in Tayninh. The 180,000 people of the city have learned to live with the war and, to some regret, to live from it.

A much advertised Tayninh industry, for example, is the making of brassware. Decoratively carved candlesticks and vases are wrought from expended allied shell casings which are a staple in the thriving black market.

New houses in the Long Hoa section, which was badly burned during an enemy assault last August, have been rebuilt with the white pine of allied ammunition cases. The sides of the simple houses have been decorated with stenciled black consignment numbers of ammunition boxes.

The New York Times

The Battle For Hamburger Hill

Ap Bia Mountain anchors the northwest corner of South Viet Nam's Ashau Valley, since 1966 a major infiltration route for Communist forces from the Ho Chi Minh Trail in Laos to the coastal cities of northern I Corps. It is a mountain much like any other in that part of the Highlands, green, triple-canopied and spiked with thick stands of bamboo. On military maps it is listed as Hill 937, the number representing its height in meters. Last week it acquired another name: Hamburger Hill. It was a grisly but all too appropriate description, for the battle in and around Ap Bia took the lives of 84 GIs and wounded 480 more. Such engagements were familiar enough in Viet Nam up until a year ago. But coming at this stage of the war and the peace talks, the battle for Hamburger Hill set off tremors of controversy that carried all the way to Capitol Hill.

The reaction in Washington came quickly. Mindful of similar assaults in the past – when hills were taken at high cost and then quickly abandoned – Senator Edward Kennedy charged that it was "both senseless and irresponsible to continue to send our young men to their deaths to capture hills and positions that have no relation to this conflict." After initial hesitation, the Army fought back, describing the battle as a "tremendous, gallant victory."

Time

'Hamburger Hill' Taken 10-Day Fight Over

American paratroopers and South Vietnamese infantrymen, in a four-pronged assault, Tuesday seized "Hamburger Hill," a 3,000-foot North Vietnamese mountaintop fortress along the rugged Laotian frontier. It was the 10th day of heavy fighting for the position.

Spokesmen for the 101st Airborne Div. said the reinforced Allied force, which was doubled overnight to include more than 1,000 paratroopers and 400 South Vietnamese infantrymen, stormed the Dong Ap Bia mountain from four sides.

Sharp fighting was reported, however, between the mountain and the Laotian border, less than two miles away. The North Vietnamese troops were said to be trying to move back into base sanctuaries in Laos.

But one battalion of paratroopers, part of the assault force, ran into the retreating North Vietnamese and maneuvered to try to trap them between the Allied forces. Helicopter gunships firing rockets and machine guns raked the retreating Communist soldiers.

Military spokesmen said the Communists lost 426 men killed in the battle for the mountain, while U.S. casualties were put at 39 killed and 273 wounded.

Tuesday's push hit the hill's defenders from all sides as the 101st's 3rd Bn., 187th Inf. was joined by the 1st Bn., 506th Inf.; the 2nd Bn., 501st Inf. and the 3rd Bn. of the Vietnamese 1st Div.

The ground assault came after heavy artillery and air bombardment. The 3,000-foot peak fell into Allied hands as A and C Companies of the 3rd Bn., 187th

101st Airborne paratroopers come under hostile fire

Inf., secured the crest on the northwest side and the Vietnamese took the southeastern knoll.

Stars and Stripes

"I've Lost a Lot of Buddies Up There"

DONGAPBIA The paratroopers came down from the mountain, their green shirts darkened with sweat, their weapons gone, their bandages stained brown and red – with mud and blood.

Many cursed Lt. Col. Weldon Honeycutt, the tough battalion commander who sent three companies Sunday to take this 3000-foot mountain just over a mile east of Laos and overlooking the shell-pocked Ashau Valley.

They failed and they suffered.

"That damn Blackjack won't stop unless he kills every damn one of us," said one of the 40 to 50 101st Airborne Division troopers who was wounded.

At least 10 died on the hill, while 125 of the enemy were reported killed.

Honeycutt, 38, whose radio code name is Blackjack, had been given an order: Take the mountain. It had been steadily pounded since May 10 by artillery, riot gas and more than 70 air strikes. It is believed to contain a North Vietnamese regimental headquarters and a supply cache.

"This is my third war and I haven't bumped into a fight like this since World War II," said Col. Joseph Conmy Jr. of Washington, who commands the Division's 3rd Brigade. "This crowd must have gotten the word from Uncle Ho."

Made 9 Assaults

Spec. 4 Anthony Toll, 20, made nine of those assaults, and the dark-haired, slender veteran of eight months in Vietnam was bitter.

"After all these air and artillery strikes, those gooks are still in there fighting. All of us are wondering why they just can't pull back and B-52 that hill," he said.

"I've lost a lot of buddies up there. Not many guys can take it much longer."

Why take the hill?

Washington Post

TROOP WITHDRAWALS ANNOUNCED

JUNE 1969

7th It is reported that battles along the Cambodian border have resulted in 399 communist casualties.

7th Da Nang comes under communist rocket fire.

8th At a meeting with President Thieu, President Nixon sets a deadline of the end of August for the withdrawal of 25,000 US personnel. Both leaders are at pains to stress that South Vietnamese troops will take their place.

10th The creation of a Provisional Revolutionary Government (PRG) for South Vietnam is announced by the NLF.

11th Instances of hand-to-hand fighting are reported during battles between US and communist forces near Da Nang.

12-15th Fifteen countries, including China and the USSR, recognize the PRG.

13th The US government defends its decision to wiretap the "Chicago Eight", who are accused of inciting the 1968 Democratic Convention riots.

13th It is reported that 242,000 bombing missions have so far been carried out by US aircraft.

14-15th A US airborne headquarters near Hamburger Hill comes under attack by the NVA.

17th According to US intelligence the NVA has moved back on to Hamburger Hill.

17th Start of a search-and-destroy operation in the Ashau Valley.

19th President Nixon says he would like to "beat" the schedule put forward by former Defense Secretary Clifford for withdrawing 250,000 US troops by the end of the following year.

21st Fighting in the Tay Ninh area continues with an attack on a US base.

23rd The US Special Forces base at Ben Het comes under siege by the NVA.

25th The South Vietnamese Navy takes receipt of 64 river patrol boats from the US.

27th Over 440 artillery rounds pour into Ben Het.

28th Forty-two per cent of the US population think that President Nixon's timetable for troop withdrawal is too slow.

Sometimes, even war has a strange beauty that man can do nothing to change. This A-1 Skyraider, weapons racks empty, returns from yet another sortie, stark against a burning sunset

Fighting Flares After Cease-Fire

SAIGON Sharp fighting broke out yesterday in the Central Highlands of South Vietnam only three hours after the end of the frequently violated cease-fire for Buddha's birthday.

The action continued into the night, and when it was halted the United States command said, the bodies of 54 North Vietnamese soldiers were found on the battlefield. American losses, from elements of the 4th Infantry Division, were put at 10 killed and 2 wounded.

The fighting near Plcimrong, about 250 miles northeast of Saigon, was the heaviest listed in battle reports this morning. There were several other clashes across the country and the United States command said that six significant enemy rocket or mortar attacks were reported during the night.

The New York Times

Reduce Vietnam Force

MIDWAY ISLAND President Nixon met with President Nguyen Van Thieu of South Vietnam today and announced that 25,000 American soldiers would be withdrawn from Vietnam before the end of August.

After the first two hours of five hours of talks on this Pacific island, Mr Nixon emerged to declare that the Presidents had agreed that troop withdrawals would begin within 30 days.

The New York Times

Premier Concedes US Planes Fly Raids in Laos

VIENTIANE Prince Souvanna Phouma, the Premier of Laos, has acknowledged publicly for the first time that United States airplanes are regularly carrying out bombing raids within his country. He said that the bombing would go on as long as North Vietnamese troops used bases and infiltration routes in Laos.

The Prince spoke in interviews with the United Press International and the Japanese newspaper Yomiuri Shimbun made public today by the official Laotian press agency. The remarks – and especially their official publication – surprised diplomats, who noted that the Prince had for years avoided the subject of American bombing.

During the interview, the Premier said:

"The bombing carried on by American planes in Laos in the frontier region is a fact that springs from the 1962 Geneva accords. At Geneva, the signatory countries guaranteed the independence, neutrality and territorial integrity of Laos.

"From the moment that one signatory does not respect the accords, it is the duty of the other signatories to intervene to enforce respect for them. If North Vietnam wants the bombing to stop, it is necessary that they withdraw their troops from Laos."

The New York Times

"You could be forgiven for thinking this was some weird form of mobile home, but we tank crews have to do the best we can under very difficult circumstances, you know . . ."

Costly Success

TAYNINH A "victory demonstration" was held at the Phukhuong district headquarters this morning.

Dozens of gawking, giggling children, a few naked, some in shorts and nearly all shoeless, filed past barbed wire and bunkers into the compound to look at a display of captured rifles, machine guns, rocket launchers and mortars lying on tables surrounded by South Vietnamese victory banners.

Most of the weapons were the spoils of a three-day battle in a ribbon of four hamlets, on the northeastern edge of this city 55 miles northwest of Saigon. Some 9,000 of the district's 180,000 people lived in those hamlets.

94 of Enemy Killed

The victory statistics included 94 enemy soldiers killed and 2 captured. The price of the victory was the destruction of 423 homes. Seventy-two homes were more than half demolished.

The New York Times

JULY 1969

2nd Allied military sources report that the siege of Ben Het is at an end.

7th The first US troop withdrawals take place.

10th It is disclosed that a group of US pacifists – it will be led by a member of the Chicago Eight – will visit North Vietnam to secure the release of three US POWs.

15th A period of covert diplomatic activity ends with North Vietnam acceding to secret talks with the US.

17-20th Head of the US Joint Chiefs of Staff General Wheeler visits Vietnam.

21st Start of Operation Idaho Canyon in Quang Tri Province. There are 565 enemy casualties by the end of the operation.

25th The US President outlines what is to become known as the "Nixon Doctrine" under which the US should not be drawn into conventional or internal conflicts in Asia.

28th US and Viet Cong forces battle for "the Citadel" a communist bastion, 25 miles north of Saigon.

30th President Nixon has talks with President Thieu during a flying visit to South Vietnam.

First GIs in Pullout Leave Saigon

SAIGON Draped in flower leis and grinning broadly, a battalion of 814 infantrymen left Saigon today in the initial withdrawal of American combat troops from Vietnam.

The soldiers stood at attention through a two-hour departure ceremony at Tansonnhut Airport and then broke into cheers as they marched towards a fleet of waiting jet transports.

The infantrymen were the first of some 25,000 troops who will be withdrawn in the first stage of the United States disengagement from a war that has so far cost 38,866 American lives.

"I only had a month to go," S. Sgt. Cleveland Brown of Jacksonville, Fla., said as he boarded one of the waiting planes. "But I'm damn glad to be getting out alive. It's been a long, hard 11 months." *The New York Times*

Ticker Tape Welcome GIs Return to "The World"

SEATTLE Rain, martial music, pretty girls, ticker tape, public speeches and the shouts of about 50 antiwar demonstrators today greeted the first GIs pulled out of Vietnam in President Nixon's effort to de-escalate the war. The 814 members of the Third Battalion, 60th Infantry, Ninth Infantry Division landed yesterday at McChord Air Force Base 30 miles away. Today they marched through the wind-whipped streets of Seattle and heard Army Secretary Stanley R. Resor tell them that their presence was "tangible evidence of the progress we have made" in Vietnam.

The New York Times

KONTUM The South Vietnamese commander in the battle to relieve the besieged Special Forces camp at Benhet said today that he had used the mountainous outpost as "bait" to draw the enemy into a trap.

Col. Nguyen Bao Lien of the 24th Special Tactical Zone, the top allied commander in the Benhet battle, said at a news conference that the enemy had taken the bait and was being "smashed." He predicted that the siege would be lifted within the week.

His statement came as a surprise to many officers who have been working closely with him since combat broke out a few miles east of Benhet in May.

Some of the American advisers to South Vietnamese units involved in the fighting chuckled when told of the statement.

"Who's he kidding?" a major asked.

The New York Times

Benhet Commander Says He Used Base As "Bait" for Enemy

Sometimes, a man's best friend is a fifty cal. These ARVN armored crewmen use their vehicle's externally mounted weapon in support

Helicopters really came of age in the Vietnam War, altering the face of battle for the infantryman and the tanker equally. Add in the comparative ease of re-supply and casevac, and it's hard to remember anything that has made so much change in so little time

Bombing Halt Has Let North Repair Supply Net

WASHINGTON (UPI) – North Vietnam has re-built all the bridges, highways and trans-shipment points that were destroyed by U.S. planes before the Oct. 31 suspension of bombing, according to Air Force Chief of Staff John P. McConnell.

"Practically everything in North Vietnam has been re-built," McConnell testified. "All the highways, the bridges, the trans-shipment points that were destroyed, and what little indus-try they have, which is not much.

"But everything is operating up there now very nearly as if it had not been even touched," McConnell said. "I would say the repair is 75 per cent completed."

McConnell's assissment was given to the Senate Armed Services Committee in closed session April 16. It was released Monday.

Stars and Stripes

Bombing pauses such as the one that came into effect on Hallowe'en only gave the enemy time to re-group and repair the damage the Air Force had managed to inflict on him.

AUGUST 1969

1st It is announced that the 27 US aircraft lost in the past week bring the total for the conflict so far to 5690.

4th The first secret session takes place between Henry Kissinger and North Vietnamese representative Xuan Thuy in Paris.

6th Eight US Green Berets are charged with the murder of an alleged Vietnamese double agent.

7th A Viet Cong raid on the US hospital at Cam Ranh Bay leaves two US personnel dead and 99 injured, of whom 53 are patients.

12th Start of a fresh communist offensive with attacks on some 150 targets.

15th US troop numbers are put at 534,200.

17-26th Fierce fighting takes place south of Da Nang.

25th Start of Operation Lien Ket 414 in Quang Nai Province. There are 710 enemy casualties by the end of the operation.

26th Operation Lien Ket 531 in Quang Tri Province. There are 542 enemy casualties by the end of the operation.

28th The Defense Department puts the total of communist troops killed between 1 January and 30 June at 93,653.

Nixon Visits GIs in Viet

President Nixon swept in and out of South Vietnam Wednesday, saying: "We have gone as far as we can or should go in opening the door of negotiations which will bring peace."

Nixon made his statement at Independence Palace in Saigon where he conferred with President Nyguyen Van Thieu.

Recounting the peace offers made by the allies at the Paris talks, Nixon said it is now time for the North Vietnamese and the Viet Cong "to sit down with us and talk seriously about ways to stop the killing."

Later at a combat base near Saigon, he told U.S. infantrymen: "Out here in this dreary, difficult war, I think history will record that this may have been one of America's finest hours, because we took a difficult task and we succeeded."

Stars and Stripes

An unusual lunch for US President Richard Nixon during his surprise one day visit to Saigon.

GI Pullback Goes for Catchup, Too

LONGBINH The United States forces in Vietnam consume more than nine tons of catchup a day and nearly six tons of sweet and dill pickles, not including relish. Their daily fresh egg consumption keeps several million chickens at full employment.

These titbits may seem trivial at first, but they provide a clue to the magnitude of the task facing officials assigned to shrinking the effort here.

In a war that costs roughly £950 a second, cutbacks in the catchup-supply rank relatively low on the list of priority considerations facing planners.

Nevertheless catchup is one of thousands of food products ranging from beef (consumed at a rate of 52 tons a day) to paprika (about 220 pounds a day) on the United States military's Vietnam shopping list. The daily grocery bill is more than £700,000.

The New York Times

Shock for a Symbol

The huge US military base at Cam Ranh Bay has long been hailed as proof of American determination to stay in Vietnam. Swiftly constructed at a cost of more than £100 million by Army engineers in the heady days of the 1965-66 buildup, the complex has 70 miles of roads, a jet airfield, a port handling ocean freighters and one of the Army's largest supply depots anywhere. Cam Ranh Bay was considered so safe that Lyndon Johnson paid two visits there.

It was a haven in an ugly war. White sand beaches stretch far at Cam Ranh. Off-duty Americans surf on the gentle swells and snorkel into secluded coves to watch brilliantly colored fish and huge lobsters. There are lighted tennis courts, and at the nurses' Saturday-night dances, the boogaloo and the popcorn are popular.

Hospital Attacked

As President Nixon began to disengage US troops from Vietnam, Cam Ranh acquired new importance as a possible exit or rear-guard enclave for departing American forces.

Then one night last week the war came to Cam Ranh Bay. Obviously tipped off about the base's security arrangements, a squad of Viet Cong guerrillas managed about midnight to slip past trip flares and guard posts on the northern perimeter. Once inside, they unerringly made their way to the army hospital. After hurling satchel charges at ward doors and windows, the guerrillas fired automatic rifles into the long, low buildings. Dashing through the darkness, the Viet Cong also blew up a chapel and a water tower. In all, the attack damaged 19 buildings. Most of the 732 patients were carried out or managed to scramble to safety. Even so, the toll was two Americans killed and 98 wounded, some gravely. The Viet Cong escaped without losing a man.

Time

Sometimes, one good man with a rifle can do more damage than a whole infantry platoon. Snipers usually occupy commanding fixed positions, but sometimes, as here, they go off in hot pursuit of the enemy, usually with just a radioman for company and support. Then, directed by a forward observer, they can act almost like air support.

Reds Attack 16 Camps Heavy Battles Flare Throughout S. Viet

Massive Communist shelling and ground attacks raged throughout South Vietnam Tuesday in the heaviest outbreak of enemy-initiated actions in three months.

The Reds assaulted at least 16 Allied camps and let loose with 137 rocket and mortar barrages. The enemy rammed their way into three of the camps' perimeters, but were driven back or withdrew in each case.

Military reports listed 447 Communists and 52 Americans killed in the incidents. The U.S. command declined to characterize the outbreak of action as the start of a new offensive.

(The Associated press said more than 800 Communist soldiers were reported to have been killed in the fighting.)

The heaviest fighting centered around An Loc, 60 miles north of Saigon. Communists attacked U.S. and Vietnamese troops within five miles of the Binh Long province capital

five times, and hit Americans within five miles of Loc Ninh, 12 miles farther north, three more times.

All eight battles began between 1.30 and 3 a.m. Tuesday and ended with the Reds pulling back before daybreak.

The fiercest clash came four miles northeast of An Loc as North Vietnamese battered for two hours at the headquarters base of the 1st Cav. Div.'s 3rd Brigade, which also houses 11th Armored Cav. Regt. troops.

The camp was hit by 107mm rocket fire in the midst of the fighting, and enemy soldiers carrying satchel charges pushed through the perimeter in at least three places. But fire from tanks, helicopter gunships and point-blank artillery pushed the Communists back.

Forty-eight Reds were found dead. Seven GIs died and 45 others were injured.

Stars and Stripes

With the **NVA** and the Viet Cong receiving more and more in the way of heavy weapons, **US** camps are coming under increasingly heavy attack from both mortars and rockets. Sappers too can cause havoc with the satchel charges they carry

Told to Move Again On 6th Deathly Day, Company A Refuses

The following dispatch is by Horst Faas and Peter Arnett of The Associated Press.

SONGCHANG VALLEY "I am sorry, sir, but my men refuse to go - we cannot move out," Lieut. Eugene Shurtz Jr. reported to his battalion commander over a crackling field telephone.

Company A of the 196th Light Infantry Brigade's battleworn Third Battalion had been ordered at dawn yesterday to move once more down the jungled rocky slope of Nuilon Mountain into a labyrinth of North Vietnamese bunkers and trench lines 31 miles south of Danang.

The battalion commander, Lieut. Col. Robert C. Bacon, had been waiting impatiently for Company A to move out. Colonel Bacon had taken over the battalion after Lieut. Col. Eli P. Howard was killed in a helicopter crash with seven others. Since the crash Tuesday the battalion had been trying to get to the wreckage.

Yesterday morning Colonel Bacon was leading three of his companies in the assault. He paled as Lieutenant Shurtz told him that the soldiers of Company A would not follow orders.

"Repeat that, please," the colonel said without raising his voice. "Have you told them what it means to disobey orders under fire?"

"I think they understand," the lieutenant replies, "but some of them simply had enough – they are broken. There are boys here who have only 90 days left in Vietnam. They want to go home in one piece. The situation is psychic here."

Then Colonel Bacon told his

executive officer, Maj. Richard Waite, and one of his Vietnam veterans, Sgt. Okey Blankenship, to fly from the battalion base across the valley to talk with Company A.

"Give them a pep talk and a kick in the butt," he said.

They found the men exhausted in the tall, blackened elephant grass, their uniforms ripped and caked with dirt.

"One of them was crying," Sergeant Blankenship said.

The soldiers told why they would not move. "It poured out of them," the sergeant said.

They said they were sick of the endless battling in torrid heat, the constant danger of sudden firefights by day and the mortar fire and enemy probing at night. They said that they had not had enough sleep and that they were being pushed too hard. They had not had any mail or hot food. They had not had any of the little comforts that made the war endurable.

The New York Times

HO CHI MINH DIES

SEPTEMBER 1969

3rd Ho Chi Minh dies in Hanoi, aged 79

5th Lieutenant William Calley is formally charged in connection with the massacre of 109 people at My Lai 4 in March 1968.

6th Ho Chi Minh is succeeded in Hanoi by a committee of leadership.

14th NVA troops are reported to be in the Mekong Delta for the first time in the conflict.

16th It is announced that a further 35,000 US troops will be pulled out of Vietnam.

18th It is disclosed that anti-war protesters will be organizing a 36-hour "March Against Death" to take place in Washington in November.

19th President Nixon announces the cancellation of the draft calls for November and December.

21st US B-52s go into action against the NVA near the DMZ.

23rd Trial of the Chicago Eight opens.

25th Nineteen die in two terrorist incidents near Da Nang.

29th Start of Operation Quyet Thang 21/38 in An Xuyen Province. There are 721 enemy casualties by the end of the operation.

Diplomats at Paris said Ho's death would not affect North Vietnamese policy in any way.

Stars and Stripes

Ho Chi Minh was born Nguyen Sinh Cung, in a village in Nghe An province, in 1890. For many decades he travelled the world, before returning to Vietnam in 1941

Ho Chi Minh Dies

SAIGON (UPI) – Radio Hanoi Thursday said President Ho Chi Minh is dead. A Vietnamese language broadcast from the North Vietnamese capital said Ho died at 9.47 a.m. Wednesday.

The Commique read over Radio Hanoi said:

"The Central Committee of the Lao Dong (Communist) party, the current affairs committee of the National Assembly, the Council of Ministers and the Front of the Fatherland are very pained to inform the people of Vietnam that Ho Chi Minh, president of the Democratic Republic of Vietnam, died at 9.47 (Hanoi time) on 3 September, 1969, as the result of heart stroke."

Radio Hanoi said North Vietnam would observe a week of mourning Sept. 4-10.

"His death is a heavy loss to the Vietnamese people and country," it said.

Death came to the goateed North Vietnamese president after a day of rumours and report that he lay on his death bed.

The son of a middle class family, Ho was educated partly in Paris but returned to the Indo-china peninsula to help organize and lead a revolution against French rule.

For 25 years he led first the Viet Minh against the French and later supported the Viet Cong against the South Vietnamese regime and later against U.S. Forces in almost continuous fighting that tore Vietnam apart.

Diplomatic circles speculated on the course North Vietnam would follow in the Vietnam peace talks and on its policy toward the two Communist giants which supported the Viet Cong – China and the Soviet Union.

Leader Mourned by a Silent Hanoi

HANOI Portraits of Ho Chi Minh were shrouded in black today and the population wore black and red armbands or badges as North Vietnam began a week of official mourning for the 79-year-old President, who died yesterday.

The real signs of mourning were in the somber faces of the people and, above all, in the funereal silence of the long lines of cyclists pedaling their way to work under a driving rain.

Despite the rain crowds gathered at street corners under the public loudspeakers, which broadcast the special communique announcing the death and giving details of the national mourning. Meetings were held to hear the communique.

The New York Times

GIs in Battle Area Shrug Off The Story of Balky Company A

THE HIETDUC VALLEY Several hundred men have been fighting here for more than a week. Today some of them shrugged when they heard of an incident that occurred early on Sunday when a company commander, ordered to move forward, told his superior, "My men refuse to go."

Several of the marines and infantrymen here said they had seen incidents in which soldiers – like those on Sunday in Company A of the Third Battalion, 21st Infantry – temporarily re-

To WW II and Korea vets, talk of infantrymen refusing to fight because it's too dangerous out there is hard to swallow, but the

fused to continue. Generally, they said, the reluctant troops, again like those of Company A, go back into battle after pep talks.

Sometimes, they added, combat-toughened men liked to test new commanders by grumbling.

No Showers and Few Shaves

Why the men of Company A refused to fight seemed simple to those interviewed. None of the explanations concerned fighting in lost causes, fighting for no apparent reason, anti-war senti-

reality is a little wider. Earlier generations of GIs fought for clearly identified causes, and that's not quite the case here.

ment, troop withdrawals or the Paris peace talks.

The elephant grass here cuts arms and faces, sometimes drawing blood that mixes with sweat and forms itchy scabs that become infected after a few days. There are no showers in this valley, and few shaves. Water is for drinking only.

The soldiers here zigzag through the shoulder-high grass wearing sweaty jungle boots, inch-thick flak jackets, three to five canteens and steel helmets and carrying 30 to 70 pounds of ammunition and gear.

Sleep is precious. Lapses into slumber compete with thoughts of enemy ambushes and mortar attacks. The two do not mix well. "Everybody gripes," said a marine private, Larry Cuellar, a 21-year-old member of Company M, which lost four men killed

and 12 wounded in 10 hours of fighting today.

"When guys don't want to go, they just make them go, and once you're out there it's OK," he said. "There's too much to think about."

Another soldier said of the Company A affair:

"A lot of guys don't want to go back in there and they say so. But they do it anyway. They complain all the while, until the shooting starts. A good company commander will take care of you out there. Word never gets out. He'll give you hell and then plead with headquarters to get you some relief. That CO must have been new. He didn't know the ropes. And word got out and now there's a big stink. But it's all a lot of bull – it really is."

The New York Times

Guarding Vietnam's Most Dangerous Pass

I was just married and only two months from reaching my 26th birthday when I received my Draft Notice. I wound up providing security for American, Korean and Vietnamese forces using the dangerous Mang Yang Pass. If that isn't enough of a distinction, I'm also listed on the Draft Rolls as the first married man to be drafted for the Vietnam War from Akron, Ohio. With luck like that, I had to be real careful but I must have done something right because I ended up as a captain.

In July 1967, I was commissioned as a Second Lieutenant in the Armor Corps. The war was pretty hot right then but they sent me first to the 1st Armored Division in Kirchgoens. I was promoted to First Lieutenant in July 1968 and one year later received the railroad tracks of a Captain. By then it was orders to Vietnam and to the Black Panther 69th Armor Regiment, America's first armored unit in Vietnam. I showed up in the combat zone in September 1969.

The 69th Armor was under the operational control of the

Fourth US Infantry Division (Ivy Division) with headquarters at Camp Inari, near Pleiku. But the outfit operated independently providing a security blanket for units using the dangerous Mang Yang mountain range.

The Mang Yang Pass was considered to be the most dangerous mountain range in Vietnam in 1969. This was where the French forces were defeated prior to 1954 by the Viet Minh. Old, burned-out French armored hulks still littered the pass in 1969.

We were there to make sure there weren't any more burnt-out wrecks. We provided the protection with M48 Patton tanks weighing 48 tons, generating 750 horsepower, and armed with 90-mm guns. I managed to never be in a frontal engagement with the Viet Cong or the NVA, but we always knew that the bad guys were right around. A couple of our tanks did get blown out by sappers and the crews killed.

*Captain
Tom Ellington*

OCTOBER 1969

4th General Wheeler, head of the Joint Chiefs of Staff, visits Vietnam to check on the progress of Vietnamization.

9th Demonstrations outside the trial of the Chicago Eight require intervention by the National Guard.

9th Defense Secretary Laird announces that US commanders in Vietnam have been told that the fighting should be assumed as much as possible by the ARVN.

10th The South Vietnamese Navy takes receipt of 80 river-patrol boats.

10th The South Vietnamese take over responsibility for Saigon's defence.

15th Nationwide anti-war protests take place on an unprecedented scale.

19th It is reported that South Vietnamese troops successfully engaged NVA forces in the Mekong Delta.

22nd US commanders insist that their tactical orders have remained unchanged since the inception of Vietnamization.

24th US troops fight engagement 28 miles north of Saigon.

31st US B-52s bomb the Central Highlands.

Green Berets Freed: Viet Murder Charges Dropped

WASHINGTON The Army Monday dropped all charges against six Green Beret officers accused of murdering a Vietnamese counter-spy, explaining that the Central Intelligence Agency (CIA) had refused to let its agents testify at their trial.

Army Secretary Stanley R. Resor ordered the action on grounds that the six Special Forces officers accused of killing alleged double agent Thai Khac Chuyen could not get a fair trial without CIA testimony.

When Armed Services Committee Chairman L. Mendel Rivers announced Resor's action on the floor of the House of Representatives, members broke into applause. About a dozen congressmen then spoke in praise of Resor's decision. None criticized it.

The six men, including the former Green Beret commander in Vietnam, Col. Robert B. Rheault, could have been sent to prison for life if they had been convicted at their courts-martial.

The secretary said all the men would be reassigned outside Vietnam.

Two other Green Berets, both enlisted men, against whom charges had been held in abeyance, were also freed by Resor's order.

Controversial from the start, the decision to prosecute the men had been appealed all the way to President Nixon by irate congressmen.

Stars and Stripes

In Phubai, War Is Mud, Boredom and Slapstick

PHUBAI "Another damn crisis," said Lieut. Paul Jensen, looking at a truckload of toilet paper. The 28-year-old supply officer from Phoenix had ordered eight boxes but received eight truckloads.

The temperature was 80 degrees at this tropical headquarters base, but "installation coordinator directive No. 210 5-4" was making the rounds. The directive, of dubious origin, but very official looking, detailed the Phubai "snow removal plan."

Another bad movie was showing at the small outdoor theater here tonight. It was part of what the soldiers call "The Phubai Film Festival, Cannes in Reverse."

The nearly 10,000 support troops stationed here have little to look forward to these days but 12 hour work shifts, monsoon mud and the nightly threat of rockets launched by enemy soldiers they never see.

A Nice Place Not to Visit

Phubai is a place nobody likes to come to but everybody likes to leave. It is about 70 miles north of Danang, the nearest "civilization". The morale of the troops here is dependent largely on their ingenuity and on the availability of such condiments of war as obscene movies, alcohol and occasionally, marijuana.

For two hours today, the men of the 24th Artillery Supply Battalion were almost in hysterics unloading and trying to give away eight truckloads of toilet paper totaling more than 10,000 rolls.

The New York Times

"Hey, Mister – we got a name for your toilet paper. We call him John Wayne, 'cos he rough, he tough and he not take no shit from nobody . . ."

GIs in Vietnam Protest

SAIGON A handful of United States soldiers took part today in the protest against the war.

In the foothills south of Danang about 15 members of a platoon of the Americal Division wore black armbands as they marched on patrol.

"It's my way of protesting," one soldier told a reporter. "We wanted to do something, and this was the only thing we could think of."

Before the day was out, four of the protesting soldiers had been wounded by Viet Cong booby traps.

At the sprawling Tansonnhut air base just outside Saigon, half a dozen airmen wore bands of black cloth around their wrists as they went about their duties.

"I couldn't let this day go by without some sort of gesture," one airman, who asked not to be identified, said. "Those people back home have to keep up the pressure until Nixon gets us out of here. It's the only way we'll ever get home."

The New York Times

Pintel-mounted .50 caliber machine guns, like this, proved excellent for all-round defence. Simple in construction, and with an effective range measured in miles, they gave comfort and succor to many a GI

US Officers in Vietnam Deny They Have Orders to Ease Up

SAIGON United States field commanders in South Vietnam contend that there have been no basic changes in their orders on strategy and tactics.

Except for increased concern with turning the fighting over to South Vietnamese armed forces, United States units are operating as they did six months ago, but with refinements in certain areas, these commanders said.

While there are some indications that the battlefield refinements, such as greater reliance on air and artillery support and small unit patrols, and fewer large-scale ground attacks, are attempts to reduce casualties, officials insist they are not based on orders but are the result of changing situations.

They do admit, however, to a single revision in strategy and tactics, described by a ranking field commander this way: "We don't ground-assault fortified enemy base areas any more."

The New York Times

Anti-Americanism in Saigon

Anti-Americanism is rising perceptibly in Vietnam, an inevitable phenomenon when half a million US troops are plunked down in the midst of a nation of 17 million people.

An odd if understandable ambivalence characterizes this particular species of anti-Americanism. The Vietnamese are at once grateful for and hostile to the US presence, which has placed enormous strains on the fragile fabric of their society. They would like to see the ubiquitous Americans go home – but not before South Vietnam is more firmly established than at present. They may find the Americans an irritant, but many would scourge them as bugouts if they withdraw too rapidly, leaving South Vietnam to an uncertain fate.

Cultural Defoliation

The signs of anti-Americanism are most obvious in Saigon. Nightly, along the city's gaudy Tu Do and Hai Ba Trung streets, GIs and South Vietnamese troops swap insults and punches – often over the favors of bar girls. In one such honky-tonk brawl earlier this month, a major in the Vietnamese Rangers chopped off the hand of a US military policeman with a machete. In June, two American military police who had rushed to a bar in response to complaints that a drunken GI was making trouble were shot to death by Lieut. Colonel Nguyen Viet Can, commander of the Vietnamese airborne battalion that guards President Thieu's Independence Palace. No charges were filed against the colonel.   *Time*

And sometimes, the thing that saved your life was how fast you could do the little everyday things like changing magazines on your M-16, or selecting the right grenade for the job. Professionals argued that there was no substitute for training, but also accepted that sometimes there just wasn't time

THE MY LAI STORY BREAKS

NOVEMBER 1969

1st Start of Operation Dan Tien 33D in Quang Duc Province. There are 746 enemy casualties by the end of the operation.

3rd President Nixon goes on television to call for national solidarity on the Vietnam war issue.

4th A Gallup Poll survey carried out in the wake of the President's speech indicates that 77 per cent of those asked are in support of the President over Vietnam. Congress is equally approving.

6th US troops are withheld from the developing battle at Duc Lop to gauge how well ARVN forces can cope.

11th It is announced that Sweden will give $45 million in economic aid to North Vietnam.

12th With demonstrations due to take place on 14-15 November in Washington, troops are standing by to assist the police and National Guard.

12th Operation Dan Tian 40 begins in Quang Duc Province. There are 1012 enemy casualties by the end of the operation.

13th Vice-President Agnew denounces US media bias over Vietnam.

13th Twenty-two US troops are killed and 53 wounded in fighting near the DMZ.

14th Police resort to tear gas to break up riot in Washington.

15th Over 250,000 demonstrators rally in Washington. In later scenes of violence the police once again use tear gas. Protests also take place elsewhere in the US and in a number of major European cities.

15th My Lai 4 survivors allege that US personnel slaughtered 567 on 16 March 1968.

18th ARVN suffers 60 casualties in fighting in the Mekong Delta.

20th Philip C. Habib assumes acting headship of US team in Paris as Henry Cabot Lodge and his assistant resign.

20th Explicit pictures of the My Lai slaughter are published.

24th Troop pull-out is announced to be running three weeks ahead of schedule.

24th It is stated that Lieutenant Calley will undergo trial by general court martial for My Lai.

30th Five US personnel die and four are injured when four helicopters are shot down by the NVA.

The Home Service

The MARS operation in Vietnam is definitely small when compared with all other Army communication services provided, but to hundreds of thousands of servicemen in Vietnam and their families back home it has been the most important service provided by the Signal Corps. After receiving the approval of the government of the Republic of Vietnam, the Military Affiliate Radio System began operation in Vietnam in late 1965, with all US armed services participating. The Army MARS program in Vietnam started with just six stations. A personal radio and telephone hookup, or "phone patch," service began in February 1966 when the Department of the Army authorized the Vietnam MARS stations to make contact with designated stations in the United States. A US contact station would then place a collect telephone call to a designated home, and for five minutes a soldier in Vietnam, perhaps one just in from a jungle patrol, could talk to his folks, who were halfway around the world. True, the reception was not always good because of ionospheric storms and weather disturbances, but who cared when an amateur radio operator in the United States was relaying to a soldier on a remote fire base in Vietnam the message "yes, she loves you and yes, she will marry you, over."

US Army in Vietnam

Had Steven Spielberg's loveable extraterrestrial been around in 1970, doubtless he would have straightway become the mascot **for the MARS operation. Soldiers were able to speak to loved ones back in the world even from remote stations out in the boonies**

250,000 Protest in D.C.

Shouting, paint-throwing extremists staged a wild demonstration at the Justice Department Saturday and police retaliated with tear gas.

The melee came after an estimated 250,000 persons had conducted a peaceful mammoth peace march and rally through the streets of the city.

Stars and Stripes

Reds Attack Bases: Winter Offensive?

Communist troops launched their first attacks on Saigon since 1968 and the heaviest enemy shellings throughout Vietnam in more than two months were reported early Friday as top Allied military men said the Reds may be ready to begin a winter offensive.

Later Friday evening Communists fired more than 100 rocket and mortar rounds into a U.S. artillery base 60 miles northwest of Saigon and early Saturday morning launched a ground attack on another U.S. camp 83 miles north of the capital, military spokesmen said.

The barrage caused light casualties but no one was killed at the 1st Cav. Div.'s fire support base Ike 15 miles northeast of Tay Ninh. U.S. artillery and helicopter fire hit suspected enemy positions around the camp, but Communist losses were unknown.

Stars and Stripes

Nixon Announces Complete Withdrawal

President Nixon told the nation Monday night he has a secret timetable for withdrawing all U.S. ground combat forces from South Vietnam but declared Hanoi could sabotage it by stepping up military pressure.

At the same time, in a nationwide television-radio address, Nixon disclosed a hitherto secret exchange of correspondence last summer with the late President Ho Chi Minh of North Vietnam which he said bolsters his contention that Hanoi is blocking the road to peace.

The Nixon address broke no new ground in the realm of peqace initiatives. It added up to a carefully-prepared appeal for homefront support of the administration's Vietnam policies.

"I have chosen a plan for peace," he said. "I believe it will succeed ...

"Let us be united for peace. Let us also be united against defeat. Because let us understand: North Vietnam cannot defeat or humiliate the United States. Only Americans can do that."

Declaring that he would not reveal any details, Nixon talked about his withdrawal program in these words:

"We have adopted a plan which we have worked out in cooperation with the South Vietnamese for the complete withdrawal of all U.S. ground combat forces and their replacement by South Vietnamese forces on an orderly scheduled timetable."

Stars and Stripes

The My Lai Massacre

It passed without notice when it occurred in mid-March 1968, at a time when the war news was still dominated by the siege of Khe Sanh. Yet the brief action at My Lai, a hamlet in Viet Cong-infested territory 335 miles northeast of Saigon, may yet have an impact on the war. According to accounts that suddenly appeared on TV and in the world press last week, a company of 60 or 70 US infantrymen had entered My Lai early one morning and destroyed its houses, its livestock and all the inhabitants that they could find in a brutal operation that took less than 20 minutes. When it was over, the Vietnamese dead totaled at least 100 men, women and children, and perhaps many more. Only 25 or so escaped, because they lay hidden under the fallen bodies of their relatives and neighbors.

So far, the tale of My Lai has only been told by a few Vietnamese survivors – all of them pro-Viet Cong – and half a dozen American veterans of the incident. Yet military men privately concede that stories of what happened at My Lai are essentially correct. If so, the incident ranks as the most serious atrocity yet attributed to American troops in a war that is already well known for its particular savagery.

Rather Dark and Bloody

The My Lai incident might never have come to light. The only people who reported it at the time were the Viet Cong, who passed out leaflets publicizing the slaughter. To counter the Viet Cong accusation, regarded as standard propaganda, the US Army launched a cursory field investigation, which "did not support" the charges. What put My Lai on the front pages after 20 months was the conscience of Richard Ridenhour, 23, a former SP4 who is now a student at Claremont Men's College in Claremont, Calif. A Vietnam veteran, Ridenhour had known many of the men in the outfit involved at My Lai. It was C Company of the Americal Division's 11th Infantry Brigade. Ridenhour did not witness the incident himself, but he kept hearing about it from friends who were there. He was at first disbelieving, then deeply disturbed. Last March – a year after the slaughter – he sent the information he had pieced together in 30 letters, addressed them to the President, several Congressmen and other Washington officials.

Ridenhour's letter led to a new probe – and to formal charges. Last month, just two days before he was to be released from the Army, charges of murdering "approximately 100" civilians at My Lai were preferred against one of C Company's platoon leaders, 1st Lieut. William Laws Calley Jr., a 26-year-old Miamian now stationed at Fort Benning Ga.

Time

DISILLUSIONMENT

DECEMBER 1969

7-8th Forty-four communist attacks take place all over South Vietnam.

7th Start of Operation Randolph Glen in the Thua Thien Province. There are 670 enemy casualties by the end of the operation.

8th President Nixon declares that Vietnamization is bringing the war to a "conclusion".

11th Head of the North Vietnamese team in Paris refuses to continue the talks because the US has not nominated Lodge's successor.

12-20th The Philippines non-combatant troops leave Vietnam.

15th It is announced that a further 50,000 US troops are to be pulled out of Vietnam before 15 April 1970.

18th Congress vetoes the injection of troops into Laos and Thailand under current budget.

21st Thailand declares that its troops will be leaving Vietnam, while the South Koreans will stay on.

27th Seventy-two communists die in battle with US troops 80 miles north of Saigon.

30th Philip Habib asks the communists if they can confirm which of the 1406 missing US personnel are dead and which are held prisoner.

31st The total of US troops killed in Vietnam stands at 40,024.

War Disillusions Many GIs in Vietnam

SAIGON It was 2.25 a.m. and the moon over Landing Zone Center was high, too high for night ambushes. But the private from Phoenix had his orders.

He slung a belt of machine-gun ammunition over each shoulder and wrapped a third around his waist. Then he smeared his face and hands with camouflage grease paint.

As he worked, he offered a running commentary on the war.

"If you'll look closely," he said, "you'll see some beads and a peace symbol under all of this ammo. I may look like Pancho Villa on the outside but on the inside I'm nothing but a peace-nik."

He picked up his rifle, slid in a fresh magazine, slammed home a round and trudged off into the moonlit paddies stretching toward nearby Danang.

Why do these man continue to fight and die? What carried them up Apbia Mountain? Or made them stick it out at Ben-het?

Conversations with scores of infantrymen throughout the country over the last several months have produced a number of answers. Most are variations on the Arizonian's theme that "I fight because that's the only way to stay alive."

The Meaning of the War

To Sgt. William Simpson, a 28-year-old reconnaissance expert from Catlett, Va., the war has no "real" meaning. After completing a recent helicopter assault in which four enemy soldiers were killed, he said:

"I'm a volunteer but this war has become only a job to me. If we're going to fight we ought to fight and not play around with a lot of sanctuaries and lulls and pauses. You could believe in the war if you could really fight it.

"As it is, I just do my job as well as I can because it's death to let up. But I don't have to like my working conditions."

Specialist 4 Kenneth McParland, a 21-year-old infantryman from Rock Valley, Iowa, does not care about the war "except that it interrupted things and I want to get out and go home."

To Private First Class Edward Stich, a 20-year-old rifleman from Queens, the war is "a big pain in the neck."

"Who needs it?" he asked one hot morning at the end of a long march. Without waiting for an answer, he continued:

"I'm just putting in my days, doing what I'm told, doing a job. One morning I'll wake up and I'll be finished and then I'll go home and tune out, forget it all."

The New York Times

Crossing rivers the hard way is all in a day's work for US infantrymen. For many, that sums up the whole war – a job to be done, and preferably done quickly. Few GIs look for anything more than a successful completion of their tour of duty

Black Power in Vietnam

Before the war went stale and before black aspirations soared at home, the black soldier was satisfied to

Many servicemen, cut off from everything they knew, felt alienated and uncared-for

fight on an equal basis with his white comrade-in-arms in Vietnam as in no other war in American history. But now there is another war being fought in Vietnam – between black and white Americans. "The immediate cause for racial problems here," explains Navy Lieut. Owen Heggs, the only black attorney in I Corps, "is black people themselves. White people haven't changed. What has changed is the black population."

When an American force stormed ashore south of Danang this summer, young blacks wore amulets around their necks symbolizing black pride, culture and self-defense. They raised their fists to their brothers as they moved side by side with white marines against their common Communist enemy.

Time

Black Power Affirmed

Personal interviews conducted with 400 black enlisted men from Con Thien to the Delta provide a measure, though by no means a scientific sample, of the attitudes of black men in Vietnam.

* 45% said they would use arms to gain their rights when they return to "the world." A few boasted that they are smuggling automatic weapons back to the States.

* 60% agreed that black people should not fight in Vietnam because they have problems back home. Only 23% replied that blacks should fight in Vietnam the same as whites.

* 64% believed that racial troubles in Vietnam are getting worse. Only 6% thought that racial relations were improving. "Just like civilian life," one black marine said. "The white doesn't want to see the black get ahead."

My Lai: Army Hears Lt. Calley

Two New York lawyers were assigned Friday to an Army probe of investigative aspects of the alleged My Lai massacre while the only man charged in the case underwent Pentagon questioning.

First Lt. William L. Calley Jr., accused of murdering 109 Vietnamese civilians, arrived tight-lipped at the Pentagon

* 56% said that they use the Black Power salute. Only 1% condemned its use.

* 60% said they wear their hair Afro style. 17% wanted to, but said their commanders refused to let them. One marine reported that he had been reduced in rank for refusing to get his hair cut closer.

* 55% preferred to eat their meals with blacks. 52% preferred to live in all-black barracks.

* 41% said they would join a riot when they returned to the US. However, a nearly equal number, 40%, said they would not.

Time

where the Army hearing is being held.

The Army panel is seeking to learn whether field officers tried to cover up any mass killings in their initial investigation shortly after the March 1968 My Lai operation.

The New York attorneys, Robert MacCrate and Jerome K. Walsh Jr., were named to add a non-military viewpoint to the work of the group headed by Lt. Gen. William R. Peers.

A spokesman said Secretary of the Army Stanley R. Resor wanted the outside counsel to insure "objectivity and impartiality" to the Peers investigation, separate from the over-all criminal probe of My Lai.

Calley was flown in from Ft. Benning, Ga., where he awaits court-martial early next year.

Accompanied by his military lawyer, Maj. Kenneth A. Raby, the young lieutenant was hustled into the Pentagon and down to the Army's secret operations center shortly after noon.

Newsmen tried to ask Calley questions but he looked straight ahead and said nothing.

Calley was leader of a platoon which went into My Lai as part of a company commanded by Capt. Ernest Medina.

Medina told reporters Thursday he neither ordered a massacre nor saw nor heard of one.

Stars and Stripes

Singer Connie Stevens continues the long USO tradition of entertaining fighting troops where they live

JANUARY 1970

3rd Seven US personnel die and 11 are wounded as NVA strikes at camp near Ducpho, south of Quang Nai.

6th Thirteen US personnel die and 40 are wounded as NVA attacks base in the Que Son Valley.

8th President Thieu declares that US troops cannot all be pulled out before the end of the year but that withdrawals must take place over a period of years.

8-9th 109 communists killed by US forces near Tay Ninh.

15th Sixteen civilians die and 21 are wounded in Viet Cong dynamite attack on refugee camp.

17th Viet Cong authorize guerrilla offensive in a bid to kill off Vietnamization.

18th Viet Cong mine explosions at Thuduc Officers Training School near Saigon kill 18 and injure 33.

26th An upsurge in military activity is announced by the US command.

26th US Navy Lieutenant Everett Alvarez Jr spends his 2000th day in captivity in Southeast Asia. He is the longest-held POW in US history.

28th A US jet escorting a reconnaissance aircraft is shot down and in the subsequent mission to rescue the crew a helicopter is also lost. An air strike is launched on the North by way of retaliation.

30th President Nixon warns that any increased aggression while US troops are being withdrawn will be responded to.

31st Communists attack more than 100 targets across South Vietnam.

Now, more than ever, support from respected members of the Vietnamese community was essential for what the American Government was trying to

Saying It Right

Are the US and its allies still trying to "win the hearts and minds of the people" in South Vietnam? Not any more, at least in those terms. According to a new directive entitled "Let's Say It Right," the allied effort is intended to "develop community spirit." Prepared by the US Command in Vietnam for military press officers, the directive bans or substantially alters 22 terms that once were used frequently in briefings for correspondents in Saigon. Instead of "search and destroy," US brief-ing officers should now say "search and clear." US troop withdrawals are to be described as "US re-deployment" or "re-placement by ARVN" (Army of the Republic of South Vietnam). A Viet Cong tax collector should be called a Viet Cong extortion-ist. Viet Cong defectors are to be called ralliers.

The term "body count" is banned. Hamburger Hill is to be mentioned only by its metric name: Hill 937. Press officers also are sternly enjoined from referring to "the 5 o'clock fol-lies," the name given by news-

Never The Twain

The Orient just ain't America and all the bitch-ing in the world won't change that fact. Many a man in Southeast Asia has become a candidate for a straight jacket by refusing to recognize this truth. There's an American way of doing things and there's an oriental way. Sometimes they are the same. More often, they're different. One way is not necessarily better than the other. Many thousands of years have contributed to this differ-ence and they haven't made the American yet who can change that during a one year tour in SEA.

Grunt Free Press

men to the frequently fanciful official recitation of the day's events. From now on, the brief-ings will simply be called brief-ings. *Time*

ARVN Rangers complete their training. As calls to phase out the US presence in Vietnam got louder, so more and more responsibility fell on the Vietnamese

Pacification in Rural Vietnam Making Big but Fragile Gains

SAIGON The road that runs south from Saigon to Cantho is clogged these days with trucks and cars that rattle along with careless abandon.

Gerald Hickey, the anthropologist who first came to Vietnam in 1962, recently compared the present security to the conditions that prevailed in the summer of 1964, before the vast American build-up was under way.

Still Many Risky Areas

"We used to drive up and down the coast and all through the delta in those days," he said. "Now people are doing it again. You can drive from Danang to Dongha now. A year or 18 months ago it would have been suicide."

None of this is to say that there are not areas that the Viet Cong dominate either wholly or in part. There are still many districts in the delta and in the north where an American driving in anything less substantial than a tank is risking his life.

And there are still many areas that the Viet Cong can rely on for sanctuary, support and supplies. Even in many of the regions where the Government presence has recently been established, the Viet Cong still conduct their business at night and collect taxes on a regular basis.

But the pendulum has swung in the direction of the Government during the last year, and the shift is reflected in the much-maligned computerized analyses prepared each month by the experts on pacification. In the past their findings have been sharply challenged, by members of Congress among others.

In some cases that security is very relative – particularly at night, when the Viet Cong are most active. In a recent speech President Nguyen Van Thieu

came up with a definition of a relatively secure area that most people agree with. It means, he said, an area that "Government representatives can visit without military escort in the daytime."

Even president Thieu would readily acknowledge that the situation can easily change at night or from one day to another.

The generally improved security is mainly a result of the enlarging and equipping of the regional and popular forces nicknamed the Ruff Puffs, which along with the regular army, have taken over a large

It was important to win hearts and minds of small people, too. The war made many, many orphans, and a lot of ordinary GIs found themselves giving up an hour or two of their spare time to help out in orphanages

share of the military side of pacification. As a result of relentless American prodding and in the absence of significant enemy opposition, they have spread out into the countryside and taken up the front-line defense of much of the rural population.

The New York Times

Big Red One Leads Phase III Cutback

SAIGON – The U.S. Army's "Big Red One," the first American infantry division to land in Vietnam, and the Marine Corps' 26th Regimental Landing Team are going home before mid-April.

The U.S. military command anounced Monday which units would leave Vietnam under President Nixon's "phase III redeployment." Along with the 1st Inf. Div. and the Marine landing team, the withdrawal will include the 3rd Brigade of the 4th Inf. Div. and three tactical fighter squadrons from the Air Force's 12th Tactical Fighter Wing.

Nixon said Dec. 15 that the

authorized strength of 484,000 men in Vietnam would be cut back to 434,000 by April 15, 1970.

The scheduled withdrawal includes about 29,500 Army spaces, 12,000 Marine Corps spaces, 5,600 Air Force spaces and 2,000 Navy spaces.

As in past troop withdrawals, "short-timers," men with little time left in their one-year Vietnam tour, will return to the United States with their units while men who have just recently arrived in Vietnam will be reassigned to other units here.

Stars and Stripes

THE WAR GOES ON

FEBRUARY 1970

2nd Anti-war protesters take legal action in an attempt to prove that the Dow Chemical Company is still making napalm.

2nd A further retaliatory air strike takes place against the North after a US reconnaissance aircraft is fired upon.

5th Eight South Vietnamese are killed and a further 31 injured when a US helicopter gunship opens fire in error.

10th Defense Secretary Laird announces that he is satisfied with the speed of Vietnamization.

13th Thirteen US troops die and 12 are wounded in an ambush near Da Nang.

14th A Gallup Poll indicates that the number of people who want the US to pull out of Vietnam straightaway has risen from 21 to 35 per cent of the population.

15th 145 communists concentrating near Da Nang are killed by South Vietnamese troops with US support.

17-18th B-52s bomb North Vietnamese and Pathet Lao troops in northern Laos.

19th The Chicago Seven (formerly the Chicago Eight – one defendant is now being tried separately) are acquitted of incitement to riot conspiracy charges, but the following day five receive the heaviest possible sentences – five years imprisonment, $5000 fine plus costs – after being found guilty of incitement to riot.

20th Fourteen US personnel die and 29 are injured in communist ambush near Da Nang.

20th Start of USAF Operation Good Luck over Laos.

21st Henry Kissinger holds secret talks with high-ranking North Vietnamese Communist Party official in Paris.

22nd North Vietnamese troops take Xieng Khouong airfield in northern Laos.

26th Defense Secretary Laird states that US air activity in Laos is confined to cutting off the flow of supplies from North to South Vietnam.

28th More than 20 South Vietnamese civilians die in terrorist incidents near Da Nang.

Nixon: "Peace Up To Hanoi"

President Nixon told Congress Wednesday the key to peace in South Vietnam lies in Hanoi's willingness to conduct serious give-and-take negotiations leading toward a compromise settlement.

"Hanoi will find us forthcoming and flexible," he declared in his first State of the World report on U.S. foreign policy for the 1970s.

Stars and Stripes

Medevac

"The greatest number of Medevac cases that my friends and I brought out of the field have been those caused by enemy booby traps."

"The casualties inflicted on our troops have been reduced in severity by the protective equipment that they have. I've seen a lot of instances where a man would have lost his life instead of having a severe wound because of a flak jacket or hard hat. This equipment does help."

"Any time a Medevac request comes over a common frequency, the first aircraft that hears about it, the pilot elects to try to make the recovery. This is

A Grunt's Best Friend

"We crawled down the hill, stopped and looked around. I saw a trail where this enemy person snuck up on us and threw the grenade. That's how he got there so quietly, because there was a trail there . . . I saw places where a couple of enemy could have sat . . . It looked like the enemy could have had a position there, because there were holes every 5-10 feet."

"We try not to make contact with the enemy, but we couldn't help it at times. We wanted to get out of the area before we got hit with a grenade. We started to move when the enemy threw the grenade. See, our purpose is not to make contact, it's to check out and see what the enemy's doing and to get out of the area. When the grenade was thrown, PFC Cummings pushed PFC Beauclaire out of the way and that's how he got most of the shrapnel."

"This other team with us had a scout dog with them, and I gotta say it was the best scout dog I've ever seen. Right before that grenade was thrown, I saw him raise up on his back legs; he was going 'spaz.' He wasn't barking, because they're trained not to. He was lurching toward the front. When the grenade was thrown, we got light fire from the front, you could tell it by the way the grass in front was getting cut down. As the grenade was thrown, we opened up to the front, the sides, and the rear. And this scout dog obeyed us, he got down; after that, he lay down quietly and any time we thought we heard something, this dog was alert. We got four con-

Most U.S. Army dogs helped guard static installations like airfields, but tracker dogs accompanied infantry patrols, too

firmed, and this dog helped us get two of them. This dog would alert us and then we'd hear movement. These scout dogs are outstanding."

Sgt Johnny P. Lee

The helicopter made the Vietnam War different from anything that had gone before. Their presence saved uncountable lives, both American and Vietnamese

another big factor in saving lives in the field. First Marine aircraft pilots have seemed to take it upon themselves to save lives. I've never talked to a helicopter pilot over here who hasn't thought this way. I'm sure this is the very biggest factor as far as the Medevac mission is concerned."

1Lt JAMES D. OPSAHL
Marine Corps Historical Center
Interview

Numbers

In a few weeks, according to the American estimate, the number of North Vietnamese and Viet Cong dead by actual body count since Jan 1, 1961, will pass 600,000 men and women. There have long been honest doubts about the accuracy of the body counts, and despite all the genuine efforts of the US military to verify tolls and improve the accounting techniques, the doubts are not likely to vanish. The odd thing is that the North Vietnamese and Vie Cong may have suffered even more heavily than the Allied tallies indicate. American figures do not include the thousands of dead enemy troops borne off he fields by their comrades, or the thousands more wounded who have later died of their wounds.

Counting their battle dead, their captured, victims of fatal disease and the 140,000 who have deserted to the Saigon cause, the North Vietnamese and Viet Cong forces have probably been drained of about 1,640,400 men during the war. Applying such a loss to the US population base (there are 21 million people in North Vietnam, plus over 100,000 Viet Cong, v. 200 million in the US), that would be the equivalent of about 15,500,000 Americans lost. And this does not even count the Vietnamese who have died in the US bombings of the

The term "Body Count" was going out of fashion by 1970, but the statistics were still all-important

North. Proportionately, the North Vietnamese have taken among the heaviest casualties in the history of warfare.

Time

MARCH 1970

2nd A new questionnaire system to ascertain levels of pacification indicates that less South Vietnamese settlements are under control than was earlier thought.

9th US Army takes over from the US Marines in the I Corps area of operations.

10th Captain E. Medina, Lieutenant Calley's former company commander, is charged along with four others with war crimes committed at Song My in March 1968.

12th In the midst of demonstrations in Phnom Penh against communist forces being based in Cambodia, the premier, General Lon Nol, orders North Vietnamese and Viet Cong troops out of his country and revokes port facilities at Sihanoukville.

14th As an anti-war protest, two seamen take over *The Columbia Eagle*, a US freighter carrying napalm, and sail her to Cambodia.

16th Anti-draft Week takes place in the US.

17th The Peers report on Song My states that successive distortions of the facts as the story passed up the chain of command meant that senior officers did not receive an accurate picture of what happened.

18th Bloodless coup removes Prince Sihanouk of Cambodia from power. General Lon Nol replaces him.

20th US, South Vietnamese and Cambodian forces take part in a combined operation for the first time.

22nd Fourteen women and children are killed by a Viet Cong bomb at a Buddhist gathering.

27-28th ARVN forces supported by US helicopter gunships conduct a large operation against the Viet Cong inside Cambodia. Officials claim ignorance of the affair.

28th US troops are given the go-ahead to cross the Cambodian frontier after communists at their commanders' discretion.

29th Thirteen US soldiers die and 30 are wounded in NVA attack near the border with Cambodia.

U.S. Official Denies Aid to Cambodia

CAN THO, Vietnam – A highly placed American official here has categorically denied a report a Cambodian officer asked for and received Vietnamese artillery fire in support of operations by Cambodian troops against North Vietnamese army soldiers inside Cambodia.

Stars and Stripes

GIs Find Marijuana Is Plentiful

SAIGON Five helicopters fluttered into a jungle clearing northwest of Saigon several months ago to pick up a platoon of American infantrymen that had been staging ambushes for 10 days.

As a pilot skimmed his craft along the treetops toward an artillery base, one of the six muddy soldiers inside pulled a hand-rolled marijuana cigarette out of his pocket and lit it. He took a deep drag and passed the cigarette on. Each soldier plus the craft's two door gunners, got two puffs.

The soldiers said later that they had found two plastic bags of marijuana in the packs of two North Vietnamese soldiers they had killed two days before. They had divided up one bag, but the other was so soaked with blood no one wanted it.

A Kilo for $5

It was an unusual example of how American troops in Vietnam acquire their marijuana. There are simpler ways.

In the village of Phuocvinh next to the headquarters of the First Cavalry Division (Airmobile), for example, a kilogram - 2.2 pounds – of marijuana costs the equivalent of $5. The prices vary, but marijuana is available just outside the gates of every major United States base this

Dust and Mud

FIRE BASE WOOD The United States Army seems to love dust. It is almost as if dust was issued to every soldier with his rifle as an essential commodity of warfare in Vietnam.

In the dry season, there is always enough dust around forward American bases to make everyone on them look like chimney sweeps. In the wet season, there is an abundance of yet another staple of the American soldier – mud.

Describing this tiny artillery outpost four miles from the Cambodian border in northwestern Tayninh Province is, for example, like describing the inside of a vacuum cleaner.

Fire Base Wood was built about two weeks ago in the middle of a grassy swamp basin in western War Zone C. The first step was to burn off the grass. Then bulldozers pushed up the

powder-fine dirt to form a four-feet-high protective ridge of earth around the base.

There is a dust storm here every time a helicopter lands and every time one of the artillery guns booms a shell into the surrounding jungle. The guns fire hundreds of shells every day.

"Fire in the hole," shouted one of the gunners. Everyone grabbed his ears, except those lucky enough to have earplugs. Then a series of booms shook a reporter has visited in South Vietnam.

100 Steps Away

A South Vietnamese reporter recently walked out of his office in downtown Saigon to see how far he had to go to buy marijuana. He walked less than 100 steps. He paid 300 piasters for a dozen cigarettes which at the black-market rate is about 80 cents.

No country-wide surveys on the use of marijuana are reported by the military to have been made, although surveys in some local areas have shown that 20 to 40 per cent of the soldiers smoke marijuana occasionally, perhaps once a week. Some 20 or 30 per cent more have tried it, these local surveys show.

The New York Times

"But where'd you find pot in Vietnam?" "What d'ya think ya bin sittin' on?" Tom Paxton

thick layer of dust about 10 feet into the air.

It isn't so bad when the small artillery pieces are fired, but when a huge gun with an eight-inch-diameter barrel cuts loose, everything on the base seems to bounce about two inches off the ground, except the dust, which rises about 30 feet.

This afternoon shirtless soldiers were creating finger paintings on each other's sweaty, dust-covered backs.

Working with the biggest self-propelled guns has always brought its share of problems, and the way they shake the earth and the dust they create are only the worst of them

Cleanliness is Brief

Each man here gets half a bucket of water a day for showers, but cleanliness lasts only until the next artillery barrage or helicopter landing.

Life here in the daytime is just miserable. At night, it is miser-

Nuoc Mam

The Encyclopedia Britannica defines that popular Vietnamese fish sauce nuoc mam as a Chinese aphrodisiac. Many local people, including more than a few Americans, don't need an encyclopedia to know this is true. They've tried it, and it works. Nuoc mam is for real. Once you get past the smell, you got it licked and it works for you. Tom S., a contract employee who's been coming to Vietnam every summer for the past six years, swears by it. Tom is in his mid-sixties and for all practical purposes he considers his love life dead in the US. But when he comes to Vietnam it's a different proposition. "I'm like a kid in a candy shop," he says. "It's unbelievable how a guy can come to life in this country." Tom douses nuoc mam over his rice, potatoes, or other food.

The Grunt Free Press

Cambodians Call for Viet's Help in Border Clash

Cambodian troops attempted to push a Viet Cong battalion back across the border into South Vietnam in a major military operation Sunday and Monday, and called in South Vietnamese Artillery fire to help, highly reliable informants reported Tuesday.

able and frightening. The men here are members of the Fifth Battalion, Seventh Regiment, of the First Cavalry Divison (Airmobile). The Seventh Regiment is General Custer's old outfit.

The New York Times

A Cambodian officer was in radio contact with the chief of South Vietnam's An Phu District, adjoining Cambodia, during the entire operation, these informants said. He directed 105mm artillery fire from the district's guns into both sides of the border where the Viet Cong were moving.

American officials in Chau Doc province, where the incident took place, said it was the first time they knew of Cambodians and South Vietnamese working together so openly to fight the Viet Cong.

Stars and Stripes

THE CAMBODIAN BORDER

APRIL 1970

1st Communists bombard and assault 115 targets across South Vietnam as a new offensive gets under way.

1st Start of Operation Texas Star in Thau Thien and Quang Tri Provinces.

4-5th US troops are involved in fierce fighting near the DMZ.

6-7th Cambodians lose 20 dead in a communist attack at Chipou.

9th Vietnamese communists are left in control of the "Parrot's Beak" area of Cambodia as Cambodian forces pull out.

10th Ethnic Vietnamese villagers living inside Cambodia are slaughtered by Cambodian forces at Prasot.

11th A Gallup Poll indicates that the number of those who support President Nixon over Vietnam has decreased by 17 per cent since January.

15th The phase-three target figure for troop withdrawals is achieved, leaving 429,200 US servicemen in Vietnam.

19th It is announced that the Vietnam Moratorium Committee is to wind up.

20th President Nixon sets a target date of spring 1971 for the next 150,000 US troop withdrawals.

24-25th At a meeting of the region's communist leaders in Peking it is agreed that they will work together in Indochina.

28th Formal presidential permission is given for US troops to move against communists in Cambodia.

29th 6000 South Vietnamese troops with US artillery and air support assault the Parrot's Beak in Cambodia.

30th US and ARVN troops are set to move against communist hideouts in Fish Hook and Parrot's Beak areas of Cambodia. They are supported by USAF Operation Patio.

Night Firing

KREK, CAMBODIA Two Frenchmen, both managers of French-owned rubber plantations here and both dressed in white shirts and white shorts, sat in big armchairs listening to the mortar shells and the submachine guns a mile away. Their manner was that of thoughtful men listening hard to music.

The three women in the living room of the villa did not want to listen since the noises told them nothing except that the Viet Cong were attacking an outpost near the plantation and that they were not at all safe. It was not the usual pleasant Sunday.

"But which side is doing what? Who is firing?" one of the Frenchwomen inquired. The men shrugged.

The shorter and heavier of the planters smiled and waved away two insects flying close to his face.

The New York Times

Reds Step Up War

North Vietnamese and Viet Cong forces attacked more than 100 military bases and towns across South Vietnam Wednesday in the heaviest coordinated shellings and ground assaults since September of last year.

American casualties were more than 40 killed and 190 wounded, including 24 troops slain and 54 wounded in a fierce sapper attack on a firebase near the Cambodian border.

The total of U.S. casualties was the most sustained in a one-day period since last Aug. 13, when 80 Americans died during a similar upsurge in fighting.

Field reports indicated the casualty figures would rise as later reports reached U.S. Command headquarters in Saigon.

Initial reports indicated South Vietnamese losses were at least as high as those suffered by the Americans.

More than 300 Communists were claimed killed.

Stars and Stripes

Setting up a firebase on the Cambodian border. Such isolated locations have become prime communist targets

A Half Step Toward Home

Even as the fighting in Vietnam suddenly flared, the US was completing its third – and largest – troop reduction since President Nixon took office 15 months ago. By next week some 115,500 fewer US soldiers will be serving in Vietnam than during the high point of the American commitment in early 1969, when the troop count reached 543,400. Like so much else about the Vietnam War, the US withdrawal is complex and at times confusing. On Pentagon recommendations, the military is cutting back on replacements rather than literally "bringing the boys home." Thus, to the Americans most interested in withdrawal – GIs already serving in Vietnam – the whole process seems little more than a numbers game.

The Big Red One Pulls Out

The special nature of the US scale-down was evident last week at Di An, 11 miles north-

SAN CLEMENTE President Nixon pledged tonight to withdraw 150,000 more troops from Vietnam over the next year and once again appealed to the North Vietnamese to undertake serious negotiations.

In a 15-minute address televised from the Western White House, Mr Nixon set forth a withdrawal plan that seemed designed to reassure his domestic critics that he intended to proceed with his withdrawal strategy yet leave himself and his military commanders wide latitude to determine the pace of disengagement.

On the diplomatic front Mr Nixon reported no progress. He fixed the blame entirely on the intransigence of the enemy and its insistence on the removal of the Saigon Government of President Nguyen Van Thieu as a precondition to meaningful talks.

The New York Times

east of Saigon. There, as a bugler sounded taps, an honor guard struck the colors of the US Army's First Infantry Division, the famed "Big Red One." It had been the first full Army division to arrive in Vietnam in 1965 and now, as part of the third-phase reduction, it was being shipped back to headquarters in Fort Riley, Kans. That did not mean, however, that its troops were going home. Only the 340-man honor guard, carrying the colors, left Vietnam as First Infantry members. The large majority of the division's 17,000 men have been re-assigned to vacancies in other outfits to complete their one-year stint in Vietnam. The transfer process is more efficient than filling such vacancies from Stateside, of course, but it does not please the individual GIs. "Man, Nixon's just foolin' the people," said one disappointed trooper. "The division's goin' home, but all of us are stayin' right here, still humpin' it."

Time

The huge numbers of Armored Personnel Carriers used by the United States Army changed the infantry role considerably. Originally conceived as "battle taxis", the APCs later took on a tactical role of their own

Four Steps to Hell

WASHINGTON A magazine account of the events at Songmy reports that the American unit involved had begun to mistreat its prisoners and "to be less discriminating" about who was or was not a Viet Cong months before the alleged massacre.

The article, written by Seymour M. Hersh, a free-lance journalist, will appear in the May issue of Harper's. It reconstructs in great detail the events at Songmy from the accounts of American soldiers in "C" Company, 1st Battalion, 20th Infantry, who were in the village on March 16, 1968.

The major new element in the article in Mr Hersh's report is that, in the words of one soldier, Songmy was "the end of a vicious circle that had begun months earlier."
He quotes the soldier Ron Crzeski, a member of C Company, as saying:

"It was like going from one step to another, worse one. First you'd stop the people, question them, and let them go. Second, you'd stop the people, beat up an old man, and let them go. Third, you'd stop the people, beat up an old man and then shoot him.

Captain Ernest Medina, the Commander of 'C' Company at My Lai

Fourth, you go in and wipe out a village."

The New York Times

173

INTO CAMBODIA

MAY 1970

1st Start of the the combined operation into Cambodia. 10,000 troops are committed. Invasion is denounced by France, China and the USSR.

1-2nd Large-scale bombing raids conducted over North Vietnam.

4th During a demonstration at Kent State University, Ohio, four students die when the National Guard opens fire on protesters.

5th President Nixon insists that US forces will not remain in Cambodia longer than three to seven weeks, nor go further than 21 miles into Cambodia.

6th Governor Reagan of California shuts down the state's universities and colleges as student unrest grows.

6th The number of allied troops committed to the Cambodian campaign reaches 50,000.

8th President Thieu of South Vietnam exempts his forces in Cambodia from the restrictions imposed by President Nixon on the US contingent on 5 May.

9th Around 100,000, predominantly students, demonstrate in Washington.

9th Allied patrol boats move up the Mekong River against communist hideouts in Cambodia.

12th It is announced that US and South Vietnamese vessels are blockading the Cambodian coast.

17th 10,000 ARVN troops enter Cambodia.

20th Building workers, dockers and office workers hold rally in support of the President's handling of the war.

20th There are now 40,000 South Vietnamese troops in Cambodia.

23-24th A South Vietnamese operation at Chup devastates Cambodia's principal rubber plantation.

27th Diplomatic relations, which were broken off in 1963, are resumed between Cambodia and South Vietnam.

31st Da Lat in South Vietnam under attack by communists.

As the Viet Cong gained strength in the south, so the riverine forces had to evolve new ways of dealing with them. Adding armor to patrol boats was an obvious step. The weapons their assailants were using were powerful enough to blow a flimsy PBR out of the water

War Is Hell

"I'd like to see the look on Fulbright's face right now," said a rotund American lieutenant colonel as he stuck a plug of chewing tobacco into his right jowl. "This is really something, ain't it?"

It was really something, everyone seemed to agree. If by no other means, you could tell a lot of allied troops were in this part of Cambodia – South Vietnamese infantrymen and their American advisers – simply because of all the US beer cans lying around.

In a stubbled rice field just outside of this village, four miles inside the Parrot's Beak area of Cambodia, the brand was Carling Black Label, and after two warm cans, the South Vietnamese commander of a squadron of armored cavalry troops flopped on a mat in the shade of one of his armored personnel carriers and promptly fell asleep. "War is hell, even in Cambodia," said an American sergeant – one of two advisers with the squadron.

The New York Times

Discipline in mixed US/Vietnamese units left a lot to be desired, but morale was still at an acceptable level. Going into Cambodia wasn't a picnic, but it wasn't a disaster, either

POW Pig

About four miles north of Chipou, as South Vietnamese planes dropped their loads of bombs and napalm on a nearby house where a sniper had taken refuge, a small, dirty pig walked boldly across a dusty rice field, past two armored personnel carriers loaded with South Vietnamese troops and up to within 20 feet of a United States helicopter – parked on the ground, next to some captured Viet Cong medical supplies. He stopped and lifted his nose.

The Americans, two pilots and two door gunners, spotted him and charged. The pig darted away and the chase was on. Three South Vietnamese soldiers jumped off their vehicles and tore after the pig. After a three-minute chase, one of the door gunners, in a flying leap, jumped on the pig, tied a piece of twine around its neck and led it back toward the helicopter. The pig squealed and strained at the twine.

"Chalk up – one POW pig," said the door gunner. They planned to take it back to South Vietnam, but their passenger – an American colonel – objected. So the pig was freed, and it ambled away in the direction of the house, now burning, where the sniper was.

The New York Times

No Ice in Cambodia

LANDING ZONE NORTH ONE, Cambodia The day after the grunts reached this roadside chunk of jungle they were cracking Cambodia jokes. And some rear-area types put in an appearance to see if anyone wanted to re-enlist.

"You say you're from Michigan huh, well whereabouts in Cambodia is that?" asked one soldier.

Another sat in the shade of a poncho rigged up on four sticks and tried to complete a limerick that began "There was a young lady from Cambodia ... "

"No ice!" exclaimed still another soldier to his supply sergeant, who responded: "Listen man, we are in Cambodia, and everybody knows there's something in that Geneva treaty that says no ice in Cambodia."

Another enlisted man, a grunt with a legalistic sense of humor, remarked:

"I'm not supposed to be here, Sarge – I forgot my passport."

A Perimeter, in Case

"Here these guys were gripin' every five minutes about wantin' to get out of Vietnam," said Sgt. 1st Cl. Lee Broome, 31 years old, of Louisville, Ky. "Now we're in Cambodia and they're gripin' every five minutes about wantin' to get back to Vietnam!"

The New York Times

GIs Attack in Cambodia

US Special Forces had actually been operating outside of Vietnam since the very start of the conflict, but now, for the first time, US troops were formally committed, in large numbers, to fight in Cambodia

President Nixon announced Thursday night that American ground troops have attacked – at his order – a Communist base complex extending 20 miles into Cambodia.

Nixon told a radio and television audience that he would stand by his order, certain to provoke controversy, even at the risk of becoming a one-term president.

"This is not an invasion of Cambodia," he asserted. "The areas in which these attacks will be launched are completely occupied and controlled by North Vietnamese forces. Our purpose is not to occupy the areas. Once enemy forces are driven out of these sanctuaries and their military supplies destroyed, we will withdraw."

The attack, commanded by American officers and augmented by units of the South Vietnamese army, began about 7 p.m., about two hours before Nixon addressed the United States and about one hour before he met with Democratic and Republican leaders of Congress to discuss his decision.

Stars and Stripes

Tears in Cambodia

After a few days the war in Cambodia took on the appearance of the war in Vietnam.

Just as the elephants in War Zone C and in northern Binhlong and Phuociong Provinces had been killed by helicopter gunners because they were laboring for the Viet Cong, so were the water buffalo in some parts of Cambodia gunned down for their circumstantial affiliations.

Just as some companies of grunts went out of their way to befriend frightened civilians in South Vietnam, so did the First Battalion, Fifth Infantry, of the First Cavalry Division (Airmobile) send its medics to Cambodian villages to stem infections and distribute captured rice.

Pigs and Chickens

Just as tank troopers of the 11th Armored Cavalry Regiment befriended stray dogs in the jungles of South Vietnam, so did they carefully gather baby chickens and even baby pigs from the battlefields and offer them the relative security of a flak-jacket nest in the bowels of their rumbling tanks.

And just as a few grunts with whatever compassion they still had, shook their heads at the discovery of a wounded South Vietnamese child, so did they unsuccessfully fight back tears at the sight of a tiny dead girl with her arm blown off.

A short time later, soldiers in another tank on the outskirts of Snoul stopped shooting to cool their machine guns.

"Give me a couple of those pills," the driver of the tank said to a reporter inside. The pills were Darvon, a tranquilizer.

"Only one left," was the reply.

"No, no," the driver said.

A border makes no difference. War came to Cambodia, and it was the same damn' war

There's a whole bottle of them down there."

The New York Times

Making All Men Equal

In the jungles of the Fishhook region of Cambodia the Second Squadron of the 11th Armored Cavalry Regiment had stopped for lunch.

"Man, it's really, really insane, isn't it?" a tank gunner said.

"But man, so is the whole entire war. All I know is that I got 79 days and they can just have it all."

For the grunt, or foot soldier, the boundaries of national geography are far less important than the boundaries of time. By far the most positive thought a soldier on the battlefield has is that he will go home at the end of one year – if he makes it.

No Political Problems

The Cambodian invasion has troubled few soldiers politically. Barely a dozen, some in the 25th Infantry Division and others in the Fourth Infantry Division, said they did not want to go. Six soldiers in the Fourth were evacuated for possible court-martial.

Even for the substantial number of soldiers who had spent two or three years in college or had college degrees before they were drafted, the significance of the political decision that put them in Cambodia was overshadowed by more basic and personal considerations.

It is difficult to distinguish college graduates from high-school dropouts on the battlefield. After a number of bouts with fear and exhaustion, rhetoric is reduced to half-sentences and offers no clues.

In the last three weeks soldiers in 11 line companies both in and out of Cambodia have estimated that 80 or 90 per cent of their men are draftees and that 30 to 50 per cent have some college experience.

The New York Times

Commanders of armored vehicles found their firepower much in demand. Unless they found themselves up against rocket-propelled grenades or 50-caliber machine guns, they were comparatively safe

Drunk on Duty

The faces of Company C, First Battalion, Fifth Infantry of the 25th Division were full of blank stares and glazed eyes. The men had been drinking beer for two days – ever since they rolled into Tayninh from Cambodia, where five of them had been killed and 35 had been wounded in eight days of fighting.

Many had been drunk since they arrived. Many had still not shaved. Some had showered and put on the same dirt-covered fatigues, like football players who never seem to be able to shed their uniforms after a game.

The atmosphere recalled one of those postfuneral affairs when everyone takes a stiff belt from the bottle and pretends to forget. The GIs played basketball and poker, watched regular movies and blue movies and howled as two Philippine dancers gyrated to the sounds of a rock band brought especially for them.

They wandered down to an impromptu "boom boom room," where Vietnamese girls smuggled on to the base as cleaning women were making half a year's salary in half a day.

The New York Times

Trading Places
Fire Support Base, Cambodia

The Indochina war could not look meaner or messier than it does here, with tanks and men and guns in the mud.

But for 29-year-old Le Van Day – one of two Vietnamese scouts with the company – the mud is not misery, nor is anything else.

A former Viet Cong infantryman, Le Van Day sees no hardships to his present life. "When I first joined this unit in the American Army in Vietnam, I felt myself suddenly to be the son of a very rich family," he said.

The New York Times

The Dump

NEAR THE TABUL RIVER, Cambodia. You could trade a case of beer for a Soviet designed rifle around here today, and lots of soldiers were doing it.

Through three layers of jungle foliage into a tiny, hacked-out landing area, helicopters lowered the brass and the press and the souvenir hunters to examine stack upon stack of Vietnamese Communist munitions. Four hundred eighty rifles were in one hut, and 120,000 rounds of ammunition were in another. Stacks or mortars were here and boxes of explosives were there.

All the munitions were new, and the grease on the rifles attested to that fact.

The search here in the so-called Fishhook area, between Cambodian Highway 7 and the border of South Vietnam, was just beginning. But members of Company C, First Battalion, Fifth Cavalry, or the First Division (Airmobile) have already found enough material to equip thousands of soldiers for months.

The New York Times

4 Die in Clash on Ohio Campus

KENT, Ohio – Four kent State University students were shot to death Monday in a football field gun battle between National Guardsmen and 3,000 rioting students. At least 15 students and two Guardsmen were injured.

The gun battle broke out after the antiwar protesters defied an order not to assemble and rallied on the commons at the center of the tree-lined campus.

Stars and Stripes

When helicopters became available in really large numbers, any unit commander worth his salt took to the air. Of course, he wanted to identify *his* units from all the others, and the best way to do that was to pop smoke

JUNE 1970

3rd President Nixon announces that of the 31,000 US troops committed to the Cambodian campaign, 17,000 have now returned to South Vietnam.

3rd Start of a new communist offensive in Cambodia. Cambodian and communist forces in battle over Kompong Thom.

8-13th US and communist forces clash in the Fish Hook area of Cambodia.

11th Over 100 civilians die and over 300 houses are destroyed as Viet Cong troops raid Thanh My (also known as Baren) near Da Nang.

12-16th Combined South Vietnamese and Cambodian forces battle with communists for the city of Kompong Speu.

16-21st The Cambodian capital of Phnom Penh is virtually cut off by communist operations.

22nd The US halts its use of defoliants in Southeast Asia.

26th Defense Secretary Laird announces that US aircraft will continue to operate over Cambodia after the ground forces have pulled out.

27th Communists are now in almost total control of northeastern Cambodia.

29-30th As promised US ground forces are withdrawn from Cambodia to South Vietnam. The campaign has cost the lives of 354 US ground troops.

The invasion of Cambodia would have been worth it if it could have brought the monstrous career of Pol Pot to an end

GIs, Back in Vietnam, Are Hard at Work – Glad but Exhausted

FIRE SUPPORT BASE EUNICE, South Vietnam Twenty-one-year-old S. Sgt. Stanley Zeager of Rocky River, Ohio – one of the more than 30,000 American soldiers sent to Cambodia – is back in Vietnam and glad of it.

"Now, oh yes, definitely!" he said today.

But he felt exhausted and so did his platoon, after setting up a fire-support base, Eunice, about three miles inside South Vietnam. They were flown here yesterday.

"The officers like to use us as their little toy, but we get the job done," said Sergeant Zeager, whose glasses are smeared with reddish dust and who looks thinner than the 150 pounds he says he weighs.

The sergeant and his outfit left Cambodia two days before the June 30 deadline announced by President Nixon.

The leader of an infantry platoon in Company B, Second Battalion, Eighth Cavalry, First Air Cavalry Division (Airmobile), Sergeant Zeager says he did not really want to go in the Army. He enlisted with a "back-of-the-mind hope" that he could "kill time in the States" at a non-commissioned officer's school.

"I could have went to college but I knew the Army was looking for me," he said. "I knew I'd be in for two years and I'd give it all I got."

Like most men in his platoon – their faces look flattened by fatigue – he believes that the use

of American forces to clean out the Communist sanctuaries in Cambodia was a good idea.

"I think it was one of the best moves in the Vietnam war 'cause it put a hurt on the North Vietnamese and the Viet Cong which could help our withdrawal here, and Stanley Zeager is in favor of that," he said.

Pfc. Rex West, the 20-year-old medic for the platoon, looked at the filth under his fingernails and sighed.

"We were so tired yesterday we hardly knew we were here, back in Nam," he said. "There are too many gooks in Cambodia. I just didn't feel right there: it gave me kind of a spooky feeling. Especially since we found all that stuff in the caches, they'll be coming back to find out

what's left and they'll be coming in mad."

A 23-year-old teacher from Pauls Valley, Okla., Sgt. Paul Hodge, said that being in Cambodia with the platoon was a horrifying experience.

"It was my first ground action," he explained softly.

New Fatigues

FIRE SUPPORT BASE SHAKEY, Cambodia The men of Company A, Fifth Battalion of the 60th Infantry, who are manning this muddy base high on a mountaintop northeast of the Fishook, wore their hair short and had their faces shaven clean today. Some got new fatigues to replace those that they were wearing 38 days ago when they left the Mekong Delta to go on what they were told would be a three-day mission.

The last hammer blows were still being struck to complete a new enclosed latrine as seven helicopters bringing President Nixon's fact-finding mission of governors and legislators set down on the pad next to the base, which gets its name from the nickname of a soldier who was killed nearby.

Cake and Cookies Waiting

Layer cake and oatmeal cookies, freshly baked, awaited the guests. The soldiers said that they hoped some would be left over because they have been living on C-rations almost all the time.

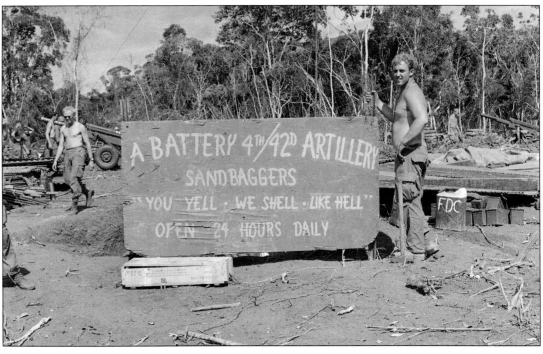

They were unhappy about losing their beards and long hair, but those who got new fatigues were pleased to get into them and throw away the mudcaked and torn ones they had been wearing.

They found some distraction from their dull routine also in a spectacular air strike against a neighboring hillside that began shortly after the visitors arrived. They said they had not seen one that near before and did not know why the hillside was being attacked.

A colonel of the First Cavalry Division (Airmobile) said it was undoubtedly "reconnaissance by fire," although air strikes are usually made only against specific targets.

Bombs and Napalm Dropped

Whatever the reason, it was spectacular. A twin fuselage Bronco observation plane first

Serving in remote firebases, GIs went to extraordinary lengths to maintain a sense of normality. VIP visits were especially welcome, both as a break in the routine and for the temporarily improved victuals

made several passes firing marker rockets, then F-100s swept in low, dropping bombs and napalm on the jungled mountainside.

Finally, the planes made several strafing passes. "If Charlie was in there," a sergeant said, "he's got a headache now." *The New York Times*

He does not believe that the South Vietnamese Army could have successfully carried out the operation without the support of American military personnel.

"How many caches did they find?" he asked. "Tell me that."

"I feel it was definitely worthwhile to do it," he went on. "It

Finding weapons was every bit as important as killing the enemy. Losing a cache like this would put the VC on the defensive for a while

kind of made me happy to capture weapons and ammunition that could be used against us." *The New York Times*

Senate Votes to Repeal Gulf of Tonkin Resolution

The Senate voted 81 to 10 Wednesday to repeal the controversial 1964 Gulf of Tonkin resolution which authorized a big U.S. buildup in Vietnam.

Sen. J. William Fulbright, a caustic critic of the resolution, wound up voting against the repealer.

The repealer was written into a $300 million foreign military sales bill that will required approval by the House and the President's signature.

Because administration forces sponsored the amendment, Fulbright and other antiwar senators contended the action violated normal Senate procedure.

Asserting he wished to "preserve the integrity" of the Senate, Fulbright voted no on the repeal of the resolution he has condemned in recent years.

The Arkansas democrat said he would vote for repeal later when a resolution of his own is brought to the floor.

Fulbright has fought the Tonkin resolution steadfastly for the last several years, contending Congress was duped into giving former President Lyndon B. Johnson a blank check for the Vietnam war.

Stars and Stripes

JULY 1970

1st President Nixon nominates David K. E. Bruce as chief US negotiator in Paris.

8th 139 communist troops die when they are attacked by US troops close to Khe Sanh.

15th President Thieu expresses his anger at those South Vietnamese who want an "immediate peace" with the enemy.

23rd US troops leave Fire Base Ripcord in the Ashau Valley after its defence has cost 64 US lives.

26th The number of South Vietnamese troops in Cambodia reaches 20,000.

Out of Cambodia – On Schedule

The last American combat troops pulled out of Cambodia Monday, leaving only a handful of U.S. advisers due to return to South Vietnam before President Nixon's deadline of midnight Tuesday.

As the Americans withdrew, Viet Cong and North Vietnamese troops renewed their assault on the Cambodian munitions depot at Long Vek, 23 miles north of Phnom Penh, the capital, and shelled Cambodian troop positions in the Siem Reap-Angkor area in the northwest.

Last to leave Cambodia were 1,800 men of the U.S. 1st Air Cav. Div., thus was ended a 60-day drive that overran huge Communist stores of munitions, food and supplies.

Bravo and Delta Companies of the 2nd Bn., 12th Cav., weary and worn, were the last to leave.

Stars and Stripes

Body Bags

SAIGON. Helicopters and planes still arrive daily at a remote corner of Tansonnhut Airfield carrying the bodies of United States soldiers, sailors and airmen.

As the copters chatter low over the white-walled compound that is the United States Army's Saigon mortuary, its commander, Maj. Ramon L. Fornier, or one of his officers, goes out to oversee the unloading of the green body bags.

That is the beginning of a soldier's last trip, which usually ends a week later with interment in the United States.

For a look at the process, the Army's Saigon Support Group authorized an unusual visit to the mortuary to view the rites accorded to the men who die here.

From Jan 1, 1961, through last Saturday, the number of battle deaths totaled 43,418, and the weekly toll is several score – an average this year of about one American killed in combat every 90 minutes.

The New York Times

The Ashau valley looks more like the surface of the moon after B-52 strikes are called in on suspected communist positions. The ferocity of the fighting in this region has forced the NVA back into Laos, but every time the allies pull back the communists simply reinfiltrate the region

A Talk With the Berets

The 11 Green Berets of the advisory team are not men who talk easily with strangers and they dislike civilians. They suspect questions, even innocent ones, which make them even more suspicious. They do not seem at ease with the 14 members of the South Vietnamese Special Forces. The Green Berets seem bored – and able to stand anything but boredom.

When they talk of the montagnards – uncorrupted by the cities, physically superior to most South Vietnamese, less sophisticated in their outlook – the Americans are fiercely possessive. They remind a visitor of the manner in which the British military once talked of the Gurkhas of Nepal.

Because the Green Berets enjoy their own toughness, they appreciate some of the more primitive aspects of the montagnards' habits. They even exaggerate them, and they hope the montagnards will never change.

A young lieutenant has a dog that he never lets off a leash except when it is in his lap. "Well," he said, "if I let it loose the Yards would eat it for sure. Wouldn't want that to happen."

The New York Times

Living in close proximity with the Montagnard people, perhaps for months at a time, the men of the United States Special Forces – the Green Berets – came to like and respect them for their honesty and loyalty

On the DMZ

QUANGTRI COMBAT BASE, South Vietnam "We planted $17 worth of flowers out there and what have we got – one damn zinnia!"

Lieut. James R. Wooten of Athens, Ga., grumbled as he looked out his screened window at the one sad flower.

That sort of thing seems to happen all the time at this dust-blown base 13 miles south of the demilitarized zone, headquarters of the First Brigade of the Fifth Infantry Division (Mechanized).

The good movies never seem to get this far north. In fact, since the projector broke down several days ago the people at this headquarters have not even been able to see bad movies.

There is an above-ground rubberized swimming pool near the service club, but when the dust is blowing, as it usually is at this time of year, taking a dip is like jumping into a mud puddle.

The Dear John Express

The PX is so small, the troops say, that it is sold out of everything half an hour after it opens.

The mail truck is known as the Dear John Express. There is so little to do that for the members of one office, excitement for three days was trying to figure out why a soldier who occasionally walked by occasionally wore an eight-inch bowie knife on his belt. He came into the office today and spoiled the fun by telling them that he was a communications man and spliced a lot of wire.

A major complaint of the troops is that no one seems to have heard of them. A soldier walked into the brigade information office and inquired: "So you guys are in the public-information business. So tell me why nobody knows we're here? Or knows that the Fifth Mech exists?"

The New York Times

Mechanized Infantry, fighting from the relative security of their vehicles, had the secondary advantage of being able to move fast when the situation demanded it. Tanks and APCs, working together, were much more efficient than infantry alone

AUGUST 1970

4th ARVN and communists clash in the Mekong Delta.

6th As David Bruce takes up his position at the Paris talks they are declared to be still in deadlock.

8th US air commanders are told to describe air raids over Cambodia as operations to protect US forces in Vietnam and help bring about Vietnamization.

11th The South Vietnamese relieve US troops of their responsibility for guarding the Cambodian and Laotian borders.

15th The South Vietnamese claim a series of successes against communist forces.

19th Cambodia and the US sign a military aid agreement worth $40 million.

24th US B-52s carry out heavy bombing raids along the DMZ.

26th Thirty-four US personnel die when two helicopters are shot down in separate incidents. 1777 out of a total of 3998 helicopters lost have been claimed by ground fire.

28th The Thais serve notice that they plan to pull their force out of Vietnam.

29th Fifteen die as the Viet Cong raid a Buddhist children's home.

30th Senate elections in South Vietnam are marked by communist raids on a number of towns.

Gunships

PHUOCVINH, South Vietnam. This war sounds different from the others. It has the usual snaps of rifle fire and booms of artillery at varying intervals, but above these is a cacophony of whirrs and putts provided by this war's jeep – the helicopter.

At Camp Gorvad here, home of the First Cavalry Division (Airmobile), one hears the putts and chugs all day long and well into the night. The First Cav. has more than 400 helicopters; a blindfolded visitor might think he was at a convention of two-cylinder tractors.

Huge banana-shaped, twin-rotor CH-46s called Chinooks ferry cases of ammunition, rations, howitzers and other supplies to jungle-locked artillery bases. Bulldog nosed UH-lH Hueys or Slicks carry everything from hot food to prisoners of war in and out of the jungle.

There are sleek, shark-shaped AH-1 gunships called Cobras that prowl above the jungle day and night looking for enemy movement or mortar muzzleflashes to pounce on with their rockets and Gattling guns.

The Tyranny of Terrain

Finally, there are tiny, bubble-domed OH-6 Light observation helicopters called Loaches that buzz in and out of jungle clearings, hovering over the treetops like hummingbirds, constantly daring enemy soldiers hidden below to shoot at them and thereby expose their positions. The most commonly heard descriptive word for loaches is "cute".

They are all part of what the army calls the "Free Forever From the Tyranny of Terrain." Without the helicopter, most commanders say, the United States Army might as well have packed up and left South Vietnam long ago. With few roads and fewer full-sized airstrips, the allies could not get very close to the North Vietnamese and Viet Cong without helicopters. Helicopter pads require only a small flat patch of ground. There is one on the top of the American Embassy in Saigon. It is called Bunker's Hill.

The New York Times

Short of Soldiers

PHUBAI, South Vietnam Faced with increasing shortages of infantry riflemen, the United States command has suspended a long-standing policy of permitting front-line troops to re-enlist in exchange for transfers from battlefields to rear areas.

Under the new rules, combat soldiers – most of them draftees – must spend their full year in front-line units.

Combat units, according to projected figures, will be operating at the end of August at 92 per cent of their authorized strength. The percentage will probably be even lower for that portion of a unit that is actually operating in the jungle. Many of the rear elements of field units are overstrength while combat platoons are understrength.

For example, one platoon of the 101st Airborne Division operating near the hazardous Ashau Valley recently set out on a combat assault with only 23 men. The authorized strength of a platoon is 44 men.

The New York Times

Three million Americans were to serve in the armed forces before the Vietnam War was over, and this huge drain on the nation started to make itself felt by the middle of 1970. To compound the shortfall, the number available for frontline duties was constantly being eroded – naturally, men preferred rear-echelon duty if they could get it

It's sometimes hard to believe it, but only twenty years before, the helicopter was still in the very earliest stages of development, and strategists largely ignored it. By this stage in the Vietnam War, all that had changed, and for good. A new generation of purpose-built attack helicopters – the AH-1 Cobra – took over the hunter/killer role that had, until then, been performed by antiquated fixed-wing types such as the A-1 Skyraider, and were supremely good at it.

When it came to moving Allied troops around, there was nothing quite like the CH-47 Chinook. Combining the legendary maneuverability of the rotary winged aircraft with the capacity to lift and transport up to a Company of fully armed and equipped infantrymen, the Chinook gave field commanders a flexibility of response that completely changed their whole way of working

AFVN

SAIGON A dozen soldiers in combat gear lounged in a sand-bagged bunker at Phuloi, north of Saigon, watching the opening segment of Burke's Law on their portable television set. On the grass outside lay their grenades, ammunition belts and rifles.

The program came over Channel 11 in Saigon, the key station of the United States Armed Forces Vietnam Network. It is one of the great anomalies of the war in Indochina.

One of the last things freshly arrived soldiers expect to hear in Vietnam is acid rock, but it is played nightly on AFVN radio.

Reaches Most Troops

While most other radio stations in Indochina broadcast propaganda, AFVN serves up "Grand Ole Opry" and "Polka Party." While Liberation Radio, the voice of the Viet Cong, is chronicaling the exploits of Ho Chi Minh, AFVN is broadcasting the adventures of "Chicken Man" and "Roger Ramjet."

With 50,000 watts of clear-channel broadcasting power, the radio programs reach 99 per cent of the troops, according to Lieut. Col. Francis K. Price, officer in charge of the network.

Sometimes it reaches them in odd situations. As tank crewmen of the 11th Armored Cavalry Regiment zipped up their flak jackets and moved up Route 7 toward a battle at Snoul, Cambodia, in early May, for example, the Beatles were singing "Let It Be" over a radio tucked between two cases of .50-caliber machine-gun ammunition in a tank.

Soldiers in a logistics unit of the First Cavalry Division (Airmobile) remember a night recently when a taped broadcast of a New York Mets game was interrupted by a mortar attack.

The soldiers dashed into their bunkers only to realize they had forgotten their radio. One soldier went back to his quarters for the radio before the all-clear signal was given.

Except for occasional programs such as documentaries on the American Legion and commercials produced by the Pentagon for itself, AFVN programing is based on preferences of the troops, determined by periodic questionnaires.

The network, known as AFVN, consists of six combination AM and FM stations, including two that provide FM stereo, and eight television stations, from Quangtri in the north to Saigon.

Colonel Price said that the main function of the network, which costs about $750,000 a year to operate, was to help morale. On television, sports, Westerns and comedy shows rank highest with the troops. Rock 'n' roll is favored on AM radio, while FM programing appeals more to older soldiers with "easy listening" music and classics. News ranks high on everyone's list of preferences.

The New York Times

SEPTEMBER 1970

1st A group of senators from both sides of the house request the President to ask the Paris delegations to consider a full ceasefire in South Vietnam.

3rd The North Vietnamese chief negotiator, Xuan Thuy, who walked out of the talks in December 1969, takes up his position once again.

5th Start of Operation Jefferson Glenn in Thua Thien Province. There are 2026 enemy casualties by the end of the operation, the last large-scale action in which US ground forces will be involved. Becomes Operation Opord 13-17 on 8 October.

7th Henry Kissinger holds secret talks with the North Vietnamese in Paris.

12th Fighting is concentrated in the north of South Vietnam and in the Mekong Delta.

17th The Provisional Revolutionary Government for South Vietnam presents an eight-point programme to the Paris talks.

21st The latest estimates show 92.8 per cent of the population of South Vietnam pacified and under the control of the government.

26th A Gallup Poll indicates that 55 per cent of the population of the US want their troops pulled out by the end of 1971.

27th Henry Kissinger holds a second secret meeting with the North Vietnamese in Paris.

28th It is announced that the recent South Vietnamese river operations in Cambodia claimed 233 enemy casualties.

Choppers Downed

An Army UH-1 Huey and a big Marine CH-53 transport chopper capable of carrying more than 40 combat-equipped troops, were downed by enemy gunfire in Laos' lower panhandle.

Two other United States helicopters were reported to have been shot down near Fire Base Fuller just below the demilitarized zone on the northern frontier and 18 miles from the border of Laos. Another helicopter was downed in the Central Highlands, the command said.

The two other helicopter losses were in the lower panhandle in Laos, delayed reports said. One, an Army Cobra gunship with a two-man crew, was downed last Friday, the command said. The other, a Marine troop and cargo helicopter, was reported lost Sunday.

The latest reported losses raised to 4,040 the number of American helicopters lost during a decade of the Vietnam conflict from all causes.

The New York Times

More Americans Are Marrying Vietnamese Despite Obstacles

SAIGON "Hey honey, what is your name?" the 22-year-old lieutenant asked his Vietnamese fiancee at the United States Consulate here, where they were applying for a marriage affidavit.

The girl giggled. In wiggly letters she carefully wrote her name: Nguyen Thi Le. The lieutenant, looking surprised, tried to pronounce it but gave up.

"You're still Lee to me, honey," he said. The couple fell silent as they went on filling out forms.

It was not an unusual conversation in the crowded waiting room of the consulate, where an increasing number of Americans, military men and civilians, are applying for the papers needed to marry South Vietnamese.

There were 455 approvals by the military in 1969. In the first eight months of 1970 there have been 397. Whether the marriages took place is not known by the American military or the consulate, since the only records are in the districts concerned.

The New York Times

By now, an entire generation of Vietnamese children had grown to young adulthood without ever knowing what peace felt like. For the city dwellers, especially, the eventual communist takeover was to be a shocking experience, but in the meantime, many young Vietnamese girls made the best of it by forming lasting relationships with American servicemen

The aircraft themselves were little more than flying ambulances; what made the difference was the dedication of the men who flew them. A Huey, coming in to land or stationary on the ground is an awfully big target, and in the right place just one rifle round would put it right out of action, but that never deterred the dust-off pilots

Orphans Slain in Attack by NVA

AN HOA, Vietnam – About 30 uniformed North Vietnamese soldiers attacked a Buddhist orphanage complex on the outskirts of An Hoa early Sunday morning, killing 12 civilians and wounding more than 50, most of them children.

After hitting the orphanage with more than 15 rounds of B40 rocket and 82mm mortar fire at about 1.15 a.m., the NVA soldiers, wearing packs and helmets, came out of the jungled hills to the northeast and systematically blasted the children's dormitories with hand grenades.

Stars and Stripes

A Vietnamese Prostitute Sees the Future as Lonely and Grim

PLEIKU, South Vietnam. Mai is not a good-looking woman, in the eyes of some Vietnamese men, for her shoulders are too big and the bottoms of her heels are not pink and soft. There are still calluses on her hands, although the frosted pink fingernails are long and curved now.

Vietnamese can tell that 26-year-old Mai is the child of peasants, a country girl who has perhaps worked in the fields. But that hardly matters to American servicemen.

She is typical of the country girls who are a majority of the prostitutes who flourish wherever there are large groups of American soldiers. She talks a little about going home to her village with her three-month-old son, of opening a shop or of becoming a dressmaker once more, although her earnings would be only a twentieth of what they are now.

Mai lives and works in a place called the American Club in Pleiku, a city in the Central Highlands. It is off limits at night to the 9,000 men of the United States forces still stationed here – far fewer than there were last year.

The club is supposed to close at 6 p.m. If there is still one man on the premises at midnight, the girls sit and wait for more to arrive. Even if there is no one, they do not want to sleep.

There is still a framed colored photograph of a smiling President Nixon above the bar, where a stuffed deer stands uncertainly near the bourbon, the cognac and the Scotch.

Of the five other girls who also live in the house, the faces of the younger ones look more hopeful, but they do not seem to know quite what they are hoping for.

Blond Curls, Blue Eyes

Yvonne, who is just 18, speaks without shyness of her blond-haired baby daughter. The child lives with Yvonne's mother, who does not mind what the neighbors say.

Yvonne speaks of the father as though he might stroll in, smiling, sit at one of the plastic-topped tables and ask once again for a whisky and coke. He writes often, Yvonne added, sending money and lots of love.

No one in Mai's family knows where she is in Pleiku, and what she fears most is that a relative will find out. But she speaks openly and without coyness to Vietnamese who ask about her life.

"I cannot make extra money now that the Americans are going," she said. "There is one GI who wanted to live with me but my boss asked him for 40,000 piasters to let me go."

"It is dull to sleep with Americans, but what can I do?" she said.

"I know that they want only one thing from me, and from them I only want money."

She thinks of herself as a poor woman still, even though she earns more than an army captain, a doctor on a hospital staff or a civil servant.

The New York Times

OCTOBER 1970

3rd A victory gathering takes place in Washington which is addressed by a junior South Vietnamese diplomat in the absence of Vice-President Ky, who was originally to have attended the event.

4th The communists launch a new shelling campaign.

7th President Nixon makes a number of proposals to the North Vietnamese, including a ceasefire across Indochina, the freeing of POWs, and the holding of talks to bring the conflicts to a close and set a schedule for the final withdrawal of US troops. The proposals are rejected by the communists.

12th Christmas is set as the deadline for the withdrawal of a further 40,000 US servicemen.

13th In a report prepared at the request of the US President, counter-insurgency expert Sir Robert Thompson explains that smashing the Viet Cong is a prerequisite for solving the political troubles of South Vietnam.

21st Fighting near Thuong Duc claims 163 Viet Cong.

23rd US sources disclose that the Americal Division has employed defoliating agents since an embargo was imposed on their use.

25th Fourteen US personnel die in incidents in Quang Tin and Quang Nam Provinces.

31st President Thieu asserts that pacification has now reached 99.1 per cent of the population.

Main Battle Tanks are awesome machines. Their very presence breathes strength and invulnerability, and there is nothing quite like them for inspiring fear in enemy infantrymen. Much of Vietnam proved to be good tank country, though of course the mechanical monsters were useless in the mountainous jungles of the west

It wasn't unusual to come across patches of land that had once been cultivated and now left to run wild again. Sometimes it meant fruit for the taking

New Proposals From President Nixon

WASHINGTON. President Nixon asked Hanoi and the Viet Cong tonight to join the allies in a standstill cease-fire throughout Indochina. He also called for an Indochina peace conference to negotiate an end to the fighting in Laos and Cambodia as well as South Vietnam.

Addressing a nationwide television audience from his oval office in the White House, Mr Nixon conceded that an internationally supervised ceasefire "in place" might be difficult to arrange and even harder to sustain.

He said, however, "An unconventional war may require an unconventional truce; our side is ready to stand still and cease firing."

He said that successful negotiations leading to such a ceasefire might well be a prelude to a large political and military settlement of the conflict and would at the very least bring "an end to the killing."

The New York Times

Mr Popularity

CHULAI, South Vietnam "There are a lot of people in the Army who would like to get you, Ron," Maj. William Gabella, information officer for the Americal Division said.

His warning was for 24-year-old Ronald Ridenhour, a Vietnam veteran who returned in August as a correspondent for Dispatch News Service. It was the letters that Mr Ridenhour sent last year to the Army and to people in Congress and in the executive branch that led to an investigation of the killing in 1968 of Vietnamese civilians at a site called Songmy and sometimes Mylai.

The Army Attitude

The men in the infantry unit accused of the killings were from Company A in the Americal Division. Its headquarters are at Chulai.

A typical attitude of some career officers in the Americal Division was shown, in Chulai, by the Deputy Provost Marshal, Maj. Robert Bromblay. In a conversation with another correspondent who had accompanied Mr Ridenhour, the major said that disclosures of the Sonmy

killings had been "bad for the Army." He inquired about Mr Ridenhour's political affiliation and questioned what his motives were in writing the letters.

Mr Ridenhour, who was a soldier in Vietnam from December, 1967 to December, 1968 was not present at the killings. He knew some men in the unit that was at Songmy because they had

Ron Ridenhour, a correspondant and Vietnam Vet, won no popularity with the Army when he exposed the My Lai massacre

trained together in Hawaii. Mr Ridenhour heard of the killings in April, 1968. He wrote a letter and mailed 30 copies of it in March, 1969, from his home in Phoenix, Ariz.

The New York Times

Aftermath of Massacre

SONGMY, South Vietnam Strangers are not welcome. Too many have already come, the people of this tired village say, always wanting to know what happened.

Songmy is the village in Quangngai Province where 500 people in one of its four hamlets, Tucung, were allegedly massacred in March 1968 by men in an American infantry unit.

The residents of Tucung, who now live in a resettlement area that opened this month, are weary and suspicious and afraid. The Government has not provided the help they need. Some say that to receive even the most meager benefits they must bribe clerks in the village office.

There are those who assert that South Vietnamese officials threaten or intimidate those villagers asked about the events of March 16.

Official No Comment

The officials refuse to comment on such accusations. How can they comment, they say, on the aftermath of an incident they know nothing about. The Government in Saigon has never acknowledged that a massacre took place and it was not discussed on radio or television.

Since March 16 many of the villagers have rebuilt their homes three times. The war has still not gone away. Their dead are buried in mass graves, and no none seems sure who lies where. And the strangers keep coming with their questions.

A 49-year-old villager, Do Truc, was sitting in his hut in the resettlement area, which is slightly more than half a mile from the subhamlet of Thuanyen, now deserted, where many died. He described life in Songmy in the last two and a half years:

"So many delegations have come here and asked again and again and again about the killings. Then, we have been summoned to the province chief's headquarters many times, and the Americans there in uniform also questioned us. Such meetings were tiring and made us heartsick."

"They do not want us to talk about the killings. They have openly threatened us. A policeman in the hamlet threatened to arrest me and my wife after I talked to one delegation about

My Lai survivors tell of how they survived by playing dead

the massacre."

A delegation, he explained, means people who are outsiders, and possibly foreigners.

His wife escaped death because she fell and was protected by the bodies of others during the shootings, he said. Their eldest daughter, aged 25, was killed and a son's leg had to be amputated because of wounds.

The New York Times

HANDING OVER

NOVEMBER 1970

2nd Seven civilians die in a communist rocket attack on Saigon.

4th The US hands over an air base in the Mekong Delta to the South Vietnamese Air Force.

5th The US bodycount is under 50 for the fifth successive week. Mines, booby traps, and mortar and sniper fire are now the major cause of casualties.

6th The South Vietnamese launch a new offensive in Cambodia.

13th North Vietnamese shoot down an unarmed manned US reconnaissance aircraft over the North. Defense Secretary Laird denounces this action and hints at retaliation.

14th The North continue to insist that they are bound by no agreement relating to the US cessation of bombing of November 1 1968.

17th The court martial of Lieutenant William Calley begins.

17th 1972 is set as the deadline for the withdrawal of the Thai contingent from Vietnam.

19th Backing up the President's recent appeal to Congress for more money for Cambodia, Defense Secretary Laird states that failure to vote the funds could delay the US pull-out.

21st A US heliborne rescue mission to Son Tay prison camp near Hanoi finds the camp empty.

21st US aircraft inflict the most severe bombing raids for two years on North Vietnam as retaliation for the shooting down of US reconnaissance aircraft. The US contends that all took place below the 19th parallel.

22nd Nineteen South Vietnamese POWs are sprung from a Viet Cong prison camp by a combined US/South Vietnamese rescue squad.

30th A step-up in fighting across South Vietnam is reported.

U.S. Bombs North

Above: As American combat troops are withdrawn from the war, the weight of the battles on the Cambodian border is taken by the Army of the Republic of Vietnam

Below: The ARVN is well-equipped with US-supplied weapons like the M60 machine guns, and is efficient when well led. But all too often, the leadership is corrupt

SAIGON – U.S. warplanes, retaliating for attacks on unarmed reconnaissance aircraft, bombed deep inside North Vietnam Saturday in the heaviest raids on the North in seven months.

Radio Hanoi denounced the new air raids on North Vietnam as a "serious act of war." It said there were two waves of attacks, including strikes in the morning in the vicinity of Hanoi and the port of Haiphong.

Defense Secretary Melvin R. Laird, however, said in Washington the planes were restricted to south of the 19th Parallel, 150 miles north of the Demilitarized Zone dividing Vietnam. Hanoi and Haiphong are more than 100 miles north of the 19th Parallel.

Laird also said the raids were ending at 7 a.m., 29½ hours after Hanoi said they began.

He added that the United States would continue to use such measures "as necessary to protect the pilots of our unarmed reconnaissance planes."

Soul Alley

Just after the 1 a.m. curfew one day last week, 300 heavily armed American and Vietnamese MPs, civilian police and militiamen, supported by 100 armored cars, trucks and jeeps, swooped down on a narrow dirt alley in Saigon and sealed it off. As their house-to-house search began, GIs groggy with sleep and drugs scampered in every direction, a few over rooftops, trying to escape. Their women followed, some stark naked, some wearing only pajama bottoms, as spotlights from two helicopters above played on the bizarre scene. When the roundup ended four hours later, 56 girls and 110 GIs, including 30 deserters, were hauled off into custody.

Known as Soul Alley, this 200-yd back street is located just one mile from US military headquarters for Vietnam. At first glance, it is like any other Saigon alley: mama-sans peddle Winston cigarettes and Gillette Foam Shaves from pushcarts, and the bronzed, bony drivers of three-wheeled cycles sip luke-warm beer at corner food stalls as children play tag near their feet. A closer look, however, shows that Soul Alley is a very special place. The children being bounced on their mothers' hips have unmistakably Afro-Asian features. A sign in the local barbershop proclaims: The Natural Look Has Arrived. Green Army fatigues hang from balcony railings to dry in the sun. Black GIs talk and laugh, their arms around slight young Asian girls.

No Whites Allowed

Soul Alley is home for somewhere between 300 and 500 black AWOLs and deserters. They escape arrest by using forged ID cards and mixing with the even greater number of GIs who are still on active duty but prefer spending nights here, away from the drabness of their barracks. There were roughly 65,000 cases of AWOL last year, and the Army estimates that about 1,000 soldiers will become deserters this year (no racial breakdowns are available).

Easy Living

For many Soul Alley AWOLS, the living is easy. Explained one: "You get up late, you smoke a few joints, you get on your Honda and ride around to the PX, buy a few items you can sell on the black market, come back, blow some more grass, and that's it for one day." Rent for the second floor of a brick house rarely runs to more than $40 or $50 a month, including laundry and housekeeping services. Hustling is the name of the game here. This gives everyone plenty of money for anything from soul food at a restaurant called Nam's to hi-fi equipment, television sets or even heroin.
Time

Koreans Weighing Shift in Role and Combat Tactics

SAIGON After five years of fighting in South Vietnam, the South Koreans are re-evaluating their role and tactics.

"The Viet Cong know all our tactics by now, maybe soon we have to change," said Lieut. Col. Lee Chan Shik, chief information officer at Republic of Korea headquarters here.

While declining to be specific – criticism has made the Koreans wary and distrustful of the press – he indicated that the Korean forces might soon assume a more defensive posture and concentrate more on shielding the population from enemy attacks than on seeking out the enemy.

Have No US Advisers

"They can do more than they're doing, but so can everybody else," said Lieut. Co. Donald Hiebert, United States liaison officer to the Korean Ninth (Tiger) Division. The Koreans have no United States advisers.

In discipline and manner, the Korean soldier may be said to re-

semble the Prussian. His camp is immaculate, with neat, well tended gravel walkways and often landscaping. At the bases, the troops are fed on imported Korean specialities, especially Kim Chi, the pickled cabbage that is to Koreans what sauerkraut is to Germans.

"They have 105 per cent discipline," Colonel Hiebert said. "If someone does something wrong they just stand him up and beat the hell out of him."

"They do everything by the book," he said. "We taught them that."
The New York Times

In the five years the Koreans have been in Vietnam, they have won a ferocious fighting reputation. But they have also been criticized for a less than gentle approach to the Vietnamese under their protection

DECEMBER 1970

1st South Vietnamese forces start a large-scale operation against the communists in the U Minh Forest in the Mekong Delta.

5th A North Vietnamese newspaper declares the country will not be intimidated by US bombing threats and will continue to shoot down reconnaissance flights.

8th NVA and South Vietnamese forces involved in fighting in the Fish Hook area of Cambodia.

10th Nixon tells Hanoi that escalation of aggression against South Vietnam will lead to US bombing of the North.

14th Six US personnel die as their patrol moves through a forgotten US minefield by mistake.

20th The 10th anniversary of the foundation of the NLF is marked by communist attacks.

22nd US troop involvement in Cambodia and Laos is forbidden by Congress.

26-27th The South Vietnamese operation in the U Minh Forest continues.

30th The US Navy bows out of the riverine war by handing over 125 naval craft to the South Vietnamese Navy. The latter has now taken receipt of a total of 650 vessels.

My Lai: The Case Against Calley

The trial had not been going badly for Lieut. William L. Calley Jr. During the first three weeks, Prosecutor Aubrey Daniel easily established that a massacre of unarmed, docile South Vietnamese had indeed taken place at My Lai. But Daniel complained of being "particularly handicapped" now, nearly 33 months after the fact, in proving Calley guilty of murdering anyone, let alone the 102 victims cited in the indictment. Most of the witnesses were vague and inconclusive as to who had issued the orders and squeezed the triggers. One of Daniel's most important witnesses, Paul David Meadlo, refused to testify at all.

Then Witness No 31 at the Fort Benning court-martial altered the trial's course in a full day of dramatic testimony last week. Dennis Conti, 21, a private first class in Calley's platoon and now a truck driver in Providence, told how he and Meadlo held a group of 30 to 40 villagers – most of them women and children – on a trail in My Lai at Calley's orders. Calley returned, Conti went on, and said: "'I thought I told you to take care of these people.' I said 'We are. We're guarding them.' Calley said, 'No, kill them.' He said to come around to this side, get on line and fire into them. I told him I would guard a tree line, with my grenade launcher, while they fired."

Steady Stare

What happened next? asked Daniel. "Calley and Meadlo got on line and fired directly into the people." What were the people doing? "They screamed and yelled. Some tried to get up. There were lots of heads and pieces of heads shot off, and flesh flew off the sides and arms and legs." Meadlo, Conti related, was weeping. He tried to give his rifle to Conti. "I told him I couldn't," the witness continued. "Let Lieut Calley kill them ... Some kids were still standing and Calley finished them off with single shots."

Time

A Silent Night in Vietnam

U.S. and South Vietnamese forces joined the Viet Cong and North Vietnamese in a Christmas ceasefire Thursday night, and the U.S. Command announced the lowest weekly death toll in more than five years.

The Americans and South Vietnamese suspended offensive combat operations throughout South Vietnam for 24 hours, beginning at 6 p.m. Saigon time. But American bombers continued to hit targets in Cambodia and Laos, where the truce did not apply.

A Viet Cong cease-fire went into effect at 1 a.m. Saigon time Thursday and was to last 72 hours. The allied commands reported only two enemy attacks in the first hours of the Communist cease-fire, both against South Vietnamese forces. One South Vietnamese soldier was reported killed.

Stars and Stripes

"Bad Yankee Go Home"

On Gia Long street in the seamy port of Qui Nhon, South Vietnam's third biggest city, two troopers from the US 173rd Airborne Brigade halted their three-quarter-ton truck. Whether they stopped to shift their load, as they said, or to grab a beer or a whore, is beside the point. Within minutes, one of a legion of larcenous Vietnamese urchins surrounding the truck had made off with a fire extinguisher.

For 15 minutes, the American GIs drove around looking for the thief. Then they came roaring back down Gia Long street. A 15-year-old student named Nguyen Van Minh was sitting on a fence outside the Tay Son High School, smoking and reading as he waited for his afternoon classes. From the back of the US truck, a soldier raised his M-16 and sent a rifle shot into the boy's forehead, the back of his skull blown away. "His brain broke out," said a stunned eye-witness.

Before long 1,500 students were demonstrating in the streets of Qui Nhon beneath a quickly scrawled sign in uncertain English: BAD YANKEE GO HOME. The signs in Vietnamese were more pointed: KILL THE AMERICANS.

The provincial chief, Colonel Nguyen Mong Hung, urged the students to remember that "without the Americans, you would have no school at all." But he was hooted down, and the crowd overturned US vehicles and wrecked bars and restaurants frequented by Americans. The demonstrations were finally dampened by drenching rains, a curfew and unsympathetic Vietnamese troops.

Time

GIs to Stay Till POWs Go Free

Defense Secretary Melvin R. Laird said Friday the United States would remain in Vietnam until U.S. prisoners of war are freed.

"Vietnamization cannot be completed as far as I'm concerned until these prisoners are freed," Laird told the Senate Foreign Relations Committee.

Laird testified on a proposal to pump $255 million in foreign aid into Cambodia, acknowledging that "A commitment" had already been made to Vietnam's embattled neighbor.

But most of the two-hour hearing was devoted to the prisoner-of-war issue and the circumstances surrounding the abortive Nov. 21 commando mission to rescue some of them from a camp near Hanoi.

Stars and Stripes

December 1970, and in spite of the troop withdrawals Vietnam is still a dangerous place for a lot of grunts. These infantrymen celebrate the festive season in a search for a Viet Cong base near Chu Lai

1971

JANUARY 1971

2nd South Vietnamese and Cambodian troops with US helicopter support struggle to lift the blockade on Phnom Penh by taking Route 4 from the communists. The fighting continues for three weeks with some allied success, but by the 25th the road is too badly damaged to use.

3rd The Ho Chi Minh Trail and missile bases are the targets for US bombing.

6th US begins a new drive against drug problems in the armed forces.

7-11th On a visit to Vietnam, Defense Secretary Laird states that US troops should be out of combat by mid-summer.

8th Defense Department seeks to justify mangrove forest defoliation by claiming that the land is now free for agriculture.

12th A group of six people, among them a clergymen, are set to face charges which include the planned abduction of Henry Kissinger. They will become known as the "Harrisburg Six".

17th A South Vietnamese raid on the communist prison camp near Mimot finds no prisoners.

18th Senator George McGovern enters the race for the 1972 Democratic Presidential nomination on an anti-war ticket.

20th Hanoi charges the US with using defoliating agents.

21st The Paris talks remain in a state of deadlock.

22-24th Fighting intensifies around Phnom Penh with the centre of the city suffering its first bombardments.

30th Start of Operation Dewey Canyon II on Khe Sanh.

30th US troops support the build-up of South Vietnamese forces on the border with Laos as they make ready for Operation Lam Son 719.

Christmas Back Home

His mother spotted him first, and as the slender young marine entered the crowded terminal at Oakland International Airport, she rushed forward and threw her arms around him. Then it was his father's turn, and the two shook hands vigorously. Finally, his eight-year-old brother stepped forward, and the marine reached out and tousled his hair. Minutes later, the family was driving home to Castro Valley, south of Oakland.

Operation Reunion

Throughout the country last week, the familiar scene was played out as families greeted long-absent sons and daughters who were coming home for the holidays. But for Robert Anderson of Castro Valley, the homecoming was special. Like thousands of other GIs, the 19-year-old marine was home this Christmas on "Operation Reunion" – a two-week furlough for servicemen who are midway through their tour of duty in South Vietnam.

The program has been a resounding success ever since it was started a month ago. Although the GIs must pay the fare out of their own pocket, the 80-odd flights offered by two charter airlines have sold out. To finance his trip, Anderson, a lance corporal stationed with the First Marine Division at Danang, had his parents draw $350 from his savings account. "It took my new car away," he said. "I was going to buy one when I got back from Nam." But it was worth it. "I wanted to see this girl," he said " – plus I wanted to get home."

Newsweek

Prisoners of War

The camera panned across a small courtyard framed by neat, low buildings, where a group of men, clad in drab prison garb, were playing basketball. The film showed seven of the men standing before a bamboo-curtained doorway, and the voice-over identified each by name, rank and branch of service. It zeroed in on two men seated at a table in a large room. "Walter Eugene Wilber," the first man said. "I'm a commander in the Navy and my family lives in Pennsylvania USA ... I had flown about twenty missions over Vietnam when I was shot down and that was in June 1968." "My name is Robert James Schweitzer," the second man said. "I'm also a commander in the US Navy. My wife and two sons are living in California ... "

It was one of the rare glimpses Hanoi has permitted inside its prisoner-of-war camps – a fifteen minute film of downed US pilots, subdued but seemingly in good health, who described austere but adequate living conditions in one supposedly typical compound and then quietly condemned the war. None of it added much to the pool of intelligence on the camps. But it was, for most of the viewers who saw it on American network TV last week, a riveting look at life inside the walls.

Newsweek

Major US Combat Role to Cease May 1

U.S. troops will cease to play a major combat role in Vietnam after May 1, but the Pentagon said Thursday that more than 100,000 combat troops will remain there in a security role.

A Pentago spokesman, Jerry W. Friedheim, mentioned the figure after Defense Secretary Melvin R. Laird said in Bangkok, Thailand, Thursday that by May 1 "a major portion of our combat forces that have a combat responsibility or a combat assignment within the country will have been withdrawn."

Friedheim said that the present force level of 335,000 U.S. troops in Vietnam would be cut to about 285,000 as of May 1, and that more than 100,000 of these will be combat troops.

Other U.S. officials said the role of the remaining combat troops will be to supply the South Vietnamese with air and artillery support, logistics and security. They said the troops might be sent out on patrol as part of their security role.

As withdrawals continue after May 1, Friedheim said, combat troops will still constitute 40 to 50 per cent of the force remaining in Vietnam.

Those that remain, Washington sources said, will be used as advisers with South Vietnamese units or will be kept in a reserve status to cope with any emergency situations posing a threat to the security of other American personnel.

Stars and Stripes

Troopers of the 196th Infantry Brigade come under fire near Hep Duc on January 10. Part of the Americal Division, the 196th was to be the last combat unit of that size to remain in-country as US withdrawal was completed

Rangers of Company 'L' (Ranger) 75th Infantry set out into the bush. The Rangers were formed in 1969 out of the various LRP- (long-range patrol) companies serving in Vietnam at the time

Out In The Bush

It is an article of faith among US Army officers that, whatever the failings of rear-area troops, the men in the front lines will, in Army slang, "stand tall."

Around a jungle clearing where the soldiers rested there were indications of higher morale than the GIs might let on. For fifteen days, the men had been struggling through tangled, prickly vines that tear ferociously at clothes and skin alike – "wait a minute" vines, the grunts call them. Two soldiers had playfully written "Merry Xmas" on a tree trunk with shaving cream. And an officer, hardly older than the grunts in his company, insisted: "Sure they bitch and a lot of them smoke grass and they don't like it here. But these men are good soldiers."

Who Likes REMFs?

After talking with these soldiers and with many others, I decided that flat statements about low grunt morale are not accurate. As much as they complain, they also boast about their work. And like soldiers in all wars, they recall exploits, tell war stories, chide and congratulate each other. They are proud of themselves and proud of each other.

"We do everything together," said one. "It's like being brothers for a year." And thy are proud to be grunts. "Those REMFs don't even know what Vietnam is all about," sneered one grunt, using the derisive acronym [Rear Echelon Mother F. ... ..] for men at support bases. An officer described one manifestation of the grunts' pride: "In the field they're always complaining they can't get new fatigues or have a shower. But if they ever have to go to the rear, all that changes. Then all they want is to look as funky as they can and terrorize the people in clean, pressed fatigues who work in air-conditioned offices."

Newsweek

ARVN IN LAOS

FEBRUARY 1971

3-4th Cambodian and South Vietnamese troops with US air support move against communist sanctuaries.

8th Operation Lam Son 719 – the South Vietnamese invasion of Laos – begins.

8th General Sitik Matak takes over in Cambodia as Premier Lon Nol has a stroke.

10th Four journalists, including photographer Larry Burrows, are killed in a helicopter accident in Laos.

12th Cambodian Brigadier General Neak Sam is killed in action.

17th Fewer Americans approve of the President's Vietnam policy than at any time during his term of office, according to a Gallup Poll.

20th It is announced that the US will finance the building of new cells for Con Son political prison in South Vietnam.

20-23rd US aircraft bomb missile sites near the border with Laos.

22nd The South Vietnamese advance into Laos comes to a standstill 16 miles over the frontier.

25th Congress acts to prevent US military involvement in an invasion of the North without congressional consent.

27th The North Vietnamese delegation in Paris condemns the decision to permit the rescue of US airmen from Laos by US ground forces.

Problems for Returning Veterans

Robert Sanchez came home from Vietnam last July with two Purple Hearts and a sense of well-being. For a month, Sanchez, 24, who had served as an infantryman with the 101st Airborne Division, was perfectly content to sit at home in Compton, Calif., "just grooving on the good living here and all the friends I had missed out there." Because he was young, Sanchez figured he would have little trouble landing a job and one day he casually dropped by a gas station to see about getting work as a mechanic. Says Sanchez: "This guy I knew there for years said, 'Sorry Bob, no jobs around here.' That didn't worry me too much. The next day I went out to some other stations, and the answer was 'no.' Then I really began sweating. I tried everything, but no one wanted me – no dishwashers, no bus boys, no mechanics, no baker's helpers – nothing."

Today, Sanchez is still unemployed – and bitter. "It makes you damn mad," he says. "I volunteered for the Army right out of high school because I figured my country needed me. For four years, my job was killing for the red, white and blue, and I reckon I done my part. But if I tell that to anybody here they just laugh at me. Now I don't try it any more. I forget about Vietnam and all that. I forgot about trying to get a job or going to school. The fact that jobs are not there is bad enough. But there's something more that we veterans have to face. It's the fact that no one gives a damn."

Newsweek

A Fragging

"One night," recalls a captain in the First Air Cavalry Division, "I went out to check our perimeter and I found everybody – I mean everybody – asleep in five bunkers in a row. I just decided enough was enough, and at the last bunker, I woke the men up and took their names. I was walking away when I heard one of the guys yell, 'I'm gonna kill you, you mother f. . . . .' I heard him pull the pin, and I went down fast into a ditch. The frag sailed right past me and went off a few feet away. As soon as the dust cleared, I was right back on top of that bunker, and I really whaled on that guy. I think I would have killed him, but people pulled me off. He's in the stockade now. I hope he stays there."

Newsweek

Drugs in the Army

"This drug situation is horrible, really horrible," says First Sgt. Ernest R. Davis, a fatherly medic who has just wound up a tour of duty at Chu Lai. "The farther north you go in Vietnam, the more drugs there are. Some of the forward fire bases are among the worst. The men are using marijuana, heroin and sometimes opium. In my unit, some of the medics were on heroin, using needles from our own stores. You could see the punctures right up and down their arms."

Newsweek

A Breed Apart

The chopper crews regard themselves as a breed apart from other soldiers, much less the folks back home. "You've got to be a complete idiot or a medal-hunter to do this job," exults one pilot. "Some cop will probably hassle me some-

The Cobra was the most potent helicopter in Vietnam

time. I'm going to tell that mother that I fired more rounds in a minute than he can buy in his lifetime. But then," he shrugs, "how can you make people understand that I have a gun that can soak a football field with bullets in a few seconds? The American public probably can't absorb that."

Newsweek

Viets Drive into Laos Along 4 Routes

At the Laotian Border, Vietnam – An initial task force of nearly 60 tracked vehicles carrying South Vietnamese airborne and armored cavalry soldiers clattered without resistance across the Laotian border at 7 a.m. Monday in one finger of a four-pronged assault to clear out Communist strongholds along the Ho Chi Minh Trail.

Simultaneously, South Vietnamese troops were airlifted into Laos along three parallel lines north and south of Route 9, according to Col. Dui Le Dung, commander of the land assault.

At 11 a.m. Monday, American artillerymen opened up from the Vietnam side of the border with eight-inch howitzers at an estimated 50 to 100 North Vietnamese spotted near a bunker complex inside Laos – the first U.S. heavy artillery support for the Vietnamese push.

The operation has been dubbed Lam Son 719 by the South Vietnamese.

Stars and Stripes

Giant Allied Push Near Laos Border

Nearly 30,000 U.S. and South Vietnamese troops have thrust into the western part of South Vietnam's two northernmost provinces to eliminate a North Vietnamese buildup along the Laotian frontier that responsible officials term a serious threat to the U.S. withdrawal from Vietnam.

The drive began shortly before midnight Jan. 29, but details of the operation were not released until Thursday by the U.S. Command for security reasons.

Stars and Stripes

The large allied push on the Laotian border includes a strong armoured element

INTO LAOS

MARCH 1971

1st A bomb set off as a protest against the invasion of Laos damages the Capitol building in Washington but causes no casualties.

1st It is announced that Operation Phoenix is to be stepped up in a drive to smash the Viet Cong in the South.

2nd The oil refinery at Kompong Som is heavily damaged by communist bombardment.

5-8th Chinese Premier Chou En-lai visits Hanoi.

6th The allies move into the town of Tchepone in Laos. Heavy casualties are reported as the fighting intensifies.

10th Around 30 per cent of the South Vietnamese forces in Laos start to return to Vietnam.

17th New Zealand draws up plans to recall some of her combat contingent from Vietnam.

20th Fifty-three US Air Cavalry troops escape disciplinary action although they have refused to obey orders.

24th End of Operation Lam Son 719 with both sides claiming victory. Saigon puts the casualty figures at 1160 allied and 13,688 enemy dead, though an AP press report alleges the former figure should be 3800.

28-31st The NVA sacks the South Vietnamese city of Duc Duc.

31st Lieutenant William L. Calley receives a life sentence later commuted to 20 years.

31st A 12-day battle begins between South Vietnamese and NVA forces at Fire Base 6 near Dak To in the Central Highlands of South Vietnam.

Into Laos

"When we were down in South Vietnam, we were told not to go out if the enemy had two 51.cal. guns working together. Out there in Laos, those guns stretch as far as the eye can see."

"I don't write home much. What am I supposed to say? That I took fire eight times today, and that if I had stayed on those LZs [landing zones] five seconds longer each time, I'd have been dead?"

"We looked out and saw little clouds. Then there were lots of little clouds and little black cotton balls from airbursts. You understand, this was at 6,000 feet. Six thousand feet."

The sign that hangs outside the headquarters of C Troop, Second Squadron, Seventeenth Cavalry shows an angry vulture crouching on a limb. The legend beneath the bird proclaims: "Patience, my ass! I want to kill something." There was a time when that slogan aptly summed up the daredevil pilots of C Troop. But a month ago, their sleek Cobra gunships were ordered into the skies over Laos, and since then, six of C Troop's twenty crack pilots have been killed and three others have been wounded. Now, for many of the once-happy warriors in C Troop, the grim facts of death in Laos have cast their job in a dif-

ferent light. Says Warrant Officer Harry Adams, 28, of Fort Pierce, Fla.: "I have a very modest ambition. I want to stay alive."

To the modern American cavalryman of the air, the plunge into Laos has been something like an old-time charge on horseback: admirably heroic, stunningly effective – and terribly costly. For four weeks now, American helicopter pilots have flown through some of the heaviest flak in the history of the Indochinese war. One day alone last week, the Army admitted to losing ten aircraft to the unexpectedly heavy North Vietnamese ground fire, and

Slugging It Out

Not long after the South Vietnamese Army plunged across the border into Laos, a Vietnamese major sat down for a private chat with a reporter in an outpost near Khe Sanh. "Aren't you afraid that the North Vietnamese might be luring your forces into a Dienbienphu-style trap in Laos?" asked the journalist. A smile of satisfaction crossed the

Left: Khe Sanh comes to life again when it is used as a springboard for allied operations in Laos. It is a largely Vietnamese affair, although American ground troops are involved

officer's face. "Nonsense," he replies. "Did the French have helicopter gunships?" And he swept his hand low over a table in a swift, darting gesture to imitate the flight of a helicopter. "Did the French have jet fighter-bombers?" His hand swooped downward. "And the French, I can assure you, did not have B-52s," he declared – and his fist thundered onto the table.

That kind of confidence seemed justified enough in the early days of the Laotian invasion – and, to a degree, even during the tough battles between US helicopters and Communist anti-aircraft guns that followed. But last week brought

another sharp reminder that the North Vietnamese do not always knuckle under to explosive American air power, and that the outcome of the war in Indochina still depends largely on foot soldiers slugging it out on the ground. Throughout the bomb-blasted moonscape of the central Laotian panhandle troops of the South Vietnamese Army (ARVN) and Communist forces waged some of the bloodiest ground battles of the war. And when the fighting died down, the ARVN troops seemed to be scurrying back toward their own border. As the Pentagon described it, the South Vietnamese were engaged in "mobile maneuvering." But in the eyes of many observers, it seemed more like a plain old-fashioned retreat.

Newsweek

Lieutenant William L. Calley, under investigation for the 1968 My Lai massacre, receives a Court Martial at Fort Benning and is sentenced to 20 years' imprisonment

Calley On Trial

Three years after the incident at My Lai, a year and a half after he had been charged with the murder of 102 Vietnamese villagers, the defendant's day in court had finally come. First Lt. William Calley, turned out in trim dress greens, took the stand at his Fort Benning, Ga., court-martial to tell his version of what happened at the Vietnamese village called My Lai 4 on March 16, 1968. And with cool military detachment, the young lieutenant did indeed admit to killing some – though far from all – of the 102 villagers he is charged with murdering. But in legal terms, Calley's account stopped well short of an admission of premeditated murder. And, as his counsel has contended from the beginning, he insisted he had been acting solely on orders from his superior at My Lai, Capt. Ernest Medina.

Newsweek

there were reports from the field that the actual losses had been much worse. As a result, the customary bravado of the American chopper pilot was beginning to wear a bit thin. "Two weeks ago," said one gunship skipper, "I couldn't have told you how much time I had left to serve in Vietnam. Now I know that I've got 66 days to go, and I'm counting every one." Another flier added anxiously: "The roles are reversed over there. In Vietnam, you have to hunt for the enemy. But in Laos, man, they hunt for you."

Newsweek

Calley Convicted

Ft. Benning, GA. - Lt. William Calley was convicted Monday of the premeditated murder of 22 Vietnamese civilians at My Lai three years ago. He is the first American veteran of Vietnam to be held responsible in the My Lai massacre.

Calley stood ramrod straight as the verdict was read, then did an about face. He was flanked by his military and civilian lawyers.

A half-hour after the verdict was announced, military police escorted him to the post stockade. "Take my word for it, the boy's crushed," his civilian attorney, George Latimer, said as they left the courtroom.

He was placed in quarters separate from those of enlisted men, and will be returned to the courtroom at 9 a.m. Tuesday when the sentencing phase of the court-martial begins.

Calley was convicted of kill-

ing one person at a trail intersection, 20 at a ditch where he admitted firing six or eight bullets, of the death of a man in white and of assault on a child believed to be about 2 years old.

He had been charged with the deaths of 102 Vietnamese men, women and children.

CALLEY VERDICT

APRIL 1971

1st Vice-President Agnew and Senator Hugh Scott take the administration's congressional detractors to task.

7th President Nixon reasserts that he will ensure an "honorable" conclusion to the conflict.

14th Start of Operation Lam Son 720 in the Ashau Valley. The South Vietnamese press labels it a "training exercise".

16th Saigon reports the siege of Fire Base 6 to be over.

18th Premier Ky admits that Lam Son 719 was not a triumph for the allies.

18-23rd The US bombing offensive intensifies against missile sites.

19-26th Anti-war protests include a Vietnam veterans' rally known as Operation Dewey Canyon III.

20th US government statistics show an increase in "fragging" – US soldiers firing on or blowing up their officers. 209 such acts took place in 1970, resulting in 34 deaths.

22-28th It emerges that US ground forces participated in the invasion of Laos.

26th The total number of US troops serving in Vietnam is put at 281,400.

29th US deaths in the conflict pass the 45,000 mark.

A gun crew at an Americal fire base wait for a fire mission. It was a firebase like this that the Viet Cong over-ran, causing the biggest single US combat loss for over a year

There are now less than 282,000 American troops in Vietnam, fewer and fewer of whom are combatants like this 5th Infantry Division M60 machine-gunner

Nixon to Pull Out 100,000 More GIs

Declaring that "our goal is no American fighting and dying any place in the world," President Nixon announced Wednesday night he will withdraw an additional 100,000 U.S. troops from Vietnam by Dec. 1.

While ordering American troop strength in Southeast Asia reduced to 184,000 men – its lowest point since November, 1965 – Nixon rejected persistent demands by Democrats that he set an early deadline for a total U.S. pullout.

But in response to growing pressure from Republicans as well as Democrats, the President asserted no less than four times during his 20-minute address to the nation that "American involvement is Vietnam in coming to an end."

Stars and Stripes

Total Surprise
at Fire Support Base Mary Ann

The war had long been "winding down" in Quang Tin province, and no one at the 23rd (Americal) Division's Fire Support Base Mary Ann had seen the enemy for quite some time. "Man, we thought for us the war was over," muttered one grunt, while another at the soon-to-be-abandoned base recalled: "We weren't expecting anything, and we especially weren't expecting what we got." Certainly no one at the woefully undermanned fire base last week expected the savagely successful enemy attack that left 33 Americans killed and 76 wounded, the largest single American combat loss in a year.

Thirty Minutes of Hell

It was Sgt. Ronald Shook's 21st birthday and his thoughts kept drifting back to Spencerville, Ohio, and to what that day would have been like back home with his folks, his friends and his girl. But even a birthday isn't that special at an isolated outpost, and Shook passed over any celebration in favor of a good night's sleep. He didn't get it, for at 2.30 a.m. Shook and the 250 other soldiers at Mary Ann were suddenly catapulted into a hell of bursting shells, shadowy demons, screaming men and death. The ferocious onslaught lasted only 30 minutes, but in that half hour the Communists succeeded in challenging once again President Nixon's hopes that the US will be able to disengage from Vietnam in a smooth and bloodless way.

Mary Ann was hit with a precision that stunned its defenders. The attackers seemed to know the location of every important building and weapon in Mary Ann; mortar shells made direct hits on the command bunker, while the estimated 40 to 50 Communist sappers ran straight for company command posts, the two 155-mm artillery pieces and the mortar emplacements, the communications shack and the helicopter fueling stations – and destroyed them all. When Capt. Victor Ferraris tried to switch on the base alarm system and then tried to phone the US mortar positions, he found that both lines had been cut. "And that means they had an intimate knowledge of the fire base," Ferraris said. It was obvious, said Mary Ann officers afterward, that the Communists had been keeping a watch on the base for weeks.

The Sappers Got In

Aided by an enshrouding fog, the sappers – naked except for loincloths but well-armed with grenade launchers, recoilless rifles and automatic weapons – crept up on the base and cut through all but the last of the many rings of barbed-wire barriers. Then, as the first rain of mortars fell on Mary Ann, the sappers rushed the base. "The way they got in was by coming in under their own mortar attack," said Captain Ferraris. "Our troops naturally ducked and the dinks advanced while everybody had their heads down."

The sappers made a steady sweep through the base, always heading for their planned north-end escape route. And before the Americans could pull together any defense, the attackers had disappeared into the fog and the jungle.

Newsweek

Calley Found Guilty
of Premeditated Murder

From the very first day of deliberation, the jury of six career officers was in agreement that Calley had committed a crime in killing, and ordering killed, a sizable number of unarmed, unresisting villagers at My Lai. They agreed as well that the central notion behind Calley's defense – that a soldier in combat loyally obeying orders cannot be held accountable – was fundamentally wrong. But whether Calley's action constituted premeditated murder under the law was another matter. Judge Reid W. Kennedy warned the panel to make certain the specific acts charged against Calley – murdering some 30 Vietnamese at a trail intersection, another 70 or so at a ditch, plus an old man and a boy – were correct in all details before they passed on to the crucial question of guilt or innocence.

A Jury of Veterans

The jury was no stranger to the dangers and difficulties of combat. Two of the jurors had served two full tours in Vietnam. Another had been badly wounded there. Still another, like Calley, had led an infantry platoon in Vietnam. Indeed, of the six, only the president of the panel, 53-year-old Col. Clifford Ford, had not seen service there – and he had won three Bronze Stars in World War II and Korea. As Maj. Walter D. Kinard, 33, of Columbus, Ga., one of the two-tour vets, put it, "We left no stone unturned in Lieutenant Calley's favor."

But Calley's order to his men to kill carried the day. On Friday, the tenth day of deliberation, the jury voted for premeditated murder – by a count of 4 to 2. It was the minimum needed for conviction.

The jury then moved on to the second charge: the killing of some 70 villagers at the ditch. Again they asked to have testimony reread – but this time, the weight of evidence was overwhelming. Of eight helicopter crewmen summoned, six had said they saw bodies strewn up and down the ditch. A half-dozen members of Calley's platoon said they had seen Calley shooting at villagers there. And Calley himself admitted he had fired at some people from a distance of 5 feet – though he could not say if his bullets had struck home.

Newsweek

MAY 1971

3-5th	A record 12,614 demonstrators are arrested in Washington.
8th	15,000 take part in a pro-war demonstration in Washington.
10-18th	US aircraft bomb targets 75 miles north of the DMZ.
11-15th	ARVN forces with US air support carry out operations in Cambodia.
12th	Fighting steps up in Operation Lam Son 720.
12th	The Pathet Lao issue their peace programme.
13th	Start of the fourth year of talks in Paris.
16-18th	NVA takes over the Boloven Plateau in southern Laos.
19-22nd	Thirty die in attack on US base Charlie 2.
23rd	North Vietnamese saboteurs wreak destruction in Cam Ranh air base.
24th	An anti-war advertisement endorsed by 29 US officers appears in a US newspaper.
26-31st	The Cambodian town of Snoul falls to the NVA.
30th	Three civilians die in a bomb explosion in Saigon.
31st	The communist offensive on the DMZ continues.

Win-the-War March

WASHINGTON Win-the-war demonstrators paraded along misty Pennsylvania Avenue Saturday and rallied at the Washington Monument, where the Rev. Carl McIntire urged President Nixon to repent his South Vietnam policy and "use the sword as God intended."

Park police estimated the crowd at 15,000 while McIntire claimed his National March for Victory had drawn about 25,000 people from every state in the Union.

Washington police estimated 5,000 to 6,000 people were in the procession that paraded from the foot of Capitol Hill to the monument to the strains of "Onward Christian Soldiers" and "The Stars and Stripes Forever" played alternately by a 26-piece volunteer band. Many who attended the rally skipped the 90-minute parade.

At the monument ground, they heard a series of speeches exhorting the United States to seek victory in Vietnam, before a late afternoon rainstorm sent much of the crowd seeking shelter.

The heavy rain came just as Gov. George. C. Wallace of Alabama began addressing the rally by telephone from Dallas, Texas.

"I, like you and many others, have become very disenchanted with our government and its no-win policy," Wallace said. "I want out of Vietnam, but I want out of Vietnam with a victory that will mean our boys have not died in vain."

Pacific Stars and Stripes

Today's Army Wants You!

It was a far cry from the World War I poster of a stern Uncle Sam captioned "I Want You." There, on prime-time TV screens, was a sexy stewardess welcoming young men aboard an airliner with breathy murmurs about the pleasures of sixteen months in Europe. Another spot featured pro football quarterbacks – one black, one white – heaving passes as an announcer intoned, "You have to make plenty of tough decisions yourself . . . "In a third, the voice of a US Army recruiter, backed by a throbbing rock guitar, told potential enlistees, "Today's Army wants to join you!"

The lively commercials – and similar ads in magazines – were all part of a thirteen week, $18 million nationwide experiment aimed at buffing up the Army's tarnished image and helping to realise President Nixon's dream of an all-volunteer army by mid-1973. The main thrust of the campaign was to stress the travel, adventure and educational opportunities available to enlistees – as well as the Army's flexible new "creative management." Results of the campaign are still being assessed – and the Army expects the real pay-off to come later this year when summer vacations are over. But preliminary figures indicate that the $18 million advertising drive may have been responsible for 2,500 new recruits – which tallies up to a cost of only $7,200 per man.

Newsweek

Beer and Soda

"The Army and Air Force Vietnamese Regional Exchange Service is the sole source of all our alcoholic beverages and the overwhelming majority of our soda. We procure this from them in Danang and transport it by water up through Qua Viet, down the Qua Viet River to a warehouse in Dong Ha, from where we do all our issuing. The purchase of snacks (various types of potato chips, pretzels, corn curls, peanuts, pigs feet, and all the other little delicacies which the troops enjoy) are purchased directly from the States and for the most part are sent in via parcel post."

"Financially, the clubs here are structured as they are in the United States. We fall under the provisions of Marine Corps Order 1746.13B."

"Perhaps the biggest difference between this system and any other, especially others in Vietnam, is that our lines of supply are so long, extending to the outer reaches of the Division itself and back to Danang, our primary source of supply."

Replacement Beer Coolers

"In addition to the logistic problems inherent in such a thin supply line, is the problem of wear and tear on most of our heavy equipment. Items such as beer coolers, ice machines, reefers, tape recorders, practically anything electronic. Items which have an average life of 5-8 years in the States have an average life of 6-9 months or at best a year over here. Consequently, the requirement for timely replacement and long-range planning is one of our paramount concerns."

"The club system conducts a program of live entertainment which is separate from the standard USO-type show. The USO show is provided by Special Services; for the most part, these shows come in and fly out the next day. Through the MACV Command in Saigon, there is a large number of civilian entertainment shows which are authorized to contract directly with the club systems. We have agents who come up, book 8-10 shows for the various clubs in our immediate area, and we pay for these out of club funds. The entertainment is extremely popular with the troops. We have various types of music, acrobatic acts, dancing girls, the full gamut of shows, which we book whenever we can to provide further entertainment."

Major Charles J. Day
US Marine Corps Historical Center Interview

27 May, 1971. 23 miles from Chu Lai. A grenadier from 198th Infantry Brigade (Light) rests during a patrol through heavily overgrown forest

JUNE 1971

2nd It is disclosed that US Brigadier General John Donaldson has become the most senior officer to be charged with war crimes.

3rd Thirteen North Vietnamese POWs are brought back to Da Nang after the North refuses to take them.

5-6th US helicopters are involved as heavy fighting takes place around Fire Base Charlie near Khe Sanh.

8th Fighting intensifies around the Cambodian capital of Phnom Penh.

9th A lieutenant is the first US officer to ask for sanctuary in Sweden.

13th The publication in *The New York Times* of the Pentagon Papers on the American involvement in Indochina rocks the US.

15th The siege of Fire Base 5 in the Central Highlands is lifted.

16th Attempts to have Congress set a date for complete troop withdrawal come to nothing.

17th Treaty gives back Okinawa, a major US Pacific supply post, to Japan.

22-28th A fierce struggle takes place for Fire Base Fuller.

28th The man who leaked the Pentagon Papers, Daniel Ellsberg, turns himself in.

Withdrawal Pains

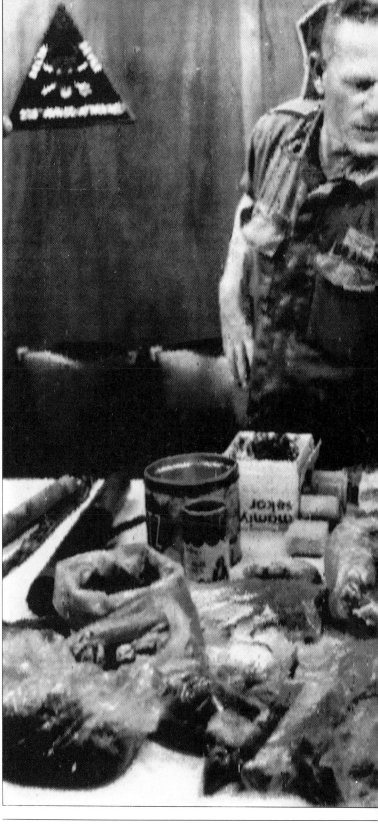

Few patrols like this mean few casualties, although Americans are still dying in VC attacks

Every Saturday morning, the top American officials in South Vietnam gather in a closely guarded room for a "weekly intelligence estimate update." Known for short as WIEU (pronounced "woo"), the session covers the full range of military and political developments, and as the US commander in Vietnam, Gen. Creighton Abrams, puts it, the discussion offers "a chance to let your hair down." But when the brass assembled for one recent meeting, it was Abrams himself who let go. "We were treated to a real Abrams broadside," reported one participant. And another witness declared: "He hit them with all eight stars" – four on each collar.

Don't Bunch Up

Abrams's wrath had been brought to the boiling point by the death of 29 GIs who were killed by a single North Vietnamese rocket at a tiny fire base named Charlie Two near the

GIs Get Viet Heroin for $2 a 'Fix'

The big new problem facing US authorities in Vietnam is drugs, with huge hauls like this one being found all the time

PHU BAI, Vietnam – It's cheap and easy to buy all along Highway 1 from the Hai Van pass to the DMZ.

It is 95 per cent pure heroin, powdery and white. It looks something like laundry detergent, but you can tell it from soap by the taste. It is very bitter, and the white particles burn like acid on the tongue.

The amount of heroin seized by military police in this area has doubled every month since September as drug prices have dropped, armed robberies have jumped and the number of drug users has increased, informed sources here said.

More than 500 vials, about 130 grams of pure heroin, were collected by the 504th Military Police Det. during the last monthly reporting period, the sources said.

More than 500 vials of heroin have been picked up in the first 12 days of the current monthly reporting period, and close to 1,000 empty vials with traces of heroin were found or seized, they said.

Another 2,000 vials of heroin were picked up by 101st Airborne Div. MPs during the last monthly reporting period.

The price of heroin in northern I Military Region has dropped since September from $5 a vial to $2 a vial or less in large quantities. A vial usually contains from one-eighth to one-fourth of a gram.

Stars and Stripes

Prisoners – A Ray of Hope

DESPITE the steady pace of Vietnamization and US troop withdrawals from Indochina, the Nixon Administration has so far made little headway in its efforts to solve the most agonizing problem of all: the plight of American prisoners of war in North Vietnam. But last week, US officials detected a faint ray of hope. Hanoi had agreed to accept the return of some 570 sick or wounded Communist prisoners – the largest repatriation of the war – and even though there was still no reason to believe that US POW's would soon be coming home, US officials treasured the thought that finally the ball might be starting to roll.

Swaps

The repatriation was first suggested by the Saigon government a month ago. The South Vietnamese also proposed that an additional 1,200 prisoners be transferred to a neutral country for an indefinite time before returning to North Vietnam. The allies' obvious hope was that a full acceptance by Hanoi might set a precedent that could lead to the release of US prisoners through a similar, third-country arrangement. But the Hanoi regime cautiously accepted only the direct return, and even that fragile accord almost collapsed. Never enthusiastic about POW swaps in the first place, Saigon became irritated at the imperious manner with which Hanoi bluntly dictated its terms for accepting the prisoners – including the specific date, time and location of the transfer. At that point, the US firmly – and successfully – stepped in, demand-ing that Saigon agree to the repatriation and guaranteeing that all of Hanoi's conditions could be met.

Barring an unforeseen snag, an unarmed civilian ship will anchor this week in the South China Sea off the Demilitarized Zone, and the prisoners will be transferred to North Vietnamese boats. And although the US is not overestimating the chances of an early release of American POWs, Washington's normal gloom over the prisoner problem has lifted a bit. "We're not holding our breath," a senior US diplomat remarked, "but accepting the return of its own men is the most substantive thing that Hanoi has done on prisoners yet."

Newsweek

Demilitarized Zone. Just before dusk, as the soldiers lined up outside the mess hall for dinner, North Vietnamese shells began to fall on the outpost. A crowd of soldiers ran for the nearest cover, a bunker that doubled as a beer club. After 50 or more men had crammed into the bunker, a Soviet-made 122-mm rocket slammed into the roof, carved through some 6 feet of sandbags, earth and timber and exploded inside. In part, the tragedy was sheer bad luck; the rockets are notoriously inaccurate, and they rarely penetrate such stout fortifications. But the slaughter was also due to GI carelessness, for the slogan "don't bunch up" is fundamental.

The bloodshed at Charlie Two was not the only high price paid for mistakes by GIs. At the huge base at Cam Ranh Bay – long considered one of the safest and most secure US installations in South Vietnam – a handful of enemy sappers breezed through the perimeter defenses last week and blew up some 1.5 million gallons of aviation fuel. Again, GI negligence was blamed. "The sappers obviously got past someone who should have spotted them," lamented one officer.

Forgetting Fundamentals

Miraculously, no lives were lost at Cam Ranh Bay. But what bothered Abrams – and many officials back in Washington, as well – was that the Charlie Two and Cam Ranh Bay attacks had demonstrated all too painfully that American troops were forgetting or ignoring most of what they had learned in basic train-ing. "They should never have happened," one Pentagon official said of the deaths at Charlie Two. "We should not have had so many men in that bunker." And that was what Abrams firmly ordered his subordinates to emphasize in the future. "He told them to make it very clear," one Army officer said later, "that people should not bunch up, not get lazy and not relax." He told them to make damned sure at all levels that the troops are not allowed to forget the "fundamentals."

Newsweek

WITHDRAWALS GROW

JULY 1971

1st The US voting age is lowered to 18.

1st The largest troop withdrawal in one day takes place as 6100 US troops leave Vietnam.

1st A new communist peace proposal calls for the withdrawal of US forces by the end of 1971, offering to free all POWs in exchange.

8th Start of further ARVN operations in Cambodia.

9th The South Vietnamese take over responsibility for the DMZ from US forces.

13th The US disclaims CIA involvement as Laotian tribesmen occupy the Plain of Jars.

15th It is revealed that President Nixon will visit the Chinese capital, Peking, the following spring.

20th It is reported that the CIA is helping Thai forces to build permanent bases inside Laos.

29th David Bruce, the head of the US team in Paris resigns for health reasons and is replaced from 31 July by William J. Porter, US Ambassador to South Korea.

The Uses of Vietspeak

Q: When is a war not a war? A: The fighting in Vietnam is referred to as an "international armed conflict," according to the Judge Advocate General's Office.
– *Army Digest, April 1968*

Every war makes its peculiar contributions to the language. There was still a sense of heroics in the neologisms of World War I: over the top into no man's land. World War II created a new terminology of mass death: fission, fire storm, and the final solution. From Korea, the first confrontation with Asian Communism, we acquired the widespread use of gooks and brainwashing.

The most vividly iconoclastic new words generally come from the GIs and so, in Vietnam, the grunts spoke of slants and slopes, of Charley (Viet Cong) and Yards (Montagnard tribesmen) and White Mice (white-uniformed local police). Where they were was "the boonies of Nam"; everything else was "the world." Officials spoke windily of "winning hearts and minds," but the GIs shortened that to WHAM. To the airmen, the jungle was Indian Country, where you might end up either in the Hanoi Hilton (prison camp) or Buying the Farm (dead).

Killing was the reality for which the GI invented the largest number of euphemisms: zapping, fragging, offing, greasing, waxing, hosing down a village (or using a Zippo Squad to set it afire). When Lieut William Calley testified that he had been ordered to attack My Lai, he did not say that he had been told to kill but to "waste" everyone in sight.

In devising such brusque euphemisms, however, the GIs hardly matched the ornate creations of their superiors at headquarters. Specimens:

* Air raid – Limited duration

The Navy Stays Put

The USS *Buchanan*, a guided missile destroyer, rolls gently in the waters of the Tonkin Gulf, 5,000 yards offshore of the Demilitarized Zone. Crew members who are not needed to fire the guns or run the ship are down in the mess deck watching Jane Fonda in Barbarella.

Last week, for the first time in two years, the ships that have been daily pounding the coast drew return fire from shore-based Communist artillery. One round hit the USS *Lloyd Thomas*, inflicting minor damage and injuring three crewmen.

Drugs and Boredom

In the style of Admiral Zumwalt's "New Navy," officers and enlisted men alike sport beards, waxed mustaches and hair long enough to have put them on report three years ago. The chief

disciplinary problems are drug abuse and racial tension, though in scope they barely match similar problems suffered in the Army. Boredom is pervasive. As one *Buchanan* sailor puts it: "I sometimes go topside and stand at the rail, watching the moon on the water. I just stand there for hours like some damn USO ad."

It bothers many of the sailors that they are fighting a passive, unseen enemy. "We've been shooting at the same place for seven years," says one radarman. "By now, the Viet Cong must have the area roped off and posted with signs that say, 'Keep out, the ship is firing.'" Still, unlike the ground units in South Vietnam, the Navy is not setting an immediate course for home. "When they talk about the US

The Army's withdrawal from Vietnam is not matched by the Navy, which will remain on Yankee Station for the forseeable future

withdrawing from Vietnam," says a chief petty officer, "they don't count the Navy, because we're not in the country. I figure we'll be staying around a while."
Time

Harassment and Interdiction sounds irritating, but when you are at the wrong end of H&I artillery fire it is deadly. This is one example of official 'Viet Speak', that curious military language designed to disguise the reality of war

protective reaction strike
* Artillery fire – H & I (harassment and interdiction)
* Murder of an enemy spy – Termination with extreme prejudice
* Defoliation – Resources control program
* Refugee camp – New life hamlet

"War does things to the language," *New York Times* columnist Russell Baker once wrote, "and the language in revenge refuses to co-operate in helping us to understand what we are talking about," so even when the US finally decided to start withdrawing its troops it created a new word to disguise reality one last time. It called the process Vietnamization.

Time

Postwar Shock Besets Veterans of Vietnam

SAN FRANCISCO The flights from Saigon and Danang reach California in 18 hours, telescoping night into day and into night again, and the big jet transports drop out of the gloom of the Pacific sky to land at Travis Air Force Base as another sunrise rims the high peaks of the Sierra Nevada range far to the east.

On board the planes are sleepy young soldiers, members of the dwindling force of American troops in Vietnam, coming home from a war in a strange land where they had served with gradations of comprehension and devotion.

They step out on the chilled tarmac and stretch and shiver. The temperature is more than 30 degrees cooler here in northern California than it had been the day before in Vietnam.

It is the first shock of re-entry for the Vietnam veteran. In the coming months, as he goes out into America and tries to pick up the threads of the life he had left behind, there will be more.

Just what Vietnam service does to a young man emotionally is difficult to define, but it is related to the shattering experience of war itself with the added ingredient that this war, unlike others, does not give many of the men who wage it feelings of patriotism, or even purpose.

The New York Times

Supreme Court OKs Pentagon Papers Release

WASHINGTON – The Supreme Court on a 6 to 3 vote Wednesday permitted the New York Times and the Washington Post to publish stories based on the secret Pentagon study of the Vietnam War.

The majority's opinion said the government had not met the burden of showing justification for a restraint. Chief Justice Warren E. Burger and Justices Harry A. Blackmun and John M. Harlan dissented.

Here are highlights of Wednesday's development pertaining to the Pentagon papers and disclosures from newly released sections of the Vietnam war study:

– The Supreme Court, in a 6-3 decision, upheld the right of the New York Times and Washington Post to resume publication of stories based on the Pentagon papers.
– Sen. Mike Gravel, D-Alaska, released a major portion of the study saying there is no justification for keeping it from the American public.
– Senate Republican Leader Hugh Scott of Pennsylvania called on Senate Democrats to determine whether Gravel violated chamber rules in releasing parts of the Pentagon study.
– The Pentagon papers disclosed early, high-level U.S. talks about using nuclear weapons in the Vietnam war if Red Chinese forces joined the fighting.
– The war study said that the night before President Lyn-don B. Johnson announced cessation of the bombing of North Vietnam in his successful 1968 bid to get peace talks started, the State Department notified U.S. war allies that the move probably would fail.
– The Pentagon papers disclosed that former Secretary of Defense Robert S. McNamara, as early as November 1961, raised with President John F. Kennedy the possibility of attacking north Vietnam.

Stars and Stripes

AUGUST 1971

2nd The US admits that an army of 30,000 CIA-maintained irregulars is operating in Laos.

3rd ARVN forces destroy two communist-held Cambodian villages.

6th The last remaining troops of the 4th Battalion, 503rd Infantry of the 173rd Airborne Brigade prepare to leave Vietnam. This was the first US Army unit to go into action in the conflict in 1965.

7th Cambodian government troops take Preykry.

15th The South Vietnamese base of Baho falls as fighting intensifies along the DMZ.

15th Cambodia demands that South Vietnamese troops be pulled out of the country after reports of their appalling ill-treatment of civilians.

18th Australia and New Zealand set the end of the year as the deadline for the withdrawal of their respective contingents from Vietnam. Australian losses are put at 473 dead and 2202 wounded.

The Hawk and the Vultures

Few of the reporters I know in Vietnam, though they often get frustrated, ever get truly angry at being treated hostilely or with suspicion by American generals or embassy officials. They accept that this hostility is born of the failure of American policy here and of the inability of those whose careers have become so entwined with Vietnam to admit it. Some of these men have been in Vietnam for a decade. They know virtually no other life but the one of trying to make American policy come out right. To admit defeat would be to throw away the linchpin of their existence. But the press has reported their failures for them, and under such circumstances, no-one can be surprised at their distrust and dislike of newsmen.

The Hawk Talks

Typical of such men was the American general advising on the northern front who agreed to talk off the record with a half-dozen Western reporters one day. He immediately made it clear that he considered us unpatriotic, because he assumed, correctly, that we had been writing stories saying the war was not going well for the allied side.

"I want you to get something straight," he said, pointing an accusing finger. "You're talking to a hawk. You know that. The only solution possible is a military solution. It's going to take a military victory to end it. We've got to prove to the North Vietnamese that they can't invade and take over." The general then said that the North Vietnamese high command does not put the same value on life as

Richard's Story

"When I was on short-time calendar was when I got all messed up in my head. I had 10 days left in my tour and they

Korean Costs

WASHINGTON A Senate Foreign Relations sub-committee disclosed today that the dispatch of 50,000 South Korean soldiers to fight in South Vietnam had cost the United States more than £1-billion in the last five years.

The agreement under which that sum was spent covered direct support for the troops, such as overseas allowances, arms, equipment and rations.

It further covered a wide range of other assistance, including modernization of South

25th The run-up to the Assembly elections in South Vietnam is marked by a communist offensive aimed at civilian targets.

29th President Thieu retains hold on National Assembly as fellow candidates for the October presidential contest Ky and Minh retire from the campaign complaining of corruption.

Australian troops, with years of counter-guerrilla expertise in Malaya and Borneo, have been amongst the most effective of Allied troops in southeast Asia. However, the last Australian combat units will be out of Vietnam by the end of 1971, leaving only advisors in-country

A **CIA** helicopter flies into the headquarters of the Clandestine Army of General Vang Pao. The CIA has been sponsoring private armies in Laos for many years, supplying them through Air America, the CIA airline. Such forces are difficult to control, but they do provide a thorn to stick into the side of the North Vietnamese, which will last until the private armies lose American support

Americans and South Vietnamese do. "They've already determined they can expend 100,000 men this year on the offensive and they don't care if they come back or not. A North Vietnamese officer has the power of life and death over his men. They shoot a man if he refuses to go on attack." Saying these things seemed to console the general.

The New York Times

ordered me to go on bunker duty with a bunch of new guys. I said I wasn't pulling no bunker duty with a bunch of new guys, they'll get me killed, but they put us out there anyway. Imagine, me with 10 days to go. I was scared. I wouldn't let any of them stand guard duty alone. They would've fallen asleep and gotten all of us shot. I sat on top of that bunker for 10 straight nights, sweating out every minute. I started smoking for the first time in my life and I still haven't broken the habit and that was two years ago."

The New York Times

Korean forces in their own country, procurement of military goods in South Korea for United States forces in South Vietnam, expanded work for South Korean contractors in South Vietnam, and financial aid.

United States support for the South Korean troops in South Vietnam has long been public knowledge. But the extent and cost of that assistance had been kept secret until the release today of a transcript of testimony by Administration officials last February before the sub-committee headed by Senator Stuart Symington, Democrat of Missouri.

The New York Times

SEPTEMBER 1971

6-18th Start of Operation Lam Son 810 near the border with Laos while B-52s bomb the DMZ.

9th The communists turn down William L. Porter's request for secret negotiations to break the deadlock. Seoul announces that South Korean forces will start to leave Vietnam in December as planned, with a view to completing the pull-out by mid-1972.

14th Start of an allied operation in the U Minh Forest. There are 400 enemy casualties by the end of the operation.

15-16th Laotian government forces retake Paksong on the Boloven Plateau.

16th Fifteen die as a Saigon nightclub is bombed by terrorists.

16-20th The communists step up their efforts in the Saigon area.

21st 200 US aircraft bomb targets north of the DMZ.

21st The passage of new enlistment legislation allows the draft, suspended since June, to resume.

23rd Captain Ernest L. Medina is found not guilty of charges relating to the My Lai massacre of March 1968.

26th US and South Vietnamese forces stave off communist assaults and counterattack on the Cambodian border.

28th China and North Vietnam sign aid treaty in Peking.

Cary

On his way into the field for the first time in Vietnam, Cary witnessed another marine cradling a dead buddy and sobbing beyond comfort. "I promised myself I'd never let that happen to me. I'd play the loner and not get attached to anyone who is going to get killed. It was like I lost all respect for love. So I built a wall around me." The wall crumbled one summer day below the DMZ. "Alpha and Bravo companies were wiped out and we were sent in to pick up the bodies. After three days in the hot sun the bodies stunk. I picked up one and the arms came off in my hands. All the time we were under fire. I couldn't help myself. I just went to pieces."

The New York Times

Vietnamese officers stand atop a PT-76 light tank captured in Laos

A Cool Dip Despite the Hot Water

A Marine makes his way up a steep hill. Such activity has always been the lot of the 'Grunt', but in 1971 it seems pointless, as there is little or no sign of the enemy. He is there, however, and loosening of discipline might well prove costly

It has been six months since the GIs of Bravo Company, Fourth Battalion, 31st Infantry, suffered a casualty or killed an enemy soldier. Now the terror of combat has faded. The men still mention the terror – it has become a word to which homage must be paid – but they don't feel it any more. Instead, they remember the blood-pounding excitement and compare that with the boredom they now endure. Six months without contact. Six months of hunting an enemy they know is nearby, but never see to catch. Every day the prospect of a fight, at once terrifying and titillating, fades a bit more and the days blur, each as deadeningly uneventful as the one before. Hump up the mountain ... hump down the mountain ... wade the "blue" (river) ... hack away the pesky "wait-a-minute" vines. The same monsoon rain at night; the same C-rations at every meal; the same jokes from the same mouths in the same faces, day after day.

Rubberlegs the Radioman

For relief, anything will do, anything that will make today different than yesterday. This was such a day. Nothing special; no blazing gunfight with Charlie. But on this morning Bravo Company found the remains of some campfires and fresh feces, the first real evidence in weeks that there were Communist soldiers nearby. "One day old, no more," said a lanky trooper. "I'd say three days," objected another with an equally expert air. They argued briefly, calmly. One day, three days – the important thing was that the enemy soldiers had been in the area recently.

Rubberlegs, the radioman, called out: "Charlie Oscar, they want you." Names are rarely used in the jungle, only nicknames. Rubberlegs got his from the rolling gait he uses to lug 70-odd pounds of radio up and down mountains. Charlie Oscar is the phonetic name for the commanding officer, Capt. Richard Hurchanik, a swarthy, rangy man with a neat mustache and a baldish head.

Newmeat Fording a River

Hurchanik spoke into the receiver for a moment, then disgustedly flipped it back to his radioman. "Goddamit," he exploded, "goddamit, goddamit." He wanted to push on and catch the enemy, but battalion had a batch of twelve new replacements, "newmeats" in GI argot, for Bravo Company. Hurchanik's instructions were to find a landing zone suitable for the choppers carrying the newmeats and wait for them.

The troops moved quickly through the jungle. But it took a full half hour to ford the river. It was less than 50 feet wide and only waist deep, but the current was swift and the men had to make their way across slowly with the aid of a lifeline. On the other side there was a large rock beach opening on to a clear, cold pool. The beach would be the landing zone. "Charlie Oscar," one of the men drawled to Hurchanik, "it would be a damned shame not to use that natural swimming hole down there," and in minutes half of the men were naked and in the water.

Homer, the young sergeant with a quick, on-off Steve McQueen grin, talked about Bravo's lack of combat. "Everybody always calls the Viet Cong elusive but you don't know the meaning of that word until you hump the bush for months looking for them." He pointed to the swimming troopers. "We haven't seen any bang-bang for so long we're getting damn lax." He pointed again, this time to the dense jungle climbing up from the bank opposite the pool. "They could be all over that hillside. They don't get seen unless they want to get seen. They could hit us right now and all we'd be is a bunch of buck-ass naked fools scrambling like ants."

Newsweek

RELEASES

OCTOBER 1971

2nd Clashes occur near Kien Thien in the Mekong Delta.

3rd Amid communist rocket attacks, President Thieu wins a second four-year spell in office in an election in which he is the only candidate. He celebrates by releasing 2938 Viet Cong POWs.

7th US B-52s bomb communist targets on both sides of the Cambodian border.

8th US ground forces complete their final large-scale operation – Operation Jefferson Glenn – of the war.

11th US troops at Fire Base Pace close to the Cambodian border allege that they are being ordered to carry out border combat missions which go against US policy, on pain of disciplinary action.

16th General Lon Nol suspends the Cambodian National Assembly.

18th Eighteen South Vietnamese troops die when a US aircraft bombs their base in error.

20th Start of a fresh ARVN offensive in Cambodia.

29th The total number of US troops remaining in Vietnam is given as 196,700.

31st Saigon frees the first of almost 3000 Viet Cong POWs.

Below: A section of the Ho Chi Minh trail as it passes through Cambodia looks more like the surface of the moon, so heavily is it marked by craters from B-52 bomb attacks. Areas of the trail were the most heavily bombed pieces of real estate in history

Right: 1st Squadron, 10th Cavalry, on patrol in Military Region 2. Originally the divisional reconnaissance squadron for the 4th Infantry Division, it has been operating under I Field Force since the beginning of the year, and is now preparing to leave Vietnam

The Artful Dodgers

Tran Van Hai, 34, has been hiding out in Saigon's labyrinthine alleyways since 1965. Reason: he is trying to avoid military service. While his wife works as a vendor, Hai does odd jobs in the neighborhood; together they make enough to care for their six children. When the police come, as they do with increasing frequency these days, he ducks down the maze of passages in his ramshackle neighborhood or hides between the wall panels of his house.

"I could not leave my wife and children," Hai explains when asked why he deserted from an army unit a few years ago. "I love them very much and there is no one else to care for them." The irony is that because he has six children Hai is now legally entitled to a deferment. Since they were born while he was in hiding, he cannot get his draft status changed without being arrested as a deserter – which would mean up to twelve months in prison and then front-line duty in an army unit.

Time

Medina Innocent On All Charges

Ft. McPherson, Ga. (UPI) – Capt. Ernest L. Medina, the last officer charged in the massacre of My Lai, was cleared of all counts Wednesday by a court-martial jury that deliberated 57 minutes.

One other officer, Col. Oran K. Henderson, is on trial at Ft. Meade, Md., but he is accused of covering up the massacre, and not with the actual killings.

Twenty five officers and men originally were charged in the March 16, 1968 incidents, 12 with participating in the actual killings, 12 with covering up, and one with both. Of that number five were tried, four were acquitted, one was convicted, and the charges against all others were dismissed.

The verdict in the Medina case came at 4.19 p.m. and the speed with which the jury reached the decision was in sharp contrast to the 13 days which another panel at Ft. Benning, Ga. took in returning the only conviction in the case – that of Lt. William L. Calley Jr.

Calley, like Medina, was charged with 102 murders at My Lai, and was convicted of 22 of them. He has his 20-year sentence under appeal.

Pacific Star and Stripes

One for One

When Sgt. John C. Sexton Jr. limped barefoot out of the Cambodian jungle two weeks ago, he became the 24th American soldier to be freed by the Viet Cong. But as Sexton's story unfolded, it became clear that he was no ordinary POW who had made it back to freedom. For one thing, although the US command in Saigon had come into possession of a letter written by Sexton shortly after his capture more than two years ago, the Army had allowed his parents to believe that their son was probably dead. What is more, according to some reports, Sexton brought with him from captivity a Viet Cong request for the release of two of their own men – a request that triggered the first de facto prisoner exchange of the Vietnam war.

The Safe-conduct Pass

Sexton's ordeal began on August 12, 1969, when he was wounded in an ambush and taken prisoner. After treating his wounds – a broken right elbow, multiple shrapnel cuts and a badly injured right eye – the Viet Cong placed Sexton in a prison camp, apparently in Cambodia. Late last month, Sexton's captors took him on a ten-day, 70-mile march through the jungle. On the last night of the journey, the Viet Cong handed him a safe-conduct pass and a crudely drawn map and sent him on his way. Weakened by malnutrition and malaria, with his right elbow paralyzed and his right eye almost blind, Sexton staggered the final 9 miles to freedom. "I thought I was dreaming," he recalled later at a base hospital. "I guess that was why I didn't sleep too well on my first night back. I just couldn't relax for fear that the dream would go away."

Spurred by Sexton's release, US officials decided to seize the opportunity and match the enemy man for man. Under pressure from the Americans, the South Vietnamese Government agreed to free a North Vietnamese lieutenant. Three days after Sexton stepped from the jungle, an unarmed US helicopter flew into Cambodia and deposited the lieutenant on Viet Cong soil in the same general area where Sexton himself had been released. "The exchange," said a US spokesman, "was made in response to a number of indications that the enemy would welcome such a reciprocal gesture. Of course," he added, "we have no definite assurance that this will lead to the release of more American prisoners, but we certainly hope so."

Newsweek

VIETNAMIZATION

NOVEMBER 1971

2nd The siege of Prakham is broken by Cambodian troops.

7th Ten Cambodian troops die in communist attack on Bamnal.

10th Communist forces bombard Phnom Penh airport.

12th 1 February 1972 is set as the deadline for the withdrawal of a further 45,000 US troops. The total of US forces in Vietnam will then stand at 139,000.

13th US intensifies bombing of communist targets when warned of an imminent large-scale North Vietnamese move into Cambodia and Laos.

The US withdrawal of ground troops is not matched in the air, and communist targets in Cambodia and Laos have come under intense attack this month

13th Cambodian forces incur heavy losses as the siege of Rumlong turns into a rout.

16th US steps up its air activities in support of the Cambodian government as the fighting gets closer to Phnom Penh.

17th Martial law is brought into effect in Thailand as Prime Minister Kittikachorn suspends constitutional rule.

19th Cambodians appeal to Saigon for help as communists get closer to Phnom Penh.

22nd Large-scale South Vietnamese offensives begin in the Mekong Delta and around Phnom Penh.

23rd US advisory personnel are reported to be in Cambodia, contrary to US policy.

27th Start of South Vietnamese offensive in the Central Highlands.

The News at 4.15

The core of the combat story that many American newspapers run as a daily staple comes from an afternoon briefing in downtown Saigon that bears about as much relation to reality as a trip through a funhouse at an amusement park.

The briefing, which has become known as "the Follies" begins at 4.15 p.m. in a sweltering un-airconditioned auditorium that is part of a euphemistic operation known as the Press Center. Press releases are passed out beforehand – one from MACV, a separate one from the American Navy that expands on items already in the MACV release (the Air Force also puts out a separate one but distributes it in newsagency mailboxes), and one from the South Vietnamese armed forces, prepared by their Political Warfare Department.

The Disappearing Battles

Their releases and answers are notable primarily for their omissions. Entire battles have gone unreported. In early September, an Associated Press correspondent, through other sources, had learned of and written about a major two-day clash that had taken place less than 40 miles north of Saigon in which 180 North Vietnamese were killed and about 200 South Vietnamese were killed or wounded. When the battle had gone unmentioned at the briefing for two days, the correspondent asked the reason for the omission.

The South Vietnamese briefer went shuffling through the mound of papers on his clipboard an finally announced "Between noon and early evening on Friday, Sept. 1, ARVN [Army of the Republic of Vietnam] elements engaged an undetermined-sized enemy force 12 kilometers north of Laikhe; 83 enemy were killed. On the ARVN side, 76 were wounded." On the face of it, this report was preposterous – it would take a miracle to produce a battle in which 76 men get wounded and not a single one dies. ARVN was simply covering up its losses again. These lies and omissions have tended to increase whenever battle losses have.

The American briefers, who smile knowingly about ARVN's doctoring of battle statistics, have not been much more forthcoming themselves with the facts of war. Their language, which has no connection with everyday English, has been designed to sanitize the war. Planes do not drop bombs, they "deliver ordnance." Napalm is a forbidden word and when an American information officer is forced under direct questioning to discuss it, he calls it "soft ordnance." In the press releases and the answers to newsmen's questions, there is never any sense, not even implicit, of people being killed, homes being destroyed, thousands of refugees fleeing.

The New York Times

Sons and Daughters

SAIGON. John and Gigi are two children of mixed parentage in one of South Vietnam's numerous overcrowded orphanages.
Their father is an American soldier. Their Vietnamese mother is a former bar girl. But they are too young to be aware of this background.

Their mother, now married to a Vietnamese, visits them every few months. She once wanted to have them back at home, but convention was against it. The children have never seen their father.

John, aged 2, and Gigi, 3, are two of the more than 15,000 children of mixed parentage left behind by the American troops after seven years of fighting in South Vietnam.

More than 500 live in "orphanages" that are in fact institutions where children are deposited by parents who cannot support them. The rest live with their mothers or other relatives.
The New York Times

A sergeant in the **LLDB** (Luc Luong Duc Biet, or **ARVN** Special Forces) takes an unarmed combat course with **CIDG** volunteers. The LLDB were better at putting down (or setting up) coups than fighting the Viet Cong, and the increasing Vietnamization of the war will see a complete shake-up of the organization, which will be renamed the Special Mission Service

ARMY AVIATORS

DECEMBER 1971

1st As Cambodian communist – Khmer Rouge – forces drive on Phnom Penh, North Vietnamese troops put the demoralized Cambodian army to flight on Route 6.

7th Communist rockets fired into Phnom Penh.

9th Refugees from outlying settlements pour into Phnom Penh as the communists push closer and closer to the capital. Communist rejection of a US request for a week's adjournment causes a breakdown in the Paris talks.

14th A combined force of Cambodian and ARVN troops backed up by US air power takes the NVA-held town of Chup.

16th It is announced that 8053 US aircraft have now been lost in the conflict.

17th Anti-government demonstrations in Phnom Penh accompany the deteriorating military situation in Cambodia.

20th Plain of Jars in Laos falls to the NVA.

22nd The USSR denounces China as being pro-US over Vietnam.

23rd Bob Hope is involved in attempt to gain freedom for US POWs.

26th Anti-war veterans occupy the Statue of Liberty.

26th US starts five consecutive days of bombing against North Vietnamese targets.

The Warlords

"Army aviators are different from other people," says Maj. Charles J. Mix, commander of the 117th. "It's the challenge, the danger, taking chances. When you're flying and you hear one of your own men at night on the ground, whispering messages into his radio set because the enemy is nearby, that's when the adrenalin really flows." But combat has become the exception now, and hardly anyone gets shot at any more. "People fight over who gets to fly combat assaults because they're so rare," says a member of the 117th. Still, as a pilot standing by his helicopter said, "The Warlords [the 117th's current nickname] are No. 1 in Vietnam, and don't forget it."

No. 1 they were and, under Mr Nixon's game plan for Vietnam, it appears that first in will be last out.

Newsweek

5 Days of Air Raids End

SAIGON – U.S. Air Force and Navy warplanes ended five days of blistering air strikes against North Vietnam Thursday, and the U.S. Command said three jets were lost during the raids.

Air Force and Navy pilots flew 1,000 sorties against assorted targets in North Vietnam during the heaviest bombing campaign in more than three years, spokesmen reported.

The "limited duration, protective reaction air strikes" ended at 3.36 p.m. Thursday, according to the command communique.

Targets of the air raids were airfields, supply depots, surface-to-air missile launchers, anti-aircraft artillery and air-defense radar sites, spokesmen said.

Most of the strikes were within 90 miles of the Demilitarized Zone, but planes also bombarded airfields south of the 20th parallel, which is 75 miles south of Hanoi, spokesmen said.

Two U.S. Navy jets – an F4 Phantom and an A6 Intruder – crashed in North Vietnam Thursday, spokesmen said, and an Air Force F4 was lost on the first day of the raids last Sunday.

One crewman of the A6 was rescued, but the other five crew members of the three downed planes were reported missing. Each jet carried a crew of two.

Stars and Stripes

The Phantoms and Intruders the Navy is currently using over Vietnam are a far cry from the A-4s and F-8s of 1964

Helicopters were the big innovation of the Vietnam War, and they have brought into being a whole new breed of aircrew, who find the current lack of enemy contact boring

Sons and Daughters

SAIGON. John and Gigi are two children of mixed parentage in one of South Vietnam's numerous over-crowded orphanages

Their father is an American soldier. Their Vietnamese mother is a former bar girl. But they are too young to be aware of this background.

Their mother, now married to a Vietnamese, visits them every few months. She once wanted to have them back at home, but convention was against it. The children have never seen their father.

John, aged 2, and Gigi, 3, are two of the more than 15,000 children of mixed parentage left behind by the American troops after seven years of fighting in South Vietnam.

More than 500 live in "orphanages" that are in fact institutions where children are deposited by parents who cannot support them. The rest live with their mothers of other relatives.

The New York Times

Beechcraft Pilot

I flew for the Army Security Agency (ASA) at Phu Bai from December 1971 to May 1972. About that time the Cong were really getting aggressive (remember, we were leaving by the hundreds) and the SAM line (the effective area for the SAMs being now located south of what had been the DMZ) was moving south until it was just north of the traffic pattern at Phu Bai. The RU-8D aircraft did not have a RHAW (radar homing and warning) system installed so the Battalion sent us south to Long Than and all of the U-21s with the RHAW gear went north.

Upon arrival at Long Than I discovered that they flew the mission at 1,500 MSL and that was right inside the small-arms limit. Being your basic coward I protested a lot about the lack of blue sky between my butt and and the ground. After a couple of missions at that altitude I was asked by the maintenance officer if I would like to be the maintenance test pilot, and I readily accepted.

Locating the Cong

As I look in my logbook I see that I flew my first mission in Vietnam on 23 November 1971 and my last on 29 July 1972.

Our mission was to locate Viet Cong radio transmitters, usually co-located with major Cong units, by the use of triangulation. To obtain the desired results we had to use fairly sophisticated navigation equipment on board the RU-8D and U-21. By using totally independent nav systems we could draw pictures of the target's location on the ground. The information was then forwarded, along with the coded message that our radio operator heard, to headquarters for interpretation and analysis. If the information was good the Corps might request an "Arc Light" (B-52 strike) on the spot that we pinpointed. For the most part though, we felt as if we had little to do with the war effort. Very few of our targets were ever bombed.

Our missions in the RU-8D and U-21 (RU-21A, D) lasted about 4 hours, most of which was spent loitering in an area waiting for the bad guys to talk. The companies were the 146th Avn Co (RR), at Long Than, 156th Avn Co (RR), at Can Tho, 138th Avn Bn (RR) at Phu Bai and the 1st Avn Co (RR) at Cam Ranh Bay. The 1st flew twelve-hour missions in the P2V Neptune, doing a similar mission.

Bugs in the Shitter

I spent a lot of my time fixing motor vehicles that had been run into the ground by extensive use and a severe lack of maintenance. When the Company CO found out that I could fix cars he assigned me to the job of Motor Officer. I had 32 vehicles in my motor pool, Jeeps, 2½-ton trucks, a 5-ton wrecker and a 5-ton tractor (that I used for my personal Jeep). When the war for us was almost over, I was given the job of standing the company down. That meant turning in all of the vehicles and company-assigned equipment. It was called Project Keystone.

Numerous things happened throughout my year that made things humorous in retrospect. The poisonous bug that bit me on the toe while I was sitting on the shitter, the food that was so bad we decided to eat C-rations to survive, the midnight rocket attacks, pilots manning machine guns on the perimeter so that the enlisted could have Christmas off.

During the flying, I concluded that Vietnam was a beautiful country and I hoped that it could see better times.

Minard Thompson
Personal Recollection

US Army Security Agency aircraft flew highly classified radio intelligence missions through the war

JANUARY 1972

1st Communist targets in Cambodia and Laos are bombed as US air activity is dramatically stepped up. The US expects a Tet offensive.

2nd President Nixon states that a force of 25-35,000 US troops will remain in Vietnam until every US POW is freed.

3rd Laotians withdraw from Long Thien base under NVA shellfire.

6th Paris talks reopen after a break of a month.

6th US troop withdrawal target is set at a further 70,000 by the end of April.

7th Eighteen US troops are injured in a mortar attack on Fiddler's Green fire base.

10th Senator Hubert Humphrey enters the race for the Presidency with criticism of the slow pace of President Nixon's withdrawal timetable.

12th Communists launch over 30 assaults across South Vietnam.

17th Targets in Laos suffer a further round of heavy US bombing raids.

The bombing of Laos continues. The Plain of Jars alone has received more bombs than Germany in World War II!

18th Seymour Hersh, who reported the My Lai massacre, asserts that a similar slaughter, this time of 90 persons, took place at My Khe 4 on the same day.

20th Thais move against communist guerrillas at Lom Sak in northeast Thailand.

21st US aircraft continue bombing in anticipation of Tet offensive.

25th President Nixon openly acknowledges that secret talks have taken place with the North Vietnamese in Paris and lists the contents of the US eight-point peace program.

28th US aircraft carry out the 20th raid inside North Vietnam since the beginning of the year.

Here Come the Cavalry

In all probability, the last US Army combat unit in Vietnam will be the 7,000-man 3rd Brigade of the First Cavalry Division (Airmobile), which is responsible for the security of a vast area of Vietnamese countryside surrounding the huge American installations at Bien Hoa, Long Binh and the Tan Son Nhut airbase outside Saigon. Recently Time correspondent Rudolph Rauch joined one 3rd Brigade company as it pushed off from a fire base 34 miles east of Saigon to begin a patrol in search of North Vietnamese infiltrators. His report:

Nobody in Charlie Company wanted to be where he was, and when we walked off Fire Base Hall and into the jungle, it was easy to sympathize. We marched as a company for an hour, then divided into three platoons. After two miles, the jungle gave way to incredibly thick undergrowth – not high enough to block out the sun and too dense to move through, either quickly or silently. Napalm strikes had killed all the tall trees whose shade once kept down the growth on the jungle floor.

Charlie Company was fresh from a weekend in the seaside resort of Vung Tau – a prized opportunity for revelry and re-laxation that comes only once every 45 days. The company has no barracks, no dress uniforms (they are stored in boxes at Bien Hoa) and no personal possessions (letters are the only personal items allowed in the field). The Vung Tau weekend, which the men enjoy in fatigues, is the only break in an endless cycle of ten- to 15-day patrols and three-day rests on a fire base with no hot showers and few other amenities.

No Hammocks

We are supposed to patrol until 5 o'clock, when the rules say that the night defensive position should be set up. If a unit moves after 5, there is a danger that a contact might run on after darkness, making air support more difficult. But at 5 it is pouring rain, and we are still in scrub, which is not good for a night position because there are no trees big enough to stop enemy mortars. It is close to 6 when we find a few trees, and everybody starts putting up his hooch. I pull out my hammock. "No hammocks," says Sergeant Henry A. Johnson, a Virginian who has a master's degree in communications. "The CO doesn't allow them. Too vulnerable to mortars. The CO believes

Viet Cong, RIP

An infantry company from the 1st Air Cavalry Division ambushed a team of Viet Cong tax collectors recently in the jungles northeast of Saigon. After collecting the enemy's weapons, the GIs dug the customary shallow mass grave for the five slain Viet Cong.

What followed was not so customary. After covering the enemy corpses with a green rubber poncho, the men who had just killed them stood with bared heads as an Army chaplain conducted a brief funeral service. Intoned

Perhaps it is the prospect of an end to the war, but US soldiers are now treating dead VC in a more respectful fashion than in the 'ear-collecting' days of old

Chaplain Michael Chona: "May they rest in peace. O Lord, we implore you to grant this mercy to our dead brothers that they who held fast to your will by their intentions will not receive punishment in return for their deeds."

It was like a Southeast Asian version of *The Grand Illusion*. The weird gallantry seemed even more bizarre after years during which both sides have sometimes collected the ears of the dead and otherwise mutilated corpses. Perhaps with the end in sight, there is some impulse to introduce a belated battlefield politesse. The new policy of helicoptering in a chaplain to hold funerals for the enemy took effect when Brigadier General James F. Hamlet assumed command of the division's 3rd Brigade. Said one brigade officer: "The general feels it is the humane thing to do."

Time

---

in being cautious."

"Line One"

When we move out at dawn next morning, everyone is a bit more nimble, perhaps because the Vung Tau hangovers are gone. We walk all morning, stopping for a ten-minute break each hour. At the noon break, the radio sputters with orders from the battalion commander to a unit that has made contact with the enemy five miles away. There was an ambush; one American was killed when he walked into an NVA bunker complex. Another is wounded and a helicopter is down. The battalion commander, flying overhead in his helicopter, says he is going in to pick up the downed pilot. His chopper is loaded with electronic gear and it is too heavy for any task that requires acrobatics. "Jesus, Colonel, be careful," whispers the radio operator, Pfc. Erik Lewis, 21. The rescue is successful.

Lewis tells me that a "Line One" (meaning a GI combat death in army jargon) "happens just rare enough so that nobody at home knows about it. But if you're out here, your peace outlook goes straight to zero." And, he adds, "I'm going to kill as many of those mothers as I can."

Time

The Cavalry were among the first Army units into Vietnam, and it looks as though the 1st Cav's 3rd Brigade, guarding major US bases, will be one of the last to leave

S. Viet Conditions on Troop Withdrawal

The South Vietnamese government asserted Thursday that the withdrawal of all U.S. forces from South Vietnam depends on Communist willingness to negotiate the withdrawal of North Vietnamese troops as well as on the release of American prisoners of war.

The U.S. government endorsed this stand, which appeared to set a new condition for a total American withdrawal.

South Vietnamese representative Pham Dang Lam told the Communists at the 140th session of the Vietnam peace talks:

"Whether all the allied forces leave South Vietnam or there remains residual forces, and how long these forces will take to disengage, depends on whether or not you accept to negotiate seriously on the problem of troop withdrawal as part of an over-all settlement, as well as on the question of the release of prisoners of war."

Stars and Stripes

FEBRUARY 1972

1st South Vietnamese forces chase communist attackers into south Cambodia.

3rd Viet Cong negotiators submit their latest peace program in Paris.

4th The last Thai troops leave Vietnam.

5th Nixon's eight-point offer is turned down by the North.

7th Laotians embark on a drive against NVA forces in the Plain of Jars.

9th US begins a further air campaign over the Central Highlands.

10th Da Nang comes under rocket attack as the Paris talks hit further snags.

12th Cambodians open an ultimately unsuccessful operation to wrest the religious centre of Angkor Wat from the NVA.

13th US B-52s carry out the highest number of missions so far in a 24-hour period.

16th According to a Gallup Poll 52 per cent of those asked are behind the President over Vietnam.

16th It is announced that a US air operation has begun over the North's Quang Binh Province and the northern DMZ.

19th Hanoi allows five US airmen held in the North to send televised messages to their families.

20th The Mekong Delta and Da Nang are the targets for multiple communist assaults.

21st Start of President Nixon's visit to China. The North Vietnamese fear a deal to their disadvantage.

24th Seventeen minutes after the Paris talks reconvene the communists leave in protest at US air raids against the North.

25th US troops clash with communists and suffer 21 injured and one fatality. This action accounts for almost half the US weekly casualties.

27th US/Chinese communique from Peking indicates that China favours Hanoi's peace formula while the US sticks by its January eight points.

29th South Korea pulls 11,000 troops out of Vietnam as part of its withdrawal programme.

The Andersen Sorties

In early 1972, all B-52 sorties in support of Southeast Asia were flown by the 307th Strategic Wing at U-Tapao, known simply to most people as "U-T". This was part of a long term involvement of B-52s in the Southeast Asian conflict conducted under the nickname "ARC LIGHT." Crews from all Continental United States (CONUS) B-52 bomb wings were assigned temporary duty (TDY) on a rotational basis to fly these missions. At the same time, the Andersen mission was to maintain B-52Ds and crews of the 60th Bombardment Squadron on nuclear alert. The host unit, the 43rd Strategic Wing, also was required to support an additional conventional warfare contingency plan for B-52s, if called upon to do so. That contingency plan was soon to be exercised far beyond the parameters envisioned by its original drafters.

Twelve Hours from Guam

The normal sortie length from U-Tapao was three and one-half hours. There was no refueling, and the crew duty day was approximately eight hours. The missions from Guam, on the other hand, required prestrike refueling and lasted approximately 12 hours. It was a more complex mission than those flown out of Thailand, and the crew duty day ran from 17 to 18 hours. This long mission and duty day meant that additional crew resources and tanker support had to be generated to support the Andersen sorties. Therefore, stateside tankers were sent to Kadena Air Base, Okinawa as the B-52Ds deployed to Andersen. Tanker operations also eventually expanded at several Thailand bases and in the Philippines, all of which would prove vital to the success of what was to come.
View from the Rock

A Boeing B-52 Stratofortress climbs into the sunset over Guam. It is setting out on a 12-hour bombing mission which will see it refuelled by tankers out of Okinawa before challenging the air defences of North Vietnam

MIG Nightmare

The first US Air Force aerial victory in four years and, more significantly, the first at night took place on 21 February 1972 over northeast Laos, about 90 miles southwest of Hanoi. Maj. Robert A. Lodge was aircraft commander.

"Red Crown called out bandits (MIGs) at our 060 degree position and proceeded to vector us on an intercept," recalls Maj. Lodge. He adds further:

"I descended to minimum en route altitude, and at approximately 1323Z [2123 local] my WSO detected and locked on a target at the position Red Crown was calling Bandit.

A Small Explosion

The target was level at zero azimuth and closing, with the combined velocity of both aircraft in excess of 900 knots. I fired three AIM-7Es, the first at approximately 11 nautical miles, the second at eight nautical miles and the third at six nautical miles. The first missile appeared to guide and track level, and detonated in a small explosion. The second missile guided in a similar manner and detonated with another small explosion, followed immediately by a large explosion in the same area. This secondary explosion was of a different nature than the two missile detonations and appeared like a large POL [petroleum, oil and lubricants] explosion with a fireball. The third missile started guiding in a corkscrew manner and then straightened out. No detonation was observed for the third missile. We had no more AIM-7s left, and broke off and egressed at low altitude."
USAF History

MARCH 1972

2-3rd South Vietnamese troops carry out operations in the Central Highlands in anticipation of communist offensive as heavy US air raids over the area continue.

7th US and North Vietnamese jets fight it out north of the DMZ. US aircraft equal the raid figure for 1971 – 86 – in just over two months of 1972.

11th Long Tien in Laos comes under severe military pressure from communist forces.

16th Quang Ngai Province becomes the target of multiple communist assaults.

17-18th ARVN operations in the Ashau Valley and west of Hue account for around 900 communist lives, while those in Cambodia uncover supply dumps.

21st Phnom Penh suffers its severest bombardment since the conflict spread to Cambodia in 1970.

23rd A US boycott of the Paris talks is announced.

30th Biggest communist offensive since Tet 1968 opens along the DMZ, forcing the ARVN to retreat. US considers, but eventually decides against, committing Marines to combat the communist push.

Bombing Ho Chi Minh Trail is Harder

DANANG "The bad guys have gone 20th century," the young Air Force pilot said. He was still shaken by a barrage aimed at his small observation plane by anti-aircraft gunners on the Ho Chi Minh Trail in Laos.

Until late 1970, the American bombers that drop hundreds of tons of bombs on the North Vietnamese truck traffic, supply dumps and anti-aircraft sites on the twisting dirt roads of the trail went largely unchallenged, except in the critical mountain passes at the entrance to the trail.

But then the enemy began to fire surface-to-air missiles across the border at the bombers over Laos. With the advent of this year's dry season, the firings became more frequent and significant numbers of missile launchers and heavy-caliber automatic anti-aircraft guns were moved farther south along the trail and deeper inside Laos than before.

The enemy has also been more aggressive in challenging American reconnaissance planes flying over Laos, and has counter-attacked vigorously when United States aircraft have flown north of the demilitarized zone to attack long-range guns and airfields for MIG-21 fighters which also began challenging American air power over Laos for the first time late last year.

First Lieut. Ray Noftsinger of Roanoke, Va., a forward air controller: "The air defenses out there are so heavy now that there are certain areas we just don't fly in. We just don't have unchallenged air superiority any more in some parts of Laos."

The New York Times

As North Vietnam moves south, so too do its weapons. It is now a risky business to mount air attacks on the Ho Chi Minh trail in the face of determined anti-air defences

Easter Offensive

With North Vietnamese tanks sniping at him within eyesight on the far side of the Cua Viet bridge at Dong Ha, Marine Captain John W. Ripley made up his mind that they weren't going to pass. The wooden trestle was afire, thin brownish smoke lacing the air, and Ripley wanted to blow it. By himself, Ripley jogged out on to the span of the bridge, 7.62-mm shells from the PT-76 tanks cutting through the air around him. It took five such trips before the captain had emplaced 500lbs of explosive. He triggered it, the span collapsed in a cloud of smoke and debris, and the enemy was stalled.

It All Came Unglued

Ripley's action, like many taken by unexpectedly embattled Americans, was a response to the "Easter Offensive," the turning point on Good Friday on 30th March 1972 which was Hanoi's final attempt to defeat US and South Vietnamese forces on the field of battle. Till now, North Vietnamese had always held some of its elite divisions in reserve and had not yet used large numbers of tanks, 130-mm howitzers, or SA-7 shoulder-mounted missiles. At Easter, everything came unglued: one NVA division struck across the DMZ at Quang Tri, two more attacked through a corner of Laos aiming at the Central Highlands, and yet another division was inserted into the A Shau Valley heading towards Hue. At Cam Ranh Bay, US Air Force pilots were abruptly wakened at 3 a.m. by a gaunt-faced sergeant who'd just heard the latest Intelligence. "It's hit the fan!" the sergeant shouted. "The bastards are coming down the pike with everything they've got!"

Every GI in [the] country remembered where he was, that cool misty morning when the NVA punched.

Robert F. Dorr

North Vietnamese swarm south in large numbers, and attempt to overwhelm the Army of the Republic of Vietnam. There are no American combat troops on the ground, but American air power is still a potent force, capable of giving highly effective support to South Vietnam

Vietnamese Returning to the Delta

Phan Van Minh, a South Vietnamese farmer, loves the land he was raised on, and all he has ever wanted to do has been to bring in a good rice crop.

The other day Mr Minh, who is 66 years old, made his way into the office of this village 95 miles southwest of Saigon and said he felt it was safe to go back to his old hamlet.

Most Houses Destroyed

The delta hamlets that are being resettled now, officials say, were among the most firmly held Viet Cong positions. They are referred to by American military advisers and some South Vietnamese officers as "mini-bases". They are usually overgrown with tall grass and trees. Most houses have been bombed or burned. There are honeycombs of bunkers and nightmarish webs of booby-traps and mines. Ten to 15 Viet Cong will hole up in such a base, the military men say.

Throughout the delta, South Vietnamese militiamen are attacking the mini-bases with machetes and axes. The Viet Cong usually flee, but casualties from mines and booby-traps have been high.

The New York Times

Nixon Suspends Paris Talks

President Nixon said Friday he personally ordered the suspension of Paris peace talks until the North Vietnamese quit using the conference as a pulpit for propaganda.

In a wide-ranging news conference Nixon also declared that he will take action if necessary to curb rising food prices. He indicated the action, would be aimed at middlemen – not farmers.

The chief executive also defended as constitutional his move for a moratorium on busing to achieve school desegregation.

Stars and Stripes

APRIL 1972

1st South Vietnamese forces cave in before the advance of thousands of NVA troops. It is believed that Quang Tri City and then Hue and Da Nang are the targets.

2-4th Refugees pour south as NVA continues its drive on Quang Tri City.

2-4th Authorization is received for Operation Freedom Train.

3rd US aircraft carrier force off Vietnam is reinforced by the arrival of *Kitty Hawk*.

5th While the push towards Quang Tri City continues, the NVA attacks into Binh Long Province from Cambodia. Mass ARVN desertions are reported from Quang Tri.

6th Start of Operation Linebacker, a massive air and naval offensive against the NVA. New NVA SAM-2s claim two US aircraft.

7th Loc Ninh in Binh Long Province falls to the NVA, which also cuts off ARVN forces withdrawing to An Loc.

7th Benhai bridge, which carries the only road joining the North and the South, is reported destroyed by US aircraft.

8th NVA attacks into the Central Highlands from Cambodia and Laos.

8th An Loc comes under siege.

9th ARVN forces succeed in beating off an NVA attack on Fire Base Pedro near Quang Tri City, but further south, relief forces are unable to reach An Loc.

10th It is reported that US B-52s are once again bombing North Vietnam, with the object of knocking out the SAM-2s.

10th The despatch of *Saratoga* and *Midway* will increase the US carrier force to six.

On Danang Flight Line, GIs Work and Sweat

The Danang air base, which has been greatly reduced in size as a result of the American withdrawals, reflected in capsule form today the heightened tempo of the Vietnam war.

"We're going at max today," an airman said as he watched the sleek planes roar off into the morning sky. He meant that the 366th Tactical Fighter Wing, known as Gunfighter, was operating at capacity.

Many maintenance men stayed with the planes through their lunch hour, leaning against the corrugated hangar walls and eating sandwiches and fruit from paper bags.

"When the tempo picks up, we are afraid to leave the aircraft," said Sgt. Harold Peters. "You never know when you are going to get a mission."

Well-informed American military sources said that the highest priority was being given to bombing the surface-to-air missile sites and their radar-controlled equipment.

These missiles, with a range of up to 21 miles at 40,000 feet, have considerably increased the risk for American planes in and around the buffer zone. They can hit planes in most of Quang Tri Province.

The New York Times

Da Nang remains one of America's most important bases, being the closest air facility to the NVA invasion from the DMZ

Reds Push South

Spearheaded by tank columns, the biggest North Vietnamese drive since the 1968 Tet offensive chewed up large chunks of South Vietnamese territory Sunday, crushed two more bases and sent hundreds of government troops retreating in disarray.

At Camp Carroll, a regimental command post eight miles below the Demilitarized Zone, some of the battered South Vietnamese soldiers threw up the white flag of surrender. Some South Vietnamese soldiers appeared to be trying to mix in with thousands of civilians fleeing south from the DMZ fighting.

But the four-day North Vietnamese campaign appeared to be broadening to other fronts. One tank column spearheaded a drive that overran Firebase Pace near the Cambodian border, only 85 miles northwest of Saigon, in the deepest southern penetration North Vietnamese armor has ever made in the Indochina war.

The fighting on the northern front continued to overshadow all other action, since North Vietnam has long desired to annex Quang Tri, South Vietnam's northernmost province bordering the DMZ on the north and Laos on west.

Stars and Stripes

Unlike the Tet offensive of 1968, the NVA invasion is a huge conventional operation, with infantry supported by armour and artillery

An Outpost, in Stillness, Awaits Foe

DONG HA – Pigs, sniffing around the corpses of North Vietnamese soldiers, were the only thing moving today in this battered town in the middle of the North Vietnamese offensive below the demilitarized zone.

Overhead, rockets sped southward and shells north. At the edge of the town was a South Vietnamese marine battalion whose job was to try and stop any northerners trying to cross a branch of the Cua Viet River.

Most of the refugees who passed through Dong Ha had come from the town of Camlo, to the west. Others were from the mountains and from little beach settlements between Dong Ha and the demilitarized zone.

On the Road to Hue

Government officials in Hue said 20,000 refugees had arrived and they expected the flood to total 100,000 in days. The Hue Citadel has been sealed off, lest the enemy send in agents disguised as refugees.

In the overcrowded Quang Tri hospital, a doctor said that he had admitted 500 civilians since the shelling began at midday Thursday.

On the Hue road, battered buses and trucks, old French cars and motorcycles made slow progress south, overloaded with people, sewing machines, beds and other possessions precious enough to carry.

Several herds of cattle in the train were periodically scattered into the rice paddies by speeding trucks taking soldiers to the front. A division was coming, the soldiers shouted to the refugees.

A young mother carried a piglet under each arm and her baby strapped to her back.

Most of the people, young or old, looked unafraid.

The New York Times

U.S. Readies Air Armada

The United States recalled two aircraft carriers to the Tonkin Gulf Monday to reinforce a massive air strike force preparing to hit back at an enemy offensive in South Vietnam's northernmost province.

The carrier *Kitty Hawk* arrived in waters off Vietnam Tuesday and the *Constellation* was steaming in from Japan to join the *Coral Sea* and the *Hancock*. The four carriers and their some 275 warplanes, combined with 250 Air Force jets at bases in South Vietnam and Thailand, will form the biggest U.S. attack force since the 1968 bombing halt.

The U.S. Command strongly indicated massive air strikes are planned against North Vietnam to retaliate for the enemy offensive across the demilitarized zone and against enemy troops and material already engaged south of the zone.

5 April 1972

Inside the Combat Information Center of USS Kitty Hawk

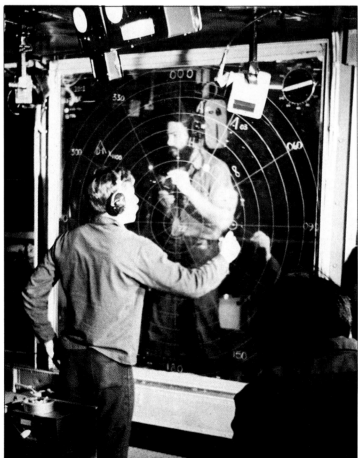

11th	Siege of Fire Base Bastogne, 20 miles west of Hue, begins.
11th	B-52s bomb the Kontum area in support of the ARVN.
12th	50 disillusioned US soldiers disobey orders to go on patrol near Phu Bai but eventually relent.
13th	Communist infantry and armour hit An Loc.
14th	While the air war escalates, the volume of communist assaults attains Tet 1968 levels.
15th	Fire Base Charlie falls to the NVA.
16th	The first B-52 raids hit Hanoi and Haiphong. The stepped-up bombing causes anti-war unrest in the US.
18th	The total of US personnel still in South Vietnam is put at 85,000.
19th	The NVA drive in the Central Highlands escalates as US naval units of the 7th Fleet come under attack from jet fighters and torpedo boats in addition to coastal artillery.
22nd	Thousands march throughout the US in protest at bombing.
22nd	Fierce fighting takes place in the Mekong Delta.
23rd	Dak To comes under attack by the NVA.
26th	Plans are announced to reduce the US presence in Vietnam to 49,000 over the next two months.
27th	The Paris talks reopen.
28th	The communists take Dong Ha and Fire Base Bastogne and move in on Fire Base Birmingham. Kontum is isolated.

Colonel Assails Newsmen

PHUBAI Lieut. Col. Frederick P. Mitchell today assailed television newsmen and other journalists who were present when American infantrymen refused orders to go out on patrol.

"All you press are bastards. I blame you for this and you can quote me on it," he said to the correspondents.

In Saigon, the United States command said, "A rumor to the effect that the area was an ambush site loaded with booby traps circulated among some members."

The command statement, without offering any direct criticism of newsmen, said "Numerous correspondents were in the area interviewing soldiers. Several soldiers told correspondents that they did not want to go into the field."

No soldier actually disobeyed orders or refused to go into the field, the command said. No disciplinary action was taken.

The New York Times

An Loc Under Siege

Moving under cover of predawn darkness, North Vietnamese troops and tanks reportedly began an assault today against the provincial capital of An Loc, 60 miles north of here, which Communist forces have besieged since Saturday.

Heavy fighting was reported in and around the city, where about 12,000 Government troops, most of the South Vietnamese Fifth Division, have been trapped by 20,000 or more Communist soldiers.

Knocking out Tanks

Several North Vietnamese tanks reportedly succeeded in penetrating into the city and its adjoining airfield, but reports from the area also said nine tanks out of a column of about 20 had been knocked out, two by United States fighter-bombers and seven by An Loc's defenders.

The assault on An Loc was one of several attacks staged across South Vietnam as the Communists' offensive entered its third week.

[In Washington, Nixon Administration spokesmen for the first time raised the possibility that, in view of the enemy offensive, the President might suspend or delay American troop withdrawals after May 1, but they said he intended to honor his commitment to reduce authorized American troop strength in South Vietnam by that date.]

The New York Times

An Loc, South Vietnam. A Soviet-built T-54 tank lies smashed on the streets of this town close to the Cambodian border. It was smashed by a US Army AH-16 Cobra gunship, flying in support of the beleaguered South Vietnamese garrison, which was to successfully hold out against overwhelming NVA attacks for 95 days

Seven Americans Die
in Rescue of Two Behind Enemy Lines

An Allied commando team snatched two United States airmen from the middle of a North Vietnamese invasion force, but the operation cost the lives of seven other Americans, United States sources disclosed today.

Despite a broken arm, a sprained back and lack of food and water, Lieut. Col Iceal E. Hambleton managed for 11 days to evade North Vietnamese troops swarming across the demilitarized zone and sometimes coming within a few feet of him.

Lieutenant Norris said that Colonel Hambleton had in the days before his rescue called in air strikes against enemy forces despite his injuries and weakened condition. The calls were made by pocket radio.

Unable to Walk

When the commando team reached Colonel Hambleton at midnight on April 13, he could not walk and was barely able to crawl to a nearby stream to wash his face.

"Hambleton was surrounded by enemy forces during most of his ordeal," said one American officer. "The search-and-rescue forces made repeated efforts to extract the men with no success. One problem was that they were caught in the North Vietnamese invasion across the DMZ. The enemy was passing through the area and it couldn't have been worse. Many times the enemy search teams were within five feet."

B-52s made several raids in efforts to divert North Vietnamese troops away from the two downed airmen. It was the first time the big bombers were reported to be used in a rescue mission.

Officers said that in addition to the B-52s, fighter-bombers and the biggest gunship the United States Air Force has, the four-engine, computerized AC-130 flew constant cover for the operation.

The New York Times

Heavy Damage as Hanoi Area is Bombed

SAIGON (AP) – The U.S. command reported Sunday's raids by hundreds of jets on North Vietnam caused heavy damage and left areas around Hanoi and Haiphong in flames.

U.S. pilots reported seeing fireballs and columns of black smoke rising into the sky from around the North Vietnamese capital and Haiphong, the seaport funnel for war material from abroad, chiefly from the Soviet Union.

A command spokesman, in confirming early Monday that areas near Hanoi had been bombed, said eight-jet B52 Stratofortresses hit Haiphong and smaller tactical jet fighter-bombers attacked near Hanoi.

The North Vietnamese claimed Hanoi itself was hit.

Late reports indicate that two tactical fighter-bombers were shot down and that all B52s returned safely, the command said. It reported the enemy fired thousands of rounds of anti-aircraft shells and about 200 surface-to-air missiles – the Soviet-supplied SAMs that American pilots call flying telephone poles.

Two U.S. airmen were listed as missing and a third was reported rescued.

50 GIs in Vietnam Refuse Patrol Duty, Then Agree to Go

PHUBAI About 50 United States infantrymen of a 142-man company refused to move for an hour and a half today when ordered to go out and patrol the rolling hills around Phubai, 42 miles south of the demilitarized zone.

"We're not going!" some shouted. "This isn't our war! We're not going out in the bush. Why should we fight if nobody back home gives a damn about us?"

"I've been here too long,", said Pfc. London Davis, 20 years old, of Bakersfield, Calif., his thumbs stuck between the bandoleer of bullets wrapped around his waist. "I'm too short [close to leaving Vietnam] for this kind of stuff. Man, I don't want to get killed now."

Pfc. William Bowlin, 20, of Walton, Ky., said: "Why should I go out there and do the fighting for the Vietnamese?"

"We're supposed to be doing defense, nothing else, not offensive," Private Bowlin said. "Going out on patrol – that's defense?"

Spec. 4, Keith Kohujek, 18, of Houston, said, "I don't want to go out and step on any booby traps and get killed. There are supposed to be booby traps all over that place. Nobody ever tells me what's going on."

The New York Times

Red Drive Slowed in Viet Highlands

The North Vietnamese drive in the central highlands slowed Wednesday and South Korean troops to the east cleared the Communists from a vital pass that may open the way for resumption of convoys to the imperiled highland cities.

Another major threat developed in the coastal highlands behind the South Koreans, however. North Vietnamese troops swarmed out of the hills into the coastal Binh Dinh Province, seized one base and pushed into three populous districts.

The North Vietnamese are north of Highway 19, where the South Koreans are operating at An Khe Pass. But should the Communists push south to Qui Nhon, the gateway to Highway 19, the route would be closed again.

In past offensives, the Communist goal has been to seize the highlands and Binh Dinh Pro-vince to sever South Vietnam at its waist. The objective in this spring offensive seems to be the same.

A Korean spokesman and John Paul Vann, the senior U.S. adviser in the highlands, announced that An Khe Pass had been cleared after more than two weeks of sharp fighting.

Stars and Stripes

INVASION

MAY 1972

1st Quang Tri City falls to the communists.

North Vietnamese artillery pounds **Quang Tri**, which fell on May 1. It was finally recaptured in **September**

2nd ARVN 3rd Division caves in and deserts southwards, while South Vietnamese Marines stand fast in defence of Hue.

4th US and South Vietnamese negotiators suspend Paris talks for an indefinite period.

5th Another attempt to reach An Loc is blocked by communist forces.

6th Civilians are evacuated from Kontum City.

8th President Nixon declares that North Vietnamese ports are to be sown with mines to cut the communist forces off from their supplies. This announcement causes immediate anti-war unrest across the US.

10th Lieutenants Cunningham and Driscoll operating from the USS *Constellation* become the first US flying aces of the war.

11th Defense Department calculations suggest that $1.5 billion will be needed to finance the mining of North Vietnamese ports and rivers.

13th First South Vietnamese counter-attack takes place near Quang Tri City. The communist attack on Kontum commences.

15th Fire Base Bastogne is retaken by the South Vietnamese.

19th South Vietnamese forces are within two miles of An Loc. Kontum is still holding out against the NVA.

20th President Nixon visits Moscow.

23rd NVA moves into the lower Mekong Delta.

U.S. Fighters Down 7 MIGs

U.S. warplanes shot down seven enemy MIGs Wednesday while carrying out the deepest and heaviest air strikes inside North Vietnam in more than four years, the U.S. Command announced.

The downing of seven MIGs in one day is a record for the Vietnam war.

The U.S. aircraft attacked both Hanoi and Haiphong, while hitting at widespread areas of North Vietnam, the command said.

It made no mention of any U.S. air losses.

The aircraft streaked to within 60 miles of the Chinese border to attack North Vietnam's northwest rail link to China.

Meantime, President Nguyen Van Thieu proclaimed a state of martial law throughout Vietnam effective at midnight Thursday, and the mayor of Saigon, Do Kien Nhieu, went on television to warn residents that an attack on the South Vietnamese capital was imminent.

Stars and Stripes

500 More GIs Out of War, 400 Marine Airmen Sent In

SAIGON The United States command withdrew 600 American servicemen from Vietnam last week, but 400 more Marine fliers entered the war zone, military spokesmen said today.

The net withdrawal of 200 Americans was the smallest since the last week of January, 1971, when there were no withdrawals. It left United States troop strength in Vietnam at 64,800 as of last Thursday.

President Nixon has ordered American strength dropped below 49,000 by June 30. An average of 2,600 soldiers must be pulled out each week to meet that deadline.

Since the command issued its weekly strength report, 700 Marine Corps airmen have been added to the Vietnam rolls, military sources said.

In addition to those stationed in Vietnam, there are 41,000 Americans in the offshore Seventh Fleet and more than 45,000 at bases in Thailand. While they participate directly in the war, they are not counted on the Vietnam rolls.

The New York Times

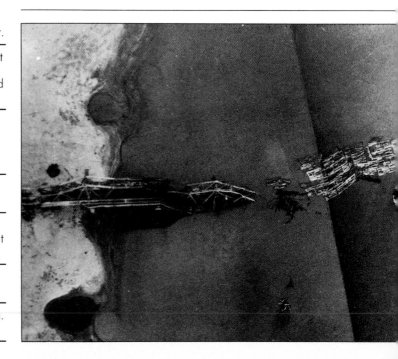

First Two Air Aces of Vietnam War Are Here for Treat

The first two American fliers to shoot down five North Vietnamese MIGs are being treated here to two days on the town for what Navy spokesmen describe variously as "a little exposure and a little reward," an information tour and a move to get them home before their luck ran out.

From their base in a donated Plaza Hotel suite, and between sightseeing trips, the men – billed by the Navy yesterday as the first all-Vietnam aces, the first "team of aces" and "the first to score a triple kill over Vietnam and the first all-missile aces" – are being made available to the news media for interviews.

Pleased to Be alive

"We're not trying to push the war," said the leader of the team, Lieut. Randall H. Cunningham of San Diego, the pilot.

"We just want to tell people that regardless of their sentiment, we're extremely pleased to be back alive and well," added his radarman, Lieut. (jg.) William Driscoll of Framingham, Mass.

One of their treats, a few hours after their arrival here from Washington yesterday afternoon, was to be taken to the restaurant 21 at 21 West 52nd Street – "courtesy Grumman," as the official Navy schedule listed it.

Comdr. William Graves, an

information officer, said that the Navy was paying no more for the fliers' trip than the standard £25 each a day for hotel and meals or £15, in this case, with the free room.

His orders from Washington, he added, were, "Make sure having aces doesn't cost the Navy money."

The New York Times

Navy Secretary Warner pins the Navy Cross to Lt. (jg) William Driscoll, with Lt. Randy Cunningham looking on

U.S. Bombers
Break the 'Dragon's Jaw'

SAIGON (AP) – U.S. warplanes have cut the heart of North Vietnam's supply network by destroying the Thanh Hoa "Dragon's Jaw" Bridge 80 miles south of Hanoi, the 7th Air Force announced Sunday. It said the bridge and stood for seven years, despite repeated air attacks, as "a symbol of invincibility and a challenge to U.S. pilots."

Officials also reported that North Vietnamese rail links with China had been cut in places and that a key railroad bridge on the edge of Hanoi had been wrecked by air strikes.

The aim of the attacks was to sever some of North Vietnam's

land routes for supplies while its ports are mined in a U.S. effort to cut down supplies from across the sea.

On the ground in South Vietnam, fighting picked up in the central highlands and the northern sector, but eased up around An Loc, 60 miles north of Saigon.

Fighting was reported continuing around Kontum in the central highlands shortly before midnight, but the South Vietnamese said that North Vietnamese forces were being contained. North Vietnamese forces had launched heavy tank, infantry and artillery assaults just before dawn against the outer defenses of Kontum. The enemy shelled South Vietnam's northernmost front with heavy, long-range guns.

Thanh Hoa Bridge was one of two vital northern bridges destroyed by 'smart' bombs, the other being the Paul Doumer Bridge seen here

Stars and Stripes

INVASION

JUNE 1972

4th   Phoumy comes under NVA attack.

6th   South Vietnamese eject communist forces from Kontum.

9th   John Paul Vann, the top US advisor in Vietnam, dies when the helicopter in which he is travelling crashes, perhaps shot down.

10th   US aircraft use laser-guided bombs to smash Lang Chi hydroelectric power installation.

12th   It emerges that ex-four star General John D. Lavelle was removed from his post in March and reduced in rank for authorizing bombing missions contrary to US policy.

12th   Saigon's Joint US Public Affairs Office shuts.

17th   First Watergate arrests take place.

19th   War correspondent Kevin Buckley accuses US troops of carrying out atrocities in the name of pacification.

20th   General Abrams is nominated as the next US Army Chief of Staff.

26th   It is established that US aircraft will not bomb within 25 miles of the Chinese border.

27th   President Thieu assumes full power in Saigon. He will rule by executive decree.

28th   It is announced that US forces in Vietnam will be reduced to 39,000 by the end of August. South Vietnamese troops with US air and naval support launch a counteroffensive into Quang Tri Province.

30th   General Frederick C. Weyand takes over from General Abrams in Vietnam.

In the magazines of a US Navy cruiser, teenaged sailors manhandle the heavy shells on to the hoist

War Seems Remote on Cruiser in the Gulf

Aboard USS Newport News off North Vietnam, Seaman Walter Olivier is embarrassed that his shipmates call him Killer. A slight boyish sailor with a shock of blond hair that falls in his eyes, Seaman Olivier pulls the small brass trigger that fires this ship's huge, computer-aimed 8-inch guns, the heaviest afloat in any navy.

As the Newport News, a 21,000-ton heavy cruiser, bombarded the darkened coast of North Vietnam, Seaman Olivier at his station far below deck wasn't sure what targets he was shooting at or whether the ship's guns were accurate.

Black and Azure

For him, as for most of the 1,150-man crew, the war seems remote and unreal, though often dangerous. "You just can't tell much from down here, so I try not to think about it," Seaman Olivier remarked.

Suddenly about eight miles from land, the Newport News swung sharply to starboard and fired a salvo of 24 rounds from her nine 8-inch guns at a petroleum storage dump. The ear-shattering explosions from the guns made the ship shudder and momentarily turned the black water around the cruiser a brilliant azure.

Within 20 seconds the Newport News was headed back toward the open sea. Lookouts on the bridge sighted several fires in the target area, and, simultaneously, muzzle flashes from North Vietnamese coastal artillery. But the enemy shells fell harmlessly several miles away.

"Two years ago I laughed at my high school history teacher when he told me to read about Vietnam because I might end up here," Seaman Buck recalled, as he ran his fingers over a peace symbol tied around his neck on a leather thong. "I figured this

On Another Street Without Joy, US Advisers Are Still Dying

US Advisers are fighting alongside their **ARVN** charges in the battle for An Loc

CHONTHANH It is only 156 miles from here to An Loc, but for two months more than 3,000 South Vietnamese troops and several American advisers have been killed or wounded trying to get there.

Route 13 has become a second Street Without Joy. That is the name French soldiers gave to Route 1 near Hue during the first Indochina war – a grinder that ate up men who stood up to move forward.

About two miles north of Chonthanh is the temporary command post of the 32nd Regiment of South Vietnam's 21st Division, the unit assigned to relieve the defenders of besieged An Loc, 60 miles north of Saigon.

The "main man on the ground" there was Lieut Col. Burr. M. Willey, the senior regimental adviser. A genial man, he was scheduled to leave in two days for a five day rest-and-rehabilitation visit to Hawaii where he would join his wife, a resident of Ayer, Mass. Colonel Willey was followed everywhere by his dog, named Moose.

Tanks Move In

A few days ago, 13 South Vietnamese tanks, accompanied by infantry, were scheduled to move up the road, swing east and then turn to sweep west across 2,000 yards of highway still held by North Vietnamese soldiers.

An absurd convoy developed. There were the 13 tanks, followed by several military jeeps, followed by eight reporters' cars and the Associated Press van, which resembles a bakery truck.

The column proceeded to a point about five miles north of Chonthanh. For weeks this had been the final point of advance. A little mound called The Ant Hill, marked the farthest that men could move and still live. It had been a bullseye for weeks.

This time, against American advice, the Vietnamese tank force and ranger infantry chose this spot to assemble.

At this point the Vietnamese began to distribute rice rations, causing the troops to bunch up around the tanks.

Colonel Willey, 30 yards ahead, rose and began to stride back toward Colonel Franklin. A shell fell a few feet from his toes and killed Colonel Willey and his dog instantly.

The New York Times

---

lousy war was all over; it's gone on much too long."

"We Should Really Pound Them"

But, he continued, echoing a sentiment heard often on the Newport News: "Now that we're here, I think we should really pound them. That's the only way to stop the war."

Another factor that helps morale, some sailors say, is that though the Newport News is considered an old ship that may soon be decommissioned, it is nonetheless very comfortable. It is completely air-conditioned, has its own closed-circuit television station, tailoring and dry-cleaning shops, and a soda fountain.

The cruiser's five galleys prepare over 1,000 pounds of meat, 1,500 pounds of fresh and canned vegetables and 100 gallons of ice cream a day. After the Newport News's late-night gunfire missions are completed and the crew is released from battle stations, there are freshly cooked hamburgers for all.

The New York Times

A massive smoke ring is left behind as a cruiser fires a high-explosive shell towards the Vietnamese coast

Nixon
Slows Pullout

President Nixon slowed the Vietnam withdrawal rate Wednesday – to 10,000 troops over two months – but said draftees no longer will be sent to the war zone unless they volunteer.

Nixon's action will cut U.S. force levels in South Vietnam to 39,000 by Sept. 1. This compares with a peak ceiling of 549,500 when he took office. The 39,000 figure does not take into account about 87,000 participating in the war from Thailand and the 7th Fleet off Vietnam.

In May and June, troops were pulled out at the rate of 10,000 a month, but with the remaining force getting ever smaller and Hanoi's army continuing its Southern offensive, Nixon opted for a go-slower approach at this time.

Stars and Stripes

JULY 1972

2nd It is revealed that the US has been using meteorological warfare – seeding clouds – in Vietnam and Laos for nine years.

7th South Vietnamese drive on Quang Tri City falters.

13th Talks reopen in Paris.

15-17th South Vietnamese enter Quang Tri City.

18th Jane Fonda delivers an anti-war speech on Hanoi Radio.

19th It is announced that the secret talks have opened once again in Paris.

19th South Vietnamese troops launch a counteroffensive in Bin Dinh Province.

21st It emerges that the defoliation Operation Pink Rose was directed against a block of rainforest as big as the city of Philadelphia.

24th The US is accused of seeking to destroy North Vietnamese flood-control dikes through bombing.

26th South Vietnamese troops are shelled out of Fire Base Bastogne.

31st Start of South Vietnamese operation in the Parrot's Beak area of Cambodia.

"Mildly Confident" On Route 13

ON ROUTE THIRTEEN South Vietnamese troops, after being stalled for three and a half months on Route 13 north of Saigon, are making what appears to be their first significant progress toward breaking through and opening up this crucial road to the rubber-plantation town of An Loc, which still has to get all its supplies and troop reinforcements by air.

In the last week, the Government relief force has pushed to a small bridge seven miles north of Chonthanh and advance elements have gone a mile beyond that and are now sweeping their way back.

The fighting is far from over, and much of it now is at close quarters, but some key officers suggest that the road may be open by the end of this month.

"This week is the best progress we've made yet," said Lieut. Col. Jerry T. Morgan, an American adviser at a muddy command post north of Chon-thanh. "I've grown mildly confident," he said.

The New York Times

US Soldiers in Vietnam an Army of Noncombatants

SAIGON Pfc Larry O. Verocker of Strealor, Ill., one of the dwindling number of American infantrymen in South Vietnam, volunteered to come here "to see what it was like."

The 20-year-old soldier has been here two months and has been on 11 patrols and never fired the machine gun he carries.

The task force of 1,200 infantry and artillerymen in which he is serving near Saigon and a similar unit near Danang are the last American ground combat units in Vietnam. They are too small to do much more than limited patroling and many officers believe their primary function at present is symbolic.

In the last week two Americans were killed in combat and the week before eight died. In both weeks, more Americans died from noncombat accidents and illness than from hostile fire.

The New York Times

The main task now for US combat troops is guarding US installations

POW-Pull Out

WASHINGTON – The Senate voted Monday the withdrawal of all U.S. forces "on land, sea, or air" from Indochina in exchange for the release of American prisoners of war.

In two critical votes, the Senate approved cutting off funds to maintain U.S. forces in Indochina in four months if the POWs are freed.

It was the first time that the Senate approved legislation cutting off funds for the Vietnam war. But it has passed policy statements in favor of ending the war by a certain date.

The Senate first voted 50 to 45 for cutting off the money and then overcame a last-moment effort by administration Republicans to kill the far-reaching antiwar amendment. That vote was 49 to 46.

Stars and Stripes

The release of American prisoners has become of prime concern to the US Government, although one problem is a lack of knowledge of just who North Vietnam has captive

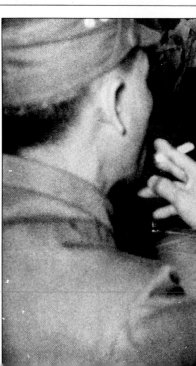

Coral and Dust

Because Andersen, the air base on Guam, was not equipped to handle the 12,000 people who were assigned during the height of BULLET SHOT, improvization became the order of the day. Overcrowding of normal living quarters had already occurred. Tent cities, recalling the days before

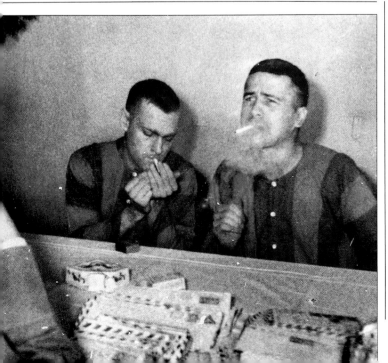

and during World War II, sprang up . . . and stayed up. These remained for months as the visible expression of a modification of an entire base's operation. Just to house a portion of the additional support element required three of the ten cities, dubbed the "Canvas Courts," where each tent held 12 men.

The Coral Dust

To erect the tents was no simple matter. After digging six inches deep or less on much of the base, a shovel hits hard Pacific coral. To drive holes for tent pegs required jack hammers. Digging trenches for water and sewer lines was a major construction task. Once completed, the tents were little protection from the blanket of coral dust which settled over everything, and they offered no relief from the heat or the whine and roar of constant jet engine operations.

"Tin City," an Andersen landmark from an earlier era, became the overcrowded temporary home for thousands of additional maintenance and support personnel. The buildings, built of steel and corrugated sheeting, were intended as temporary spartan quarters for short duration TDYs. These H-shaped buildings, with a central latrine facility, were designed to hold 80 people while allowing the minimum floor space required by regulations for living quarters. Into these buildings were crammed 200 people. There was no air conditioning, and the only ventilation was from inadequate fans at each end of the bays. The temperature in these structures regularly exceeded 110 degrees

A B-52D on Guam is given its massive bombload before the mission to Vietnam

in the noonday tropic sun. These were the sleeping quarters for those night shift workers who were loading bombs and maintaining the aircraft the crews flew in combat.

A Long Day

A normal bomb wing engine shop would be hard pressed to overhaul five jet engines a month. At Andersen the requirement was 120 jet engine overhauls each month. The feats performed by maintenance technicians to insure on-time launches of aircraft became legendary. On one occasion, a tire change which would normally require two and one-half hours was accomplished in 15 minutes on the taxiway for a bomb-laden aircraft with engines running. On others, electronics specialists stayed aboard the aircraft to repair equipment in flight. These were voluntary gestures made without benefit of knowledge of the specific mission or possible hazards. It also meant an extension of at least 12 hours to what had already been a long, hard work day.

USAF
"The View from the Rock"

COMBAT TROOPS GONE

AUGUST 1972

2nd Massive communist artillery barrage hits Quang Tri City. South Vietnamese forces go back to Fire Base Bastogne.

7-8th The number of air raids declines because of bad weather.

11th The return of the 3rd Battalion, 21st Infantry to the US means that there are no more US ground fighting units left in Vietnam.

13th Thousands of tons of ammunition are destroyed at Long Binh by Viet Cong raiders.

16-18th Hopes rise that a conclusion to the conflict may be in sight as Henry Kissinger visits Saigon and the North's chief negotiator returns to Hanoi.

19th Que Son and Base Camp Ross fall to the communists.

22nd Communist artillery appears south of Quang Tri City.

27th US aircraft flatten North Vietnamese barracks near Hanoi and Haiphong.

28th The USAF gets its first ace of the war – Captain Richard Ritchie. Cunningham and Driscoll were USN.

Captain Richard S. Ritchie (front, right), seen here at Udorn, Thailand, is the USAF's first Vietnam ace

29th President Nixon sets 1 December as the target date for reducing US troops in Vietnam to 27,000.

30th Some 2000 NVA shells rain into positions near Quang Tri.

31st The US weekly casualty figures of five dead, three wounded are the lowest recorded for the war.

Reds Send More Men South

Pentagon officials say thousands of fresh North Vietnamese troops have crossed the Demilitarized Zone into South Vietnam during the past "week or so."

The new troop movements puzzled Defense Department analysts, who admit they don't quite know what to make of North Vietnam's strategy. They said the reinforcements barely offset the number of Communist troops killed in recent weeks.

"It looks like they're pouring good money after bad," said one expert. "You reinforce success. You don't reinforce failure, but it looks like that is what they are doing."

Stars and Stripes

All Over Vietnam, GIs Still Have a Role

SAIGON "My mother wrote to me and said, 'if you ain't over there, why aren't you here?'" said Specialist 4 John Walling, an infantryman from Lexington, Ky.

"I still can't see where they can say we aren't here," he continued.

Specialist Walling is one of the last 570 or so American combat soldiers in South Vietnam. His job is to help guard the 16-mile perimeter of the big army rear base at Longbinh, just east of Saigon.

The last long-range infantry patrols by American troops were made earlier this month and, in a well-publicized announcement, the army said that all organized combat units had been withdrawn from South Vietnam.

Advising the ARVN

The three infantry companies left at Longbinh have the job of keeping Communist commandos from penetrating the

A Navy CH-46 crew-chief in the Mekong Delta is typical of the American personnel still serving in Vietnam

base, not of going out and looking for a fight. But they are still here.

American advisers – usually officers – come into closer contact with the South Vietnamese, but even they live in separate "advisory team compounds" on the Vietnamese bases, where they eat American canned rations, and watch American movies. At Laikhe, a combat base 30 miles from Saigon, the advisers often spent two weeks at a time or longer with their counterparts but could return to a tree-shaded mess and be served hot American meals by South Vietnamese waitresses in white uniforms.

Of the 800 fighter-bombers the Americans are flying over Indochina only a handful – three squadrons, about 70 planes – are based in South Vietnam, all at Bienhoa. But the United States Army still has 700 aircraft – most of them helicopters – in South Vietnam, and they are scattered from one end of the country to the other. Of the 23,000 United States soldiers left in South Vietnam, 5,800 belong to these units of the First Aviation Brigade, whose head-

quarters is at Longbinh.

Helicopters Taking Fire

Some of these – particularly the seven Air Cavalry units, which are equipped with Cobra helicopter gunships and light observation helicopters – have a direct combat role. Each of the "Cav" units has about 27 helicopters, and their job is to seek out enemy troop concentrations, bunkers, fighting positions and supply caches and to fire at them with air-to-ground rockets and rapid-firing cannon.

The pilots wear black cavalry hats with silver cordlike bands when they are off-duty.

"They're seeing quite a bit of action lately," said the First Aviation Brigade's operations officer, Col. James T. McQueen. "They're taking fire from Strella missiles and automatic weapons just about every day."

"We've only had one man killed in the last 30 days but we've had a lot of people get shot down," he continued. "In the last month three aircraft were lost in combat. That's only half of the number the month before."

The New York Times

More Americans Wed Vietnamese

SAIGON Marriages between Americans stationed here and Vietnamese women have risen to a peak rate since the beginning of the North Vietnamese offensive four months ago, even though the number of Americans now in South Vietnam is less than one tenth what it was in 1969.

In April, applications for marriage papers and for visas for war brides and fiancees reached such a level that the United States consulate here for the first time had to assign a Foreign Service Officer to the work full time.

In spite of huge losses in battle, the North Vietnamese are pouring large numbers of troops into the South

In the first six months of this year alone, American Consular statistics record 940 marriages between Vietnamese and Americans, of whom only 213 were serving in the armed forces.

"Up until recently, a career military man could assume whenever he left Vietnam that he would probably be back eventually for another tour," one official said.

"But now it is by no means a sure thing, and many Americans back in the States who left girls here get to thinking that if they ever want to see the girls again, they had better start the legal work involved in getting the girls out and marrying them."

The New York Times

AIR WAR

SEPTEMBER 1972

2nd Phuc Yen air base in North Vietnam is smashed by US bombing.

6th South Vietnamese troops pull out of Tien Phuoc, near Da Nang.

8th The Defense Department admits that the crippled American destroyer *Warrington* may have struck a US mine.

10th Communists raid Tan Son Nhut and Bien Hoa airports near Saigon.

12th US intelligence agencies report that the North Vietnamese have 100,000 regular troops in the South.

15th South Vietnamese now in control of Quang Tri City. The battle has cost 8135 and 977 North and South Vietnamese dead respectively.

16th New communist offensive opens in Quang Ngai Province.

17th Three US pilot POWs freed by the North.

19th A sixth MiG victim makes Captain Charles D. DeBellevue the war's top flyer.

26th With the rainy season coming, the US decides to deploy F-111s to Thailand to give better air cover.

28th The weekly US casualty figures contain no fatalities. This has not occurred since March 1965.

29th US air raids eliminate a tenth of the North Vietnamese Air Force.

A US air raid smashes into the administrative and operational buildings of a North Vietnamese airfield less than two miles from the centre of Hanoi. North Vietnamese airpower was decimated during the raids of September 29

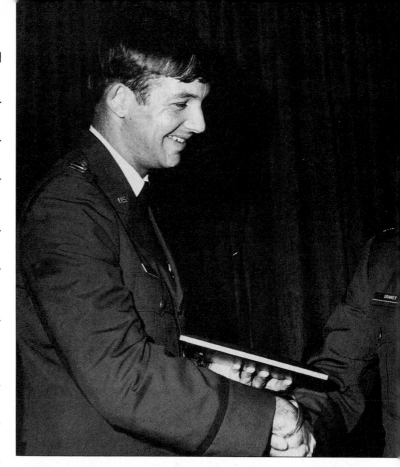

Flier Becomes Top Ace of War
With Sixth MIG

SAIGON The United States Air Force announced today that Capt. Charles D. DeBellevue of Lafayette, La., has been credited with shooting down six North Vietnamese MIGs, making him the leading ace of the war.

Captain DeBellevue, 27 years old, is a weapons systems officer flying in the back seat of F-4 Phantom fighters. Since much of

Thai Base for Pilots Who Bomb Vietnam Is Like a Small US City

UTAPAO AIRFIELD Thailand This is not just a base but a small American city, built for the more than 50 B-52 bombers that fly from it every day to drop 30 tons of bombs apiece on targets in North and South Vietnam.

Eight thousand American airmen here fly what amounts to a small air force of the eight-engine bombers and scores of KC-135 tankers to refuel them. But until today American authorities in Thailand have refused to allow news correspondents to visit the base because it is under Thai sovereignty.

The B-52s, which have a 185-foot wingspan – so long the tips of the wings droop – have been flying from the two-mile long American-built runway at Utapao since 1967. Other American fighter-bombers, tankers, gunships and spy planes have been using bases at Udon, Ubon, Nakhon Phanom and Korat since the late Nineteen-Sixties.

Both Ta Khli and Utapao are spacious, tree-shaded bases and American soldiers are free to go off base to the bars in the town. The base newspaper, Gunfighter Gazette, even has tips about how to check bargirls for venereal disease. There are post exchanges and restaurants on base. The movie theater where Colonel Rutter gives his briefings was showing The Godfather and The French Connection.

The New York Times

Draftee On Trial In Officer Deaths

FORT ORD, Calif. A black draftee went on trial in a court-martial here today, accused of premeditated murder in the deaths of two white officers killed by a hand grenade as they slept in their bunks at Bienhoa Army base in South Vietnam.

This is the first trial in this country to grow out of the rash of "fragging" cases in which soldiers threw fragmentation grenades to kill or maim their superior officers or enemies. Several cases have been tried in Vietnam. Department of Defense sources said that 551 such incidents occurred in the four years ending in July, and

that 86 deaths resulted.

The defendant in the court-martial here is Pvt. Billy D. Smith, 24 years old, who grew up in Watts, a section of Los Angeles that has become symbolic of black revolt.

The New York Times

Hanoi Frees 3 POWs; Wife and Mother Greet 2

HANOI An American mother clasped her son, and an American wife embraced her husband here tonight in a room hot with television lights, at the release ceremony for three American prisoners of war, pilots shot down

over North Vietnam.

Mrs Olga Charles, who had flown from San Diego, Calif., had had her hair washed and set in a downtown Hanoi beauty shop today. She fought through a wall of Vietnamese and European TV technicians and

cameramen to embrace her husband, Lieut. (jg) Norris A. Charles, 27 years old. He wore a neat gray civilian suit.

The New York Times

Captain Charles DeBellevue, an F-4 Weapons System Officer, is presented with a plaque after becoming the top scoring US Ace of the Vietnam War

the fighting between aircraft over North Vietnam is done by radar, the second crew member of Phantoms, who mans the radar, is credited with downing planes as well as the pilot.

The New York Times

Foe Now Holds Large Part of 5 Northern Provinces

SAIGON "The other side is building a nation in the hills," a high American officer said, ruefully summing up developments in the last six months in the five northern provinces of South Vietnam, known as Military Region I.

"The way they're going, they'll soon have two-thirds if not three-quarters of the physical geography of the region," he

continued.

South Vietnamese troops took a major step in reversing the Communist trend in the northern region last Friday when they recaptured the Citadel in the heart of the capital of Quangtri Province, and some officials were saying they had greatly reduced the enemy threat to Hue.

But the greater part of Quang-

tri Province remained either controlled or strongly contested by the Communist forces and the Saigon military command continued to report 50 to 75 North Vietnamese killed each day in the hills west of Hue, indicating that more than a few enemy soldiers were still in the area.

The New York Times

Pilot: Navy Flew Illegal Strikes

WASHINGTON – A former pilot implicated the Navy Thursday in unauthorized bombing attacks on North Vietnam, senators said.

"If this fellow's testimony was right," said Sen. Stuart Symington, D-Mo., "more than one service was involved in preplanned bombing raids regardless of reaction."

"I am greatly disturbed by what I heard," said Sen. Richard Schweiker, R-Pa., after listening to William Groepper, a former navy lieutenant and A7 Corsair pilot, at the closed-door inquiry of the Senate Armed Services Committee.

Schweiker said the allegation should be traced up the chain of command.

"I think we should talk to

McCain," he said, referring to Adm. John McCain, who at the time was the overall Pacific and Indochina air war commander.

The probe had focused on the firing of Air Force Lt. Gen. John D. Lavelle for unauthorized raids he ordered last November through March, before the White House ordered renewed heavy bombing of North Vietnam. The inquiry has also been into civilian control of the military.

Stars and Stripes

A Vought A-7 Corsair and a Grumman A-6 Intruder from USS Constellation are seen at the time it is suggested that the Navy was flying unauthorized strikes against North Vietnam

OCTOBER 1972

1st Twenty sailors die and 37 are injured when a shell goes off in the barrel of a gun aboard the US heavy cruiser *Newport News*.

3rd The total bomb tonnage expended by US planes since February 1965 is put at 7,555,800. This is over three times as much as was used by the Allies during World War II.

7th South Vietnamese forces come under attack along Route 13 north of Saigon. Thirty-six Cambodians die as communists destroy a bridge near the centre of Phnom Penh.

8-11th In the light of a favourable North Vietnamese offer, Washington starts Operation Enhance Plus – the provision of South Vietnam with $2 billion worth of hardware.

11th US aircraft hit the French, Indian and Algerian legations in Hanoi. A senior French diplomat is killed.

12th President Thieu declares that peace will only come when the communists have been exterminated.

12th Ben Het Special Forces camp is showered with 1500 rockets and taken by the communists.

12-13th Racial violence flares aboard US Navy ships.

16th Communists bombard roads around Saigon.

17th The fact that senior US military and diplomatic personnel are meeting in Saigon fuels the rumour of an imminent ceasefire.

22nd President Thieu turns down the US/North Vietnamese ceasefire programme. With a ceasefire in the offing both sides in the conflict scramble to seize as much territory as possible.

24th A suspension of bombing above the 20th parallel is ordered by Washington.

29th It is decreed in Saigon that all South Vietnamese must have a national flag on pain of arrest.

29th Communists are steadily taking over settlements around Saigon.

31st Khmer Rouge forces continue the fight against the Cambodian government as the Vietnamese communists move into the Mekong Delta and Saigon areas.

The "Impersonal War" of the B-52 Bomber

ANDERSEN AIR FORCE BASE, Guam Six hours and 14 minutes after taking off from this Pacific island base, Capt. Terry Jennings' B-52 shuddered and 32,500 pounds of high-explosive bombs plummeted toward South Vietnam.

A few seconds later a ground controller radioed, "good job," – the bombs were right on target.

There was not a flicker of reaction from any of the six crewmen, no sign of satisfaction or any trace of excitement - an attitude, of course, that has been common in bomber crews for years.

For the crewmen, sitting in their air-conditioned compartments more than five miles above the steamy jungle of South Vietnam, the bomb run had been merely another familiar technical exercise. The crew knew virtually nothing about their target and they showed no curiosity.

Only the radar-navigator, who in earlier wars would have been called the bombardier, saw the bombs exploding, and those distant flashes gave no hint of the awesome eruption of flames and steel on the ground. No one in the plane, including this correspondent, heard the deafening blast.

200 B-52s in Theater

In many ways, Captain Jennings and his men are typical of the scores of crews that have

33 Hurt in Racial Clash Aboard Carrier Kitty Hawk

HONOLULU – A fight involving black and white sailors aboard the attack aircraft carrier Kitty Hawk off Vietnam Thursday left 33 men injured, three seriously, the Pacific Fleet Command reported Friday.

Two of the injured were flown to shore-based hospitals for treatment and another was scheduled to be flown ashore, a Navy Spokesman said. The remainder were treated for minor injuries aboard the ship and returned to duty, he said.

The Navy said "order has been fully restored" aboard the carrier and that it is "continuing to perform its mission at Yankee Station" in the Tonkin Gulf.

Stars and Stripes

Cruiser Heads for Philippines After Explosion That Killed 19

SAIGON The cruiser *Newport News* steamed out of the Vietnam war zone today and headed for the Philippines with the bodies of 19 sailors killed in the worst United States naval disaster this year.

Ten men in the crew were wounded by the explosion in an eight-inch gun turret that rocked the 21,000-ton warship shortly after midnight. Many of the 1,300 crewmen were shaken from their sleep by the blast.

The explosion occurred while the 700-foot cruiser was firing at North Vietnamese positions in Quangtri Province just below the demilitarized zone. Her position at the time was given as 13 miles northeast of Quangtri City.

The New York Times

Boeing B-52s cover every parking space on Andersen Air Force Base, as the 43rd and 72nd Strategic Wings build up strength for an all-out effort against the North

been sent to Guam since February in a build-up that has brought a number of B-52s bombing Indochina to about 200 – four times more than were in the theater at the close of last year. Some of the big bombers are based at Utapao, Thailand.

They are intelligent, steady, family men doing a job they've been told to do. Because they are professionals, they take pride in doing their work well. But neither Captain Jennings's crew nor any of the numerous other pilots and crewmen interviewed displayed the kind of enthusiasm for their assignment that bubbles through conversations with fighter pilots. "It's a job," the bomber men often say.

The New York Times

Continuing Cost of War

For the first time in seven years, a week passed without a single US soldier dying in combat in Indochina. But in that same week, ending Sept 16, 4,625 North Vietnamese troops reportedly died, as well as 409 South Vietnamese soldiers. Another 1,710 ARVN fighters were hospitalized.

In that same week US military aircraft flew 1,590 sorties in South Vietnam. The South Vietnamese flew another 883 sorties of their own in the South. There were an additional 230 B-52 bombing missions, mostly in the South. The tonnage of bombs dropped in Indochina by US planes since Richard Nixon became President is nearly twice the amount dropped by the Allies in Europe, Africa and Asia in all of World War II.

Time

'Peace at Hand' – Matter of Weeks: Kissinger

WASHINGTON – Presidential adviser Henry Kissinger said Thursday "peace is at hand" in Vietnam.

Kissinger announced that a settlement of the Vietnam war, the longest in U.S. history, could be signed "within a matter of weeks or less."

In Huntington, W. Va., President Nixon said Thursday night he is confident that differences blocking a final Vietnam peace settlement "can and will be worked out."

Speaking for the first time publicly about what he termed "a significant breakthrough" in the Vietnam negotiations, Nixon told an airport rally that, "I am confident we will succeed in achieving our objective – peace with honor and not peace with surrender in Vietnam."

Stars and Stripes

AIR RE-SUPPLY

NOVEMBER 1972

1st Twenty-two US personnel die when a helicopter crashes in the Mekong Delta.

1st 200 Laotian troops die as their garrison is taken by the communists.

7th Richard Nixon is re-elected President of the United States of America.

8th South Korean troops, in compliance with the wishes of Saigon and Washington, withdraw from the fighting.

10-12th It is alleged that a mutiny takes place among communist troops who are against the coming agreement.

11th The massive Long Binh US military base is handed over to the South Vietnamese.

15th US pacification chief Willard E. Chambers quits, expressing extreme dissatisfaction with those running the war effort.

20-21st A further round of secret Paris talks opens.

22nd The US loses its first B-52 of the conflict, brought down by a SAM.

23-25th Secret talks appear to be deadlocked.

30th B-52s bomb Quang Tri Province and North Vietnam.

Saigon Gets Longbinh

SAIGON The United States Army today turned over its huge headquarters base at Longbinh, 16 miles north of Saigon, to the South Vietnamese Army. The transfer symbolized the end of direct United States Army participation in the Vietnam war after more than seven years.

About 19,000 Army soldiers remain in South Vietnam, working chiefly as advisers to Saigon Government troops, as helicopter crewmen, and as maintenance, supply and office staff. Under ceasefire proposals being considered, they would have to leave South Vietnam along with about 10,000 Air Force personnel, 1,300 Marines, 1,800 sailors and 100 Coast Guardsmen within 60 days after the signing of an agreement.

Movies for the Viets

The 50-square-mile Longbinh base was headquarters for United States Army, Vietnam, or USARV (pronounced Use Are Vee), a command established on July 20, 1965, during the rapid American buildup.

Its small remaining headquarters staff, commanded by a major general, moved into United States Military Assistance Command offices in Saigon today.

With today's turnover of the Longbinh base, three Army infantry companies that had been providing perimeter security were to be replaced by South Vietnamese units. An Army spokesman said no American Army troops would remain on the post after Dec 1.

A large property disposal yard there has been turned over to American civilians. Recreational facilities, including basketball and tennis courts, swimming pool and a large new movie theater, were turned over to the South Vietnamese.

The New York Times

Helicopter crewman are about the last non-advisory Army personnel in Vietnam

First B52 Shot Down

SAIGON – The United States lost its first B52 bomber to enemy fire in the Vietnam war Wednesday and disclosed that another $15-million, F111 fighter-bomber had vanished, the fourth in less than two months, on a mission over North Vietnam.

While the U.S. command here declined to say what caused the B52 loss, military sources here and in Washington said the big plane was hit by enemy fire during the heaviest B52 raids of the war over North Vietnam.

The eight-engine strato-fortress crashed near Nakhon Phanom in eastern Thailand shortly before midnight while trying to make it back to is base at Utapao, 400 miles to the southwest. All six crewmen bailed out and were rescued, the command said.

Stars and Stripes

US Cargoes Keep Saigon Field Busy

SAIGON No. 59397, a four-engine C-141 jet cargo plane of the Air Force's 63rd Military Airlift Wing, rolled to a stop on the tarmac, at Tansonnhut Air Base at 10.42 a.m. after a 3-hour-40-minute flight from Kadena Air Base on Okinawa.

The hatch below the tail swung down. Side flaps opened. Maj. Darrel D. Shinn, 33 years old, the plane's commander, stepped out of the crew door, "General cargo, replacements," he said.

On the pallets that rolled out of the innards of the plane were truck and jeep fenders, five-gallon cans of insecticide powder, radio parts and cases of rifle-bore cleaner – all rather pedes-

A C-141 Starlifter takes off from South Vietnam during the intense resupply effort intended to build South Vietnamese military strength before the final American departure

trian war material.

Speed-Up Followed Visit

The Air Force began speeding up deliveries of supplies to air bases at Saigon, Bienhoa and Danang on Oct. 24, the day after Henry A. Kissinger left Saigon after conferring with President Nguyen Van Thieu on a peace settlement. The airlift has been called one of the largest of the war, but Air Force officials say it is smaller than peak shipments when Americans were at top strength here.

Under the peace proposals, all American military men would have to leave within 60 days. Weapons, thereafter, could be replaced only on a one-for-one basis.

"The time-compression factor is important," said Col. John B. Voss, chief spokesman for the Seventh Air Force. Deliveries have increased roughly tenfold since just before Mr Kissinger's visit, but in September and early October, supplies were vir-

tually a dribble.

More than half the handlers of ground cargo at the three bases had been sent home, and the remaining ground crews, and some handlers brought in temporarily, are now working overtime.

The New York Times

GI Found Not Guilty of Killing Officers

FORT ORD, Calif. A military jury found Pvt. Billy Dean Smith, the first soldier brought to trial in the United States in a "fragging" incident, not guilty today of charges that he killed two officers with a grenade in Vietnam.

Private Smith, a 24-year-old black from the Watts section of Los Angeles, was acquitted of six counts of murder, attempted murder and assault. However, he was found guilty of assault-

ing a military policeman who arrested him soon after the fragmentation grenade exploded on March 16, l971, at the Bienhoa air base near Saigon. "Fragging" refers to assaults with fragmentation grenades.

The jury, all career officers, reduced Private Smith's enlisted man's rank from E2 to E1 and ordered that he receive a bad conduct discharge on the assault charge.

The New York Times

239

LINE BACKER II

DECEMBER 1972

4th Resumption of secret talks in Paris.

6th Massive communist rocket assault hits Tan Son Nhut airport.

10th US bombing of the DMZ moves into its fourth day as the task of drawing up the final agreement gets under way.

12th Pathet Lao offers a ceasefire proposal.

16th Henry Kissinger publicly discloses why the secret talks have failed to reach an agreement.

16th It is announced that should a ceasefire come into effect the US military headquarters will move from Saigon to Thailand.

18th Bombing of North Vietnam restarts as Operation Linebacker II. The Hanoi and Haiphong area will bear the brunt of the 40,000 tons of bombs expended.

18th A fierce struggle is in progress for Fire Base Anne, near Quang Tri City.

18th The last Australian military personnel leave Vietnam.

19th Two die and three are wounded as the USS *Goldsborough* is comes under fire.

19-20th The bombing of the North is condemned by the international community.

21st Forty-three US airmen are missing in action since 18 December.

22nd Bach Mai hospital in Hanoi is a victim of US air raids.

24th It is disclosed that 11 B-52s have now been lost.

25th The figure for US troops in Vietnam is given as 24,000.

25th Da Nang airbase comes under fire.

25th It is revealed that the equivalent of 20 Hiroshima A-bombs was expended against North Vietnam between 18 and 24 December.

26th US bombs Hanoi on an unprecedented scale.

27th The battle around Quang Tri is still in progress.

28th South Vietnamese troops fail to retake Artillery Base November in the Central Highlands.

30th US bombing north of the 20th parallel is suspended pending a reopening of secret talks.

No More "Clowning Around"

ANDERSEN AIR FORCE BASE, Guam "The flight crews are different now," said the young Air Force sergeant, a ground crewman. "Before, when they came back, they were always clowning around. Now they're shaken. They just get out of the plane and into the bus and go to the debriefing."

Since 1965, when the United States began bombing in Vietnam, the crews of the B-52 bombers had flown what some fliers call a "milk run" and others a "bus ride" over South Vietnam, where they faced little opposition from air defense.

The crewmen flew for about six hours from here to Vietnam, used radar to find targets they couldn't see, pressed a button to drop their bombs into a rectangle 3,000 by 9,000 feet, turned around and flew six hours back to their huge base on this tropical island. Their only enemy was boredom.

On Dec. 18 all that changed. For the first time the B-52s were ordered to bomb North Vietnam steadily, including the Hanoi-Haiphong area, where they face what an Air Force spokesman here called "the greatest air-defense system in history."

The Big Battalions

Today, the flight crews are the targets for concentrated salvos of surface-to-air missiles, or SAMS. There is evidence that the North Vietnamese gunners have new, more accurate, and more explosive SAMS supplied by the Soviet Union. In addition, Soviet-built MIG fighter-interceptors appear to have been more active in the defense of Hanoi.

One result, clearly apparent at the air base here, is a partial change of tactics by the Air Force. Before the Christmas pause in bombing, missions were flown by single B-52s or cells of three. Now, to prevent Hanoi from concentrating its fire on such inviting targets, the planes often swarm out in much larger numbers.

"It's like flying through a Fourth of July celebration," a pilot said in describing a night raid to a friend here. "The sky is lit up all around you."

"There I was," said a tall young pilot with a mustache. "There were SAMS to the left of me, SAMS to the right of me, SAMS in front of me . . ." His voice trailed off, and he shrugged.

Another young pilot said: "I was about two miles back and there was this flight in front of me and they got hit with a salvo of those new SAMS. No 1 dove forward and No 3 veered off to the right in evasive action." He motioned with his hands as fliers have since the days of the Wright brothers.

"But No 2 stayed right on course and got it right in the belly and they got blown right out of the sky," he said, holding his left hand palm down and jabbing a finger up into it.

First Combat Losses

In the 12 days since President Nixon ordered the resumption of the bombing, Washington has officially conceded losing 15 of the B-52s to enemy fire, the first losses in combat they have suffered. Hanoi says it has shot down 33.

The New York Times

A B-52 carrying a full load of 108 bombs refuels on the way to bomb North Vietnam

---

On Target

The first victory credited to a gunner came on the night of 18 December. S/sgt. Samuel O. Turner, normally stationed at March AFB, California, but on temporary duty with the 307th Strategic Wing based at Utapao airfield, Thailand, was the tail gunner aboard a B-52D, part of the heavy bomber force hitting targets in the Hanoi area. Turner describes the engagement:

"As the attacking MIG came into firing range, I fired a burst. There was a gigantic explosion to the rear of the aircraft. I looked out the window but was unable to see directly where the MIG would have been. I looked back at my radar scope. Except for the one airplane out at 8 o'clock, there was nothing."

USAF
"The View from the Rock"

JANUARY 1973

2nd US bombing of targets south of the 20th parallel restarts.

8th Defense Secretary Laird expresses the opinion that "from a military viewpoint, the Vietnamization programme has been completed".

8-19th Henry Kissinger and Le Duc Tho of North Vietnam have further talks in Paris and announce an agreement.

15th President Nixon orders a halt to all military activity against North Vietnam itself, but the war continues in the South.

18-26th Both sides scramble for territory before the ceasefire takes effect.

23rd It is announced that the US/Hanoi agreement has been signed with a ceasefire to begin at 0800 on 28 January, Saigon time.

24th Henry Kissinger states that hopes are high for a similar cessation of hostilities in Laos and Cambodia.

27th As a result of recent supply operations South Vietnam has the fourth largest air force in the world.

27th The North Vietnamese presence in the South is put at 145,000.

27th The end of the draft is announced in the US.

27th Lieutenant Colonel William B. Nolde is the last US combat death in the conflict, killed 11 hours before the ceasefire deadline.

27th The US, North and South Vietnam and the Viet Cong sign "An Agreement Ending the War and Restoring Peace in Vietnam", which includes the setting-up of an international control commission.

28th A ceasefire proposal is put forward by Premier Lon Nol of Cambodia only to be turned down by Prince Sihanouk.

Kep Airfield near Hanoi is bombed. It was the destruction of Vietnam's defenses and war industries during Linebacker II that brought Hanoi to the conference table

Army Freezes Orders; No More GIs to Vietnam

WASHINGTON (UPI) – The Army Wednesday cancelled all orders for Vietnam "effective immediately" because of the ceasefire scheduled to be signed in Paris Saturday.

"No individual will be permitted to return or continue to RVN (the Republic of Vietnam) without prior Department of the Army clearance," the order said.

An Army spokesman said he could think of no circumstances under which such clearance would be given.

The spokesman said the order would have an immediate effect on "about 2,000" officers and enlisted men who already had received orders to proceed to Vietnam.

Stars and Stripes

It's All Over

SAIGON – The Vietnam war ended Sunday. It came to a halt at 8 a.m. as a cease-fire agreement went into effect.

Church bells rang out and the Saigon government voiced its gratitude to the Americans who helped it survive.

The cease-fire was underwritten a dozen hours earlier by the signing of peace agreements in Paris. A night of deadly fighting in various parts of South Vietnam preceded the hour of truce, however.

This last-minute effort to grab land left details of positions to be straightened out in the spotted pattern of disputed holdings that already mark the map of South Vietnam.

Stars and Strips

VIETNAM ACCORD IS REACHED; CEASE-FIRE BEGINS SATURDAY; POWs TO BE FREE IN 60 DAYS
Transcript of the Speech by President on Vietnam

Following is a transcript of President Nixon's televised address to the nation last night on the Vietnam war, as recorded by The New York Times:

"Good evening. I have asked for this radio and television time tonight for the purpose of announcing that we today have concluded an agreement to end the war and bring peace with honor in Vietnam and Southeast Asia.

"The following statement is being issued at this moment in Washington and Hanoi:

"At 12.30 Paris time today, Jan 23, 1973, the agreement on ending the war and restoring peace in Vietnam was initiated by Dr Henry Kissinger on behalf of the United States and Special Adviser Le Duc Tho on behalf of the Democratic Republic of Vietnam.

"The agreement will be formally signed by the parties participating in the Paris Conference on Vietnam on Jan 27, 1973, at the International Conference Center in Paris. The cease-fire will take effect at 2400 Greenwich mean time, Jan 27, 1973. The United States and the Democratic Republic of Vietnam express the hope that this agreement will insure stable peace in Vietnam and contribute to the preservation of lasting peace in Indochina and Southeast Asia."

Prisoners of War in Hanoi talk through the bars as the prospect of release, after eight years in some cases, becomes real

---

Bombing Halt Brings Relief to B-52 Crews in Guam

ANDERSEN AIR FORCE BASE, Guam – The halt in the intensive American bombing of North Vietnam has brought a touch of relief, but only a little let-up in action to the B-52 flight and ground crews here.

"It was good word to get," said one officer of President Nixon's order to cease bombing above the 20th Parallel in North Vietnam. Since they started hitting Hanoi and its environs on Dec. 18, the bomber crews had been on the receiving end of probably the most intensive anti-aircraft fire in the history of aerial warfare.

The United States has admitted the loss of 15 of its B-52s in southeast Asia, there being 150 based here and 50 flying from bases in Thailand. The North Vietnamese have said they have shot down 81 American planes in the last two weeks, 34 of them B-52s.

A B-52 gunner, asked if he felt relieved that he would not be flying over the Hanoi-Haiphong area of North Vietnam, replied:

"Yeah, I just hope they accomplish something this time." He meant the peace negotiators who are scheduled to resume their talks in Paris on Jan 8.

Still Working

But he and other fliers were skeptical. They expressed concern that the North Vietnamese would use the time provided by the peace talks merely to rebuild their air defenses and to recover from the damage done during the recent bombing campaign.

"I think we were really hurt-ing them," a flier said. "Now they can pull themselves back together again and we'll sure catch hell with what they throw up at us the next time."

There was a raucous New Year's Eve party at the officers' club here last night, with people and furniture being dunked into the swimming pool. But New Year's Day saw everyone at work this morning as the seven-day week continued in force.

The New York Times

243

POWs ARE FREE

FEBRUARY 1973

5th Direct talks begin between the political wing of the Viet Cong and the South Vietnamese government. There is little progress.

6th Supervisors from the International Commission of Control and Supervision (ICCS), who have been delegated to oversee the ceasefire in place, start to take up their positions. They come from Canada, Hungary and India.

ICCS members are initially flown about in **CIA** planes like this, but the planes are soon transferred to the **Commission**

7th Canada becomes the first Western nation to recognize North Vietnam.

12th Prisoners of war are exchanged as part of the peace settlement.

14th Operation Homecoming swings into action: the first US prisoners held captive by the communists are flown back to California.

20th US warplanes begin a series of missions over Cambodia in support of the forces of the military government of Lon Nol, being pressed hard by the communist Khmer Rouge.

21st In Laos, a ceasefire is agreed between the communist Pathet Lao and the government

26th The South Vietnamese government accuses the communists of building up their forces within South Vietnam, against the terms of the Paris Accords.

Prisoner Flabbergasted by News From Home

CLARK AIR BASE, the Philippines – There was general sympathy here today for one former prisoner of war who, after calling his wife in the United States, was said to have walked down a hospital corridor saying, "My God, she did it, she did it, she did it."

A fellow prisoner asked him sympathetically, "What did she do?"

The reply: "She bought a motorcycle."

The New York Times

First 2 POWs Land in US, "Grateful, Overwhelmed, Proud"

SAN DIEGO The first two of the returning United States prisoners of war stepped on to their native soil with a salute tonight after an hour's delay while their plane circled an airfield with wing flap trouble.

Comdr. Brian D. Woods, 40-years old, of the Navy, a native of San Diego, and Maj. Glendon W. Perkins, 38, of the Air Force, from Orlando, Fla., were flown back early so they could be at the bedsides of their critically ill mothers.

The Air Force C-141 medical evacuation transport carrying the two pilots from the Philippines touched down at the Mira- mar Naval Air Station at 9.28 p.m., Pacific Coast time, after circling the airport for almost an hour.

The airport ceremony was brief so the men could hurry to their mothers' bedsides.

"This homecoming is not only for myself and Glendon Perkins, but for all the POWs," said Commander Woods to the group of about 100 spectators, mostly newsmen.

"We are grateful and overwhelmed. We are proud to be Americans. We are proud to have served our country and our Commander-in-Chief."

The New York Times

Negotiators in Laos continue to Haggle Over Truce Details

VIENTIANE, Laos Representatives of the Laotian Government in Vientiane and the Communist-led Pathet Lao were still haggling over details of an imminent Laotian cease-fire settlement today. It appeared certain that the cease-fire would go into effect before the end of the week, but a high Government source said it could take years to reach a political settlement.

The main outlines of the cease-fire agreement, various well-informed sources said, include the following elements: The cease-fire in Laos will be exactly like that in South Vietnam. Both sides will remain in place, creating a "leopard spot" pattern of control zones.

The New York Times

As it is what you hold at the ceasefire that counts, the communists do their best to occupy as much ground militarily as they can before it comes into effect

---

All Freed POWs to Get Lifetime Baseball Pass

Each prisoner of war returning from Indochina will receive a gold-plated lifetime pass good for any professional baseball game, Bowie Kuhn, the commissioner of baseball announced yesterday.

Mr Kuhn said that the action, effective at the start of the 1973 season, had the endorsement of Joe Cronin, president of the American League; Chub Feeney president of the National League, and Henry Peters, head of the minor leagues. The Associated Press reported.

The New York Times

Amid Cease-Fire Battles, Peasants Remain Stoical

SAIGON The Vietnamese are a remarkable and stoical people.

A group of peasants were squatting patiently in a hamlet near Tay Ninh yesterday while Government and communist troops fought furiously with machine guns and grenades around the peasants' home nearby.

They chatted with an American visitor about the rice crop. Dry weather had cut the yield but the price was up. On Friday the Viet Cong had killed an old woman who was too deaf to understand their orders to evacuate her house.

What is their worst problem these days, they were asked.

"The price of fertilizer is too high," one replied.

No Sense of Jubilation

As an official cease-fire – but a considerably violated one - came into effect in South Vietnam there were almost no scenes of jubilation.

For one thing the Government of President Nguyen Van Thieu had forbidden celebrations, fearing that Viet Cong agents would turn them into demonstrations. In any case, celebration in so equivocal a situation does not seem to fit the Vietnamese character.

The New York Times

The Return

CLARK AB, R.P. – One hundred fifteen American pilots, released a few hours before from the darkness of a Hanoi prison, landed under an overcast sky at this base late Monday and walked into the sunlight of a vibrant, triumphal welcome – one in which the spirits of many returnees seemed to flow brighter than those of the 2,000 persons who turned out to greet them with cheers, banners and chants.

Several hours later 26 other Americans, including a civilian who had been a Viet Cong prisoner for a month less than nine years, were brought from Saigon on a C9A medevac plane after an earlier release had been stalled by hours of tense negotiation. All but one man walked from the plane. The 19 servicemen and seven civilians, tired but happy, were greeted by the tireless crowd. One greeter waved an American flag at them.

Stars and Stripes

CEASE FIRE

MARCH 1973

18th The longest-serving US POW, Major Floyd Thompson, is released. He was captured in March 1964.

29th The last US troops leave Vietnam, as President Nixon announces "the day we have all worked and prayed for has finally come".

JUNE 1973

4th Congress passes a bill blocking funding for military activities in Southeast Asia, including the bombing of Cambodia.

JULY 1973

1st US Navy minesweepers begin clearing mines from North Vietnamese ports.

AUGUST 1973

15th All US bombing of Cambodia ends.

DECEMBER 1973

3rd Viet Cong raiders destroy 18 million gallons of oil in storage tanks near Saigon.

US Ends Its Vietnam Role After a Decade

SAIGON The last American troops left South Vietnam today, leaving behind an unfinished war that has deeply scarred this country and the United States.

There was little emotion or joy as they brought to a close almost a decade of American military intervention.

Remaining after the final jet transport lifted off from Tan Son Nhut air base at 5.53 p.m. were about 800 Americans on the truce observation force who will leave tomorrow and Saturday. A contingent of 159 Marine guards and about 50 military attaches also stayed behind.

The fighting men were gone, but United States involvement in South Vietnam was far from ended.

The New York Times

Thousands See Release of Last POW

HANOI As tens of thousands of North Vietnamese watched and smiled and waved, the last 67 American prisoners flew out of Hanoi to freedom today.

Despite a few minor hitches in the final ceremony, several of the North Vietnamese officials seemed to be in an almost playful mood and they drew praise from American officers who flew here to accept the release of the prisoners for "straightforward and professional" negotiating.

The New York Times

Viet Cong Captive Tells of 7-Year Ordeal

WASHINGTON Douglas K. Ramsey, a 38-year-old Foreign Service officer who spent seven years in Viet Cong captivity, told today of forced marches, isolation, beri-beri, malaria, meals of monkey, dog and bear meat, crude cages, shackles, chains and the jungle burial of a fellow prisoner.

But Mr Ramsey repeatedly emphasized during a two-hour meeting with a small group of newsmen today – the first since his release last month – that his handling, under the circumstances, "would not constitute gross mistreatment."

He made an effort, he said, to judge each of his captors individually, and added that they "ranged from saintly to something out of Marquis de Sade."

Humor in Adversity

Mr Ramsey, who is from Boulder City, Nev., seemed fit. One of the few visible signs of his imprisonment was a slight limp in his left leg – a result of a severe case of beri-beri in 1966, he said.

His description of prison life was facile and punctuated with easy humor, all the more remarkable, a State Department official said later, considering that he did not have one sustained conversation during the last five years of his captivity.

In all, Mr Ramsey related, he spent six of his seven years in isolation – usually living in crude cages that did provide enough room to exercise.

He explained that three things kept him alive during the years that he was trundled from prison camp to prison camp in South Vietnam and Cambodia, while his captors tried to keep ahead of American and South Vietnamese military offensives.

Perhaps most important, Mr Ramsey indicated, was that "I developed a compulsive neurosis vis-a-vis exercise." For a time, he said, he would try to jog in place for seven miles.

A second aid was his ability "to overcome constant nausea," he said, and to force himself to eat. He cited the case of a fellow prisoner, badly weakened from malnutrition and disease, who could not bring himself to eat his regurgitated food and thus grew even weaker.

Mathematical Puzzles

"A third thing," Mr Ramsey said, "for which I can't take credit, was the fact that after the third year, time began to move very rapidly." He said that the "last three years passed more quickly than the first 10 months."

To help pass the time, he explained, he did mathematical puzzles and games in his head.

He also spent hours multiplying numbers in his head, he said, "and finally worked up to where I could multiply four digits by four digits."

His most critical period, he said, came in 1967 in a Viet Cong prison camp somewhere in the jungles west of Saigon. He con-tracted cerebral malaria in the mosquito-infested area and spent 60 hours in a coma.

"When I woke up," Mr Ramsey related matter-of-factly, "I found that every single superficial blood vessel in my head, arms and legs had swollen shut." He was fortunate, he said, because the prison-camp doctor arrived "literally within 60 seconds after I went into convulsions." His pulse rate dropped to 34, he said.

The New York Times

The mining of North Vietnam's ports and the subsequent strangling of the country's trade did much to bring Hanoi to the conference table. After the ceasefire, Operation Endsweep was designed to clear North Vietnamese waters of mines, using minesweeping helicopters as well as conventional mine counter-measure vessels

1974

JANUARY 1974

27th South Vietnamese government estimates there have been 13,788 deaths in its forces since the ceasefire of January 1973.

MARCH 1974

18th Khmer Rouge forces win an important symbolic victory when they occupy the former Cambodian royal capital, Oudong.

APRIL 1974

4th The House of Representatives refuses a measure to increase military aid to South Vietnam.

AUGUST 1974

9th President Nixon resigns, and is replaced by Gerald Ford.

SEPTEMBER 1974

16th President Ford offers an amnesty to draft dodgers from the Vietnam War period.

Saigon Hears the Fighting at Its Edge

SAIGON A heavy column of black smoke rose over the edge of Saigon today as advance Communist forces moved close to the city limits.

South Vietnamese Air Force helicopters fired rockets into the Communist positions on the Saigon River at Newport, a former United States port complex on the road to Bien Hoa. The Communists fired back with AK-47 automatic rifles and the noise was clearly audible inside the city.

Only a few lightly armed South Vietnamese combat policemen and militiamen guarded the road on the northeastern edge of the city. They made no effort to dig in and several Government officers simply stood around watching the helicopters firing at the Communist forces.

Seize End of Bridge

The Communist troops, who had seized the far side of the Newport Bridge over the Saigon River, were believed to be part of major North Vietnamese units moving rapidly toward Saigon from Bien Hoa, 15 miles to the northeast. Another group of

North Vietnamese troops at Ban Me Thuot sweep aside the last vestiges of South Vietnamese resistance

Communist troops reportedly had occupied a crossroads two miles beyond the bridge on the way to the biggest South Vietnamese ammunition dump at Cat Lai.

The Communist advance blocked all traffic at the large Hang Xanh Intersection, the main gateway to Saigon from the north. Combat policemen wearing flak jackets, helmets and mottled green and brown uniforms stood behind barbed-wire barricades, forcing all traffic back into the city.

It was the closest fighting to Saigon since the Communists' Tet and spring offensives of 1968.

The Communist troops this morning apparently had only small arms and no mortars or anti-aircraft guns. If they had fired a few mortar shells into the city, it appeared that the few nervous Government soldiers would have instantly fled.

The New York Times

US Will Receive 130,000 Refugees

WASHINGTON Robert J. McClosky, Assistant Secretary of State for Congressional Relations, said today that about 130,000 Vietnamese refugees would be brought to the United States.

"We have authority from the Attorney General, using the so-called parole procedure, to bring

Vietnamese refugees, fleeing the fall of Saigon in 1975, crowd aboard a USAF C-141 bound for the safety of Clark Field in the Philippines

into the United States something on the order of 130,000," Mr McClosky said on the NBC interview program Meet the Press.

He said that if all the Vietnamese who had been in some way associated with the United States in the last 15 years were to be evacuated, the number "would run up to a million."

"I think it fair that we could absorb the figure that we are talking about in the present situation but I would think that a figure of a million is something

that probably we could not absorb and probably not very realistic," he declared.

Mr McClosky said that foreign policy in Vietnam by "different administrations has failed. It failed for a variety of reasons but I do think that we can master these problems," he said.

However, he added that the United States had not suffered permanent setbacks in other areas because of Vietnam.

The New York Times

Saigon's Gold-Mine PX is Going Out of Business

SAIGON The PX is closing. The institution that symbolized the American presence to Vietnamese more than any other will shut its doors for the last time in a few days, knowledgeable United States officials said today.

Already the rows of Johnny Walker Scotch, at £4 a bottle, the cases of bourbon, the fifths of gin, rum and cold duck have been crated for shipment back to the United States. Everything

else is on sale at half-price.

There wasn't much left today in the supermarket-like post exchange at Tan Son Nhut air base: Some cartons of Dr Pepper, cans of Hawaiian Punch, potato chips, Salem and Marlboro cigarettes.

Gold Mine for Some

Once the hundreds of PXs at every United States Army, Marine, Navy and Air Force base in Vietnam provided a gold

mine for smugglers and black marketeers, supplying everything from Welch's Grape Juice and fruit cocktail to tape recorders and Japanese cameras.

So big was the institution of the PX in the lives of American soldiers here that they called the United States the "Land of the Big PX."

The New York Times

Minh Named in Move to End War; Red Forces Within Mile of Saigon as Tanks and Artillery Close In

SAIGON As overwhelming Communist forces moved to within barely one mile of Saigon's city limits this morning, South Vietnamese leaders acted at almost the last minute to install Gen. Duong Van Minh as President to end the war on Communist terms.

A ceremony was scheduled for later today, at which outgoing President Tran Van Huong will formally hand over the Presidency to his neutralist successor, reliable informants said.

There seemed some possibility that the Viet Cong themselves may send a representative to the ceremony.

Late last night, the Hanoi Communist party newspaper Nhan Dan published the text of a resolution passed by the National Assembly here autho-

rizing President Huong to transfer all power to General Minh. The naming of General Minh to power was thought to remove

the last major obstacle to meeting Communist demands.

The New York Times

South Vietnamese UH-1s without fuel lie useless at Tan Son Nhut as the field is occupied by victorious communists

249

1975

JANUARY 1975

1st Khmer Rouge forces launch direct attacks on the besieged capital, Phnom Penh.

FEBRUARY 1975

3rd The Saigon government orders the closure of critical newspapers.

MARCH 1975

13th Communist forces capture Ban Me Thuot, a strategically important provincial capital in the Central Highlands.

14th President Thieu orders the ARVN to retreat from the Central Highlands.

26th The communist offensive is in full swing. Hue, former imperial capital, falls to the communists.

29th Da Nang, former major US base in the northern provinces, is taken by the communists.

APRIL 1975

1-7th During non-stop advances, communist forces occupy almost half of South Vietnam's land area.

5th Khmer Rouge attacks almost break into Cambodian capital Phnom Penh.

7th Saigon shelled by advancing communist troops.

12th US Ambassador is airlifted out of Phnom Penh.

16th Phnom Penh falls to Communist forces.

21st President Thieu resigns.

21st The last concerted resistance from the ARVN, at Xuan Loc, collapses.

28th General Duong Van Minh is sworn in as head of state of South Vietnam.

29th Helicopter evacuation of last remaining Americans in Saigon begins.

30th President Minh meets communist officers who refuse to accept anything less than unconditional surrender. By mid-afternoon, communist forces have taken over in the city.

The panic as the North Vietnamese approached Saigon saw many trying desperately to escape by any means possible. South Vietnamese government employees knew they were in for a rough time if they stayed, but what nobody knew was that the southern communists would also be swept aside as the North occupied the south and put their own people into power

Americals Flee Saigon

The United States pulled out of Vietnam Tuesday. All but a handful of Americans fled the country aboard Marine helicopters by early Wednesday and left it up to the Vietnamese to find peace.

The Americans were ordered out Tuesday by new President Duong Van Minh to meet one of the Communists' major conditions for peace talks – an end to the U.S. presence. Political sources said the Communists and the Saigon government had agreed in principle to call a cease-fire.

President Ford then ordered Marines to evacuate the last Americans assigned to the U.S. Defense Attache's Office within 24 hours. Ford promised in his statement that force would be used only to protect lives.

The last Americans in Saigon are lifted out by Marine Corps helicopters

It's Over

The Saigon government surrendered unconditionally to the Viet Cong Wednesday, ending 30 years of bloodshed.

The surrender was announced by president Duong Van "Big" Minh in a five-minute radio address.

As he spoke, the city of Saigon fell quiet and shellfire subsided.

Minh said:

"The republic of Vietnam policy is the policy of peace and reconciliation, aimed at saving the blood of our people. I ask all servicemen to stop firing and stay where you are. I also demand that the soldiers of the Provisional Revolutionary Government (PRG) stop firing and stay in place.

"We are here waiting for the provisional revolutionary government to hand over the authority in order to stop useless bloodshed."

On the same Saigon radio broadcast, Gen. Nguyen Huu Hanh, deputy chief of staff, called on all South Vietnamese generals, officers and servicemen at all levels to carry out Minh's orders.

"All commanders," Hanh declared, "must be ready to enter into relations with commanders of the Provisional Revolutionary Government (Viet Cong) to carry out the cease-fire without bloodshed."

South Vietnamese officers said they had no other choice.

The surrender came within hours of the evacuation of all Americans except a handful of newsmen from Saigon and the closing of the U.S. Embassy which was later looted along with the residence of U.S. Ambassador Graham A. Martin.

South Vietnamese officers complained that the U.S. evacuation had panicked the army and that many top officers and most of the air force had pulled out, leaving the armed forces depleted and Saigon an open city, as Communist-led forces closed in.

Stars and Stripes

Aboard the USS Blue Ridge, command ship for the evacuation, a correspondent said the Navy announced 4,582 persons, about 900 of them Americans, had been lifted out by the evacuation that began at mid-afternoon Tuesday. Forty ships of the U.S. 7th Fleet were gathered on the South China Sea for the task.

Former Vietnamese Premier, Vice Air Marshal Nguyen Cao Ky, natty in his khaki safari suit with maroon scarf around his neck, stepped aboard the command vessel. He said nothing to reporters.

Stars and Stripes

You know the war is over when a tank batters down your door

Reporter's Notebook: Tenderness, Hatred and Grief Mark Saigon's Last Days

ABOARD USS Mobile in the South China Sea Like a failed marriage, the Vietnamese American relationship of the last generation has ended in a mixture of hatred and suspicion, coupled with a strong remnant of tenderness and compassion on both sides.

It ended with an embittered Saigon policeman pistol-whipping an American reporter and with Government troops and policemen taking potshots at American cars and buses, or sometimes just at any "big nose" – non-Asian.

The tens of thousands aboard the huge evacuation armada sailing away from Vietnam have told endless stories of heroism, loyalty and love in the last hours.

But for millions of Vietnamese and not a few Americans the dominant memory will be sorrow and betrayal and guilt.

There was scarcely an American in the final weeks who was not forced to share personally in that intense feeling of guilt. For each of them had what Vietnamese call a big nose – the only real passport to salvation. Caucasian features could do almost anything: cash checks, cut through the maddening bureaucratic impediments that had been erected both by Saigon and Washington and, most of all, get a few Vietnamese to safety.

The New York Times

251

INDEX

254